T0385510

THE GREAT REVERSAL

By the same author

Taiwan: A Short History of a Small Island That Will Dictate Our Future (2024)

China Incorporated: The Politics of a World Where China is Number One (2023)

Xi: A Study in Power (2022)

China Through European Eyes: 800 Years of Cultural and Intellectual Encounter (2021)

China in Five Cities: From Hohhot to Hong Kong (in English and Chinese) (2020)

China (2020)

The Trouble with Taiwan: History, the United States and a Rising China (with Kalley Wu Tzu-hui) (2019)

The Future of UK–China Relations: The Search for a New Model (2019)

Contemporary China (third edition, 2015)

China's Dream: The Culture of Chinese Communism and the Secret Sources of Its Power (2018)

The World According to Xi: Everything You Need to Know About the New China (2018)

China's World: The Foreign Policy of the World's Newest Superpower (2017)

China and the New Maoists (with Simone van Nieuwenhuizen) (2016)

CEO, China: The Rise of Xi Jinping (2016)

What's Wrong with Diplomacy? The Future of Diplomacy and the Case of the UK and China (2015)

Berkshire Dictionary of Chinese Biography (chief editor) (four volumes, 2014–15)

China and the EU in Context (editor) (2014)

Shanghai 2020: The City's Vision for Its Future (2014)

The New Emperors: Power and the Princelings in China (2014)

Carnival China: China in the Era of Hu Jintao and Xi Jinping (2014)

Hu Jintao: China's Silent Ruler (2012)

Ballot Box China: Grassroots Democracy in the Final Major One-Party State (2011)

China 2020: The Next Decade for the People's Republic of China (editor) (2011)

Friends and Enemies: The Past, Present and Future of the Communist Party of China (2009)

The Rise of the Dragon: Inward and Outward Investment in China in the Reform Period 1978–2007 (2008)

Struggling Giant: China in the 21st Century (2007)

The Purge of the Inner Mongolian People's Party in the Chinese Cultural Revolution, 1967–1969: A Function of Language, Power and Violence (2006)

THE GREAT REVERSAL

Britain, China and the 400-Year Contest for Power

KERRY BROWN

YALE UNIVERSITY PRESS
NEW HAVEN AND LONDON

For information about this and other Yale University Press publications, please contact:
U.S. Office: sales.press@yale.edu   yalebooks.com
Europe Office: sales@yaleup.co.uk   yalebooks.co.uk

Set in Minion Pro by IDSUK (DataConnection) Ltd
Printed in Great Britain by Clays Ltd, Elcograf S.p.A

Library of Congress Control Number: 2024938424

ISBN 978-0-300-27292-5

A catalogue record for this book is available from the British Library.

10 9 8 7 6 5 4 3 2 1

Dedicated to the memory of my grandfather,
Edwin Wilberham Cole, 1901–82

Contents

CONTENTS

Plates and Maps

Plates

1. Queen Elizabeth I's letter to the emperor of Cathay, 1602. Lancashire Archives, Lancashire County Council.
2. Willow Pattern plate by Spode Ceramic Works, 1800–20. © Victoria and Albert Museum, London.
3. Printed Chinoiserie wallpaper from Ord House, Berwick-on-Tweed, Northumberland, 1720s. © Victoria and Albert Museum, London.
4. Henry Dundas, first Viscount Melville. Replica by Sir Thomas Lawrence, *c*. 1810. © National Portrait Gallery, London.
5. *Chien-Lung's Court* by William Alexander, n.d. The Huntington Library, Art Museum, and Botanical Gardens. Gilbert Davis Collection. © Courtesy of the Huntington Art Museum, San Marino, California.
6. *The European Factories, Canton* by William Daniell, 1806. Yale Center for British Art, Paul Mellon Collection.
7. Li Shigong, Chen Laoyi and Robert Morrison. Engraved by Jenkins from a painting by George Chinnery, 1828. From Eliza Morrison, *Memoirs of the Life and Labours of Robert Morrison*, vol. 1, London, 1839.

8. Admiral Sir Charles Elliot from Maitland Dougall Photographic Collection, *c.* 1852–80. Courtesy of the University of St Andrews Libraries and Museums.

9. Sir Henry Pottinger by Lowes Cato Dickinson, printed by Charles Joseph Hullmandel, published by Joseph Dickinson, after Samuel Laurence, December 1842. © National Portrait Gallery, London.

10. Pa-Li-Kiao's bridge on the evening of the Battle of Palikao. Niday Picture Library / Alamy.

11. Charles George Gordon in Chinese mandarin dress, *c.* 1864. Granger / Shutterstock.

12. 'Chinese Customs'. Original drawing by IMP for a cartoon published in *Vanity Fair*, 27 December 1894. Courtesy of Special Collections & Archives, Queen's University Belfast.

13. 'A Legacy of Discord'. Cartoon of the Boxer Rebellion by Sir John Tenniel in *Punch*, 1900. GRANGER – Historical Picture Archive / Alamy.

14. Weihaiwei, China, 1898. From *Cassell's History of England*, century edition, *c.* 1900. Design Pics Inc / Shutterstock.

15. Chinatown, Limehouse, London, 1890s. CPA Media Pte Ltd / Alamy.

16. Major General Maltby discussing the arrangement of surrender with Japanese at Peninsula Hotel, 25 December 1941. *Mainichi.*

17. Joseph Needham and Lu Gwei-Djen's father, Lu Shiguo, in Nanking, 1 March–4 April 1946. Needham Research Institute.

18. Clement Attlee meets Mao Zedong in China, 1954. Hulton-Deutsch / Hulton-Deutsch Collection / Corbis via Getty Images.

19. The British embassy in Beijing, 1967. *Room for Diplomacy*. Open Government License v2.0.

20. Mao Zedong greets Edward Heath during his visit to Beijing, 1 October 1975. Keystone / Getty Images.

21. Deng Xiaoping meets Margaret Thatcher in Beijing, 24 September 1982. STR / AFP via Getty Images.

22. Queen Elizabeth II and Prince Philip visit the Great Wall of China, 14 October 1986. Tim Graham / Getty Images.

23. The hand-back of Hong Kong, 1997. David Brauchli / Sygma via Getty Images.
24. David Cameron drinks beer with Xi Jinping at a pub in Princes Risborough, 2015. Associated Press / Alamy.

Maps

Acknowledgements

I would like to express my gratitude to King's College London, for granting me a year's sabbatical from 2021 to 2022 to undertake the research for this book. I am also grateful to the staff at the British Library, the library of the School of Oriental and African Studies in London (where the China Association archives are kept) and the Maughan Library at King's College in London; also to the directors of Jardines for access to their archives kept at Cambridge University Library.

I would like to thank the editorial team at Yale University Press, and in particular Joanna Godfrey for commissioning this book and for help in its writing; Katie Urquhart for her assistance; Clive Liddiard for his meticulous and careful copy-editing; and the two anonymous reviewers who gave detailed and valuable feedback on the first draft of this work. My thanks, too, go to Professor Ken Dark for feedback, in particular on the discovery of the two skeletons in London, reportedly of Chinese origin, from the era of the Roman occupation of Britain.

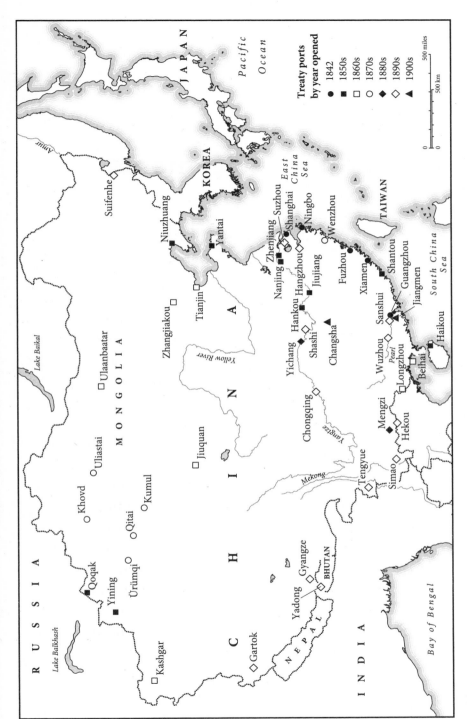

1. Treaty ports.

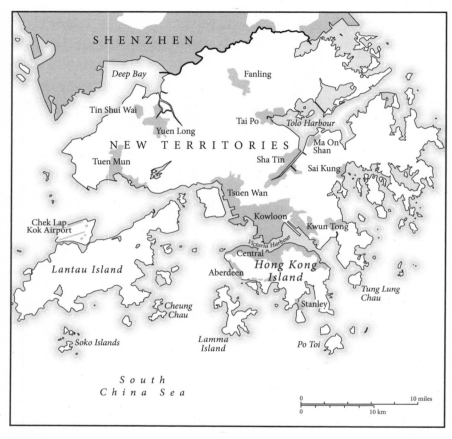

2. Hong Kong.

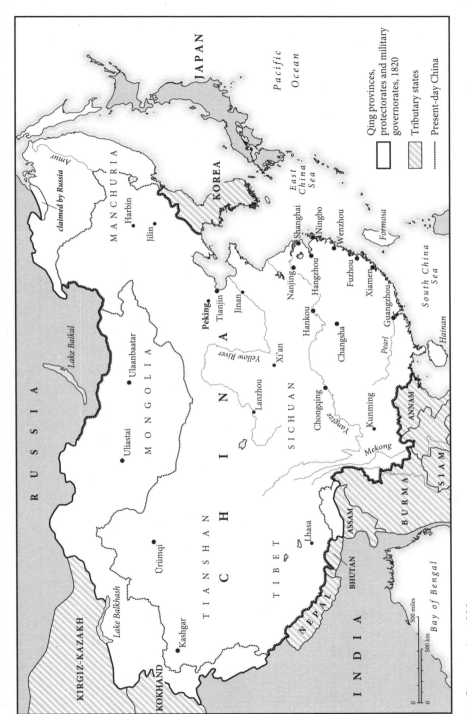

3. Qing empire, 1820.

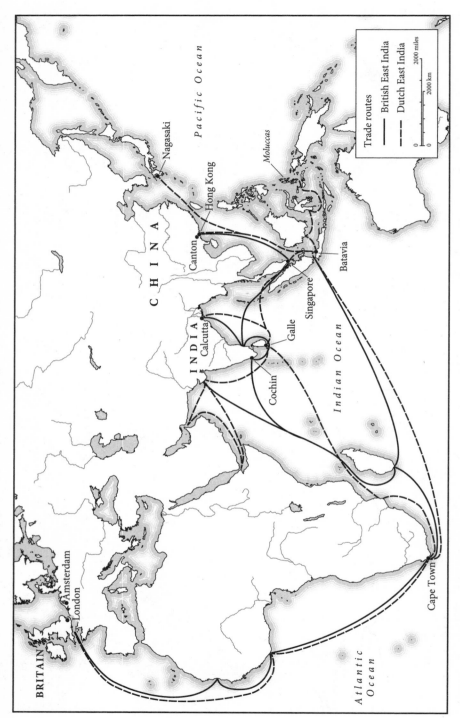

Pacific Ocean

Nagasaki
Hong Kong
Canton

C H I N A

Moluccas

Batavia

Singapore

I N D I A
Calcutta
Galle

Cochin

Indian Ocean

BRITAIN
Amsterdam
London

Cape Town

Atlantic Ocean

Trade routes
British East India
Dutch East India

2000 miles
2000 km

4. East India Company routes to China.

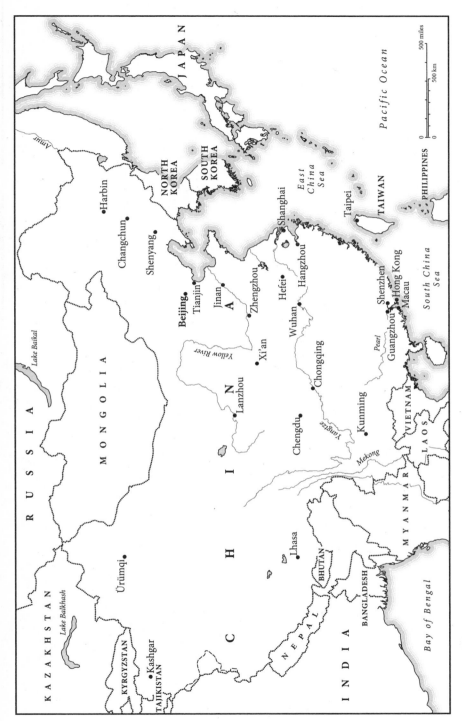

5. China, 2023.

Introduction

The Great Reversal: Britain's China Story

For years I have been hearing it. Either on long train journeys when I was living in China and working as a teacher in the 1990s, or while I was serving as a British diplomat in Beijing a few years later and attending formal Chinese government functions. It was about the century of national humiliation: the period when China was put down, humiliated and defeated by foreign forces. Sometimes it would be in pictorial form, with images of Qing-era soldiers from the nineteenth century being fired on by foreign soldiers. At other times it would be while listening in on the lectures given to local schoolchildren by their teachers in Beijing as they stared at the sombre ruins of the Summer Palace, razed to the ground in 1860 by marauding, vengeful foreign troops. Often it would be while wandering around museums covering the country's modern history. Here displays show the way in which colonisation and the impact of invasion from the 1840s onwards are woven into the tale of how, after all this suffering, China today is able to stand erect, renew itself and resurrect itself, promising never again to be brought to such a low point by the actions of outsiders. As a British person, it was hard to ignore the recurring actions of my own country and its major role in this lamentable tale. Not that those recounting it to me in the present were resentful or ever made a point to me personally. But I became aware early on that Britain figured in the story of this country in a major way.

That China has a story about its past should not be surprising. If anything distinguishes the early decades of the twenty-first century, it is the desire of people everywhere – in an ever more complex world – for stories. These create a sense of purposeful structure and meaning. They humanise issues, so that audiences can relate to them. They embody interpretations about values and aims. A newspaper editor in China in 2017 recognised this by labelling the national leader, Xi Jinping, the 'storyteller-in-chief'. This historic relationship with European powers – and in particular Britain, with all the trauma and tragedy attributed to it – was one of the most important tales he told. It was important enough to make an appearance at the top of the national State Constitution, the core document of governance. There, in the preamble, it states: 'After 1840, feudal China gradually became a semi-colonial, semi-feudal country. The Chinese people, wave upon wave, waged heroic struggles for national independence and liberation and for democracy and freedom.'[1]

That narrative was reinforced through patriotic education campaigns, widespread since the 1990s. In these, the Opium Wars (called Anglo-Chinese wars in this book) and the horrors of first British and then Japanese military aggression reinforced the sense of national victimisation that I had noted in my own personal experience of living in China and interacting with people over the years. Through this, the government conveyed to the domestic audience the notion of the moral rightness of the country's renaissance and reawakening today. From their first days at school, Chinese students learn that theirs is a nation that was hard done by and exploited almost to the point of destruction by greedy, unprincipled foreign actors. Self-respect, self-reliance and a strong form of nationalism are the morals that are drawn from this, making it a living story in the present – not just something about a departed, remote past.

INTRODUCTION

The more I heard this story (however sceptical I was of its content), the more I realised something: Britain has no corresponding tale to tell about its relations with China. If they are taught any history at all, children at schools in the United Kingdom today are more likely to learn about local, or European or American history. China is regarded as a subsidiary issue, a part of the vast, complex narrative of the British empire. It touches on contentious matters like the role of colonisation and imperialism. This lack of a more widely known national narrative about such an important country – and one with which Britain has such a key relationship – is a puzzle, because despite their great geographical distance from each other, the fact is that in previous centuries Britain and China were very closely linked. China's epic struggle with modernity, where an ancient civilisation tried to industrialise and reform its economy, society and politics, is one of the great sagas of humanity. It is a story that continues to this day, touching the lives of hundreds of millions, shaping our age and radically impacting on the nature of the world we now live in. At perhaps the key stage in this vast story – the very beginning – Britain was at the forefront, influencing China in ways that continue to resonate. This means that Britain's China story is not just about two countries, but is about forces, trends and shifts that fundamentally altered the path of humanity, and that form a major part of the whole tale of modernity and the shaping of globalisation itself.

The pitting of Britain against China during the period of the industrial and scientific revolutions of the eighteenth and nineteenth centuries brought two radically different cultures, world views and economic systems face to face with each other. It made the East and the West acknowledge the need for a relationship, despite their profound differences. In the twenty-first century, as the US and China try to forge a way of working with each other (and come to understand that there is no other option), the Sino-British story has deeper relevance than ever. It is one relationship that shows more than any other the shifting tectonic plates of power over the last four hundred years.

Power shift: The great reversal between Britain and China

Britain's reticence about a recognised and publicly accepted narrative of its history is not just an academic matter: the refusal to know this history – or the effort to try to forget it – carries with it real costs. Rather than a story, the UK currently has ambiguity and confusion. Examples abound: in 2015, during the state visit of Xi Jinping to Britain, a 'golden era' was famously declared by both sides. After a long time spent arguing and failing to see eye to eye over issues like Hong Kong, human rights and trade access, finally the two old foes were putting things on a new footing. And yet, only a few years later, a leader from the same political party that had declared this new era, Rishi Sunak of the Conservatives, announced that the 'golden era' was over. Huawei, a telecoms company from China that had been welcomed to Britain in the 2000s as a technology partner and provider, was banned from 5G work and told to exit communication systems by 2028. Even more confusingly, Britain declared in a policy review that China was a systemic competitor and the greatest economic threat to the country – even as trade ministers post-Brexit talked up the rich opportunities to come from doing more trade with the Chinese.[2]

Faced with this confusion, Britain appears like a character in a play that is still searching for a plot. All good stories need some identifiable structure – even if no more than a beginning, a middle and an end. In this retelling of the British story about China, I will argue that not only is there a plot, characterised by idealism and disappointment, love and hate, greed and charity, but also that it has undergone a dramatic and unexpected twist in recent years. As in a long-running television drama, suddenly the whole basis of the series has been turned on its head. Completely new dynamics have appeared. That seismic change is down to the massive role that power and access to sources of influence have played in the narrative. This was never a tale of harmony and balance, but rather a story about the use of force, and the forging of the desires of one party over those of the other. From the earliest times until recently, those forces were overwhelmingly on Britain's side. But in a remarkable twist, since 2000 there has been a radical and irrevocable change. The plot we see unfolding now is one where there is still a power imbalance – but the roles have been reversed. We are in the era of an altered game.

In this complex, multifaceted story there are four thematic areas where power has been exercised and made real: economic, technological, geopolitical and intellectual/cultural. Those four themes provide the great underpinnings of the story that follows, existing like massive pillars holding up a huge monument or building. They function in much the same way as do leitmotifs in an opera or differently coloured elements in a frieze: drawing together the various parts of the whole, however different the times and the people being referred to. Focusing on them makes the often contrasting (and sometimes contradictory) British story of China tellable. Without them, we would stare at unknowable chaos.

Let's start with the first – the economic area. Here we should not be distracted by the single question of scale. Many economic historians in the last few decades have declared that until at least 1800, Qing China's wealth and its overall economic size exceeded that of any other part of the world.[3] Adam Smith (1723–90) acknowledged this in his monumental *Wealth of Nations*: China crops up with surprising frequency throughout his argument. True – symptomatic of its shadowy presence in other areas of cultural and political discourse at the time – China never quite merits Smith's sustained attention (no doubt due to a contemporary lack of extensive information). But it is far from absent. China may well have had *scale*: it was, he stated at one point, 'a much richer country than any part of Europe'.[4] But it clearly lacked quality and effectiveness, because, while 'the greater part of Europe [is] in an improving state . . . China seems to be standing still'. As he wrote earlier, it 'has long been one of the richest, that is, one of the most fertile, best cultivated, most industrious, and most populous countries in the world. It seems, however, to have long been stationary.' Despite that, 'though it may stand still, [it] does not go backwards'.[5] The idea of the static, stagnant nature of China – not just in the economic realm, but also in the cultural and political – was one that British commentators would return to in the future. John Barrow (1764–1848), one of the men who accompanied the first ever formal embassy from Britain to China – the famous Macartney delegation – made the application of this notion to China a core feature of his writings. The energy and invasiveness of British capitalist practice meant that when the economies of the two countries came into direct contact, it was the methods and philosophies of Britain that generally prevailed, as they found themselves operating against what was seen as a passive, backward-looking entity that was ill equipped to engage with modernity without serious changes.

The same might be said of technology. The great twentieth-century sinologist Joseph Needham (1900–95), in his monumental multi-volume work *Science and Civilisation in China*, documented and described the huge achievements of early inventors and thinkers in the imperial era. Long before him, commentators from Britain were struck by the ways in which there were strands and threads of innovation in the past of the country they were encountering. All were also impressed by how these had sputtered out and stalled. As the British grew more involved in the country, this issue of the massive benefits their technological advancement brought for managing and controlling the new place they were dealing with became key. The introduction of the iron, flat-bottomed warship *Nemesis* during the First Anglo-Chinese War and the use of new kinds of rifles in the second were simply the most obvious examples of the benefits of the technical and scientific assets that Britain could deploy to get its own way. This was about more than just the use of new materials and methods: it involved different ways of organising people, both in battle and trade; and new ways of thinking which industrialisation brought with it. A more Marxist interpretation for why Britain was so willing to engage in the affairs of China from the start of the nineteenth century was simply that the country needed new markets for the wool, textiles and other goods that it was now making in factories and workshops. China was no more than a destination for excess capital, created by the energies of new processes – themselves the result of the new scientific way of thinking. Some of the most moving and poignant descriptions of Anglo-Chinese conflict in the Victorian era are of Chinese defending themselves with pre-modern bows and arrows, and simple human shields, against the devastating industrial armaments that Britain had pioneered. Mao Zedong (1893–1976) paid Britain a backhanded compliment during the revolution of the twentieth century, by declaring that power grew from the barrel of a gun. The British established that this was true – along with the more fundamental rule that the gun was the result of fresh and novel perspectives: almost right up to the end of the Qing era, China had barely begun to engage with these.

The third space for imbalance in Britain's favour was geopolitical. In seeking to understand the conflict between Britain and China, one of the most intractable problems lies in making sense of their markedly divergent attitudes towards international relations and their respective roles in the world. Both places clearly saw themselves as important powers. They also regarded the issue as being about more than just their economic or population size, or their material living standards. They each felt that they were representative of a particular view of the world and of order, and both sat in dominance at the heart of their separate zones. They were in the business of expressing their influence and power through values, not just blindly pursuing interests and satisfying their material needs. For Britain, its concept of itself as a nation state was shaped and formed by the political philosophy of Enlightenment Europe, and the Westphalian notion of the nation state. From this emerged a whole way of thinking about equality, respect and the need for universally accepted rules of engagement with others – notions that remain with us to this day. For the Ming and Qing Chinese, however, there was a very different set of concerns, involving complex ideas not about equality, but rather about concepts of tribute and hierarchy in order to preserve harmony. These notions derived principally from classical Chinese thinking on statecraft, but also from the nature of the Chinese state as it had evolved and developed, often in radically different forms, over the previous centuries. China's politics had a profound sense of the need to preserve stability, whether the threat derived from humans or nature. Relations with its bordering neighbours were captured through a much studied and analysed formal diplomatic language and accompanying set of protocols, where ritual and symbolism were as important as material transactions. This is well illustrated by the fact that before 1860, the Chinese did not even have any equivalent to the foreign ministries found elsewhere: the government simply assumed that its way of conducting relations with the outside world was so well understood that it needed no formal institutional set-up (it established one only as a result of the Second Anglo-Chinese War). Time and time again, British interlocutors complained about the cultural haughtiness and the constant insistence on engaging in such acts as kowtowing to the Chinese emperor that captured this excep-tionalist mindset in their opponents. More practically, Britain came to China with a set of relationships and alliances that placed it in a shifting coalition where the latter was almost always isolated. This issue became more striking as the nineteenth century ended and the Qing became the subject of a struggle for different zones of foreign influence. Geopolitically, Britain was a far more networked power, with a range of partners with whom it at least shared a common conceptual framework in terms of international relations and rule of law – even if, in practice, it often had conflict with them.

Very finally, there is the far more complex area of cultural and intellectual dominance. A good illustration of this is the simple matter of how Britain and China had knowledge of each other. In the twenty-first century, we are used to hearing British people berate themselves for their lack of knowledge of this vast power that they are having to engage with as never before. But the record shows that this is a very new phenomenon. British testimony about a place known and understood as China goes back, at least in the English language, to the 1580s. But any mentions in Chinese-language sources of a specific island nation on the edge of Europe called 'England' occur far later and are much sparser. The British were largely seen by the Chinese of the late Ming and the early Qing as mere Europeans. They were often labelled 'barbarians', even though there has subsequently been much argument about whether this English word captures the real meaning of the Chinese character employed. It was not until the era of the Anglo-Chinese wars that the Chinese felt the need to know about this place that was figuring increasingly in their lives and started to study it in any depth. The first British academic post for sinology – while later than that of Paris (which established a chair in Chinese studies in 1818) – was created in 1837, at University College, London. There Samuel Kidd (1799–1843), once a missionary, studied and taught for two years. The first direct translation from Chinese to English of important classical works occurred in 1809, when the remarkable scholar and linguist then based in India, Joshua Marshman (1768–1837), rendered part of Confucius's *Analects* into English. The even more remarkable scholar Robert Morrison (1782–1834) completed (in the most difficult circumstances imaginable) the first comprehensive Chinese–English dictionary in 1814. There was a tradition of British study of China which had depth and extensiveness long before this was remotely reciprocated. This is not to deny that there were Chinese who came to Britain to study. But as a broad rule, until the post-1978 era, British people (albeit a narrow and often elite subset) knew far more about China than the Chinese did about Britain.

In these four areas, as the twentieth century closed and the new century proceeded, the advantages have largely shifted towards

China. From being a smaller economy in the 1990s, China in 2023 stands at four times the size of Britain. In technological areas – without in any way wishing to belittle Britain's ongoing achievements – China has produced artificial intelligence, telecoms, automotive and other methods that have either reached parity with or overtaken Britain. Its three thousand or more universities receive research and development funding from the government on a level that would be hard to comprehend for cash-strapped British institutions. Most of the latter, in any case, are increasingly bankrolled by international student fees, including a large number of Chinese. In geopolitics, China is increasingly being seen as contesting and even undermining the Western order, with its vast Belt and Road Initiative, the 120-plus countries where it figures as the largest trading partner, and its set of relationships in Africa and Latin America that give it global reach and clout. Finally, it is the Chinese who, through language study and overseas stays, tend to know more about Britain than the other way around. It is estimated that 200 million speak English to some level. Those in Britain that speak Chinese that were not originally from China or of Chinese heritage number in the low thousands.

Landmarks: The great moments of Britain's China story

In the narrative that follows, happily there are not just generic themes of economy, technology, geopolitics and culture, but a number of key landmark dates. These act as useful boundaries, marking off separate stages as the relationship has intensified. They have been drafted into service, therefore, to structure the long story I am about to tell.

The beginning is inevitably somewhat blurred – a mixture of myth and reality, with no clear starting point. It is as though through the late sixteenth century, during the height of Elizabethan exploration and curiosity, Britain was slowly travelling towards China, seeing its contours and epic qualities from afar, sometimes through fog, via the confusing testimony of intermediaries. But then things sharpen up around 1600, when there is at least direct contact. The first well-documented visits by

British merchants to Ming China (1368–1644) started around 1635. For the following century, in the first decades of the new Qing Dynasty (1644–1911/12), there was a game of sporadic, sometimes quite intense, initiation and exploration. More ships and traders found themselves, by design or accident, on the great coasts of southern China looking for profit or adventure, driving the story forward.

This early phase ends with the arrival in 1741 of a Royal Navy ship carrying George Anson. This conferred a new element of officialdom on the links, which up until then had been dominated by private traders. This is a story where we have to look both ways: we have to pay attention to the situation as the British and Chinese saw it in China itself, but also to the ways in which this perception was relayed back to (and played a role in) Britain's own domestic political and cultural space. There the idealisation of China – this barely known, remote, strange place, described in sparse accounts and encountered by very few – reached new heights. That was reinforced by the arrival in people's daily lives of tangible signs of China's presence and influence – tea, porcelain, silk and, of course, ideas of gardening and aesthetics. This phase peaked around 1790. By that time, embassies from the Netherlands and Russia, in particular, had been sent to make contact and to gather knowledge about China. And all the while the British empire was intensifying its commitment to and involvement in India and neighbouring China. Thanks to such direct contact at a deeper and more committed level, there was far more empirical evidence and lived experience on which to base the relationship. More complex feelings and attitudes grew up. These are eloquently and intelligently attested to in the reflections of Lord Macartney following his frustrating, enormously significant embassy of 1793–94. This stage of deeper knowledge and the framing of China in British discourse reached its peak in the 1830s.

The tensions and contradictions that arose over this period of familiarisation – whether from perceptions of unbalanced trade, unfair treatment or cultural clashes – came to a head in the explosive period from 1838 and resulted in war. The First Anglo-Chinese War set in train a new kind of relationship and a consolidation of the deep power imbalances in Britain's favour. These were codified and normalised in treaties, a growing network of treaty ports (specific designated areas where British and eventually other foreigners were allowed to trade and operate in China with special privileges), and a host of other interventions and interferences by the new quasi-colonial partner. A part of China's sovereign territory was ceded in perpetuity to Britain, the so-called 'fragrant harbour' of Hong Kong (though most of the city territory was eventually ceded on leases – a point that will be covered later). As I will show, there were many ways in its early years when this chaotic, often lawless frontier place, so rich in symbolic importance, failed to live up to the original meaning of its name in Chinese. But the city indicated a mutual link – one that carried different kinds of meaning and different understandings on both sides. These were to work themselves out over the following century and a half. The era of the wars continued with the Second Anglo-Chinese War of 1856–60, a further demonstration of raw force, but one that carried the real possibility that Britain might end up with a collapsing China and far more responsibility than it wished for.

Ironically, therefore, after the landmark date of 1860, we enter four decades when Britain changed from being the constant harasser and interferer in Qing China, to something like a defender. It shifted, with great reluctance, from a position of strenuously defended neutrality during the Taiping Rebellion (1850–64) against the Qing to military supporter, assisting (albeit in ways far less impactful than subsequent imperialist propagandists were to claim) in the final defeat of the Nanjing-based insurgency. Through entities like the predominantly British-managed Chinese Imperial Maritime Customs Service and the Salt Administration, and by insisting in the Treaty of Beijing (1860) on China setting up a foreign ministry (the Zongli Yamen), Britain expanded its networks across almost the whole of China. This loose arrangement has confused interpreters, forcing them to use terms like 'informal empire' to acknowledge the depth of interference, along with the resistance to any deeper administrative involvement. The principal objective of British interests at this time, it is often claimed, was simple trade. But this ignored the complex of ideas and world views which underpin trade, and the whole issue of the attempt to promote legal, administrative and political thinking in China.

From the Boxer Rebellion of 1900, a further landmark date, we see the start of what might best be described as a Chinese fightback. The Boxers themselves were a complex, hybrid movement. But most evidence suggests that they were partly motivated by profound anger at foreign (and particularly British) involvement in the affairs of their country. The undignified scramble for concessions and other benefits by Germany, Russia, Japan and others had forced Britain, too, to engage in what looked like a carve-up of a passive, suffering China. The Boxer Rebellion itself, with its violence and chaotic shape, manifested a new form of more active Chinese nationalism. That was to grow over the following decades, fuelled by the increasing evidence of foreign self-interest and ruthless behaviour against a China unable to defend itself. The gargantuan indemnities extracted – not just after the 1900 events, but by the Japanese when they defeated China in the 1895 war – created a whole system of finance and a new way of once more embedding British and other interests deep in the existing Chinese state and body politic.

Over the following three decades, there were further key inflection points, all of them related to the evolution and rising challenge of Chinese nationalism. The collapse of the Qing dynasty itself in 1911–12 ushered in a period of almost continuous crisis. Britain's potency in terms of its military and economic instruments of influence began slowly to wane. Events like the Paris Peace Conference of 1919, the London Imperial Conference of 1921 and the Washington Conference a year later all opened up China's affairs to international, rather than purely British, involvement. But Britain remained, at least in symbolic terms, the key carrier of the colonial mission and message. Strikes and boycotts of British goods were the instruments by which

Chinese nationalism – whether represented by the new Kuomintang (KMT) party or the nascent communist movement – tried to fight back. There was a slow dismantling of the extraterritoriality privileges and the so-called treaty ports – with the northern port city of Weihaiwei (one of Britain's possessions in China ceded in 1898) belatedly returned to the Chinese government in 1930 and the Salt Administration handed over in 1931. Total reversion occurred a decade later, when all extraterritoriality was scrapped.

The era of 1931 to 1949 was dominated by conflict and war. Britain's China story over this period was one in which the actions of others overshadowed their bilateral links. For China, the epic struggle against Japan consumed the nation from 1931, reaching full war status in 1937. This period fundamentally reshaped and reframed China; it created a situation of huge instability and uncertainty, in which, at least for the latter half, Britain was an ally – but an ally with very limited capacity to help in China's existential struggle, since it had to deal with its own colossal fight against Nazism back in Europe. For China, the war clarified finally and irrefutably the fact that Britain, as a European power, would always prioritise its interests there, and that its global pretensions were fading and unreliable. In Singapore, Malaysia and Hong Kong, the potency and reach of British military power had been dramatically exposed as limited to nonexistent. From this era, it was America that became the more dominant force: it ended a century over which Britain had been the principal foreign actor in China. That situation persists to this day.

The year 1949 marked a natural turning point. After a civil war, the establishment in Beijing of the communist-led People's Republic of China (PRC) heralded a new phase. By accident rather than design – and in order principally to preserve its interests in Hong Kong, over which it had managed (despite American opposition) to resume control after 1945 – Britain maintained and nurtured an uneasy, isolated relationship with the new regime in Beijing. Though this lacked official status, from 1950 to 1972 (when diplomatic links were finally established) it did furnish the two sides with a means of contact and communication that neither America nor much of Europe had. Britain had representation throughout this period in Beijing and, until 1966, in Shanghai. It had business interests until those were extinguished, on the ground at least, in 1959. This is the era of delegations, many of them sympathetic to the Chinese new politics. In Britain, too, a new sentiment – one that often separated left and right; more established businesses and newer arrivals – created a far more divided, ambiguous attitude towards this new partner.

Full diplomatic status was concluded between Britain and the People's Republic in 1972. Shortly thereafter, in September of that year, US President Richard Nixon visited Beijing. Thus Britain's ability to be to some extent an intermediary, with a unique presence in China, came to an end. American direct engagement and involvement with the country intensified from this period. Britain itself had to craft a policy and an attitude towards China which accepted the new geopolitical reality of the world around it. The means to that end came largely through trade. All of this was energised by the reforms in the People's Republic itself from 1978. These seemingly presented new opportunities for influence and dialogue. As part of the process, the negotiations between 1982 and 1984 to resolve the Hong Kong issue, culminating in the final framework agreement, were of enormous importance. They were best symbolised by the meetings between Britain's key political figure at that time, Prime Minister Margaret Thatcher, and the Chinese paramount leader, Deng Xiaoping. But the 1984 resolution resulted in a long coda before its final act of full retrocession in 1997. That interlude covered the first and only state visit to China by Queen Elizabeth II in 1986, the Tiananmen Uprising in 1989 along with the agonised problems this gave rise to, and then the epic battle between the last governor of Hong Kong, Chris Patten, and his compatriots about how to manage the transition of the city to its new owners.

The final landmark was 1997, which ushered in a move to a new era of 'engagement' and an attempt – by the British at least – to reset relations. This period, as I will argue, is striking because of the ways in which the four great areas of imbalance – economic, technological, geopolitical and cultural/intellectual – shifted from Britain in favour of China. It is in this era – an era that witnessed both the golden age referred to above and its rapid demise – that we now live, working out daily the implications of this great transition.

Who are we, who are you: The terms 'Britain' and 'China'

For all Europeans – right from their first encounters with China at the time of the Venetian Marco Polo (1254–1324) in the thirteenth century – the greatest problem was the gulf between what they perceived in (and learned about) this new partner and their own traditions and cultures. Interpreting this difference proved an epic and often inconclusive undertaking. Jesuit missionaries in the sixteenth and seventeenth centuries spent many years in the Ming and early Qing dynasties – some of them (like the great Matteo Ricci, 1552–1610) in the imperial court. But the contrast between their own Christian beliefs and world view and those of the Chinese they interacted with often made them grapple with explanations and theories that ranged from the bizarre to the unworkable. We will see that, as late as the 1660s, some in Britain constructed arguments that the Chinese were descendants of one of Noah's sons stranded in the country during the great flood. Others believed isolation had stopped the Chinese from engaging with the outside world in ways that would have served to make them easier to relate to. Orientalist or not, for those British who physically ventured into this brave new world now available to them through sea routes and more robust ships, the first impression was of the immense antiquity of the place. Everything else seemed alien, too: the flora and fauna, the architecture of the buildings, the clothes people wore and, of course, the way they spoke. What were they to make of this place, where the rulers were literati selected through a national meritocratic examination, and where the emperor existed behind walls of seclusion and mysterious ritual? For some, this fundamental difference was stimulating and exciting; for others, it aroused deep insecurity and antagonism. Very rarely did it leave people unmoved.

This issue of difference and how to make sense of it is made much more complex because neither of the parties in the relationship was static over the four centuries they came to know each other. From the sixteenth century to today, the entity that is now called the United Kingdom underwent frequent changes and transitions. These are reflected in the story contained in this book. At the outset, it is principally England's relations, until the accession of James VI of Scotland to the English throne in 1603 created a common monarchy for those two countries. The 1707 Act of Union in the reign of Queen Anne formalised this, creating the United Kingdom of Great Britain. Ireland was added to this Union in 1801 – a situation that was revised when the Irish Free State came into existence in December 1922. The six counties of Northern Ireland, however, were taken into the Union in the late 1920s. Though aware of the evolving nature of the entity from 1707, for the purposes of this book – where the principal focus is on the combined relations of England, Scotland, Northern Ireland and Wales with an external partner – I will most often use the term Britain, serving as a shorthand for 'Great Britain'. Where necessary, I will be more specific if I talk of particular places or strands of history.

For China, the issues are perhaps even more complex. Here we do not have the relative stability of islands with some settled natural boundaries, as is the case with Britain. Instead, we face portions of a vast landmass where the frontiers between each often shifted over history and where the component entities sometimes contracted and sometimes expanded. The natural barriers to this immense territory were the great Tibetan plateau, the huge deserts of the northeast and the arid northern wastes extending up to modern Siberia. The Yuan dynasty from 1267 to 1368 had witnessed Mongol rule extend into

Central Asia and as far as the edges of Europe. But after its collapse, the Ming dynasty – when the first substantive contact with the West and Britain occurred – witnessed a massive contraction. The China that existed at this time did not include in its administrative territory Inner Mongolia, Xinjiang or Tibet. Nor for that matter was much jurisdiction exercised over the island of Taiwan. The reign of the sybaritic Wan Li emperor (1563–r1572–1620) in the sixteenth century – a ruler who disappeared from even his own courtiers for almost two decades and governed by proxy – was soon followed by the slow implosion of that dynasty and a messy transition to the Qing. The Qing dynasty, after it finally managed to secure its powers, underwent a process of expansion, so that it became more akin to an empire than a nation state. The areas now covered by Tibet, Xinjiang and Inner Mongolia were conquered. Taiwan was also brought (reluctantly) by the ruling emperor of the time, the great Kangxi (1654–r1661–1722), more closely into the Qing sphere of influence. A softer zone around the periphery of the new empire area came into being; where there was no direct rule but a great deal of Chinese cultural and political influence. Often these 'tributary' or neighbouring states were where the British and Chinese first experienced serious tensions and conflict as they sought to exercise influence by using their very different approaches to administration. It was the British designs and actions in the Indian areas bordering the Qing that most unsettled the Qianlong court when Lord Macartney appeared there in 1793, espousing the cause of the pacific intentions of the country he represented.

The Qing, after its final great appropriation of land and influence in the middle of the eighteenth century, maintained relatively stable borders until its demise in 1911–12. What was less stable was the uniformity of the government within, which progressed from a large degree of centralisation in the high Qing era of the three great emperors, Kangxi, Yongzheng and Qianlong (from 1661 to 1796) to a slow fragmentation and erosion. Insurgencies in the middle of the nineteenth century created potential alternative Chinas – states that

Britain could be obliged to (and sometimes did) engage with, such as it briefly did in the 1850s with the Taiping. This process deteriorated until there was something akin to administrative anarchy in the early twentieth century. The fall of the Qing itself, though long predicted, resulted in a situation in which Great Britain did not formally acknowledge the new republic until 1914. Even then, there were divisions through the next two decades – initially between the southern and northern parts of the country, run under very different systems and groups; there were then further divisions into areas operated under specific provincial warlords. The Japanese carved up much of the extant state in the 1930s, bringing into existence a Manchurian puppet administration and then – with staggering levels of violence – appropriating much of the coastal region of the country. In the Second World War, China split into this Japanese-controlled zone, the nationalist KMT zone and a smaller communist-influenced area. Inevitably these were highly unstable formations. Only in 1945 and with the ending of hostilities in China's favour did a relatively unified government come into being. But civil war from 1946 and the final victory of the communists in 1949 once more resulted in division. Despite the constant declarations of a 'One China' principle, in 2023 at least, we continue to be in the same era as began in 1949, where there are two entities – the People's Republic of China and the Republic of China on Taiwan – that rest on contested claims about which, ultimately, is the legitimate ruler of the Greater China area.

While these different Chinas engaged with different Britains over the centuries, there was one feature that remained the same. Right up to the modern era, any interaction that Britain had almost always raised questions not about what was being engaged with and witnessed, but about who the British themselves were. The way that China operated, its hybrid belief system, the curious combination of an often highly centralised state and almost anarchic conditions in much of the rest of the country, its strong sense of history and culture that contained little – or often nothing – about the West (and in particular about Britain itself): all this sparked curiosity or defensiveness on the part of the British. Similarly for the Chinese, the increased role that Britain played in shaping and influencing their country – and its habit of getting its own way and of moulding China to its own advantage – inspired deep soul-searching. For both sides, their mutual link made them ask questions not just about the other, but about who they were themselves. To this day, even the manner in which the People's Republic subscribes to Marxism while operating like a full-blown capitalist economy disrupts the more commonly accepted tenets of modernity. This matter of how the British dealt with aspects of China's difference, even as the Chinas they were dealing with changed and as they themselves changed, will be a constant undercurrent in the story this book will tell.

Sources for the storytelling

Finally, a practical issue. The story of Britain's relations with China consumed the lives of a huge number of people; preoccupied many more; and had an impact not just on individuals who might claim British or Chinese identity, but also on those from other places. The written sources alone that attest to this story – set down either by those directly involved or by bystanders, commentators and others – would take many lifetimes to read. I have only been able to scratch the surface of this immense mass of words. An enormous debt is owed to the scholars, from the nineteenth century onwards, who started to make sense of what this narrative meant and how to tell it – figures like H.B. Morse, who worked originally in the Imperial Customs, and who then pursued a career akin to a chronicler, producing two vast tomes about the East India Company's work in China and the foreign relations of the imperial Chinese court. These works are now over a century old. Many have followed in his footsteps, working on different parts of the overall story. As many of these works as I could easily lay my hands on are in the bibliography.

There are rich archival sources. I have looked at material contained in the Jardine Matheson collection held at Cambridge University Library; at the China Collection at the School of Oriental and African Studies (SOAS) in London, which largely derived from the holdings of the Swire company; and at the remarkable online archives where the Foreign Office papers on China are digitised, covering the years 1919 to 1980. There are also the very early works, most of them also available online, along with materials relating to the earliest trading and political relationship with China, which are held at the British Library. Huge amounts of this material have been placed online, thus removing time constraints by obviating the need to get to a particular place, in order to refer to documents within the designated hours. These combined sources are the foundation of what follows. They and innumerable others testify to the fact that whatever the Sino-British relationship has been over the last four hundred years or so, it has been constantly written about and attested to.

1

Partners at the Edge, 1550–1720

Edmund Scott, a trader based in the Dutch East Indies headquarters in Batavia, where today's Jakarta is located, was clearly a man with a temper. In the years 1603 to 1606, according to his own testimony written and published on his return to his native Britain, his greatest ire was directed towards his neighbours, who were not Christians, but 'Heathen dogs' from China. 'A long time we lived in fear of fire,' he raged, 'but now we felt the brunt and smart of it, and if God most miraculously had not preserved us, we had all perished both lives and goods.' The Chinese were keeping 'a victualling house', brewing the fearsomely potent arrack, 'a kind of hot drink that is used in most of those parts of the world, instead of wine'. In his retelling of what happened, Scott's fury welled up in the words he used: 'This offspring of the devil, and heir of hell, had two outhouses' in which they undertook their brewing business. For some reason, they had dug deep holes under Scott's house, and while using these had started a fire, which ended up destroying most of the British trader's merchandise.[1]

'When I saw that these damned Chinese would do us little good, but rather harm, I was almost in despair', wrote Scott. But he was not about to accept passively what fate had served up. An initial

22

investigation of one of the suspects had involved the threat of hot irons on the man's skin. His passing of the blame onto someone else had been enough to prevent him receiving the full horror of extensive torture. But his compatriot, a goldsmith who was fingered as the main culprit, was not so lucky:

> Because of his sullenness, and that it was he that fired, I thought I would burn him now a little, for we were now in the heat of our anger. First I caused him to be burned under the nails of his thumbs, fingers, and toes with sharp hot Iron, and the nails to be torn off, and because he never blemished at that, we thought that his hands and legs had been numbed with tying. Wherefore we burned him in the arms, shoulders, and neck, but all was one with him: then we burned him quite through the hinds, and ... [with] Iron tongs [took] out the flesh and sinews.

These were only preliminary horrors. After taking 'hot searing irons' to his shin bones, and breaking his fingers, Scott tore the Chinese neighbour's toes with pincers. Then he broke the man's fingers. 'Yet for all this,' Scott went on, 'he never shed tear, no nor once turned his head aside, nor stirred hand or foot: but when we demanded any question, he would put his tongue between his teeth, and strike his chin upon his knees to byte it off.' Getting no satisfaction any longer from this sadistic orgy, Scott had the man with his broken body carried away and stuck on a pole, where he was shot to death: 'Between our men and the Hollanders, they shot him almost all to pieces before they left him.' The lugubrious truth is that one of the earliest, if not the earliest, direct, first-hand accounts of interaction between a British and a Chinese described unimaginable levels of abuse and force.

The history of Britain's relations with China contains, from its earliest, fragmentary beginnings, characters and opinions that are akin to archetypes. If Scott, with his venting of sadistic cruelty on the

Chinese goldsmith, serves as the forerunner of all those people who used violence over the coming centuries, then the next extensive record of interaction reversed the power dynamic. The East India Company (EIC) had been established on the last day of 1600, with a charter approved by Queen Elizabeth I giving it a monopoly on all English trade with countries east of the Cape of Good Hope and west of the Strait of Magellan. Those that violated this ran the risk of having their goods forfeited. The twenty-four directors under the first governor, Thomas Smythe, started to plot out ways of identifying and benefiting from the kinds of rich opportunities for trade that they knew the Dutch, Portuguese and other Europeans were finding in the distant East. For the next 233 years – until the final disbandment of its privileges – the EIC was central to interaction with China. And yet, in the early days – as proved by the factory (in this context meaning company base, rather than a place for manufacturing) at Hirado in Japan, run by the British from 1613 to 1623 – access to the Chinese market was challenging and offered paltry returns.

This had little impact on our second archetypal figure, represented here by the idealist Richard Cocks. Sent as the manager of the EIC interests in Japan, he was faced with competition from the Dutch (who were well entrenched there) and with barriers increasingly thrown up by the rulers of Japan themselves. Their deep distrust of the actions of the predominantly Jesuit Christian missionaries was leading to the rapid closure of the island nation to the outside world. On 15 October 1615, Cocks cheerily wrote that Dittis – a man of Chinese heritage whom he had grown to know and trust and who was based partly in China and partly locally – 'doth assure me on his life that our pretence to get trade into China cannot but come to good effect which God grant'.[2] Cocks gave Dittis numerous payments to nurture and cultivate this prospective trade. His faith remained undimmed, despite no subsequent hard evidence that things were proceeding particularly well. A year after his initial optimistic expectations, on 11 August 1616 he wrote, 'I thought good to note down as we passed along the river side our business concerning procuring a trade into China was a great hope to take effect, for that the great men [sic] [Dittis] hath taken 3,000 pesos.'³ A little later, on lending the ever-helpful local two bars of gold, Cocks stated that his expectations of trade with China stood higher in hope than ever. But despite the odd morsel, and the concession finally of two ships to be sent each year to the southern city of Fuzhou in China from 1621, the EIC seniors were far more sceptical. When the decision was taken in 1623 to dissolve the Hirado factory for poor returns, one of them wrote to Cocks from Batavia that 'the Chinese [Dittis] hath too long deluded you, through your own simplicity, to credit unto him'.⁴

The unfortunate Cocks died in March 1624 on board a ship sailing back to Britain, no doubt none the wiser about who precisely he had been dealing with. We now know through the work of modern scholarship that Dittis was recognised as 'a man of mystery',⁵ who may have been little more than a pirate. The records in Chinese that exist refer to Andre Dittis as a name given by the Dutch and others to someone who was the chief resident Chinese in Hirado. The Dutch themselves seem to have been more than aware of his shady side, with one account stating that 'he is a sly man', but one with 'a magnificent house at Nagasaki and here'.⁶ Other records from China say that Dittis and his brother, Whowe, were 'the greatest smugglers in Formosa [the former name for Taiwan]'.⁷ Under his Chinese name of 'Li Tan', Dittis occupies a shadowy place – the first of the third archetype we will encounter in these pages: the mediator, a sort of go-between, who flits to and fro between the two worlds of Britain and China, sometimes creating more darkness than light, and pursuing aims that are frequently opaque and hard to clearly divine.

Of the dark past

There is no clear beginning to the links between the British Isles and the Chinese empires of the past. In archaeological digs in 2002, two skeletons of people who appeared to have Asian DNA were found in Lant Street, on the edges of Roman London. The findings were 'cautiously accepted', with potential links via slave trading between India and China and the movement of people onwards from there into Europe. This was an early, fascinating glimpse of contact. The only other potential connection was recorded in the work of Rabban Bar Sauma, a Uyghur Nestorian, who in 1289 was appointed by the Mongol court newly established in Yuan China (1271–1368) as ambassador to West Europe. He reportedly met Edward I (1239–r1272–1307). Another brief strand of evidence states that an Englishman served as an interpreter and messenger in the Mongol invasion forces that came to Europe from the 1220s to 1240.[8] This ghostly figure slips back into the great anonymity of early history almost as soon as he emerges. After that, silence reigns for several centuries.

It is a curiosity that while Britain showed barely any consciousness at all of the great empire on the other side of the world, other Europeans were not innocent about China. In the years around 1516, the Portuguese Fernão Pires de Andrade had visited the Ming court, reigniting the direct contact that had existed two centuries earlier in the time of the explorer Marco Polo. On reaching the Chinese, Pires was eventually briefly jailed for his efforts; but the outcome – the eventual creation of an informal settlement on which the Portuguese might establish some business links at Macau around the middle part of the sixteenth century – meant that there was a tangible connection between the two continents. After this, from the time of the Spaniard Saint Francis Xavier (1506–52), the predominantly Jesuit missionaries had made the heathen of Ming China one of their chief targets. Their work was heroic, often tragic and painstaking, and resulted in the creation of new forms of knowledge, translations and the dissemination in European languages other than English of information about the remote, little-known, mysterious world on the other side of the globe.

The British in the time of Elizabeth I (1553–r1558–1603) were initially preoccupied with their struggles in Europe, and with the exploration by figures like Sir Walter Raleigh and Francis Drake of seas and routes to their west and south. Conflict with the Spanish meant that Europe itself was almost an excluded market for them. This period of partially enforced early globalisation saw interest in the wider world, and the chances it offered for enrichment and influence. In the literature over this very early period, this place so far away – partly prefigured in Latin and other European-language sources – comes slowly (and often with significant blurring) into sharper focus. There were the fanciful tales of Sir John Mandeville, whose book of marvels and travels written some time in the 1350s in Latin referred to 'the Great Khan, who is a great emperor, indeed the greatest in the world, as he is lord of the great isle of Cathay'.[9] All of this would have been edifying, had it not been for the near certainty that Mandeville never existed and that his work was a concoction of fabrication, hearsay and heavy borrowing. The later and more historically grounded compendium of sailors' and merchants' tales by Richard Hakluyt (1553–1616), assembled over the period 1589 to 1600, contained fleeting mentions of 'the Tartars', a term thenceforward fixed in often shifting and vague ways to what today would be labelled the Manchurian and Mongolian parts of contemporary China and its ethnic inhabitants. Hakluyt declared in his 1600 dedicatory epistle to the second edition of his work that 'I have brought to light certain new advertisements of the later alteration of the mighty monarchy of Japan, and the new conquest of the Kingdom of Korea, as also of the Tartars adjoining on the east and northeast parts of Korea.'[10] But in terms of testifying to physical visitation by the British of this remote, fabled place, the record was more about disappointment and failure. A letter by Anthony Jenkinson in Hakluyt's collection, written in Moscow in 1559, refers to 'our voyage towards Cathay [meaning China]' being curtailed by 'the incessant and continual wars, which are in all these brutal and wild countries'.[11]

The Tudors could not be accused of being indolent in their attempts to achieve first contact. But they were impeded by a couple of fundamental problems. The first was that no one seemed clear on whether they were looking for one place or two. The terms China and Cathay are sprinkled across the literature and used interchangeably. Things were only finally settled in the somewhat surprising work of the writer Robert Burton (1577–1640). There, in his dense, erudite *Anatomy of Melancholy*, published in variant texts from 1621 to 1638, he offered a final judgement: amidst a fulsome passage discussing cures for melancholy and the importance of air to life and well-being, he declared that 'Riccius [Matteo Ricci, the great Jesuit missionary to China] hath written, China and [Cathay] be all one, the great Cham [Khan] of Tartary and the king of China be the same.'[12] In this way, finally, in the minds of literate English people, two people became one.

As for the second matter, this was the prosaic issue of how to get to this place. William Bourne (1535–82) in his treatise from 1574 on navigation, *A Regiment for the Sea*, after presenting tables that recorded longitude, sea tides and other nautical information, had discussed routes to Cathay. He acknowledged that – even though he had set down five possibilities – 'there were some people who were doubtful whether there be any such place.'[13] One route was that which the Portuguese took, 'by Cape Bon Sperance' – the Cape of Good Hope. The other would be 'through the Strait of Magellan and so into the South Sea'.[14] The third is the northward route, 'unto the place called Merra Incognita' and via Iceland. 'Being at Merra Incognita you must discover thereabouts where that you may find sea for to give you passage',[15] Bourne airily states – hardly reassuring advice for those brave enough to take a journey thousands of miles into the unknown. A fourth, northeast passage is so vague that he says little specific about it. The final route would be via the pole, something that even he admits is 'a mere foolishness and a thing impossible'.[16] At least by 1592, the English mathematician Emery Molyneux and the geographer Edward Wright had created a globe which physically marked out the various ways that could be followed from one side of the then known world to the other. According to one account, this venture can be seen as an early example of intellectual collaboration, because it was based on the Ming mapmaker Luo Hongxian's *Extended World Chart* (*Guang Yutu*), brought back indirectly, via Thomas Cavendish on his tour around the world of 1586–88.[17] There is an even earlier map than this, kept today in the British Library, though by Ludovico Georgio and published in Antwerp in 1584, rather than a British product.

Those that attempted the passage to China from Britain did not fare well. Sir Hugh Willoughby perished in his attempt in 1554. Richard Eden and Richard Chancellor's attempt over 1554 to 1555 ended when they met the coast of Muscovy (the duchy centred on today's Moscow). Martin Frobisher may well have been furnished with Bourne's learned treatise; but if so, he managed to get only as far as Baffin Island, east of Greenland – and therefore in entirely the wrong direction. Francis Drake's circumnavigation of the globe allowed him, while in Malacca, to come across a Chinese man called Pausaos from Anhui province in central China. Perhaps this was the earliest documented contact between named British and Chinese individuals. For Edward Fenton in 1582, the endeavour to use the southern route to reach China went in the right direction, but ended up in Brazil.

In the ship captained by John Newbury in 1583, a letter was carried, the first of four from Queen Elizabeth I to her counterpart, the Wan Li emperor (though the latter's immense sense of status and power meant that he would hardly have regarded her as remotely being his equal). Here she had written that Britain's intention was to propose trade 'which consisteth in the transporting outward of such things whereof we have plenty and in bringing in such things as we stand in need of'. This succinct expression of the desire for commerce was followed by another cool acknowledgement of reality: 'We are borne and made to have need one of another, and that we are bound to aide one another.'[18] The letter never reached its destination, as Newbury was taken prisoner by the Portuguese. But such setbacks only seemed to stoke British enthusiasm. The names of those attempting to reach China increased as the years proceeded. Adrian Gilbert in 1582, John Davis in 1585 and then the already mentioned Sir Thomas Cavendish in 1586–88 in his own voyage around the world. In his subsequent account, Cavendish wrote that 'I navigated the island of the Philippinos hard upon the coast of China of which country I have brought stateliness and riches of which I fear to make report of lest I should not be credited.'[19] Such tantalising glimpses inspired other travellers and seekers of riches, such as Ralph Fitch. He managed to complicate the picture by mentioning an account of Tibet given by someone who knew someone who had been there – another new and intriguing place.

The second missive to the Wan Li emperor from Queen Elizabeth's hand (or at least the second that was physically sent) was despatched in the three ships fitted out by Sir Robert Dudley bearing the evocative names of the *Bear*, the *Bear's Whelp* and the *Benjamin*.[20] Two merchants on the ships, Richard Allen and Thomas Broomfield, carried a Latin epistle. Here the sovereign continued the ardent protestations of hope and mutual benefit that she had alluded to over a decade and a half earlier, expressing her desire for 'the greater increase of mutual love and commerce between us and your subjects, by these present letter of ours'.[21] She hoped that 'the stations, ports, towns, or cities of your Empire' would be open and that the merchants 'shall have full and free liberty of egress and regress and of dealing in trade of merchandize with your subjects'.[22] But Dudley's mission got no further than those of his predecessors, perishing in transit. In 1602, a year before the end of her reign, a final letter issued from Queen Elizabeth's hand to be carried on an EIC ship under the captaincy of George Waymouth. A copy of this is today kept in the Lancashire Archives. Like its two predecessors, it did not reach its intended recipient.

Even if Elizabeth's ornate letters in their various translations (Latin, Greek, Portuguese) had been delivered, it is highly unlikely that they would have attracted much attention. The long reign of the Wan Li emperor, famously described in historian Ray Huang's wonderful account, had resulted in his complete disengagement from his court.[23] Matteo Ricci, after long residence in China, had finally reached the Ming capital Beijing in 1601 and gained first-hand experience of this. Despite fluent written and spoken Chinese, and an acculturation to local circumstances that meant he sometimes wore the clothes of a Confucian scholar rather than his priestly garb, his presentation to the imperial throne itself resulted in him bowing down to an empty seat. Wan Li had disappeared into a world where his only contact was with eunuchs and concubines in the secluded inner palace. The court operated on almost mechanical, bureaucratic lines, where representatives issued edicts in the name of the living (but absent) emperor and regulated life with no active input from him.[24] Britain's rulers were sending messages to people who would never have even looked at them if they had been successfully delivered.[25]

Tea time: Trade and the origins of Britain's love affair with a Chinese drink

Being undelivered, the Elizabethan letters led to no trade. It was the East India Company, made permanent in 1609 after its initial temporary establishment, that became the main vehicle for future attempts at real, physical links with China. This was to prove a backbreakingly hard endeavour, and not just because of the newness of the terrain being explored. The failure and closure of its factory in Hirado was only the first of a series of setbacks. In 1623, conflict with the competing Dutch resulted in the Amboyna Massacre, when a dozen English merchants were tortured and then executed on the island of that name.[26] This struggle for new markets and trading opportunities between the Dutch and the British continued in Asia for much of the next three decades. The region became a site for competition between European nations and their hunger for imports and exports. Britain was venturing into seas already of deep interest to other powers – something that provided an added edge of danger and unease, because it was not just the suspicions and hostility of indigenous peoples that was problematic, but the intentions of neighbours closer to home.

The British persisted, despite this. In 1634, the EIC ship the *London*, captained by Matthew Willis, a Briton with a British crew, landed in Macau. Through the mediation of the Portuguese there, they managed to gain direct contact with the Chinese, though little came of it.[27] It was left to a private entrepreneur based in London, Endymion Porter, who approached Sir William Courten (somewhat ironically, in view of the fact that the main obejective was to thwart the Nethrlands, a Dutch immigrant) to finance a full, formal trade tour of the Far East. There was a highly domestic motive behind this: the travails of the reigning monarch Charles I (1600–r1625–1649) and his seemingly perpetual fights with parliament (fights that ended up, after the Civil War broke out in the 1640s, costing him his life) made the money-making potential of the trip of interest even to a king.[28] Despite the EIC's monopoly on business, its profits had been declining since the Amboyna Massacre, prompting a search elsewhere for quick returns. The hopes of Charles I and others for such enrichment were pinned on the non-EIC Courten ships as they set sail on 1 April 1636. The fleet was composed of the *Dragon*, *Sun*, *Katherine* and *Planter* and was accompanied by two smaller vessels, the *Anne* and *Discovery* (the last returning to Britain part way through the journey, as it proved too slow). On its arrival in Goa in October the same year, the fleet had a frosty reception, on account of the new competition it brought: 'You bring ruin to the honourable company [the EIC] whom I serve', stated William Methwold, the company's representative there.[29]

The Weddell voyage, as it came to be called, after its captain John Weddell (1583–1642), was the first full trading mission to attempt to deal direct with Ming China (and also the last, in view of the dynasty's demise in 1642–44). It did so in the most difficult circumstances. EIC opposition was the least of its problems: the Portuguese, in the figure of Macau's Governor General Domingos da Câmara de Noronha, were highly antipathetic. Almost from the moment they arrived, Noronha's unwelcome British guests irritated him, with the Portuguese complaining that the ships' crews were 'full of greed, all hatched on the [Willis] vessel *London*'.[30] Weddell's designs on undertaking trade into Canton from Macau were seen as posing a serious diplomatic threat, with the Portuguese arguing that their smallholding on Chinese territory was loaned to them, and was not one over which they had any sovereign authority. That meant they had no right to allow other nations to use its facilities and engage in their own business. Via the Macau authorities came the far stronger resistance of the Chinese themselves, who, on 7 September 1637, made the Portuguese complain to the British that 'the [Chinese] Mandarins are much disturbed and anxious seeing your ships where our vessels have never reached, and they send us many orders that we do command your worships to quit their kingdom, compelling us to make your worships put out to open sea, and deliver their ports from you'.[31] This was hardly a case of being greeted with open arms.

We are fortunate to have a good first-hand account of this historically crucial encounter, written by Peter Mundy (1596–1667). He was a merchant trader, present on the vessels to appraise the opportunities that the voyage was planning to discover. His diary offers the first proper account by an English person of what this new land felt and looked like. In Goa, in January 1637, Mundy met an Englishwoman – someone who appeared to have already been where their fleet was heading. 'She came from England some eighteen or nineteen years since', he wrote of the encounter, when 'she was a maidservant to one Furbisher a carpenter, who was passing thither'. She had been cast away on the coast of China, in order for the ship to save costs, and there had survived in Macau by marrying a local Portuguese.[32] This unfortunate individual was the earliest person from Britain recorded as physically visiting China, though in the most unhappy of circumstances. For Weddell's own new venture, the ships moved up towards Canton, where they had a chance to see their new potential partners. In September 1637, Mundy records another important first – the drinking of 'a certain Drink called Chaa . . . which is only water with a kind of herb boiled in it. It must be Drunk warm and is accounted wholesome.'[33] Within decades, 'chaa' – better known to English speakers as 'tea' – was to have a profound impact not just on Anglo-Chinese relations, but on culture and life in Britain down to today.

Mundy was able to observe the use of chopsticks in eating food, and the curious ways in which 'the better sort of women . . . have their Feet straight bound up from their infancy, so that they become very short and small'.[34] He even indulged in a little, very early anthropological analysis: 'The Chinese [is] a great [and frequent] eater, drinker and gamester, so that some will play away all that they have.'[35] In China 'there are more people on the water than in the land' – a reference to what must, for a British person, have been immensely busy coastlines and waterways. On 11 August 1637, a local mandarin 'who is Governor of all the towns and villages hereabouts, as also of their junks, sent order all about that nothing should be sold us'.[36] With constant delays and excuses, Weddell's fleet was shot at from a fort on the shore. Happily, the Chinese manning these weapons were not good gunners, so that 'their own shot Dropped down out of the Mouth of the Piece close under the wall'. Weddell told the Chinese on 15 August that 'we were Englishmen and came to seek a trade with them in a fair way of merchandizing'.[37] But that cut little ice with the nervous locals. And when John Mountney and Thomas Robinson, members of the crew, were sent to Canton to try to speak to the officials there three days later, 'they were brought to the chief Palace where they were willed, according to the custom, to . . . kneel, and then present their petition'.[38] This prototype of the kowtow (the Chinese-style genuflection) would, like tea, subsequently gain a prominence and symbolic importance in the future relationship.

The Chinese were adamant, stating in their reply that: 'They [the British] must return to their Kingdom and that we would not allow them to come and disturb our lands.'[39] Despite the warnings, the aforementioned Mountney, Robinson and a third man (perhaps Mountney's brother or relative Nathaniel) went to Canton to trade on 24 August. For their exertions, these three were to end up being detained as hostages. Nevertheless, goods were loaded onto the ships over the coming weeks, even as further warnings proceeded from Chinese and Portuguese junks nearby. Clearly desperate to see the back of these rapacious new arrivals, five Chinese vessels carrying fireworks were sent to destroy the British ships on 10 September, causing them to withdraw to near the island of Formosa a day later. Far from achieving an abatement, the actions of the Chinese meant violence only increased: in the following days, the British returned to burn five small junks and pillage a town. Worse than that, in a skirmish with the Chinese they gained the unwanted distinction of being the first British to kill a native of the empire on local soil. The whole venture suffered a torrid fate thereafter. Ordered to leave China by the authorities with its cargo, having promised never to return (an undertaking Weddell agreed to),[40] the *Dragon* and *Sun* sank in the Indian Ocean. The *Katherine* disappeared without trace. Only the second in command, Richard Swanley, survived, returning to England and ending up fighting on the parliamentary side against Charles I in the Civil War. After all this, Weddell's recorded parting words as he set sail from China's shores were ominous. Despite his promise to the Chinese officials not to come back, he vowed that: 'We shall fight your people with blood and sweat to the end.' This stands as a sombre epigraph for the decades and centuries that followed.

After such a fiasco, the EIC's ventures into the Chinese world continued sporadically in the coming decades. In 1644, three of its vessels – the *William*, the *Seahorse* and the *Hind* – arrived in Macau, leaving the crews dismayed by the poverty of the city.[41] Fourteen years later, two English ships, the *King Ferdinand* and the *Richard and Martha*, were at Canton.[42] After the first mention of the island of Taiwan in 1623, British ships started to enter the ports there in 1672. This gave birth to the idea that this location could be an entrepôt for trade with the larger entity across the waters. It was only finally in 1676 that a factory was established in Amoy, today's Xiamen, the first actual permanent British presence on Chinese soil. From here, in 1678, 12,000 pieces of silk were despatched to the English market.[43]

But British interests soon became entangled with the larger politics of the newly established Manchu Qing dynasty. Koxingha (1624–62, sometimes known as Zheng Chenggong), the Ming-supporting rebel, had his principal power base around Xiamen, on the island of Taiwan and in parts of coastal southern China. With his death in 1662, leadership of the rebels passed to his son, Zheng Jing, who was forced to relinquish Amoy in 1680. That marked a temporary end to the English efforts. The Amoy trade did, however, prompt one of the earliest mentions of England (under the guise of 'Ying-kuai-li-won') in contemporary Chinese documentation.[44]

Britain was behind its European competitors. During the 1660s, the Dutch were sending missions to the new Qing court, meeting the very young Kangxi emperor in June 1669, and building relations there to assist their trading ambitions. They described the ruler as

> a young man of middling height, quite white, about sixteen years old, modestly dressed; he wore a blue damask coat with a little embroidery on the front, back and shoulders and yellow boots. He looked their [the Dutch] horses over especially carefully, and could hardly take his eyes off them, laughing and talking about them to the First Councillor.[45]

Compared to this contact, the British were laggards. But they did derive some benefit from the Dutch diplomacy. The Kangxi emperor's benevolence meant that in 1685 foreign trade was permitted, and the Amoy base reopened. One account from the time records how the British now 'should have liberty to settle a factory in "Amoy", or any other place in the great Emperor's dominion'.[46] Slowly, however, the kinds of issues that were to loom so large over the coming decades started to cast a shadow: there were sporadic outbursts of violence, in the wake of the anger and frustration felt by seamen and merchant traders towards the Chinese (in 1685, a local was shot by the British) and resentment at the unreasonable behaviour of the Manchu officials. Around the same time, a drunken sailor 'got into the Custom house during the night, and broke open a lock where concerns of the Emperor lay; which, if done by a Native would have been punished with instant death'. The ship's managers, the supercargoes, negotiated with the local official (called a *hoppo*) who permitted the culprits to have '100 Stripes with a Catt of nine Tails and Pickle, to their satisfaction',[47] administered in public, but at British hands. This is the first recorded instance of extraterritoriality for British in China – another issue that was to figure hugely in the centuries ahead.

Despite expending great risk and effort, early trading experience proved frustrating for Britain. Returns from Amoy were meagre. The appointment by the EIC in 1699 of a president in charge of a council for Chinese affairs – a position first occupied by Allen Catchpole (a man who can thus lay claim to be the first formal consul to the Chinese empire) – and an attempt to sell wool into the Chinese market from the island of Chusan (today's Zhoushan) did little to help matters. There were two simple challenges. First, English products that appealed to the Chinese were few and far between, so it was hard to find things to sell them. That impacted on the second issue, which was that the Chinese demanded payment in silver for the products they sold (increasingly tea, silk and porcelain), rather than an exchange of goods. The net outflows of bullion from Britain to China figure as the earliest of the trade deficits that continue into the twenty-first century. By 1703, the Amoy factory had been abandoned. The problems were compounded to some extent by the EIC's domestic travails back home. By an Act of Parliament of 1693,

William III (of the Netherlands province of Orange), holding fast to his Dutch preferences for more liberal trade, allowed at least some competition by letting a second company work in the Far East. For the next few years uncertainty prevailed, with the two British entities often clashing with each other. The experiment proved short-lived, and a decade later the companies were allowed to amalgamate. That cleared the way for the EIC to finally open a more permanent location for trade in China – fatefully in Canton. This city was to prove the most important interface between Britain and China for the next century or so, and was the location of some of the great dramas of the crucial middle part of the China–Britain story. Within a year of the factory opening in 1715, the British and Chinese were able to indulge in one of their few common passions – the creation of bureaucratic structures. The supercargoes formed a local council to engage better with Chinese officialdom. Ironically, it was bureaucracy like this that provided the first real space where these vastly different powers were able to evaluate and slowly get to understand each other, working out ways in which they could collaborate.

The idea of China: 'The only wise nation under the sun'

There has always been China, the physical place, with its vastness, diversity, complexity, cultural difference and geographical remoteness. And then there has been the *idea* of the place in the minds of those engaging with it – an image they held of China as outsiders that was often prone to either idealism or demonisation. Lack of direct contact between Europeans and Chinese meant imagination played a strong role. At the very start, in the Elizabethan era, there was a ready market for speculation like this about a wider world beyond the British Isles – one that offered material and imaginative returns: a place where dramatists, poets, writers and artists were able to construct a sort of fantasy country. This phenomenon of imagination versus reality, in different ways and guises, has continued down to the present. The China dream is nothing new to the British: it has always been deeply embedded in the relationship, and has proved far more complex and multifaceted than the othering and exoticisation critiqued in the work of post-modern theorists like Edward Said. The British imagination of China had a reality of its own. It constitutes almost half the story of the relationship.

In the very beginning, ideas about China were mediated via other languages – sometimes several of them. It was the Portuguese explorers and traders, and then the Italians through the Jesuit missionaries, who had the earliest modern contact and who produced full accounts. The first English-language book explicitly about China, Richard Wille's *The History of Travaile in the West and East Indies*, from 1577, was a translation via Italian from Portuguese of a travelogue by the soldier Galeote Pereira.[48] A year later a small pamphlet appeared, *The Strange and Marveilous Newes Lately Come from the Great Kingdome of Chyna, Which Adjoyneth to the East India*, which regurgitated much of the information already conveyed by Wille's book. In 1588, the work of Juan González de Mendoza, *The Historie of the Great and Mightie Kingdome of China and the Situation Thereof* was translated into English by Robert Parke. Under the guise of 'Quinsay', this introduced the great city of Hangzhou, source of silk, to the English-speaking world.[49]

The works of the greatest contemporary playwright, William Shakespeare (1564–1616) himself, were largely bereft of any knowledge or awareness of the Ming, apart from one stray mention in *Twelfth Night* (written probably around 1601–02) where one of the main characters, Sir Toby Belch, declares: 'My lady's a [Cathayan], we are politicians.'[50] But Shakespeare's illustrious contemporary, Ben Jonson (1572–1637) was more fulsome. In a 1609 masque (a short play, usually for ceremonial occasions) called *The Key Keeper*, commissioned to mark the opening of the new bourse in London, there is a section singing the praises of trade. 'O your Chinese!' the passage goes, before proceeding to deliver one of the earliest idealisations of China in the English language:

The only wise nation under the sun. They had the knowledge of all manner of arts and letters many thousand years before any of these parts could speak. Sir John Mandeville was the first that brought science from thence into our climate and so dispensed it into Europe and in such hieroglyphics as these.[51]

Earlier on in the same piece, a shop boy had acknowledged the other side of the Chinese coin – the abundance of the country's goods and wares:

What do you lack? What is't you buy. Very fine China stuffs of all kinds and qualities? China chains, China bracelets, China scarves, China fans, China girdles, China knives, China boxes, China cabinets, caskets, umbrellas, sundials, hourglasses, looking-glasses, burning glasses, concave glasses, triangular glasses, convex glasses, crystal globes . . .[52]

The list goes on, four hundred years ahead of the time when indeed supermarkets in Britain were replete with these sorts of goods, most of them manufactured and exported from China.

Later in the century there were dramatic representations of matters about China on the London stage. Of these, the drama by Elkanah Settle from 1676, *Conquest of China by the Tartars: A Tragedy* was probably derived from an Italian source. The plot recounted the dramatic collapse three decades earlier of the Ming, and their replacement as supreme rulers of the Chinese empire by the Manchus. Settle's verse work contains plaintive laments from the conquered: 'Is it not enough, ye Gods, our bleeding land/ Groans at the wounds from our Invader's hands.'[53] So, too, is there determined stress placed on the all-powerful qualities of whoever it was that ruled this immense empire: 'The Mighty will from whence all power does grow [i.e. the way in which the king in the drama describes his own authority] plac'd the sun above, and me below.'[54] The play ends with a declaration against the 'lazy kings' who had ruled the empire in the previous dynasty (a swipe, no doubt, at the inactive, mostly invisible Wan Li, intended recipient of the epistles of Queen Elizabeth and King James). But now 'fate grants the High Command/ of this Great Empire to a Martial Hand'.[55] These were not baseless statements, even if their accuracy may have been more accidental than deliberate: 1676 was during the early phase of the great Kangxi emperor's reign. He was indeed to rule by 'Martial Hand'. But as the next chapter will show, it was to be over forty years before a British person was finally to clap eyes on him. And by then, his period of conquest and consolidation was already almost over, and he had only another year to live. China figures in the works of the great poet John Milton, too – though very fleetingly, and once more as 'Cathaian' rather than China itself.[56]

While not dramatic, the collections of the aforementioned Hakluyt and his great editor (and adorner) Samuel Purchas (1575–1626) often hailed as much from imagination as from any grain of reality, even if they were ostensibly records of real journeys. Purchas's monumental assemblage from the 1610s, *Purchas His Pilgrimage* (1614) and *Purchas His Pilgrim or Microcosmus* (1619), was rounded off the year before his death in 1625 by *Hakluytus Posthumus, or Purchas His Pilgrimes*. Purchas was a somewhat shy figure who, after graduating from Cambridge, lived most of his life enjoying the quiet benefice of Leigh-on-Sea on the Essex coast. He perhaps derived his stories of distant lands by listening to and being inspired by the yarns of itinerant seamen. It is the fourth book of the 1614 tome that carries the main description of the great Far Eastern empire, though the information conveyed as far as China goes mostly came from sources that were several centuries out of date. Marco Polo's *Travels* of the thirteenth century inspired the famous descriptions of the mighty khans in Purchas's work – the greatest of all being 'Cingis Can [Genghis Khan] . . . [who] ruled them with such modesty and justice, that they loved and feared him as a god, his fame reducing all the other Tartars in other parts under his obedience'.[57]

The unique belief system of the Chinese was something Purchas gave very early recognition to: 'They have books, written by certain wise-men or Philosophers two thousand years since or more, of political and moral Philosophy; the Authors whereof they honor for Saints, especially one Confucius, to whom the Mandarins do therefore once in the year offer sacrifice.'[58] And their leader 'is absolute Monarch, and in revenue exceedeth all the Princes in Europe, and Africa together which ariseth out of that which is properly called Census, the poll-money of his subjects.'[59] Purchas's evocative description, via Marco Polo, of the great summer city of Xanadu (located today in Inner Mongolia) was to inspire Samuel Coleridge's poem 'Kubla Khan' almost two centuries later. In another strange parallel, at the time he wrote the work, Coleridge was under the influence of opium, a drug that had started to figure massively in the trade between Britain and China, and which was to loom large over the coming decades.

China's remoteness and difference was as much about the language the country's inhabitants used as anything else. If there was one issue above all others that prompted confusion and rampant speculation, it was what exactly this unusual script was. The first recorded appearance of a sample of Chinese writing was the copy of a cheap edition in the original classical language of the *Four Books* of Confucianism, acquired by Thomas Bodley, founder of the Oxford Bodleian Library, in 1603 via Amsterdam. 'No English scholar was able to decipher [Bodley's text] for over two centuries after its acquisition', one contemporary historian has explained.[60] Indeed, the earliest translation of Confucius into English was not produced until 1691, and even then derived from a Latin rather than a Chinese original.[61] The Bodleian Library managed to acquire more material over the coming century, much of it through the good offices of merchants of the EIC like John Dacres. They provided the Oxford scholar Thomas Hyde (1636–1703) with texts picked up on their journeys.[62] For a few months around 1687, Hyde had the good fortune to host in Oxford the first person of Chinese heritage ever recorded to have visited Britain, the Christian convert Michael Shen Fuzong (*c.* 1658–91). Hyde wrote warmly of how the young man helped him decipher – through Latin, the common language they shared – the small accumulation of texts from China. 'My Chinese Michael Shin Fo-cung (for that was his name)', the scholar wrote in later correspondence,[63]

> was bred a Scholar in all the Learning of their country, read all their Books readily, and was of great honesty and sincerity, and fit to be relied upon in everything; for indeed he was a very knowing and Excellent man, very Studious and Laborious in all things, and could speak Latin, whereby I conversed with him very freely and easily.[64]

It is one of the most moving, and heartening, aspects of the British–Chinese story, that for all the drama, trauma, turbulence and violence over the centuries, there are also innumerable, individual testimonies, very much like this, of the mutual affection and warmth between different people, despite the vast contrast in their backgrounds and world views. Shen was to die, tragically young, soon after his departure from Britain back to continental Europe in 1691.

For others, however, the differences in terms of China's system of governance and the vastness of its territory that were starting to be revealed by the accounts of travellers were troubling, as was its hybrid belief system, stories of which were beginning to filter through in the works of Jesuits. One of the most richly speculative and unusual early examples of how best to manage these differences and make China more familiar and part of European historical narratives was a 1669 tract by John Webb (1611–72). Webb was an architect, and early in his career had been an associate of Inigo Jones, working as his assistant for a while. Indeed, as a Royalist, after the Restoration of 1660 he lobbied to be Jones's successor as surveyor of works – efforts which went unrewarded (the position was eventually awarded to Sir Christopher Wren).[65] Three years before his death, he produced *An*

Historical Essay Endeavouring a Probability that the Language of the Empire of China is the Primitive Language. This tour de force of high-flown speculation began as it intended to continue, with one of the most audacious acts of historical revisionism ever committed. 'We may certainly conclude that Noah carried the primitive language into the ark with him', declares Webb, going on to claim that the ark had made landfall 3,952 years before the date he was writing, according to his computation, and 'rested on high mountains . . . of inaccessible altitude' within China's territory. As a result of this, the Chinese were descendants of some people in the ark and spoke the most ancient human language.[66] Webb's argument to support this is elegantly simple: 'From the East came the first knowledge of all things, and the [Eastern] parts of the world were the first civilised, having Noah himself for an Instructor, whereby the further East to this day, the more civil, the further West, the more savage.'[67]

Beneath these claims lay the fact that China's newly discovered antiquity had been a great disruption to Renaissance scholars like Webb, people who believed in the age of the world since creation being no more than 6,500 years. How to account, therefore, for this place where there were claims of dynastic history going back almost to the limits of this timeline, and documents that pre-dated most of the written history of ancient Europe? This history now being discovered somehow needed to be appropriated and made consistent with European thinking and beliefs. In Webb's words, the fact that 'the language of the empire of CHINA is the PRIMITIVE Tongue which was common to the whole world before the flood' showed that they had a shared common point.[68] But in his essay, beyond the wild speculation about the ark, there is also some factual acknowledgement of the country's early inventions (paper, gunpowder and the newly discovered, and soon emulated, wonder of porcelain) and a little knowledge of specific Chinese words: ' "Xiangti" [Shangdi] by which they signify the Supreme Governor of Heaven and Earth', he wrote, using a term still in currency in Mandarin today.[69] As so often, fact and fiction, empirical reality and speculation, got woven into the attempts to understand what China was, and what meaning it might have for those looking on from outside.

A more restrained, empirical approach can be found in an essay for the Royal Society by Robert Hooke (1635–1703), one of its founders and a man of deep and extensive learning. Barely a few months before Shen Fuzong set foot on Britain's shores, in *Some Observations and Conjectures Concerning the Chinese Characters* (1686), Hooke noted that 'the Chinese court language is said to be of this kind [an artificial language], invented and spoken by the Literati and Mandarins through the whole empire of China, differing from all the other languages spoken'. He was right here, for the Mandarin language was the language of the court bureaucrats and the specific elite discourse they would continue to use over the following centuries. But taking an approach more in line with modern linguistic philosophers, he went on: 'I conjecture . . . the names of the characters by which they write and express their meaning [are] arbitrarily imposed by them, as we in Europe set names to Arithmetical Figures, not as we pronounce words, written with literal characters.'[70] That Chinese characters did not seem to operate in the phonetic way as European alphabets did (something subsequently shown to be erroneous, since parts of characters do, in fact, carry some phonetic information, though not always) was one assumed difference with European languages that reared its head this early. Encountering written Chinese certainly puzzled and intrigued British scholars, opening up new ways of thinking about how language operated. One explanation for this – that they worked in the same way as Egyptian hieroglyphics and were related to them – proved hard to shift. As late as 1760, the Royal Society sent enquiries to the EIC in Canton about whether these writing systems were the same.[71] Only in the early nineteenth century, with the birth of more sophisticated language studies, was it accepted that Chinese was radically different from, and unrelated historically to, the Indo-European languages.

But it was not academic interest in what Chinese spoke and wrote (or its sporadic appearance in literature) that most brought China into the lives and worlds of British people in the sixteenth and seventeenth centuries. The tasteless beverage that Peter Mundy had tried on his tour with Weddell in 1637 – 'chaa' (tea) – proved by far the most important influence. The first mention of the drink being consumed in Britain was in September 1658, when a London periodical, *The Gazette*, spoke of 'that excellent and by all physicians approved China Drink called by the Chinese Tcha, by other nations Tay, alias Tee, [which] is sold at the Sultan's Head, a coffee house'.[72] Two years later, on 25 September 1660, the diarist Samuel Pepys, while undertaking work in his office in London, 'did send for a cup of tee (a China drink) of which I never had drank before'.[73] He does not record either a favourable or unfavourable reaction. In 1662, the new wife of reinstalled British monarch Charles II, Catherina of Braganza, reportedly brought a small tin of the drink when she relocated from her native Portugal to London.[74] Such royal patronage may have given tea cultural cachet and influence. Whatever its significance to Britain's trading relations with China (and they were to prove to be vast), tea in Britain was as much about the introduction of new ideas of taste, refinement and a culti-vated way of life. The drink, and the paraphernalia associated with it, was to be one of the main means by which, at least in the early phase, China itself became associated with sophistication and high culture.[75] This was reinforced by the introduction of porcelain, initially brought back in the mid sixteenth century by Portuguese sailors, before then becoming one of the main items traded by the EIC. Shakespeare in *Measure for Measure* had Pompey say about his mistress's crockery, 'They are not China dishes, but very good dishes', testifying to their appearance in the fabric of everyday life.[76] The first porcelain shop opened in London in 1609.[77] The aristocrat Robert Cecil, around the same time, became an avid collector of Chinese plates and goods.[78]

No less a figure than John Ovington (1653–1731), chaplain to King James II and the EIC, was to testify to the great virtues of the beverage in 1699, when, in *An Essay upon the Nature and Qualities of Tea*, he made clear that drinking it was not just a matter involving physical taste. Not that this was unimportant, for tea, as he wrote, 'is generally acknowledged to be both pleasant and medicinal, at once to delight the palate and correct the disease'.[79] *Singlo* tea, he says, 'tastes very crisp', whereas *Bing* (imperial) tea has 'a very pleasant' smell.[80] Above all this, however, tea encouraged a healthy mindset and lifestyle. It, the good chaplain explains, has 'the Ascendant which it gains over the powerful Juice of the Grape, which so frequently betrays men, into so much Mischief and so many follies. For this admirable tea endeavours to reconcile men to sobriety'.[81] Morality and not just appetite was on the side of the tea drinkers.

There was to be much more written about tea in the future. With the opening of Thomas Twining's coffee house selling imported tea in Devereux court, London, in 1706, one of the core features of metropolitan social life was established, creating a whole new social activity – sitting down with others in cafes and talking while drinking tea. What this all testified to was the fact that even this early, something had originated in China and been introduced into British life, in ways that were to prove profoundly influential, and yet go largely unrecognised. This was perhaps the reason that Ovington complained (as did others) of the 'subtlety of the Chinese', able to create things that influenced others in such seemingly mysterious and ineffable ways.[82]

That note of complaint about the 'subtlety' (meaning at the time something akin to trickiness, and lack of transparency) attributed in this period to the Chinese marked, very early on, the other side of the British ideas and feelings about China – the notion of them being in some ways problematic, alien, people living in an ossified system that was enclosed and resistant to the outside world, and hard to fully understand and appreciate. This negativity was very light at first. Daniel Defoe (*c.* 1660–1731), the great, protean journalist and novelist, covers both extremes of the spectrum (as he did in so many other areas). In two of his works, he presents powerfully critical views of China, and then equally committed positive views. *The Farther Adventures of Robinson Crusoe*, published in 1719, the same year as the much more widely read and famous *Adventures*, contains a long complaint by Crusoe about the Chinese he meets:

> Their armies are badly disciplined, and want skill to attack, or temper to retreat; and therefore, I must confess, it seemed strange to me, when I came home, and heard our people say such fine things of the power, glory, magnificence, and trade of the Chinese; because as far as I saw, they appeared to be a contemptible herd or crowd of ignorant, sordid slaves, subjected to a government qualified only to rule such a people.[83]

To add to the problems, these people 'think they know more than all the world besides.'[84] Defoe was the ultimate ventriloquist however. In the earlier *The Consolidator* (1705), a curious fable about travel to the moon, the narrator gives fulsome praise to the Chinese who, he says, 'all men know . . . are an ancient, wide, polite and most ingenious people.'[85] In China, 'we find knowledge as much advanced beyond our common pitch, as it was pretended to be derived from a more ancient original.'[86] This land was 'peopled long before the flood', which had not, contrary to Webb's argument, destroyed them. 'It is no such strange thing', therefore, 'that they should so much outdo us in the sort of eyesight we call general knowledge, since the perfections bestowed on nature, when in her youth and prime, met with no general suffocation by that calamity'.[87] There is a strong argument, however, that even here, the grandiloquence of his praise is underlined by what one scholar called a bitter hostility.[88]

But of all the debates from the earliest phase of British–Chinese relations, it was a totally made-up word, the neologism *Sharawadji*, that had most impact – a term whose origins and actual meaning to this day remain imperfectly understood. Sir William Temple (1628–99) was its inventor. A diplomat, courtier to Charles II (before arguing with him), scholar and essayist, he expressed perhaps better than any other an appreciation (which almost verged on the idolatrous) of China and ideas about Chinese culture and the positive difference it could make. His essay 'Of Heroic Virtues' from the 1690s talks of 'the great and ancient Kingdom of China', a place whose inhabitants 'esteem themselves as the only reasonable and civilised people'.[89] In this nation, Confucius – one of 'the great heroes' – is revered as 'a very extraordinary genius, of mighty learning, admirable virtue, excellent nature, a true patriot to his country and lover of mankind'.[90] Temple went on, 'No King is better served and obeyed, more honoured or rather adored, and no people are better governed, nor with greater ease and felicity'.[91] In the purely aesthetic realm, Temple's already high excitement about what China might offer grew in intensity. In 'Upon the Gardens of Epicurus' from around 1690, he spoke of the ways in which 'for Europeans, the beauty of buildings and planting is placed chiefly in some certain proportions, symmetries or uniformities'.[92] But 'the Chinese scorn this way of planting . . . Their greatest reach of imagination is employed in contriving figures where the beauty shall be great and strike the eye, but without any order or disposition of parts that shall be commonly or easily observed. And while Europeans have no word for this, the Chinese use the term *Sharawadji*.'[93]

For all its phonetic suggestiveness, there is no word in Chinese that easily relates to Temple's neologism.[94] But its lack of clarity and fixed reference was useful in trying to combine a constellation of different ideas and impressions, many of them vague and still being formulated, about how best to speak of Chinese notions of pattern and order, as opposed to those which could be categorised as European. In 1712, writing in the *Spectator*, Joseph Addison developed Temple's idea by speaking of

Writers who have given us an Account of *China*, [who] tell us the Inhabitants of that Country laugh at the Plantations of our *Europeans*, which are laid out by the Rule and Line; because, they say, anyone may place Trees in equal Rows and uniform Figures. They chuse rather to shew a Genius in Works of this Nature, and therefore always conceal the Art by which they direct themselves.

Addison goes on: 'They have a Word, it seems, in their Language, by which they express the particular Beauty of a Plantation that thus strikes the Imagination at first Sight, without discovering what it is that has so agreeable an Effect.' In a contribution to the ongoing debate about the natural and the artificial, Addison argues that in British gardens 'We see the Marks of the Scissars upon every Plant and Bush', trimming things into 'a mathematical Figure'.[95] In China, however, everything was free, flowing, natural. This offered another vista onto beauty and the organisation of the natural world.

Gardens were to become in the following century a key location of Chinese influence, both in their design, and in the flora planted in them. Physical links with China were to result in seeds, plants and shrubs being brought back from this new kind of world – a development that impacted on and shaped the receiving nation. As we shall see, fierce debate swirled around Temple's claims about the virtues of Chinese aesthetics. Writers like Horace Walpole saw no such admirable artlessness originating from China, but muddle and ugliness. But – rather appropriately, seeing as we are talking of gardens and plants – the idea had been sown. This at least showed the fecundity and fruitfulness of some aspects of the new cross-pollination of ideas between China and Britain. These were only to intensify in the decades to come.

2

Coming Within Sight, 1720-87

In his 1676 play *Conquest of China by the Tartars*, Elkanah Settle (1648–1724) has the line: 'Think how large pow'r/ is seated in a Chinese emperor.'[1] A thought like this may have passed through the mind of the Scottish surgeon John Bell (1691–1780), as he visited the court of the Kangxi emperor in 1720. Quite how Bell had ended up tagging along with a Russian delegation is unclear. In his account, published in Glasgow over forty years after the event, he offers little background. He just happened to be in Moscow, and it seemed someone suggested joining a trip travelling east. Evidently of an adventurous disposition, he obliged.

Over time, foreigners being given an audience with the emperor grew to become something carrying colossal symbolic importance. 'The Chinese emperor', historian of imperial China Yuri Pines has written,

> was the single most powerful human being in the world. His[2] exaltedness was, above all, symbolic: by the mere fact of his singularity, the emperor personified the supreme principle of the realm's unity, while in his capacity as the 'Son of Heaven' he acted as the sole mediator with and representative of the highest deity.[3]

In the embassy of 1793, Lord George Macartney (1737–1806) at least managed to see Qianlong, Kangxi's grandson, at an even more advanced age. In the nineteenth century, the disastrous Amherst embassy of 1816 failed even to clap eyes on the Jiaqing emperor (1760–r1796–1820), despite this being the precise objective of their visit. After this, there were no more than a handful of subsequent meetings until the Qing collapsed and emperors were no more. In the era after the Treaty of Beijing was signed in 1860, which stipulated more formal relations, Thomas Wade (1818–95), while British minister in China, met the Tongzhi emperor when he came of age in 1873.[4] Sir John Walsham, one of Wade's successors, met the Guangxu emperor soon after he had ascended the throne in 1891, and the following year there was a meeting with Walsham's replacement, Sir Nicholas O'Conor.[5] Sir Claude MacDonald in 1900, and Sir Ernest Satow on 2 February 1904 had been able to see the same emperor, though this time an almost wholly humiliated and disempowered figure, under the control of his formidable grandmother, Empress Dowager Cixi (1835–1908). 'She looked cheerful,' Satow was to write in his diary, 'but the Emperor though apparently in good health looked more girl-like than ever.'[6]

Bell was the first person from the British Isles to record his impressions of seeing the incumbent of the imperial throne. He had come overland to the capital of the Qing, getting an early sight of the Great Wall, the appearance of which 'running from one high rock to another, with square towers at certain intervals, even at this distance, is most magnificent.'[7] His arrival in China made him feel that 'everything now appeared to us as if we had arrived in another world'. But this was as much due to the alterations in the weather, Bell concluded, rather than anything seen in the environment around.[8] They had come, after all, in winter, when it must have been dry and bitterly cold. On being told what to do before he was granted an audience alongside his Russian colleagues, Bell had none of the issues with the Chinese-style genuflections expected on the day, simply recording that 'all the company' were required 'to kneel and make obeisance nine times to the Emperor. At every third time we stood up and kneeled again. Great pains were taken.'[9]

But the efforts were rewarded. Bell records how the emperor sat cross-legged on the throne, dressed in a short, loose coat of sable, the outward fur lined with lambskin interwoven with figures of golden dragons, 'with five claws on his head in a little round cap, faced with black fox skin, on top of which I observed a large beautiful pearl in the shape of a pear which, together with a tassel of red silk tied below the pearl was all the ornament I saw about this mighty monarch.'[10] Mighty indeed, but not overbearing. For Bell could not 'omit taking notice of the good nature and affability of this ancient monarch on all occasions. Though he was now in the eightieth year of his age, and sixtieth of his reign, he still retained a sound judgement and sense entire, and seemed more sprightly than many of the princes, his sons.'[11] Bell had got the empror's age wrong, for at the time of meeting he was only sixty-six. He had a number of occasions to observe this august personage, concluding that 'he is a prince eminent in prudence and valour. His countenance is open, his disposition generous, and he gives great application to business.'[12] The Scotsman departed a happy visitor, praising his hosts as civilised and hospitable people.[13]

Thirty-five years earlier, the great and wise figure he had just seen in the flesh had issued an important edict. This had allowed the country to finally open up to trade after the resolution of the long struggle with the Ming loyalists of the previous dynasty. As this new trade increased, so too did the need for a set of mutual rules of engagement. For the Chinese that involved having some way of controlling these novel figures now appearing in their midst, greedy for trade, somehow linked to events in the wider world around the Qing as their ambitions led them to explore other parts of south and southeast Asia. Ever since 1699, the preference was to do business in Canton. In 1716, three ships had arrived there from the EIC, most of their cargo being silver, with which to buy local goods.[14] The EIC overlords back in London had issued firm instructions: 'We . . . expect that laying aside all misunderstandings, you [the captains of the vessels] will contribute your utmost endeavours, all the while you stay at Canton, to promote our interests.' This resulted in the first agreement, around 1720, with an official named in the English-language material as the *hoppo*, the local key bureaucrat on the Chinese side who collected customs and duties from traders, and who had power over issuing the permits and export approvals. For the British merchants, their demand was to have communication free of insults, and freedom to arrive and leave.[15] The merchants were seeking simple, unique things – tea, chinaware and silks – on which to build their hopes of making great fortunes.

Such great fortunes begin with small steps. The first invoice for tea was issued by the EIC in 1669 – for a mere two canisters with a combined weight of 143 pounds (lbs) or 65kg.[16] By 1720, this had risen to 196,000 lbs (89,000kg) of tea, with a value of £129,000. Within forty years that would increase to 2.6 million lbs (1.2 million kg), at a value of £831,000.[17] For the smooth running of this burgeoning trade, the Cantonese authorities established what were called *cohongs* – groups of trusted local merchants, who eventually were to act as guarantors for the ships of the British and other nations and be the sole route to doing business locally. In time, these figures would become some of the wealthiest people on the planet. Wu Bingjian (1769–1843), better known as Houqua, was among the best known, a man who, as a member of a *cohong* in the early decades of the nineteenth century, amassed wealth estimated to be the equivalent of around £680 million today.[18] The system proved a contentious one, often beset by issues surrounding the bankruptcy and dwindling size of the *cohongs*: they were usually expected to consist of some twelve individuals, but illness and death sometimes meant they were half that size, with no prospect of approval being given by the Chinese government for new members. A further controversial issue was the way in which they were increasingly used by their own government as a shield against direct dialogue between foreigners and local officials. These problems were to contribute to the tensions that led to the Anglo-Chinese War of 1839.

On top of this, there was the matter of the conduct of the British when finally they arrived at Canton, often after months at sea. Initially accidents were the biggest headache, with no common legal viewpoint by which to try to manage the fallout from these. In 1722, a Chinese boy was killed by a mate on the *King George*. That unfortunate incident was handled by the simple payment of compensation to the boy's family, as the act had been unintentional. But such early informality in dealing with difficult issues was clearly not sustainable. As time went on, and engagement intensified, the management of incidents like this became increasingly hard.[19] Finally, as ever, there were domestic and geopolitical matters. Kangxi's death in 1724 after a long and illustrious reign resulted in the elevation of one of his sons, who assumed the name of the Yongzheng emperor (1678– r1722–1735). Almost immediately, he started the persecution of Christians. The missionaries from other European countries up until then favoured in Beijing were either expelled or placed under intense surveillance, with tight restraints on their activity.

Yongzheng's main issue for the traders was the prohibition he introduced in 1729 against the sale of opium. Opium, the drug produced from poppy seeds farmed in neighbouring India, increasingly figured in the coming decades as one of the most important, and contentious, issues between China and the outside world – Britain in particular, because of its interests in India and its role as one of the world's most powerful trading nations. The drug functioned as a counterpart to tea, both in moral and economic terms. While tea was seen as healthy and beneficial, opium went on to be regarded as a source of unremitting evil, ill health and social instability, and as one of the key instruments by which the British, in particular, enforced their will against the wishes of suffering Chinese. But it also proved to be the only trade in which Britain was able to reverse the massive deficits it ran up when doing business in China. The trade itself featured very lightly at first: the earliest reference of a ship's carrying the drug as cargo from Indian to Chinese ports was in

1703/1704.[20] But by the middle of the nineteenth century, the opium business had become a key issue and the main cause of conflict – so much so that, to this day, the wars of this period are called by the Chinese the 'opium wars'.

The 1730s saw the continuation of an often messy, unstable situation, one in which ways of doing business were still being improvised and where there were no formal institutional structures for dialogue, or well-understood rules for interaction. Amoy returned to the picture, figuring as a potential alternative market and port to Canton – until, that is, the Chinese authorities closed it down. The taxes that were imposed on imported goods were often prohibitively high and frequently arbitrary.[21] It did not help that there was a lack of unity among the local British, despite all the imprecations of the EIC court of directors (as it was then known) back in London. The merchants on the ground were tough characters, people who were often troublesome and highly individualistic, and not given to niceties. They were unlikely to be the sort of figures that would give the Chinese encountering them a positive idea of what British people were like. An early example was Edward Barlow (1656–1703), a perennial traveller who kept a diary of his voyages through the East and West Indies. Barlow was clearly a highly irascible character. Far more seriously, notes found recently also indicate that he was a rapist.[22] The violence of his character comes through in his bitter complaint about the Chinese, whom he castigated as 'very subtle and unjust in their dealings, and very hard to be trusted thinking themselves above all other nations in greatness'.[23] His views of the EIC were little better. 'In their warehouses,' he grumbled in 1701, 'we have our goods much abused in waste and breakage, and found great wants of our weights and fall of our commodities, and no allowance or consideration of anything by the Company.' The seamen, he ended, 'are forced to take what the Company are pleased to give them'.[24]

With this current of discontent and ill feeling, it was unsurprising that such violent events as the shooting of a local Chinese woman by a sailor called Gough in 1736 should have occurred. This was followed by an unpleasant altercation between the Chinese and English around the factory in Canton the following year. The reality was that, until much later, the key mediators between the complex, highly distinctive and different cultures of Britain and China in the earliest phase were those individuals with the least aptitude to create and then reinforce deeper understanding, either among the Chinese or back in their homeland.

The Royal Navy appears

If there was one clear area that represented Britain's global aspirations and power in the early modern period it was its navy. Though this force had been instrumental in defeating competitors for territory and trade back in Europe, it was not until 1742 that a ship of the Royal Navy found its way to Chinese shores after arriving in Macau (then under Portuguese management). It was to prove an unhappy encounter. Captain George Anson (1697–1762) aboard HMS *Centurion* was assessed by the local Chinese, according to one account, as 'a mere military officer'.[25] In 1741, his ship of war docked at Macau (then under the control of the Portuguese as a separately managed territory), looking for supplies. Irritated by the local *hoppo*'s refusal to grant him permission to proceed on a smaller boat up the Pearl River, he issued a series of threats. When his right to advance was finally (albeit reluctantly) granted, he arrived in Canton city itself and promptly demanded an audience with the viceroy (the most senior local official in the province, perhaps equivalent to the term 'governor' today). Initial impressions of this new place were intriguing. Close to Macau 'before sunrise we were surprised to find ourselves in the midst of an incredible number of fishing boats, which seemed to cover the surface of the sea as far as the eye could reach'.[26]

The inhabitants of these boats had a further surprise in store: their indifference to the foreign ship of war in their midst. 'The inattention, and [lack] of curiosity, which we observed, in this herd of fishermen' struck the commodore as weird. 'A ship like ours had doubtless never been seen in these seas before, but though many of their vessels came close to the ship, yet they did not seem at all interested about us.' This alone brought about a change in Anson's attitude, for he interpreted it gravely as 'an incontestable symptom of a mean and contemptuous disposition ... a sufficient confutation of the extravagant panegyrics, which many hypothetical writers have bestowed on the ingenuity and capacity of this nation'.[27]

Anson's words were for a publication in Britain, seven years after the events they were recording, and aimed at an audience there awash with warm feelings on account of the Chinoiserie craze then sweeping the country, which the captain, with his direct experience, wanted to correct. Even so, it is easy to see why, with this antagonistic mindset, his discussions with local officials did not go well. Demands for duty and a refusal to accept the unique official status of the warship in Macau had forced him to seek higher authorities in Canton. But on arrival there, the issue was the novelty of whom he claimed to represent (the British state, rather than a commercial entity) and what status to give his vessel. 'Such a ship as the *Centurion*,' he admitted, 'fitted for war only, had never been seen in these parts before.' That meant that 'the merchants were to some degree terrified, even with the idea of her'.[28] The EIC was of no help. Only direct contact with the viceroy was going to sort things out, as far as Anson was concerned. Via the initially reluctant *hoppo*, his missive received the desired response, and finally 'a Mandarin of the first rank appeared'.[29] To this benighted individual the commodore delivered his unambiguous message: 'They must be convinced that the *Centurion* alone was capable of destroying the whole navigation of the Port of Canton.' Anson followed up this arresting assertion with the claim (reportedly in jest) that 'if they delay of supplying him with best provisions, his men should be reduced to the necessity of turning cannibals, and preying upon their own species, it was easy to foresee that, independent of their friendship to their comrades, they would, in point of luxury, prefer the plump, well-fed Chinese to their own emaciated shipmates'.[30] It is unsurprising that, in the Chinese account, his comments – maybe the first attempt at cross-cultural humour between the two nations – were received in icy silence.[31] Quickly furnished with what he desired, he was on his way, evidently much to the relief of almost everyone who had had to deal with him, including the local British merchants. He was subsequently to serve as first lord of the admiralty from 1751 to his death a decade later, once back home.

It is not clear how these hot words were conveyed to the local officials, because one of the fundamental challenges of the time was the lack of a direct means of communicating with each other. According to the historian H.B. Morse, the first record of a local hybrid lingo, Pidgin English, to try to bridge this language gap was in 1715. Before the deployment of this, Portuguese was the dominant common language.[32] While sufficing for dealing with transactions and the payment of duties, or even simpler disputes, Pidgin was hardly likely to be of service as issues got more complex, and higher-level ideas needed to be communicated. As the scholar John King Fairbank noted,

this language amounted to a translation of Chinese into a restricted international vocabulary. Since all aspects of life, from table-talk, to homicide and philosophy, were discussed during the East India Company period in this medium, it is small wonder that cultural understanding did not proceed more rapidly.[33]

Those using this cobbled-together language were called the linguists, a group of much-maligned and blamed individuals appointed on the Chinese side. Condemned to the fate of translators down the ages of having great responsibility, but no real power, their task was a thankless one. They tended to be blamed whenever there were any problems, even if those problems had nothing to do with them. That gives great significance to the support of the EIC for one of its young employees, James Flint, to learn the Chinese language itself. An allusion to this figure was first made in 1740, when a Captain Rigby (of the *Normanton*) left Flint in China to start his studies.[34] Flint was not the earliest to be recorded as able to speak some Chinese: in 1734, a certain Andrew Reid had learned enough to accompany supercargoes to Canton's city gates to explain one of their griev-ances.[35] But Flint was seemingly the first to take a systematic approach to acquiring the language and the first to be used by the EIC thanks to his facility in communicating direct with the locals.

Under the new Qianlong emperor (1711–99, r1736–96), from 1736 a number of changes were made. These were mainly assertions of control and attempts to restrain the role of foreigners and the scope of their activities in China. The *cohong* monopoly was formally adopted in 1754. In 1755, the study of the Chinese language by non-Chinese was banned. But the most significant measure was that restrictions were placed not on *how* trade was to be carried out, but on *where*. When the *Earl of Holderness*, a British vessel, arrived to trade in Ningbo and Chusan (today's Zhousan island) in 1757, it was initially granted permission to do so on terms far more favourable than in Canton. But this business was quickly curtailed by the viceroy, who, after appealing for guidance to the central court, precipitated the famous and hugely influential edict of the same year, which forbade foreign trade in all but the southern city of Canton. All busi-ness conducted at places like Ningbo, Chusan and Amoy was stopped with immediate effect. Canton became the limit of foreign activity and experience of China for much of the next century, until the whole system was destroyed by the First Anglo-Chinese War.

What references to Flint that exist mainly concern his involve-ment in the response to this new development, when he made a sea voyage up the coast from Ningbo to the capital to lodge a protest there against the rules. He succeeded in being the first person from

Britain to set foot in Tianjin, the port city adjacent to Beijing and its main source of supplies. There he promptly used his language skills to persuade a local official to present a letter of protest to the emperor. In his own brief account, while in Canton he had 'told [the local officials] that I was come first in the small vessel, to deliver a petition to the . . . Mandarins of Che-Kiang [presumably modern-day Zhejiang, the province where Ningbo is located], for them to represent to the Emperor the grievances we lay under in Canton'. When they refused to take his petition, he sailed north and there, faced with a similarly recalcitrant official, said he would 'go as far as the foot of the great wall and he must take care of himself for I would acquaint [the Beijing officials] of my having been here'.[36]

It is unclear just how much Chinese Flint was actually able to speak. Chinese documents from July 1759 say that he knew how to speak just a little, and that he himself acknowledged that he knew 'only how to speak these few sentences of Mandarin, the rest of my speech is all written in the petition'.[37] What is certain is that for this all-important document, he had fatefully managed to employ a local person (Liu Ya-pie, originally of Sichuan) to translate it into Chinese.[38] The message did get through to Qianlong, who issued decisions that resulted in the *hoppo* in Canton being demoted and other punitive measures being doled out to the local administration. The EIC supercargoes based in the city soon found out that, in a vast and seemingly centralised polity, there was often plenty of scope for local officials to create distance from their overlords in the north (a lesson many others have since learned). For once the imperial orders had been fulfilled, the Cantonese mandarins took vengeance on the community they hosted and which had dared lodge a complaint against them at headquarters. For Flint, his efforts to mediate were rewarded by his being hauled before the local viceroy, banished from the country to Macau for four years, and then, on pain of death, being sent back to Britain with a solemn order never to darken the shores of the country whose language he had taken years to learn.[39] The Tianjin resident who had helped him translate the petition fared far worse, being executed. The gloomy outcome of the Flint affair hardly offered encouragement for people from Britain who might have wanted to learn Chinese. There are sketchy records of him, as a much older man, being initially consulted before the Macartney embassy in the 1790s; but beyond that, there is simply silence.

Learning Chinese was never to become a mainstream activity for the British, despite the valiant example of figures like Flint. More representative of the supposed dangers involved in learning this seemingly fiendishly difficult script was the example from 1759 of another EIC employee who was rewarded for his hard work (in the eyes of contemporary observers at least) by being made 'prostrate with illness and [driven] out of his mind'! Today we can see this as a good instance of correlation not being the same as causation.[40] But for the more enlightened of the EIC local leaders, some facility in the language was non-negotiable. Frederick Pigou, a supercargo who as early as 1754 had suggested that a formal British government embassy needed to be sent to Beijing to iron out the increasing number of problems occurring, had written that 'with permanent residence in Canton and a settled residency . . . the residents, especially the Chief, would in time have an Interest in the country, which now, hardly one supercargo has'. Pigou went on that 'they will then learn to speak the Chinese language, which is often of great use, and although more difficult than languages more usually are, yet not to the degree commonly supposed for experience shows, many men have learned it, and boys can in two years or less'.[41]

This expression of a worthy aim was to prove optimistic. In 1794, after Macartney's mission, the shrewd lord had, in his third report on the outcome of his visit to Beijing, acknowledged – as Pigou had earlier – that without skills in the local language, the EIC agents 'will be always at the mercy of men [the Chinese linguists] sufficiently inclined to impose upon them through dishonesty or to betray them through fear'.[42] It remained the case that few British people decided to invest the time and effort in learning Mandarin, even long after restrictions had been lifted and there had been numerous predecessors to follow. In March 1828, the local English-language newspaper, the *Canton Register*, established at the end of the previous year, had complained that 'of the foreigners who have visited [China] for the last century, not one in a hundred has been able to converse with the people of government but through the medium of a few interested and generally ignorant natives, who have spoken only a jargon composed of a few words to express the names and prices of the articles of commerce'. The *Register* continued, 'the true cause [of this lack of Chinese by Europeans] has been a want of patronage on the part of senior merchants, who regret too late their ignorance, and a love of ease too incident to the young and inexperienced'. This was compounded by the fact that 'the Chinese government and merchants have always thrown every possible difficulty in the way of learning their language from a belief that ignorance is weakness'.[43] This issue never seemed to improve, for in the early twentieth century, long after most of these impediments had gone, and when there were far more incentives and support available to learn for those who wanted to, of the 180 Hong Kong Shanghai Bank British staff employed in greater China at the time, only 5 per cent had Chinese-language abilities.[44]

Life in Canton

The infrastructure of trade dialogue, primitive as it was, did function to some degree by the 1760s. And for a Britain about to enter into the most intense period of its imperial expansion and its own domestic industrial modernisation, there were more reasons why the Qing Chinese empire was no longer so remote and marginal. The consumption of tea was rising to the point where it had almost become a national staple drink in Great Britain. So, as we shall see later, had the aesthetic taste for things perceived as Chinese, even if they were in origin more home grown and British in their creation. For a global, naval power, with colonies in the Americas and expanding interests in India, Britain – by accident as much as design – was almost fated to come into increasing contact with China. Indeed, 'accidental' was the overwhelming characteristic of most aspects of this evolving relationship. Things happened through an almost organic process, where pressures and influences elsewhere (the opium trade in India and the private traders who came to service this trade are good examples) left their mark on how the Chinese and British related to each other, and how they developed some level of mutual understanding.

William Hickey (1749–1830), a lawyer who is best remembered today for his vast diaries, passed through the Far East as a young man in 1769. He gives a vivid first-hand account of what the English factory in Canton looked and felt like to live in before the diplomats, soldiers, missionaries and others had come to interpose upon the scene. For Hickey, his arrival in Macau was an inauspicious start. The city was in its long decline, a 'miserable place where there is a wretched, ill-constructed fort belonging to the Portuguese in which I saw a few sallow faced, half naked and apparently half-starved creatures'.[45] Canton suited him far better: 'The view of the city as you approach is strikingly grand, and at the same time picturesque.' In an early example of the use of parallels closer to home to make sense of things, he compared the scene upon the water to that of the Thames below London Bridge.[46] The boats of the city were not as monumental as those back in Britain, but this was an environment where the differences were as much about the nature of society and the way people behaved, as about external physical appearances. Gender roles, in particular, captured his attention. 'Females of higher order are entirely secluded', he noted, but 'poor women are made to execute the most laborious and menial services . . . These are frequently seen tugging at an oar, having one infant receiving its nourishment at the breast and another slung behind her.'[47]

The British were now present in some numbers in the city – at least in the part of the year when they were allowed to reside there (usually the autumn and winter months, before they left for residence in Macau, to return for the next shipping season the following year). The local laws forbade women from accompanying their husbands. This was largely due to deep-seated patriarchal attitudes on the part of the Chinese authorities and a desire to ensure that the men's living conditions felt impermanent, underlining the fact that their sole reason for being there was to undertake business, not to settle and live. This rule was in place until the end of the *cohong* system in 1843, though it was frequently violated. Hickey himself records one such early incidence – a Captain Elphinstone, who brought a girl from Madras with him, but attempted to evade detection by having her wear the 'garb of a boy'.[48] As mentioned above, rather than places of manufacture the factories were extensive trade buildings: the goods from the boats were taken off and placed in storage there for onward sale (though relatively simple processing work on goods was also sometimes undertaken). Of the factories, the British one was the most extensive and the grandest. The only downside was its location next to the unromantically named Hog Lane, where, according to later testimony, sailors seeking refreshment after months of deprivation and sobriety at sea went to indulge themselves on the local grog, or alcohol, concocted by the Cantonese. This potent brew often reduced them to a malleable stupor, so that they could be robbed and mugged.[49]

The whole era from the creation of the *cohong* system in 1757 was about the establishment and issuance of rules by the Chinese, and constant conflict and tension over their implementation by the British. All trade was to be with the *cohong* merchants, who were told to set a common price on goods, after an early period of competition in 1780. Duties and charges for imported and exported goods were paid through them. There were restrictions on movement by foreigners while in China: they were largely confined to the area around the factories and some small islands, where they were able to go for rest and recreation without coming across locals. Firing of guns was prohibited. Foreigners committing crimes were to be punished according to Chinese law.[50] On the British side (inevitably) there had to be committees. The EIC in 1757 set up a Council of Supercargoes to act as one arena for governance. By 1779, the main problem was dealing with drunken sailors. Rules issued to ships that year instructed crews hell-bent on getting merry in their temporary new home not to shout, to keep within the bounds of sobriety and decency, not to break into groves (private woods) or molest Chinese, and not to smuggle.[51]

Despite these restrictions, life was not so bad in the six to seven months a year when merchants were in Canton. While the warehouses and living quarters for all foreigners (including the Dutch and others) covered a modest amount of space,[52] people were reasonably well accommodated. Each warehouse had four rooms on the floor above the factory, with the public apartments facing the river and offering a view over well-tended gardens. 'All supercargoes and any guests that honoured them dined daily in the great hall at 2', Hickey recorded.[53] There as many as thirty would 'sit down to a capital dinner consisting of fish, flesh and fowl, all of the best, with a variety of well-dressed made dishes being served up in two courses, followed by a superb dessert, the wines, clarets, madeira and hock all excellent, and made as cold as ice'.[54] Three hours was expended on this repast alone. Astonishingly, people had time and appetite for supper later in the day, at about 10 p.m. Hickey also gives a verbal tour of the factory: 'In one long gallery we found upwards of a hundred persons at work, in sketching or finishing the various ornaments upon each particular piece.' Here people as young as six worked side by side with those in old age.[55] The English visitor was also able to visit the house of one of the *cohongs*, Pankeequa (Pan Wenyan in today's Pinyin): on the first evening of hosting visitors, he and his guests used the English style, eating with knives and forks; on the second evening, the Chinese style, with chopsticks. 'The entertainment was splendid', writes Hickey, the victuals supremely good. At night, brilliant fireworks . . . were let off in a garden magnificently, lighted by coloured lamps, which we viewed from a temporary building erected for the occasion and where there was exhibited slights of hand, tracks, tight and slack rope dancing, followed by one of the cleverest pantomimes I ever saw.[56]

The locals were, however, less hospitable than their wealthy *cohong* compatriots. When travelling into town, Hickey was followed by children who yelled out epithets, the meaning clear enough in the hostility of their delivery, even though the literal meaning, being in Chinese, was incomprehensible to most foreigners. Some threw sticks and stones at the foreigners. This charmless depiction of the behaviour of Cantonese people towards outsiders was to be noted many times in the future. For them, familiarity had clearly bred a great deal of contempt – something that intensified as time went on and their clashes with British and other Europeans grew more violent and dangerous. For Hickey, who was only at the early stages of his global journey, the lengthy eating bouts and the very restricted social life in the city ultimately proved unappealing, and he soon felt restless to get on his way: 'Canton afforded little variety except for the first few days, after which there was nothing but repetition of the same round.'[57] This serves as a prototype of a lament made by expats over the centuries since, where so much of local life was either tedious to them, or simply inaccessible due to cultural or linguistic reasons.

Journey to Tibet

There was a larger context in which this insular world existed. Between 1757 and 1764, Britain had gained sovereignty over Bengal and control of the opium regions there, meaning the EIC was able to re-establish its monopoly over opium production. This British involvement in China's massive neighbour, and its assumption through the EIC of more and more of the governing responsibilities of various kingdoms and provinces, was something the Chinese were aware of, though they would have had no knowledge of the bold proposal of Robert Clive of India in 1763, after his military successes in the new empire, to launch an invasion of China itself. Thankfully, at least for the Qing, he was deterred by cooler minds in London from such an epic venture.[58] Even so, the encroachment on an area of direct interest to them was closely monitored in Beijing. The Qing assimilation of Tibet in 1720 only intensified the scrutiny and brought this unique, complex and isolated terrain directly next to British interests into a much closer relationship with the Chinese state. What that relationship was remains a subject of fierce debate to the present day. The term 'suzerainty' ended up being the label most used for these links: a recognition of special influence falling just short of complete sovereign control. In a region largely devoid of the neat borders and the tidy demarcation of geographical space between recognised states established in Europe over the previous century or so, this sort of more amorphous arrangement was not unusual. That was the whole basis of the pre-modern tributary system, with its complex rules of protocol, performance of subservience and acknowledgement of power hierarchies centred on the Qing, where symbolism rather than set borders, and deference rather than sovereignty was the priority.

If the nature of Chinese influence in Tibet confused the British, the way they operated in India created as much bafflement in return. The EIC, not the British government, increasingly ran the affairs of various Indian states, and while a non-state player, it was one that behaved exactly like a state one. What was this entity, the Chinese must have wondered, that had an army, control over an economy, all the infrastructure of a centralised government, and yet said it was a purely commercial vehicle? Even today, the metamorphosis of the EIC in India into this behemoth is mystifying, as is the fact that this arrangement lasted until the Mutiny of 1857, which finally necessitated direct British government intervention. Warren Hastings (1732–1818), governor general of the recently constructed state of

Bengal for the decade after 1774, was the most influential adminis-trator over this period, developing an intense interest in the countries adjacent to Britain's new imperial acquisition. Of these, Tibet offered rich possibilities, and for this reason was the object of two missions by the young Scotsman George Bogle (1746–81), the first in 1774, with a second five years later.

Bogle's succinct, witty account of these explorations is an under-appreciated classic. The open-heartedness and generosity of spirit on show are all the more striking in view of the novelty of what he was attempting. For while there had been some knowledge of this remote, mountainous kingdom since the sixteenth century, when Samuel Purchas, in his vast assemblage, mentioned the 'Thibetans', it was still as close to 'terra incognita' as one could get. Europeans had succeeded in reaching the place – for example, the Jesuit António de Andrade (1580–1634) in 1624 (though he may have been preceded some centuries before by the Italian Friar Odoric in around 1325). But no Briton had ever set foot there.[59] While at Fort William in Bengal, Hastings had pondered ways of rectifying this situation, finally devising a plan of reaching out to the Teshi Lama (today known as the Panchen Lama, the second in the Tibetan monastic hierarchy, after the Dalai Lama). Bogle, the man he chose to undertake this great venture, had been born in Daldowie, Scotland in 1746. After graduating from Edinburgh University, he arrived in India during the hard year of the Great Famine of 1770. Appointed a secretary of the Select Committee in Bengal (which governed the EIC affairs locally) in 1773, he quickly gained Hastings' trust and confidence, to the point where this major new mission was assigned to him. In Hastings' letter of appointment for the voyage, he had written that the Tibetans, 'a simple, well-disposed people, numeric and indus-trious, living under a well-regulated government', might be brought within the Indian sphere of influence, thereby opening up new trading arrangements with them.[60] As so often, it was commercial gain, not scientific curiosity, that most spurred the British on.

There was, beyond this generic knowledge, very little else that was known for them to structure the mission on – not least what precisely the nature of their relationship was with the Qing. Hastings raised the question of 'whether the Dalai Lama is still a vassal to China',[61] one of several issues that Bogle would need to establish as he made contact. The Scotsman's voyage started well, for on transiting from Bhutan (where he complained about the '3000 spectators' watching his every move) he wrote that the Tibetans were 'much better bred and more affable than their southern neighbours'.[62] Arriving at Shigatse, Tibet's second city, on his first encounter with the Teshi Lama, a figure ostensibly divine, Bogle recorded that

> although venerated as God's vice regent through all the eastern countries of Asia, endowed with a portion of omniscience and with many other divine attributes, he throws aside, in conversation, all the awful part of his character, accommodates himself to the weakness of mortals, and behaves with the greatest affability to everybody.[63]

The first impressions proved accurate, for he recorded with some feeling later that 'I never knew a man whose manners pleased me so much or for whom upon so short an acquaintance I had half the heart's liking.'[64] Recently historian Kate Teltscher has written that this remarkable encounter between Bogle and his main intended interlocutor was striking, because it was 'neither violent nor exploitative', despite the context in which it occurred.[65] This warmth and humanity are reflected in many other descriptions in Bogle's book. After meeting the governor of part of Tibet, he writes of how his 'looks and manners are exactly those of an overgrown country farmer, smelling strongly of tobacco'.[66] As for the Tibetan custom of polyandry (one woman, several husbands) 'in this country ... the elder brother marries a woman, and she becomes the wife of the whole family. They club together in matrimony as merchants do in trade.'[67]

One of the aims of Bogle's mission was to establish via this land route trade not just with Tibet, but with the great Qing empire beyond. That was something left in the hands of the now friendly Teshi Lama, due to visit Beijing at some point and be granted an audience with Qianlong, a man Bogle understood (erroneously, it seems) to have 'a violent and imperious temper'.[68] Departing Shigatse on 7 April – a promise by the lama of his best efforts to intercede on behalf of the British at the Chinese court successfully secured – Bogle felt that his whole visit had had 'the appearance like a fairy dream'. The lama was, in the end, unable to set out on his imperial visit to Beijing for another three years, dying tragically soon after he reached the Qing capital in 1778, his mission unfulfilled. Bogle followed soon after, passing away after a second brief visit to Tibet in 1781.

The isolated mountain kingdom was not to be left alone, however, being visited by another British emissary in 1783. Samuel Turner's account of this mission makes it clear that it was a more nakedly political one. Carrying a second message from Warren Hastings to the Tibetan authorities, Turner's shrewd insight when talking to the regent, in power during the infancy of the new Panchen Lama, was that these people, despite their ostensibly close relationship with the Qing, were 'averse to own any immediate dependence upon the Chinese'.[69] 'They look upon the Chinese', he later commented, 'as a gross and impure race of men.'[70] Despite his discussing the potential for trade on his visit, and his conclusion that 'from time immemorial [Tibet] has been the resort of merchants' and the 'proper field for a variety of mercantile projects',[71] the extreme youth of the Panchen Lama meant no treaty was forthcoming. After a further twenty-eight years, in December 1811, Cambridge graduate Thomas Manning became the first British person to penetrate the holy city of Lhasa itself. He did this in disguise, and under constant fear of being at some point found out and evicted. He did, however, meet the Dalai Lama himself, who was at that time a seven-year-old infant who had 'the simple and unaffected manners of a well-educated princely child.

His face was, I thought, poetically and affectingly beautiful. He was of a gay and cheerful disposition.'[72] Like Turner, Manning was also to observe that he felt the Tibetans 'would view the Chinese influence in Tibet overthrown without many emotions of regrets'.[73]

Tibet was only one of several places and regions where Chinese and British power started to brush against one another. These borderland zones became increasingly important as spaces where the different attitudes and world views of these two forces came into contact with each other, performing complex operations of assessment and appraisal. The Qing court was ill equipped to make much sense of the way these foreigners behaved, often using the 'yi' character to refer to foreigners, a term subject to much debate, due to its connotation of 'barbarian' in English translation (this will be discussed in more detail in chapter four). From time to time, more overt symbols of British statehood passed by, in the form of the ships of the king's navy. The second naval ship after the Anson visit of 1742–43 was the HMS *Argo* in 1764. HMS *Seahorse* appeared in 1775, arousing bickering about whether it needed to be measured as a commercial ship in order to pay the appropriate dues, rather than receive exemption (an argument in this case resolved peacefully).[74] HMS *Discovery* and *Resolution*, deprived of their commander Captain James Cook after his murder on Hawaii earlier in the tour, were allowed to refuel and refit at Macau in 1779. These warships were often an indication of trouble afoot. In 1781, British ships were in conflict with French vessels in the vicinity, the spillover of the strife between the two nations brewing in Europe that would continue for the next three and a half decades. And in 1784, the first ships from the newly independent nation of America appeared, freed from the shackles of Great Britain. The first was flatteringly called *The Empress of China*, sailing from New York under John Green.[75] The situation among these foreigners was complicated. The Chinese would have had no idea that it was tea – or rather the import duties on tea – which had played such an important symbolic role in the revolution against

British rule in the States in the years leading up to 1776, when independence was finally attained. One of the landmark events in this struggle was the Boston tea party of 1773, when goods (tea) on which taxes were to be paid to Britain, but which originated from China, were tipped into the waters. But after achieving full independence, America was surprisingly quick to want a piece of the trade in this huge, remote market. The one thing America didn't do directly was engage with the opium business.

The troublesome nature of the British was visible not so much in the conflicts on the periphery of the Chinese empire and in the waters around China's coast, as in the way some of them behaved internally. The *Lady Hughes* Affair of 1784 typified this. *Lady Hughes* was a private ship and nothing to do with the EIC. Despite the fact that the EIC had a monopoly on trade between Britain and the Far East, there were no restrictions on British vessels and their merchants getting involved in country-to-country trade within the Asian region, so long as none of it went via Britain itself. This sort of regional trade was the main, and eventually only, means by which opium was shipped from its source into China, offering a convenient but somewhat hollow excuse for the EIC to claim to be unconnected to this sordid business. A gunner of the *Lady Hughes* was the cause of what escalated into a major dispute when he fired a salute and, in the process, accidentally killed two Chinese. With the EIC refusing to take any responsibility for the behaviour of a crew member who was not an employee and in effect had no relationship to the company, Captain Smith of the vessel itself was ordered to present himself in Canton for examination by the local officials. When he did so, he was promptly detained until an elderly sailor volunteered to be handed over, in the expectation of a fair trial and immediate release because of the accidental nature of the incident. At this point, things started to go badly wrong.

This was because of the two sides' radically different understanding of law and due process – something that had become more starkly apparent as their commercial relations grew. The author of one of the earliest books on Chinese governance, Peter Auber, phrased it well when he spoke in 1834 of 'the laws of China ... [being] compared to a collection of consecutive mathematical problems, with this additional circumstance of perplexity that a just and entire comprehension of each section individually requires a general knowledge of those that follow, no less than those that precede'.[76] The jurisprudential traditions in China and Britain had many contrasts, one of the most striking concerning ideas about responsibility: the Chinese approach stipulated that a whole group or community stood responsible for a crime committed by any one of its members; by contrast, the British side clung to the notion of clear individual responsibility and innocence for everyone else. In the *Lady Hughes* case, the Cantonese officials took the surrendered sailor as a scapegoat for the crime, regardless of whether he had actually committed it or not, and briskly executed him. The consternation among the British at what they perceived as gross injustice meant that this was the last time a person from Britain was offered up to the Chinese authorities for punishment until the end of British privileges, over a century and a half later. Extraterritoriality – the doctrine that foreign subjects in China were answerable to their own courts and legal system, not to the Chinese – was adopted informally before 1843, and then codified in treaties thereafter. It meant that the British, and others, were literally above the local law. This principle served as one of the greatest points of contention and resentment on the Chinese side, demonstrating to them almost daily that they were no longer masters in their own home.

Searching for reciprocity: British and Chinese views of each other

What did the Chinese think of these new actors suddenly so present within their country, so keen to purchase some of their goods, and yet also growing an import trade in a drug that was soon acknowledged as harmful? Anson's visit in the early 1740s had inspired an imperial edict in September 1743 which, contrary to the captain's own somewhat grand claims about putting the Chinese in their place (recorded above), said he had 'begged for water and rice'.[77] 'We await', the account went on, 'a convenient monsoon [when] we shall order them to quit our harbour.' On the arguments about the opening of other markets for trade, rather than Canton, the Beijing authorities in August 1756 simply stated that 'for the sake of pacifying the strangers [we shall] permit them to come to trade. However, if foreigners are hereafter allowed to have another market, we fear that in the course of time, those who remain in our interior will increase in number.' This was deeply undesirable, so the opening of Ningbo was refused.[78] It was in this document that James Flint was mentioned. The Qianlong emperor himself in February 1758 wrote that 'if we treat [foreigners] with courtesy they become more arrogant, if we awe them with power they naturally fear us'.[79] These were shaky principles on which to ground a sustainable response to a power that was clearly highly motivated, active in regions all around China, and showing itself technologically increasingly capable. As the historian John King Fairbank noted, the original response of China to the West 'was to treat [it] as though it were not the West at all, but merely a new form of Inner Asian barbarianism'. This was a 'poor preparation for contact with the modern [world]. It left China to deal with the industrial West through institutions and preconceptions developed over 3000 years of contact with pastoral nomads.'[80] At the epicentre of this interaction in Canton, however, the officials had already formed very clear ideas of who these new people were. 'You English', stated the governor in 1781, 'are a lying and troublesome people, for other nations that come to Canton are peaceful and do not hurt anyone, but you English are always in trouble.'[81] That view would not shift for many decades.

Such ill feeling was, from the beginning to the middle of the eighteenth century, not reciprocated in Britain. Far from it. From the 1736

English translation of the French scholar Jean-Baptiste Du Halde's monumental compendium of knowledge about China transferred back to Europe by the Jesuits (*A Description of the Empire of China and Chinese Tartary*), to the construction of the Chinese-style house in Stowe in 1738 (one 'built on poles, after the manner of the Chinese, odd and pretty enough'),[82] to the production of soft-paste porcelain in London, Staffordshire and Derbyshire from 1745 to 1755, interest in and enthusiasm for Chinese materials and aesthetics became so intense that it merited a specific term: Chinoiserie. Styles and characteristics imputed to China manifested themselves in the design of wallpaper, in furniture, in gardening and in architecture.[83]

The principal proponents of the import of Chinese ideas about landscape design or furniture aesthetics were people who had surrendered to the ideal of China with no direct engagement with the place. In the case of Sir William Chambers (1723–96), the Scottish–Swedish architect whose *Dissertation on Oriental Gardening* (1772) was to prove so influential, he had the great advantage of having visited the country three times in the 1740s while working for the Swedish East India Company. The impressions these direct encounters left were very deep. His chief observation was elegant and simple, and operated along the same lines as Sir William Temple, half a century before: 'The Chinese gardeners take nature for their patterns, and their aim is to imitate all her beautiful irregularities', he wrote.[84] This was because Chinese gardeners 'are not only Botanists but also Painters and Philosophers'.[85] He was appreciative of the ways in which, in the landscaping he had witnessed in the country, straight lines were avoided, and a constant element of invention and surprise was present. The 1753 description (in French) by Father Jean Attiret of the garden at the Yuanmingyuan (the ill-fated Summer Palace, which was to be infamously sacked by principally British and French troops a century later) had already introduced this notion of 'beautiful disorder', of an aesthetics which wandered 'as far as possible from the rules of art'.[86] Chambers was behind the erection in Kew Gardens,

London in 1761–62 of the pagoda, modelled on the Great Pagoda of Nanjing.

Not that there was universal appreciation of the new fashion. One architect, Robert Morris, complained in 1750 that Chinese taste 'consisted of mere whims and chimera without rules of order'.[87] In 1780, the writer Horace Walpole (1717–97) issued a far more coruscating attack, around the time when the craze was showing signs of waning:

We have heard much lately as Sir William Temple did, of irregularity and imitations of nature in the gardens or grounds of the Chinese. The former is certainly true; they are as whimsically irregular as European gardens are formally uniform, but with regard to nature, it seems as much avoided, as is the squares or oblongs, and straight lines of our ancestors.[88]

Walpole hammered the point home when talking of images he had seen of the Chinese emperor's pleasure palace (presumably the Summer Palace mentioned above): 'Except a determined irregularity, [I] can find nothing in it that gives me any idea of attention being paid to nature.'[89] Despite this scepticism, Chinese influence was discernible in the work of the hugely influential cabinet maker Thomas Chippendale (1718–79), who in 1754 advertised himself as producing work 'in the Chinese and gothic taste'.[90] China rooms were created at Claydon House, Buckinghamshire, in the 1760s, and wallpaper in the Chinese style (also from about 1760) still survives at Dalemain House, Cumbria. These efforts were unrelated to notions of authenticity. They were intrinsically interpretive, a production arising from the play of ostensibly Chinese images (some of them via French works like that of Du Halde) and English imagination. Ironically, even those that were made in China tended to be produced according to British expectations, rather than anything local.

Intellectually, engagement with China figured in the works of, for instance, Oliver Goldsmith (1728–74), whose *Citizen of the World* (1762) described the views of a visiting Chinese mandarin to Britain. This operated as a satirical device, ending up inevitably being more about its intended target – English mores and habits – than about anything else. The great essayist, lexicographer and cultural figure Samuel Johnson (1709–84) operated as a more significant, penetrating voice. Over his career, he shifted from being idealistic about Chinese matters to a more critical stance later on. A preface he wrote in 1733 to Jerome Lobo's *Voyage to Abyssinia* typifies the early position, with Johnson writing of the Chinese as 'perfectly, completely skilled in all sciences'.[91] In 1738 and 1742, he also produced two essays for *The Gentleman's Magazine* specifically on China, writing in July 1738 that 'the Antiquity, Magnificence, Power, Wisdom, Peculiar Customs and Excellent Constitution' of the Chinese 'undoubtedly deserve the Attention of the Publick'.[92] Chinese learning and ethical thinking attracted his praise, and in his second, 1742 essay he wrote of Confucius: 'His whole doctrine tends to the propagation of virtue and the Restitution of Human Nature to its Original Perfection.'[93] Towards the end of his life, he spoke to his biographer James Boswell of his strong desire to see the Great Wall of China. But his final comment on the country was a negative one: 'The Chinese', he stated on 8 May 1778, 'have not an alphabet. They have not been able to form what all other nations have formed. It is only more difficult from its rudeness, as there is more labour in hewing down a tree with a stone than with an axe.'

As in the previous century, there were manifestations of Chinese influence on stage. A China festival was promoted, unsuccessfully, by the great actor David Garrick (1717–79) in 1754, consisting of plays and public performances. But five years later, Arthur Murphy's *The Orphan of China* was to enjoy huge success. As with Elkanah Settle's production from a century before, it is hard today to make much sense of the play: it focuses on the transition between the Ming and the Qing, though this time with names and events that are difficult to reconcile with any corresponding historic figures or facts.[94]

The general idealisation of China in this earlier, more naïve era, when contact was so limited, included a brief period when its political system was also lauded: 'Amongst the several models and plans of government which ancients formed, we shall perhaps meet with none so perfect as the Chinese' went one description in 1775.[95] But this was to last only until sustained, direct intercourse removed some of the more callow impressions spread about the place. One imbalance was that while there were some (albeit a small number) of British who had been to China, the number of people who originated from China and were physically present in Britain at this time was minuscule. This was partly because of imperial commands from Beijing that no natives of the country were allowed to leave their homeland, and that punishment awaited those who violated this and tried to return after their lives abroad. Of those recorded, an artist called Chitqua, possibly from Canton, arrived in London in 1769. The Royal College of Physicians still has a ceramic attributed to him, and he exhibited at the Royal Academy Summer Exhibition in 1770. His first attempt to leave Britain to return to China was traumatic, because 'he found that the sailors looked upon him as a passenger likely to bring ill luck to the ship, and their threats so terrified the artist that he begged the carpenter, in case he was killed, to make a coffin in order that his body could be taken ashore'.[96] Johnson's biographer, James Boswell, had met Chitqua in 1769, and had him read some Chinese to him. 'It was', Boswell said, 'just what Mr Johnson told me of another Chinese – a sound like the ringing of a small bell.'[97] A Chinese boy, Huang Ya Dong, also a native of Canton, was brought to Britain around 1770 by the EIC merchant John Blake. He is immortalised in a portrait by Sir Joshua Reynolds that still hangs on the walls of the great Kentish stately home, Knole Park.

The greatest single influence on Sino-British relations in the period up to 1787 was not cultural or necessarily commercial, but rather domestic legal. In 1784, in order to deal with the rampant smuggling of tea into Britain (brought about by high tariffs), the Commutation Act reduced duties from 75 per cent to a uniform 12.5 per cent. The impact of this move was dramatic. It resulted in a tripling of trade with China within a few years, largely destroying the illicit trade and making people far more willing to import openly. The upsurge in demand magnified the various problems in the supply system that had been accumulating until then: the restrictions on places to trade, the limitations of the *cohong* system, and the arbitrariness of many of the Cantonese authorities' regulations and claims. After this act, Britain dominated the Chinese tea export trade. This alone caused the British elite and the public to take an interest in China. It accounted for most of the profits of the EIC, and made a major contribution to Whitehall tax revenue. It was this act that led to the idea of embassies being sent to China to try to resolve the problems through direct government-to-government links. In this way, the era of dominance by traders and merchants alone came to an end, and the time of the diplomats and officials commenced. For the first time, not just commerce, but high politics entered the mix, with what was to prove explosive and profoundly far-reaching consequences.

3

A Time of Diplomats

Macartney and Amherst, 1787–1830

William Alexander (1767–1816), a native of Maidstone in Kent, was not the main artist for the first embassy to be sent to the mighty Qing emperor's court, which has gone down in history as the Macartney mission (after the lord who led it in 1792–94). Instead, that position belonged to Thomas Hickey. Alexander himself was merely the draughtsman.[1] And yet, while Hickey produced almost nothing during his months in the stimulation of this wholly new visual environment, Alexander's output was prodigious. Today, his prints dating from his tour are in the Maidstone Museum archives, along with others he made on more local, parochial themes. But in his watercolours, painted on board the vessel *Lion* as it slowly passed along the Chinese coast from Macau up towards the Bohai estuary, he was able to portray instances of this strange new landscape. Like Peter Mundy over 150 years before, what struck him were the boats: the vast numbers of small vessels in the rivers and waters around the coast. On 2 July 1793, he wrote that 'the ship at this time surrounded with Chinese fishing boats . . . I counted 700 of them in sight at the same time, and each containing an average of 12 persons . . . this gave us a strong idea of the populousness of this immense country'. But unlike in the time of Captain Anson in the 1740s, these people were not indifferent to the new kind of vessel among them. 'Boats', wrote Alexander on 4 July, 'are constantly swimming about the ship to admire [our vessel]'.[2]

Once in Beijing, Alexander's main issue was the scorpions that suddenly appeared in the visitors' sleeping quarters in the Summer Palace, and the heat. The latter necessitated desperate measures: 'I wound a bandage of green silk and sat without my coat *a la Turque*, with a fan, which I found of infinite service. Some others looked equally ludicrous with goggle spectacles to defend them from the dust.' Despite having come so far, however, at the key moments of the voyage – the visit to the Great Wall and the meeting with the Qianlong emperor himself – Alexander was not allowed to be present. Reasonably enough, he found that the artist being absent at these seminal moments 'was not easily to be accounted for'.[3] If there was compensation, it was that the landscape he finally observed once the mission concluded its business in Beijing and its members made their way overland back to the south clearly deeply impressed him. On reaching the province of Zhejiang, he wrote that 'the surrounding country is beautiful with plantations of mulberry trees like English orchards, the foliage of these are the source of a strong yellow and orange fruit, and the numerous canals which branch off from the principal one on which we are sailing give altogether a charming appearance of the scenery'.[4]

Most agreed even at the time that the mission – despite exposure to these wonders – had been a failure. The reasons for that failure were much pondered afterwards, and will be discussed later. But what is indisputable is that this single visit produced lots of new ways of seeing, and created new kinds of knowledge about this novel place. These included relatively prosaic (but fundamental) things, such as the profound insight Alexander gained into the nature of the Chinese landscape and its appearance. Much of what was learned was either totally new or else broke paradigms that had existed up to then. This knowledge was conveyed through the numerous different books published after the embassy that recounted what had happened over the few months that Macartney and his colleagues had been in China. A different level of understanding about this place, and what it might mean to Britain, had been created. The implications of all this were to prove profound. In many ways, Macartney's visit created the modern idea for the British of a China that was neither the ideal that so many had dreamed and written of before, nor the fearsome spectre that others had concocted. Instead, it was a place that could be related to: one that had values, perspectives and ideas which were different, but distinctly human and humane.

It has to be remembered, however, that the issues prompting the embassy in the first place were prosaic ones to do with market access and trade rules, rather than with searching for new forms of understanding and knowledge. There had been a growing awareness since the establishment of the Canton system in 1757 (by which all trade with the outside world from China had to happen through Canton and various restrictions were put in place) that the status quo – where merchants from Britain dealt solely with *cohong* agents in China, who then relayed messages to and from officials, rather than allowing any direct contact – was no longer workable. The EIC supercargoes were increasingly convinced that their complaints about what they regarded as pernicious, ever-changing rules and duties demanded by the Canton officials would only be properly addressed if they sought intervention from higher authorities in Beijing. This was a very early occurrence of the conviction by some foreigners that local problems in China would not be resolved unless the central authorities were invoked and waded in – a conviction that persists to this day, despite plenty of evidence to the contrary. In order to aid their lobbying, the appointment of a person of appropriate status direct from Britain, representing not the EIC but the British state itself, was regarded as an increasingly viable idea. Indeed, it was proposed as early as 1754 by one of the main supercargoes in Canton, Frederick Pigou, though at that time nothing transpired. With the passing of the Commutation

Act in 1784 and the unleashing of yet more trade, with renewed energy the EIC urged London to take up the idea, believing the time had come to finally do something to expand its business even further, and convinced that the British state needed to take the lead.

The Cathcart and Macartney missions, 1788–94

The British in Canton were pushing at an open door. Henry Dundas (1742–1811), first Viscount Melville, was the chief lieutenant to Prime Minister William Pitt the Younger (1759–1806). In the mid-1780s, he held an informal position somewhat grandly named Lord of Trade. Because of its increasing importance to British interests, Dundas had developed a deep interest in India. It was via this route that China came within his purview. One of the main complaints of the EIC was the failure to find any market for their chief British export, wool. This was unsurprising in the case of southern China, as it had a perpetually warm climate; but surely, the EIC argued, entry to a more northerly port in the Qing empire would mean access to far colder climes, and a ready consumer base for sturdy British woollen clothing. It was to actively explore this possibility that the notion of a formal mission first started to be discussed.

Britain was not doing something wholly novel in this respect. Between 1520 and 1795 there were seventeen European government missions to China. Six of these were from Russia. But the first attempt by Britain did not come until 1787, when Charles Allan Cathcart (1759–88) was selected as the plenipotentiary. A lieutenant colonel in the British army, Cathcart had been a patron and friend of the potter Josiah Wedgwood (1730–95), himself a famous developer of technology originally sourced in China for his porcelain ware.[5] Cathcart had stated on his appointment that, while he was 'averse to idle parade', much of the success of his mission 'depends on the decorum with which it shall be conducted'.[6] It was clear that the British had already learned the lesson well that their Chinese interlocutors were highly status conscious. They were also aware that, for some reason, the British were not regarded with quite the high esteem they felt they deserved. As Dundas acidly wrote, Cathcart should 'impress upon the minds of the Chinese that the British subjects were controlled by British laws [and] that all mariners were not a rabble'.[7] The whole endeavour was therefore designed to be as much a diplomatic performance as a pure trade and political negotiation mission. Dundas, as architect of the terms of reference for Cathcart's proposed voyage, set out firm objectives: to clear away 'lack of open access to the tribunals of the country and the fair execution of its laws'.[8]

The embassy was to be undertaken in the name of King George III (1738–r1760–1820), for, as Cathcart wrote to Dundas on 20 June 1787: 'The only chance of success in negotiating with the court in Peking [would] arise from the Mission being in the name of the King'.[9] It was to demand 'a small track [sic] of ground or detached island in some more convenient situation – a place of security as a depot for our goals'. Dundas continued that 'our views are purely commercial, having not even a wish for territory' just for its own sake, and attempted to convey the idea that for the British, trade and politics were entirely separate projects.[10] But in an indication of how misleading this message was, Cathcart was ordered not to mention the burgeoning opium trade in his talks, but to impress on the Chinese the idea that the British state, which he served, was to promote and grow 'the open market'. In that context, if the unhappy subject of the drug trade came up, the British visitor was to state that this was a matter for free trade, and that 'the sale of our opium in Bengal must be left to take its chance there', unattached to any direction from Britain's government.[11] Continuing the tradition of Elizabeth I and James I, George III had furnished the embassy with a letter.

All of this preliminary effort proved to no avail, however. Cathcart died en route in the summer of 1788 and, with no viable deputy, his embassy was aborted even before it had entered the waters around China. But this mission was merely a prelude, it turned out, to one of the seminal events in the development of global modernity – the first official British delegation to reach China. Learning from the preparations for Cathcart, the EIC made it clear that one of the chief aims of the new proposed mission was to 'create a favourable impression of the British character'.[12] The person appointed to do this was indeed someone with immense international experience, who might stand as one of the chief players in Britain's early modern globalisation. Born in 1737 in County Antrim, in today's Northern Ireland, and a graduate of Trinity College, Dublin, George Macartney had served as envoy-extraordinary to the court of Catherine the Great in St Petersburg, where, after some strenuous negotiation, he had secured a treaty of commerce. Other posts he held were chief secretary for Ireland, governor of Grenada, and then, from 1780, governor of Fort St George in Madras, a position from which he returned to Britain in 1786. It is hard to think of anyone from this period with a similar range of experience across so many different cultures and contexts.

Nor had Macartney's life been without drama and incident. He had been incarcerated in Paris as a prisoner of war in the late 1770s, and was an associate of Dr Johnson, who had accorded him the praise of being 'in some degree a literary man'.[13] After returning from Madras in 1786, he had even fought a duel with a certain Major General James Stuart (who had been disciplined by him while he was in India), sustaining a painful injury. He was thereafter plagued by gout: he would suffer the effects of this complaint during his later visit to China, meaning that the whole experience – with the long periods of confinement at sea and the discomfort of carriage travel within China – was as searing for him physically as it was culturally and intellectually. For Dundas and the EIC, as they turned their minds increasingly to a second attempt at an embassy in the late 1780s and early 1790s, Macartney's personal attributes and his lengthy experience meant he was a man worth considering. It was hardly a surprise, therefore, when he was formally offered the role in 1791.

The Macartney embassy he led spawned such a large number of different interpretations and accounts that the challenge for those writing about it afterwards is more what to exclude than what to put in. It was the first direct encounter between the modernising British state at a key moment in its evolution and the Qing, which was also experiencing a portentous transition from the Qianlong era (which had lasted for six decades and had been a period of relative stability and success) to the far less certain reign of the successor Jiaqing. Both nations were charged with a sense of importance and an accompanying desire to receive recognition and validation of their status from others. But their aims and the dynamics driving them economically and geopolitically were very different. Arguments about how best to understand the nature of the misunderstanding between the two sides have continued to the present. One reading by the American scholar James Hevia argues that much of the dissonance that occurred when Macartney presented himself at the Qing court was about fundamentally different cultures of power. The two sides had 'incompatible views of the meaning of sovereignty and the ways in which relations of power were constructed'.[14] The various clashes about the kowtow, the meaning of gifts given and what the two sides' ultimate objectives meant boiled down to an attempt by both to insist on a specific set of mutually incompatible meanings and a world view that supported them. For the French scholar and diplomat Alain Peyrefitte, however, the whole incident could be seen as a prime illustration of the 'clash of civilisations' – a seminal moment in which different views of progress, history and politics came starkly into conflict with each other and set up the trauma of the ensuing decades. 'There is', writes Peyrefitte, 'perhaps no more striking instance in the clash between advanced and traditional societies than the proud encounter at the end of the 18th century between Britain and China – the first country to be gripped by the industrial revolution and the most brilliant of all civilisations rooted in custom.'[15]

What is certain is that the drama of the whole episode allows us an opportunity to see, in sharp detail, the deep differences that divided one polity (which privileged a sense of tradition, stability and order) against another (which was undergoing transformative change). Britain in 1792 was experiencing a huge transition to a new kind of economic, social and eventually political structure. It was in the midst of a long industrial revolution, some of the products of which Macartney, with very limited success, gifted to his august host as adverts for British technological prowess. It seems these were hardly the paradigm changers that were intended – Qianlong had seen other products of Western manufacturing and was unimpressed by the novelty claimed for them. But it was also clear that both sides had more fundamental differences. Not the least of these was the lack of a clear common language in which to communicate. This raised one of the hardest practical issues that had to be solved before the mission even set off: who would be the interpreters? The EIC-trained linguists were unacceptable to the Chinese because they were people who had violated the internal laws forbidding foreigners to learn the local language. That meant reliance on other groups – either long-term Jesuit missionaries in the capital (whose sheer length of service in the country meant they inevitably did learn to speak the language, but who were suspect, hailing as they did from European countries with which Britain was often in conflict) or the Chinese themselves. The latter also raised issues of divided loyalties – and in any case, the British would not be able to find them until they reached their destination, creating the problem of what to do if no one suitable was available. A mute embassy was hardly optimal. George Staunton (1737–1801), appointed as Macartney's secretary for the mission, found the solution: Li Zibao, a Chinese Christian convert at the Catholic Seminary in Naples, who agreed to accompany the delegation back to his homeland.[16] On the voyage over, Staunton and his son (also called George) learned some Mandarin – though, as the father complained, 'he had the mortification of finding that he could scarcely understand a word of what was said to him', whereas the son, while working less hard, through 'senses more acute, and . . . organs more flexible, proved already a tolerably good interpreter'.[17] Staunton junior was indeed to go on to be one of Britain's most important early sinologists.

Macartney himself undertook a profound re-education before the embassy (and a process of re-evaluation immediately after it). He was to prove a highly reflective and self-questioning emissary, and by no means a slavish follower of diplomatic form. After embarkation from Portsmouth on 21 September 1792, he read all that he was able to lay his hands on while undertaking the long sea voyage across the Atlantic, via Brazil and the Cape of Good Hope on the older, long-established route. His fleet consisted of the *Lion*, *Hindustan* (this ship largely laden with gifts for the emperor) and *Jackal*. This last ship soon disappeared from view, only rejoining the others months later in the Sunda Strait, between the main islands of today's Indonesia. The voyage was not an easy one, and there were numerous deaths on board as the boats progressed slowly to their destination. But while this drama was going on, the chief representative was able to read and reflect, preparing for the first formal state-to-state encounter between the two great countries.

Much of his thought must have been devoted to working out how to implement the objectives of the whole endeavour. These had been devised by the EIC and Dundas after lengthy discussion, and were therefore highly deliberative. The main objective was to open up free trade at Canton. Secondly, there was a need for more ports to trade from (in particular in the north, to sell wool in colder climes). The EIC's wish list included 'a port or ports to the northwards of Canton, in the expectation of extending our commerce generally, particularly for trade in tea'.[18] Duties needed to be eliminated or reduced. The EIC also wished Macartney to 'use every endeavour for the purpose of introducing new articles of British manufacture into China'.[19] There was also a demand for greater diversity of goods exported back to

Britain. A depot similar to Macau for the Portuguese would be desirable. And the EIC also wanted its agents to be no longer responsible for the behaviour of private traders, who were increasingly a law unto themselves and beyond control.[20]

The story of the embassy once it reached China is easy enough to trace (at least in outline) because so many participants, including Macartney himself, left excellent first-hand accounts. After its arrival in Macau in June 1793, the *Lion*, *Hindustan* and *Jackal* moved up the coast towards Zhousan, off the coast of Zhejiang, where they arrived on 3 July. They reached a town called Tengzhou in Shandong a few days later, when their hosts – two officials called Wang Wenxiong and Qiao Renjie – came on board. Here the interminable arguments began about the ritual procedure to be followed when meeting the emperor. By 5 August, the delegation was at the mouth of the Peiho (today's Haihe) River, where, a day later, they met the governor of the local province. On 11 August, still arguing over ritual issues, and when and how to present the gifts the embassy had brought, Macartney and his delegation of about eighty came to Tianjin. By 21 August, they had managed to skirt the great walls of the capital, Beijing, on their way to the Summer Palace and the place of their residence on the outskirts. Here, three weeks later, on 14 September, they were taken to the summer residence of the Qianlong emperor in the city of Jehol (today's Chengde, about 140 miles northeast of the capital) and Macartney at last had his fabled audience. For him, the great emperor was 'a very fine old gentleman, still healthy and vigorous, not having the appearance of a man more than sixty'. But he also injected a touch of scepticism into the pomp and ceremony of what he was observing: 'Thus, then, have I seen the "King of Solomon in all his glory"'. The scene made him remember an event from his childhood when he had observed a puppet show, 'which made so strong an impression on my mind that I then thought it a true representation of the highest pitch of human greatness and felicity'.[21] But he needed to remind himself that, as had been the case when watching the puppets as an infant, everything he had witnessed had been a performance and *only* a performance. It was an astute early insight into the underlying vulnerability of Chinese power under the late Qing. And in the end, it proved devastatingly accurate, as the British subsequently used force and violence to expose its fragility.

At least for now, however, the performance continued. A few days later – after a second and larger audience in an open field, with games and a banquet, and with other emissaries from Korea and nearby countries present – the group was despatched back to Britain, largely empty handed. Qianlong's infamous letter of rejection, so often repeated it needs only a summary here, thanked the embassy for the trouble it had taken in coming – and then rejected the demands for free trade, for further ports to be opened and for some form of permanent representation. The numerous gifts presented to the Chinese ruler had failed to make much of an impact, though they had been painstakingly unpacked and assembled in a display place in the Summer Palace. Qianlong was in the twilight years of his reign – one that had lasted for almost six decades. The challenges of a proactive relationship with this truculent, ambitious and new player from so far away were not ones that a ruler as old as he (or the Qing he led) was willing to embrace voluntarily. History was to prove that he had good reason to be wary of these visitors from afar, for his descendants would end up largely serving at their behest.

On 3 October, after finally realising that the Qing authorities wished the embassy to depart Beijing and that there would be no further chance of discussion or negotiations, Macartney wrote: 'having been selected for this commission to China, the first of its kind from Great Britain, of which considerable expectations of success had been formed by many, and none more than myself, I cannot help feeling . . . disappointment most severely'. The embassy had failed to achieve an opening-up of trade to China or direct intercourse between the Chinese and British governments: in fact, it had failed to meet a single one of its overtly stated aims. Macartney's journey home – which took almost nine months – offered a period for more reflection. He wrote in his journal: 'I have now, however painful for me, been obliged to dismiss from my mind many of the flattering ideas which I had entertained at the commencement of my Embassy.' Macartney stands as the first realist in affairs relating to China – someone who had needed to move through the initial distant hopes to see, far closer up, how challenging and difficult it would be to forge a new relationship with this very different power.

Many of the participants alongside the ambassador left either contemporaneous records or reflections penned many years later. This gives anyone seeking today to learn what the embassy was like a disarming array of perspectives, as though it were not one event but several. It is true that the visit was multifaceted and worked on many levels. All those who wrote were united, however, in their awareness of the historic importance of what they were undertaking. For some, the tone in which they conveyed this was humble, almost demotic, and their concerns more humdrum and prosaic. Samuel Holmes, sergeant major of the 12th Light Dragoons, was one of Macartney's guards, a 'worthy, sensible, but unlearned man', who left an account recording just how physically gruelling the journey had been.[22] His description of the journey out, and of the activities in China itself, was dominated by a list of fatalities and illnesses, rather than a record of any splendour and ritual. Sickness came early, when fever struck many of the crew in the Sunda Strait. Later, closer to China, they were prone to 'prickly heat', which left the bodies 'of some amongst us . . . one entire sore from head to foot'.[23] On 12 June, Mr Tortle, purser of the *Lion*, died 'and [was] buried the same day near the watering place'. On 23 June, George Martin, a caulker's mate (someone dealing with maintenance), passed away. On 26 June, a crew member from the *Jackal* fell overboard as the topsails were being reefed. 'By the direction of his cries, he survived some time though the sea ran mountains high' before he succumbed.[24] The crew of the *Lion* 'remained in very sickly condition and from the time we anchored on July 6', wrote Holmes, 'we buried five seamen, and had sixty on the surgeon's list'.[25] The journey had put things into perspective for the sailor: 'We should think nothing of the hardships of [future] soldiery, having so severely felt that of sailoring.'[26]

For others, like Sir George Staunton, Macartney's deputy, the main focus was on the larger economic and political implications of what they had learned on their voyage, and what the nature of Chinese governance and diplomatic power was. The aim of the whole endeavour, as Staunton stated, was policy oriented – to put British trade with China on 'a less precarious and more advantageous footing'.[27] This knowledge was therefore crucial if that were to be achieved. Staunton and his young son, also called George, had been present at the imperial audience, where the boy had put his study of Chinese on the voyage out to good use by saying a few words directly before the emperor and eliciting his praise and approval. Staunton senior added the homely detail about this encounter that the great leader was wearing 'a velvet bonnet in form not much different from the bonnet of a Scottish highlander'.[28] His prognosis after the whole tour was that Chinese merchants, unlike their British counterparts, had little real freedom, and did not know how to stand up for their own commercial self-interest. They were 'bred in awe which the heavy hand of arbitrary power had impressed upon their minds', making them timid and cautious.[29] Nor had the level of science and technology he had seen impressed him. 'The state of physic is extremely low', he remarked at one point. But he also showed an appreciation of the source of the Chinese court's wariness of the British. Macartney himself had been told of the news of British military activity against the Gurkhas in India. Staunton noted that because of incidents like this, 'the British nation was felt to be too powerful not to require some management towards it, even from the proud empire of China.'[30]

For Aeneas Anderson, assistant to the ambassador, the mission had delivered mostly disappointment; it had gained an insight into the country, while being cut down to size. He writes much like many other British tourists taken from the comfort of their home environment and exposed to the horrors of the foreign. He notes the cautiousness of some of the delegation towards Chinese food, which was known to be 'indifferent', while arrival in Beijing had shown that the houses in the capital, though pleasing enough on the exterior, were 'most wretchedly furnished within'.[31] The Summer Palace was 'a very mean, inconvenient building of no more than one storey'.[32] And while the Great Wall of China did impress him, he went on to reflect on how it would fare now that it had lost whatever defensive purpose was imputed to it, believing that it would end up 'an enormous length of ruins and an awful example of decay'.[33] Even sight of the emperor (Anderson was one of the members of the parade sent to be present at the first meeting with Qianlong) was underwhelming: he came 'in a very plain palanquin, borne by 20 mandarins, and were it not for the circumstances he would not have been distinguished from a common mandarin'.[34]

For Macartney's main secretary, John Barrow, the key issue was cultural differences, and in particular the lack of any modernity in the country. He wrote in his account of a China he had experienced which was a monument to ossification and worship of tradition for the sake of it. This was to have an enormous impact on British ideas and perceptions of China in the nineteenth century. While appreciative of the efforts the Chinese hosts had made, Barrow's views of the overall cultural level of the place were damning: 'With respect to any branch of learning or speculative science little improvement seems to have been made in the last two thousand years.'[35] The mission he was part of had found a nation 'worn out with old age and disease'; a place 'where millions could be set to work at the nod of a despot';[36] and the present state of which meant 'they are totally incapable of appreciating anything great or excellent in the arts or sciences'.[37]

On the long voyage home to Britain on the *Lion*, Macartney was far more reflective in his personal journal (published over 170 years later). Unlike today's plenipotentiaries, who find themselves caught up in the ever-increasing pace of events, with almost instantaneous communications with their home countries (however distant) and multiple sources of information to distract and occupy them, he had time to think. Despite the splendour of the diplomatic theatre he had witnessed, the country he had seen was a 'nation in general . . . far from being easy or contented'.[38] Using a strikingly symbolic language, his shrewd eyes had

> often perceived the ground to be hollow under a vast superstructure, and in trees of the most stately and flourishing appearance I discovered symptoms of speedy decay . . . The Chinese are now recovering from the blows that had stunned them; they are awakening from the political stupor they had been thrown into by the Tartars [the ruling Manchu].[39]

Qianlong, after all, in Macartney's eyes, despite all the trappings of grandeur around him, remained a 'true tartar'.[40] This was rule by a tiny minority over a vast mass of people. How could it be sustainable? The question was not whether it would end, but when they would awake, when the regime would fall and what might happen afterwards. Perhaps that was why Macartney had noticed undercurrents of uneasiness and nervousness in the haughty, outwardly self-confident officials around him during his stay. These were signs of a 'fundamental caution and circumspection of the government, which is awake to the slightest alarms'.[41] It was clear that already, some of the great sources of asymmetry between Britain and China were readily apparent. In science, 'the Chinese are certainly far behind the European world'. There was evidence of an understanding of mathematics and astronomy, but this was 'very limited'. 'A great part of their astronomy is mere astrological trifling.'[42] He also noted how far behind the Chinese appeared in terms of medical or surgical skill.[43]

Macartney was not risk averse and was willing to make a few predictions. He assessed the Qing state to be like a great, old ship somehow kept afloat, but constantly precarious. Perhaps this was inspired by his many months at sea. But his compatriots also came in for criticism. He observed how in Canton, the British 'keep aloof [from the Chinese] as much as possible', wearing 'a dress as different from them as much as possible' and proving 'quite ignorant of their language', so that 'we therefore almost entirely depend on the good faith and good nature of the few Chinese whom we employ'. Nevertheless, he saw a future time when things might be different: 'By proper management, we might not gradually and in some years [sic] be able to mould the China trade (as we seem to have done the trade everywhere else) to the shape that best suits us.'[44] The British, after all, had something the Chinese seemed not to possess – a transferable ideology (early capitalism) which could shift across environments regardless of their cultural differences and find something common between them – financial profit through the operation of markets. In order to promote this set of ideas and practices, Britain might need to use force, deploying 'a few frigates', which in 'a few weeks [would] destroy all their coast'. There were other options: 'We might probably be able from Bengal to excite the most serious disturbances of their Tibet frontier by means of their neighbours there, who appear to require only a little encouragement and assistance to begin.' It was just a question of political will. Macartney saw one other important fracture that might be manipulated, 'the thread of connexion between this Empire and Formosa [Taiwan]' that 'is so slender that it must soon break of itself, but a breath of foreign interference would instantly snap it asunder'. He had witnessed a fragile empire, in a dangerous neighbourhood.

Macartney was not talking about these issues flippantly: he realised that stakes were high. But unlike his Chinese interlocutors, whose interests and priorities were defensive and insular, he at least dared to think of the possibilities of greater openness. The break-up of China, he wrote, 'would occasion a complete subversion of the commerce, not only of Asia, but a very sensible change in the other quarters of the world'. But it would offer opportunity, and 'Great Britain, from the weight of her riches and the genius and spirit of her people' would 'as the first political, marine and commercial power on the globe' be able to deal with this. Britain stood, even were China to fall apart, 'the greatest gainer by such a revolution', rising superior to every competitor.[45] In this way, Macartney was an accidental and unconscious prophetic revolutionary. For in the coming century, it was indeed the management of a China that was almost perpetually broken and damaged, but that never quite got sucked into the abyss, that worked best and provided the greatest opportunities for Britain. Its weakness created a space for others to get rich. Its vulnerability meant it would never be able to push back against British incursions and demands. Macartney was a humane and cultivated man. But this was his inhumane and harshly realist prognosis. And while not the conscious, explicitly stated policy of the British state, now newly – albeit imperfectly – linked to its Chinese counterpart, that was the great aim: a China that worked for British interests; a China which did not fall apart so that it threatened those interests, but which never grew so strong that it might oppose them.

Aftermath

Macartney's return to Britain was inauspicious. Some decades later, Peter Auber (1770–1866), secretary to the directors of the EIC, pithily summarised the embassy's outcomes: in China it 'was received with the utmost politeness, treated with the utmost hospitality, watched with the utmost vigilance, and dismissed with the utmost civility'.[46] On its final return to Britain, Macartney and his colleagues were regarded as failures. The poet John Wolcot (1738–1819), writing under the pseudonym Peter Pindar, penned a sarcastic ode, lambasting the lord and his reported servile behaviour before the Chinese emperor:

And now I hear the lofty Emperor say,
'Good folks, what is it that you want, I pray?' —
And now I hear aloud Macartney cry,
'Emperor, my court, inform'd that you were rich,
Sublimely feeling a strong money-itch,
Across the Eastern Ocean bade me fly;
With tin, and blankets, O great King! to barter,
And gimcracks rare for China-man and Tartar.[47]

Such lilting doggerel was the response to a venture which had seen itself having far loftier aims. As Staunton wrote, the purpose of the mission was not conquest 'or enlarging our dominions . . . nor for the purpose of acquiring wealth, nor even for favouring the commerce of [British] subjects but for the sake of increasing knowledge of the habitable globe'.[48] That was why, in addition to the painters Hickey and Alexander, there was also James Dinwiddie, who participated as a science advisor; Hugh Gillan, a medical doctor; and the botanist David Stronach (who continued the work of the first known flower and seed collector to visit China, James Cunningham, who had visited from 1698 to 1700, bringing back samples for Sir Hans Sloane). These men – along with all the other witnesses from the mission who wrote of what they had learned about Chinese governance, diplomacy, culture, society and politics – were in the business of creating new ways of knowing and understanding difference through encounter with a place that clearly was seen as embodying this. It was as though the West and the East were finally placed side by side like parallel texts, and an enormous act of comparison was taking place.

Macartney's work had clearly uncovered something fresh and new. This is nowhere more apparent than in the exposure it gave the group to a landscape which, in terms of architecture, signs of human intervention and design, and in its natural layout and contents, was completely novel to them. The journey from Beijing back down south was, after all, the first of its kind by the British in this new, largely unexplored land, and it provided a glimpse of a place until then forbidden and closed off. They were venturing into virgin territory. The great cities of Hangzhou, Nanjing and Suzhou were finally physically exposed and available to them. Sometimes the observers drew parallels with what they already knew and understood to make sense of the terrain they were in. Staunton himself had felt Suzhou reminiscent of Venice.[49] For Barrow, his recollection of their journey by canal was more poetic:

> We sailed for two days in our little barges through one of the most wild, mountainous and barren tracks [sic] of country that I have ever beheld. Abounding more in the sublime and horrible than the picturesque and beautiful. The lofty summits of the mountains seemed to touch each other across the river and at a distance, it appeared as if we had to sail through an arched cavern.[50]

Such descriptions of a feeling both of awe and of fear and dread before nature had parallels with the work of Barrow's contemporary, William Wordsworth. They certainly accorded with the ways in which the unruliness of Chinese aesthetics was impacting on the Romantic movement developing in Europe.

Despite this acquisition of knowledge, however, the brute fact remained that, in practical terms, the embassy had changed nothing. The same high duties were still required of British ships in Canton – only more of them than ever before, because of the upsurge in demand for tea. As the historian Earl Pritchard said, China 'had converted England into a nation of tea drinkers', despite all the efforts to exercise influence in the other direction.[51] Between 1764 and 1800, British trade with China increased by 264 per cent.[52] Tea accounted for the bulk of this growth. In the early eighteenth century, the EIC purchased 400,000 lbs (180,000kg) a year. By 1800, this had grown to 23.3 million lbs, rising to 26 million lbs (12 million kg) after 1808, half the total for Europe.[53] This trade was profitable for the EIC. For it at least, the Macartney embassy had not caused any rupture in business as usual – even if that involved perpetual small-scale arguments and clashes. In a follow-up attempt to iron these out a little, a further letter from George III was sent in 1805, co-signed by the president of the Board of Control in the government at the time responsible for EIC affairs, Lord Castlereagh, requesting a further embassy be allowed to visit Beijing. This elicited a polite, emptily dismissive reply from Qianlong's successor, the Jiaqing emperor: 'Your majesty's kingdom is at a remote distance beyond the seas, but it is observant of its duties and obedient to its laws . . . Our celestial nation regards all persons with eyes of charity, and always treats and considers your subjects with the utmost indulgence and affection.'[54] The message was clear. There was no need to send such a delegation. In any case, the Napoleonic Wars back in Europe acted as a major distraction. They even had a small spillover effect on Far Eastern affairs. In 1808, Admiral William Drury of the British navy briefly took control of Macau from the Portuguese, in order to prevent the French from taking opportunities there. And in 1814, the British warship HMS *Davis* seized an American vessel during a flare-up between Britain and its newest major liberated colony (a British force two years earlier in Washington had undertaken the first and last land attack on the American capital). In the background there were always British interests in India. In 1815, as the duke of Wellington and his forces finally laid Napoleon's grand European plans to rest at Waterloo, the British invaded Qing China's neighbour, Nepal.

The kowtow and Amherst 1816

Marx's dictum that history occurs first as tragedy and then as farce is nowhere more apt than in its application to the first and second embassies sent from Britain to the Qing. The earlier one, at least, had a certain drama and grandeur. The second, led by William Pitt Amherst (1773–1857), was an unmitigated failure that ended in chaos when the delegates failed to stay in Beijing for even one day or to gain sight of the emperor. Having set out months earlier from Britain with a set of objectives, it took just a few hours for all their hopes to be reduced to naught.

What linked the two ventures was the never-ending argument about kowtowing. This made such an indelible impression that to this day, 'kowtow' (from the Chinese *ke-tou* – to lower one's head) is a well-known part of the British lexicon, and is still applied when attacking those who are seen as too obedient to the desires of others. Kowtowing was not unknown to the British. Peter Mundy had referred to the ritual when he met mandarins in 1637.[55] For Macartney, there was the action itself (in its highest form consisting of three kneelings and nine kowtows, where the supplicant had to kneel from a standing position three times, each time touching the floor with their head three times) and there was the meaning imputed to it, which implied submission and recognition of superiority towards those before whom it was performed. The Chinese documents ascribed great importance to the action and to the attitude its performance (or non-performance) indicated. 'Now when your King sends you to congratulate His Imperial Majesty on his birthday', an edict of 14 August 1793 stated, 'you should obey the established ceremonials of the Celestial empire. If you refuse to perform this ceremony, you will call into question the sincerity of your King who sends you here from afar over the seas to congratulate his Imperial Majesty on his birthday.'[56]

While appreciating this, what Macartney wanted, as is made clear in the record of his long arguments with the Chinese, was a corresponding sense of reciprocity. He did not want to undertake a demonstration of subservience – something unacceptable to the nation he represented; instead he sought something showing mutual recognition. He therefore demanded that Chinese officials perform a similar act of obeisance before a portrait of George III that the delegation had brought with it. The refusal of the mandarins to do this ended up with lengthy discussions. Only after this did compromise ensue.

When meeting Qianlong, Macartney bowed his head three times, at least according to the English-language records. The Chinese, however, say that he performed the full ritual.

While Macartney's mission had to navigate such delicate issues while lacking expertise and linguistic ability, the Amherst embassy a quarter of a century later could have no such complaints: Amherst had a plethora of home-grown talent at his disposal. In the years since he had impressed the Qianlong emperor, George Staunton the younger (1781–1859) had acquired such expertise in Mandarin, both written and spoken, that he had translated the Qing's complete legal code into English. Thomas Manning, the first British person ever to set foot in Lhasa (mentioned in the previous chapter), was also employed, though only after Amherst had made it clear to him that he needed to desist from wearing Chinese costume, as was his habit, and from acting in an eccentric manner. Finally, there was the great scholar Robert Morrison, a Protestant missionary (who will be considered in more detail later) who in 1814 had published the first ever English–Chinese dictionary. This was a formidable array of talent – probably the best that Europe could offer at the time. But ironically, it ended up working against the visitors. Part of this was due to the refusal, in Chinese eyes, of Staunton junior to acknowledge that Macartney had ever kowtowed, despite supposedly being a first-hand witness. On a report in Chinese of Staunton's protestations of not being able to remember something clearly from so far back, the Jiaqing emperor had written 'detestable equivocation' in the margin.[57] The other experts irritated the Chinese with their ideas and assumption of knowledge. As so often since, Amherst may well have wondered why he had so-called advisors to hand, when they only seemed to make his life more difficult.

Staunton's steer was consistently not to engage in the kowtow act. In a letter to Amherst, he stated that 'I feel strongly impressed with the idea that a compliance therefore will be unadvisable, even although the refusal should be attended with the hazard of the total rejection of the embassy.'[58] Arguments about this single act became the central issue for the whole embassy. While Amherst was given similar aims as Macartney had been (to open more trading ports, to allow greater market access, to reduce tariffs and to constrain the powers of officials and the arbitrary use of those powers in Canton), furious debates about whether or not he would perform the ceremony indicating 'sincere' obedience before the imperial throne took up most of the days before his arrival in Beijing. Henry Ellis, an official on the tour, left a contemporary account of the embassy: it had arrived with little fanfare in Beijing in the dead of night on 29 August 1816. Its members had barely been able to settle into their accommodation before Amherst was told that the emperor wished to see him immediately. Protesting that he needed at least some time to rest and wash and prepare himself, Amherst refused. At this point, the forceful persuasion of the anxious mandarin caused the situation to veer into farce. As Ellis wrote:

> All proving ineffectual, with some roughness, but under pretext of friendly violence, he laid hands upon Lord Amherst, to take him from the room; another Mandarin followed his example. His Lordship, with great firmness and dignity of manner, shook them off, declaring nothing but the extremest violence should induce him to quit the room for any other place but the residence assigned him.[59]

With both Amherst and his colleagues persisting in their argument that they were in no fit state to have formal meetings immediately after their arrival from such a long and arduous journey, the mandarins reported the emperor's fury, and his demand that they immediately leave Beijing. This they did, travelling back on the land route to meet their vessels, which had earlier been sent to meet them in the south (another cause of irritation to the Chinese, who said they had not sanctioned this).

As if the bad blood arising between the two nations from this fiasco in Beijing was not enough, the actions of Captain Murray Maxwell (1775–1831), who was in charge of Amherst's awaiting fleet, served to make things even worse. He managed to get involved in a fight with local vessels when he was refused entry to Canton to pick up his charge. Promptly firing back, he reportedly killed forty-seven locals. This tragedy summarised the whole chaotic mission. The Jiaqing emperor, condemned by the British for his 'weak and capricious' behaviour,[60] initially sent a vaguely conciliatory letter after the embassy, as it made its way down to Canton. But in a subsequent edict issued in 1817, he proceeded to blame the failure of the venture on the British and his own officials.[61] If there was any mitigation for his behaviour, it lay in the weighty and distracting domestic issues preying on his mind at the time. Amherst and his colleagues would not have known this, but there were growing signs of internal dissent and disharmony at the Qing court. The White Lotus Rebellion of 1796 to 1805 had prefigured this, spanning the years after Qianlong had abdicated as emperor in favour of his son, and putting immediate pressure on the new young ruler. Described by one historian as consisting of 'more or less millenarian or apocalyptic groups that combined elements of folk Buddhism, Manichaeism and devotion to the monotheistic Eternal Mother', the rebellion's suppression involved a scorched-earth policy which, while ultimately successful, left strands of resentment that were to flare up almost half a century later in the far more devastating Taiping uprising.[62] There had also reportedly been two assassination attempts on the emperor's life, the second in 1814. Whatever the British were looking at in their visit to China, it was not, as Macartney had earlier predicted, a secure leader ruling over a happy, contented place.

Ellis himself found that their point of departure, Macau, served as an apt enough symbol of the situation they had found themselves in. The rundown, dilapidated city was now 'the narrow limits to which Chinese jealousy had confined European excursions'.[63] More exciting was the visit they made on their way home to the island of St Helena. Here Amherst managed to achieve what he had failed to do in Beijing by setting eyes on an emperor, albeit an exiled, imprisoned one. Napoleon Bonaparte (1769–1821), incarcerated in this isolated spot after his defeat at Waterloo, 'rather declaimed than conversed', wrote Ellis, 'and during the half hour Lord Amherst and I were with him, seemed only anxious to impress his sentiments upon the recollections of his auditors, possibly for the purpose of having them repeated'. His style of speaking was 'highly epigrammatic' and he 'delivers his opinions with the oracular confidence of a man accustomed to produce conviction'.[64] Ironically, through an accident of fate, Thomas Manning had been the only British person whose passport Napoleon had signed, due to his need to interrupt his studies of Chinese in France and leave the country when war broke out with the British in 1803.[65]

As with Macartney, the group's reception back in Britain was a mocking one. One pamphlet wondered why the EIC was willing to be humiliated in order to trade, and how a representative of Britain who had failed so spectacularly was able to return home to no punishment. The anonymous author referred to the story of a king of Russia who had had the hat of a French ambassador who had called on him and irritated him nailed to his head. The clear implication was that Amherst had, at least symbolically, received similarly degrading treatment at the hands of the Chinese.[66]

Some subsequent – albeit lower-level – visitors had more positive experiences in China than Amherst. One anonymous account from 1822 records having been shipwrecked off the coast of the large island of Hainan (off the southern coast of the Chinese mainland) in 1819. Despite apprehension about what the natives might do when they turned up on shore, 'we were agreeably surprised to find that all our fears . . . were groundless and premature, as they did not attempt to offer the least violence or molestation'.[67] On walking about this island, the British were 'met everywhere with the greatest civility and politeness, for this people appeared to be in a high state of civilisation and their manners were singularly harmless and inoffensive'. There was one downside, however, because 'their extreme curiosity was . . . sometimes disagreeable'.[68] After a brief stay, the British managed to find their way to Canton, and from there back to their homeland. But their testimony of life at the margins of the Chinese empire showed that there was no single monolithic narrative about the attitude of the country's inhabitants to outsiders.

Despite the Amherst debacle, events in the following decade did not deteriorate greatly, but reverted to the patterns of trade that had prevailed in the decades before. There was the occasional unhappy occurrence. For instance, two Chinese died after coming under fire from the British ship HMS *Topaz* in 1822 – a man-of-war, not a trading vessel. After a brief stoppage of trade, the matter was resolved by the offending ship simply disappearing, leading the local officials to consider the matter closed. Over the longer term, more important events were the decision from 1821 by British merchants to use Lintin Island near Canton (today called Nei Lingding Island) as a trading point for opium ships, and the appearance of the merchants James Matheson (1796–1878) and William Jardine (1784–1843). The increase in opium trading through the decade and the struggle by the Chinese authorities to combat it were also emerging themes. The newly established *Canton Register* recorded on 30 November 1827 that 'His Excellency the Governor [of Canton] ordered the opium lately seized to be burnt at the gate of his office.'[69] To these events should be added the first stirrings of missionary activity – a kind of moral counterpoise to the venality and opportunism of the opium business, and one that only reinforced the confusion and bewilderment of the Chinese who, on the one hand, were dealing with people who said they wanted to save their souls, but on the other were damning them by supplying substances that were addictive and destructive. The 1820s proved to be the lull before the storm, appearing, on the surface, to be a decade of no major events and no real significance.

Knowing China: The Chinese origins of English Romanticism

Macartney and his colleagues had started a practical process of broader knowledge acquisition, ushering in an era when there were far wider sources and a greater complexity of materials informing British views of China.[70] These had influence far beyond the purely commercial and political, reinforcing the powerful cultural appeal that China and attitudes or beliefs about the country already exerted on a domestic audience. The work of translators and poets such as Thomas Percy (1729–1811) and the EIC merchant James Wilkinson had started off this phenomenon, earlier on introducing English versions of works such as the first Chinese novel to be rendered into English, the *Hau Kiou Choaan, or The Pleasing History* in 1761.[71]

Along with the work of landscape gardeners, architects and artists, these had served to embody a notion of Chinese aesthetics which was regarded as novel and striking because, as the historian Arthur O. Lovejoy pointed out in an influential essay on the Chinese origins of Romanticism, it encouraged rebellion against order and tightly controlled design:

> A turning point in the history of modern taste was reached when the ideals of regularity, simplicity, uniformity, and easy logical intelligibility, were first openly impugned, when the assumption that true beauty is 'geometrical' ceased to be one to which 'all consented, as to a law of nature'. And in England, at all events, the rejection of this assumption seems, throughout most of the eighteenth century, to have been commonly recognised as initially due to the influence of the example of Chinese art.[72]

Writers like the great poet William Wordsworth (1770–1850), an early exemplar of the power of Romanticism in literature, mentioned the 'paradise of ten thousand trees,/ Or Gehol's matchless gardens . . . Chosen from a widest empire where 'the Tartarian dynasty composed/ (Beyond that mighty wall, not fabulous,/ China's stupendous mound) by patient toil/ Of myriads and boon nature's lavish help'.[73] Wordsworth had a direct contact with this remote place he wrote of, for his brother John had worked in the later 1790s as a merchant in the Far East, profiting from the opium trade.[74] There was another direct connection with the business of building British influence in China through the brother of Jane Austen (1775–1817), Frank, who served in the Royal Navy in Canton from 1809 to 1810.[75] A short story by EIC employee (and friend of Thomas Manning) Charles Lamb (1775–1834), the 1822 'Dissertation upon Roast Pig', was even directly set in China itself, though a version that was almost wholly contrived and fanciful. Lamb writes whimsically of a house burning down with pigs in it, which then gives the owner the idea of roast pork, the subsequent production of which needs him to constantly be setting fire to his home.

Fanciful, too, is the best way to describe the 'respectable farmhouse' rented by the prince regent (later to be George IV, 1762–r1820–30) at Brighton in 1787. After his full purchase of it that year, he was, through the good offices of the architect John Nash, to transform this into the ornate pavilion which exists to this day. A very late monument to Chinoiserie, and perhaps the most celebrated ever produced in Britain, the wallpaper, furniture and decorative detail of the interior certainly originated from China, though ironically some of it may well have been produced by local craftsmen on wholly alien specifications for their foreign patron's notion of what China should be, rather than what it actually was.

A similar act of cultural adaptation and adornment occurred with the creation by Josiah Spode (1733–97) in Staffordshire around the late 1780s of the blue underglaze transfer-printing technique. This was forever afterwards associated with the Willow Pattern, images portraying a purportedly Chinese tale about two lovers separating, committing suicide and then transforming into doves. While the precise origins of this ersatz tale are unclear, what is incontestable is its ubiquity. As one scholar wrote, '[It] would be difficult to find any inhabited space on the earth's surface, where an Englishman [sic] had lived, without some evidence of the willow-pattern plate.'[76] The story even figured as inspiration for part of the plot of novelist George Meredith's 1879 novel, *The Egoist*.

Beyond the realm of China in the imagination, there were more practical ways of making sense of the new sources of knowledge and understanding that the greater access to China gave rise to. Staunton himself had been one of the founders of the Asiatic Society in 1823, set up to help promote this. At the heart of this new era of knowledge acquisition was the act of translation, the gaining by some British for the first time of a facility in spoken and written Chinese, and the direct access that gave to understanding China. The pioneers in this field were people like the formidable William Jones (1746–94), a judge at the Supreme court of Calcutta. Jones was a linguist of genius, and in addition to Persian, Sanskrit and Greek was competent in most European languages, and instrumental in postulating a common root for all of these – something that became known as the Indo-European family. Through the use of a Latin–Chinese dictionary, Jones was able to translate some Confucian passages and other classical Chinese texts into English around 1790.[77] The Baptist missionary Joshua Marshman, based at Serampore in Bengal, was the first to produce a direct translation from Chinese into English of parts of Confucius's *Analects* two decades later in 1809. It is appropriate that – in the new era of more positivist, empirically driven knowledge acquisition, when understanding the Chinese through texts in their own languages was key – a professor of Chinese should have been appointed in 1805 to instruct British students. This, however, occurred not in Britain, but at the East India Company's Fort William College in Calcutta; and the appointee was not a Briton, but Johannes Lasser, an Armenian Christian born in Macau, who had been taught Mandarin as a child.[78]

George Thomas Staunton, veteran of the Macartney and Amherst embassies, produced his own scholarship. While his translations were valuable and important, it was the missionary Robert Morrison who had a claim to be the real father of a distinctive school of British sinology. Before him, the reliance by the British on sources of knowledge of the Chinese language in continental Europe was typified by the fact that the first European academic chair to be established was in Paris, in 1818, a position given to Jean-Pierre Abel-Rémusat. Britain had to wait for another two decades before Samuel Kidd, a Protestant missionary who had previously worked in China, occupied the first chair of Chinese studies, at University College London, in 1837. King's College London was to follow a few years later. Morrison was an extraordinary figure. Born near Newcastle in northern England, his background and upbringing were humble. His learning of Chinese was, in the beginning, part of a plan by the London Missionary Society, which wanted him to be one of four people sent out to work in China.[79] In the end, the newly ordained Morrison was to travel out alone in 1807, after initial studies in London with a teacher called Yong-sam Tak and after transcribing Chinese manuscripts held at the British Museum. Morrison's continuation of his studies when he finally arrived in Canton, via New York, was furtive and clandestine, since such study was still prohibited under laws put in place by the former emperor.

Morrison's first residence was at the old French factory in Canton, where he lived from September 1807. 'As an Englishman, he dared not to be known, and it was as an American that he remained', his wife's posthumous biography of him recounts.[80] When he did walk through Canton, children called out names after him, giving him the same harrowing welcome extended to other foreign visitors over the decades, and continuing the tradition of Cantonese inhospitality to outsiders. A fellow missionary, the German-British Charles Gutzlaff (1803–51), complained in 1838 about how, when in the city, foreigners had to 'expose themselves to insults from the natives, and even on the walls of the factories themselves abusive placards have been stuck up to degrade Barbarians in the eyes of the flowery natives'.[81] Despite these practical impediments, over the following years Morrison achieved one of the great feats of nineteenth-century intellectual life. To do so, despite his Christian commitments (which were immensely powerful in framing his sense of mission and purpose), he eventually adopted the dress, habits and even to some extent the lifestyle of the local Chinese. His studies at points made him so ill that he was 'unable to walk across his room'.[82] Over the following decade, he issued the first grammar of Chinese in English, and the first full English–Chinese dictionary (funded by the EIC, published in 1814); founded an institution for the education of foreigners in Chinese matters (the Anglo-Chinese College in Malacca); and produced a translation of the Bible in Chinese, a copy of which he was able to present to George IV when he was granted an audience in April 1824, while back in Britain for a two-year visit.[83] Morrison was to be the first of many to lament the lazy nature of his compatriots with regards to attempting to get a deeper understanding of the place with which they traded so much, and which more were now visiting or going to live in. 'How preposterous is it', he wrote in a letter in December 1818, 'that a living language, one of the oldest in the world, and known by one third of our species, should be entirely neglected in England.'[84] This is a lament that could be validly made two hundred years later.

Morrison's life and achievements are worth paying attention to and celebrating because they made China and the Chinese infinitely more knowable for British people. After his monumental labours, at least the basic means of comprehension – a dictionary and an accessible grammar showing how the Chinese language worked – were available to those British with the incentive or interest to try to learn. In effect, Morrison supplied the most fundamental interpretive tools that could make another culture and country intelligible – the means to understand its language. And while he was to have plenty of complaints about the Chinese in terms of their (in his view) enclosed, often hostile and reactive behaviour (he had, after all, been a participant in the Amherst embassy), towards the end of his life he alluded to an awareness of a deeper cultural wisdom and sympathy between the two peoples. 'It is not', he wrote then, 'a mere knowledge of the words of the language that is so important, but a knowledge of the character and sentiments of the people.'[85] But without an understanding of words in the first place, that further act could never happen. Morrison must stand therefore for the significance and impact of his work as the greatest sinologist Britain has ever produced. His work was partially continued by his son, who, having been born and brought up in China, acquired native fluency in writing and speech, and put this to use for the British over the following decade or so as a translator.

The British desire to know and understand China was not reciprocated. The dearth of material about Britain in the great corpus of early modern Chinese literature is striking. Xie Qinggao, a merchant, travelled in Europe from 1783 to 1793, and on his return to China, together with a scholar called Yang Bingnan produced *Records of the Sea* (*Hailu*, 海录), though this did not appear until 1820. The sections on the British referred to their maritime prowess: 'Wherever there is a region in which profits could be reaped by trading, these people strive for them, with the result that their commercial vessels are to be seen on the sea.' Such a remote and distant power need not strike fear into the Chinese, Xie counselled, despite the fact that 'although the country is small it has such a large military force that foreign nations are filled with fear'. The main issue was the way in which the interests of this seagoing nation were slowly encroaching on the space around China, in the region of its network of tributary nations.[86] These were to prove prescient observations, for it was precisely through Britain's growing involvement with India and the sourcing of opium there that so much trouble would come China's way in the next decades, fundamentally changing the relationship between the two powers, and profoundly impacting on China's understanding of its identity and global role.

4

The Era of Conflict

The First Anglo-Chinese War, 1830–43

I n 1830, the Select Committee of the British Parliament on Foreign Trade was holding an enquiry into the affairs of the EIC. Relieved of its complete monopoly on trade in India by charter in 1813, it did manage to maintain exclusive rights over the China market. However, increasingly strong support for free trade and the lobbying of powerful merchants in-country necessitated a rethink. The committee's report gives a snapshot of British views at the start of a decade that was to see dramatic changes. 'The People of China', the report opined, were 'intelligent, industrious, and persevering, and although said to be in some measure independent of foreign trade, owing to their extensive inland commerce, [they are] highly sensitive to its value.'[1] In a claim that was to become commonplace thereafter, the authors went on, it was not they who were the problem, but their government, which was 'anti-commercial'.[2] As one witness later remarked to the committee, somewhat optimistically, 'The Chinese if left by their rulers to themselves would perhaps be the most industrious and commercial people in the world.'[3]

Even with these issues, however, the EIC had had rich pickings, between 1815 and 1830 generating £15 million in profits from tea alone.[4] From this, the British government gained revenue of

£3.3 million in duty. That was why the monopoly mattered: because it contributed directly to the state's bottom line. The committee heard long-familiar complaints about the corruption of local officials, the impediment to trade from the arbitrary imposition of rules, and the constant hostility of the local people. But those directly involved with the business offered a different perspective, complicating the picture. Mr John Aken, a ship's captain, had nothing but praise for the people he dealt with in Canton. Trading compared to elsewhere was easy there, he said. 'Is there as much facility in transacting business in Canton as a port in England?', the members of the committee asked. 'Yes,' replied Aken, without much hesitation, 'and a great deal more.'[5] There was recognition that the EIC monopolistic arrangements in China, under scrutiny by the committee, did provide some advantages. As one of the senior partners in a leading house in Canton, W.S. Davidson, said, it 'formed a counterpose of inestimable value against the Hong [cohong] monopoly', in an environment where individuals would be crushed if they acted alone. This was a case of one monopoly being the best way to deal with another.[6]

But the problem was for too many British that the EIC was every bit as capricious and keen to wield its powers as its Chinese counterpart, stopping business whenever it felt its own interests threatened. A trader in India, R. Richards, pointed out that while in India originally the company had had a function because it was, to all intents and purposes, operating as the government there, filling an administrative void. This was not the case in China, Richards elaborated, where the officialdom was perfectly functional, but just not that sympathetic to the aims of foreigners. In addition to this, he went on, the Chinese were 'free traders' despite appearances, and what the British most needed to do was open up the market there. The best way to do that was through company competition, not through bringing yet more government-style intervention in.[7]

The committee was evidently more impressed by the arguments of free traders like Richards. The EIC lost its monopoly on Chinese trade on 22 April 1834, bringing to an end a history of over two hundred years. That unleashed forces which proved powerful and turbulent. Almost immediately, a new framework needed to be set in place. The Select Committee of the EIC based in Canton managing British interests in China was no longer fit for purpose. A government superintendent of trade was appointed, the first being Lord William Napier (1786–1834), a former Royal Navy officer. Someone who figures as a minor tragic figure in the overall story of Sino-British relations, he was described sarcastically by one historian of his brief tenure in post as 'an expert breeder of sheep who . . . had no previous diplomatic or administrative experience'.[8] In the Blue Book assembled with official (but often highly edited and carefully redacted) material and set before parliament later on to prepare its members for the debates on China in April 1841, the reprinted orders originally given to Napier in his new role were clear enough. The problem was their implementation. The British government ordered that, on arrival in China in July 1834, he was to 'cautiously abstain from any unnecessary use of menacing language', and to conform 'to the laws of usage of the Chinese empire' – though with the all-important caveat that 'such laws shall be committed towards you . . . with justice and good faith'.[9] He may as well have been asked to construct a square circle, for his situation quickly proved an impossible one.

This was in large part not because of what he was trying to do, but of who he was and what he was meant to be representing. The fact that his formal instructions issued direct from the Foreign Office in London, rather than the EIC, was the best indication of this and marked a seismic shift. This single administrative detail showed that London now regarded the relationship as a state-to-state one, rather than purely commercial, despite the fact that China clearly did not share the same understanding. For them, Napier was not the first ever British state-appointed representative to try to transact official British business direct with the Chinese government while being permanently based in the country, but an unwelcome interloper. The tough, lapidary tone of orders emanating from the foreign secretary and one of the key players in the Sino-British story, Henry John Temple, third Viscount Palmerston (1784–1865) showed that Britain was determined to get this status accepted, come what may. His attitude to China was clear enough right from the start. In instructions to Napier in August 1834, he wrote, 'When was it ever known within the last century that the Chinese authorities ever evidenced a disposition to encourage fair foreign trade?'[10] Palmerston warmed to his theme in subsequent messages, demanding a 'more active principle' for dealing with the Chinese than that which had been used by Macartney and Amherst, figures whose efforts now were representative of failure. 'What advantages or what power did we ever gain by negotiating or humbling ourselves before these people, or rather their government?', the viscount asked. These new, more forcefully articulated sentiments broadly indicated the approach that was to be adopted for the following hundred years. Increasingly, under the influence of this ethos, while talking was initially fine, if words failed to persuade, then force was to be deployed.[11] This was to be the method of persuasion that the British adopted for the rest of the nineteenth century; and its first test was to get permanent state-to-state direct contact accepted.

When reading these despatches from London to Napier today, what is striking is the time lapse that is built into them. In the era before telegraphic traffic and faster modes of communication, six or seven months might pass from the writing of a message to its receipt. It was only in 1845 that Peninsular and Oriental (P&O) steam services introduced a Southampton to China line. This took seventeen days and greatly narrowed the time lag.[12] Napier's period in China was, in any case, so brief that the demands from headquarters in London sent at the start of his appointment had no time to reach him before he died. His immediate attempt to go to Canton and speak direct to officials, rather than through the loathed *cohongs*, was resisted. He was issued with a simple instruction: 'Obey and remain, or disobey and depart.'[13] The Chinese even managed to devise a transliteration of his name which had characters meaning 'laboriously vile'. Even once he got to the city, he was forced to depart after a brief detainment, having sought to make official contact. And after using the *Andromache* and *Imogen* ships at his service to bombard the Bogue forts nearby (in what is today called the Pearl River), he died on 11 October 1834, his demise brought on, according to his temporary replacement, John Francis Davis (who would go on to be the governor of Hong Kong from 1844 to 1848), 'by the heat and confinement of Canton, and by the harassing and distressing annoyances which he experienced from the Chinese'.[14]

A brief lull in 1835, when Arthur Wellesley, first duke of Wellington (1769–1852), was foreign secretary, produced more emollient and conciliatory language. But in China itself, the continued refusal by the local officials to recognise that the chief superintendent of trade appointed by the British government had any authority and to confer any legitimacy on the post became a major sticking point. This proved to be an extension of the older arguments about forms of power and sovereignty, and which rules might prevail in terms of how they were understood and operationalised – arguments that had figured in intercourse between the two powers from the Macartney era onwards. The difference this time was that Britain, after almost four decades of industrialisation and economic development, was far stronger and better able to assert its will than it had ever been before. The new chief superintendent, Sir George Robinson (1797–1855), recognised as much when he wrote to Palmerston in December 1835 that direct contact with the Chinese government 'can only now be achieved by a demonstration of force on the part of the British government'.[15]

Robinson was able to report decent trade, and some stability in the coming few months. But his masters in London were evidently not happy with so much effort being expended for seemingly so little return. On 7 June 1836, Palmerston, now back as foreign secretary, sacked him, abolishing the position and reducing the representation there to a chief of commission. This role was handed to Charles Elliot

(1801–75), a Royal Navy official who had transferred across to more purely diplomatic work. Due to the time lapse in communication, Robinson was blithely unaware of this move for a number of months, and carried on doing what (at least judging by his reports back to London) he thought was a good job long after he had actually been removed from it.

One of the easy assumptions to make is that British and Chinese confrontation as it built up over the 1830s was somehow inevitable, and that the key actors on both sides had a clear vision of where they were heading with each other and what their gameplan was. Reading the words they wrote as this whole episode unfolded, particularly on the British side, it is clear that this was not the case, with confusion being more common than clarity. With his initial instructions to Elliot in July 1836, Palmerston began counselling 'caution in interfering . . . with British merchants' and not assuming 'a greater degree of authority over British subjects in China that which [sic] you in reality possess',[16] meaning that Elliot, while put in a position of power, was also being told he had few grounds on which to exercise that power. In September 1837, to the lords of the admiralty, Palmerston had also contradicted his earlier, more bullish, sentiments towards the Chinese, by ordering that they 'be very careful that the officers and men belonging to the ships under their command do not in any way offend the prejudices of the Chinese people, nor violate the laws and customs of the Chinese empire'.[17] Even as late as June 1838, he instructed Elliot that 'Her Majesty's Government cannot interfere for the purposes of enabling British subjects to violate the laws of the country to which they trade'.[18] The message from the modern British state was clear: there was official business and there was the business of citizens, and the two did not necessarily run along the same tracks. Palmerston's position on the opium trade was a largely amoral, pragmatic one. He resisted the use of state power to enforce the private commercial interests of actors like Jardine or Matheson (by then among the main traders in the region), and clearly had a sceptical view of those trading commercially with the Chinese and always trying to force their business interests on the latter. But his approach was ultimately to be disingenuous, asserting that Britain respected laws, and using Chinese inconsistency in the application of their own laws as grounds on which to attack them.

This act of correction was through what Palmerston somewhat euphemistically called 'moral influence'.[19] This boiled down to the threat (and if necessary the actual deployment) of violence. 'It is useful', Palmerston had written in 1837, 'that the Chinese should be aware of the nature and extent of Her Majesty's naval power.'[20] Such nicety of expression did little to shield the fact that although the British state, through its naval assets, came with 'peaceful purposes', its aim was (as the wars from 1839 to 1842 showed) to ensure that its will and power prevailed. The asymmetry of capacity between the two countries here could not be disguised and was to prove decisive.

Charles Elliot's challenges

During the 1841 parliamentary debates about the wars against China, about which there was great controversy and considerable opposition, one of the main points of attack made on Palmerston was the lack of precise instructions given to Elliot. Some of the orders had placed restrictions on the choices Elliot had at his disposal, sternly admonishing him not to use British state and military power for commercial interests, even as they had also told him to promote and aid these aims. There were plenty of other restrictions. Elliot, as a British state representative, like his predecessor Napier, was 'not at liberty to receive any such communications [from the *cohong* merchants], except from the Viceroy direct', because the former did not work for the Chinese state, and the latter did. He was also to avoid using the written Chinese character 'pin' (which translated as 'petition') when trying to address mandarins (if he ever got access to them), because it would give the impression of an inferior addressing a superior, rather than communication between equals. Trying to achieve these aims while also observing the restraints imposed on him by London meant that Elliot had an impossible job. It was one that became harder the longer it went on, so that as we look over the record of his time dealing with China, it is remarkable that he was able to function at all.

He was no doubt fortified by the fact that in his previous career he had also been asked to perform thankless tasks. Before arriving in Canton in 1834, he was 'protector of slaves in British Guiana' from 1830, a role where he complained 'my office is a delusion. There is no protection for the Slave population; and they will very shortly take the matter into their own hands and destroy the Property . . . I am desperately unpopular, although I am sure I have not intended to do my duty captiously'.[21] Popularity would not come his way in China either: one commentator in 1843 compared what he called the correct bearing of Elliot's replacement from 1841, Sir Henry Pottinger (1789–1856), with the 'bowing, scraping, or chin-chinning like our later plenipotentiary'.[22] Another stated that in his negotiations 'Elliot has tried fair and conciliatory measures for too long'.[23] Then there were those who saw him as being too much in the pocket of the business community. Captain Elliot, wrote one, 'appeared to identify the English nation with the criminal cause of the smugglers'.[24] Even Queen Victoria (1819–r1837–1901) was eventually goaded to fury by what was regarded as the very poor terms of the Convention of Chuenpi, the agreement that marked the first attempt to end the war, ceding Hong Kong Island to Britain in 1841: in a letter to King Leopold of Belgium, she complained about her local representative's 'unaccountable behaviour'. The convention ended up being rejected by the British government in London; a new one was demanded, for which further war proved necessary.

In the copious despatches he sent back to London, Elliot comes across as an often conflicted, more complex person than the inevitably unfair modern portrayals of him in Chinese state propaganda. The 1997 film by Xie Jin had Elliot played, with impeccable stiff upper lip and steely determination, by British actor Simon Williams. In real life, he was pitched into a situation where events accelerated so fast that, by 1839, things were impossible to control fully. The lengthy pause needed for communication to pass between London and Canton exacerbated this. His ultimate dismissal – after infuriating Palmerston by his perceived refusal to follow orders – was a final piece of tough justice. Not only were the orders given him general and vague, but they frequently arrived long after events had moved on and they were no longer relevant. Strikingly, in the many accounts of this period written afterwards, the voice of Elliot is absent. Sent to Texas to be chargé d'affaires in the new republic there, and thence to be governor of Bermuda in 1846, he retired in 1869 and returned to Britain. He maintained his silence about his role in the China business right up until his death, several years later.

Elliot's seeming equivocation was not due just to the orders he was given, nor to the remoteness of the location in which he found himself. A far deeper cause was the utterly contradictory situation that British trade was now in. It was, in essence, constructed on an edifice which involved double standards and hypocrisy. At the heart of this lay opium. The business had grown during the eighteenth century, as British control over India increased. Opium was not introduced into China by the British: that had happened far earlier, around the eighth century, during the Tang era (618–907), via Turk and Arab traders. Originally eaten raw, as a medicine, it was in the seventeenth century that the Chinese started mixing it with tobacco and smoking it. To begin with, the volumes were small – in 1750, around four hundred chests were shipped between India and China. But by the turn of the nineteenth century, the situation had changed: in 1816, 3,000 chests of the drug were imported; by 1825 this had risen to 10,000; and by 1850 that figure had doubled again.[25] The EIC did not, after the very early period, convey these goods to China: it had prohibited their carriage from as early as 1733. But commercially it benefited massively from the trade, because the revenue generated from the business helped finally to address the huge balance-of-payment issues that had arisen from the British addiction to tea and the failure to find goods and commodities to import into China to compensate for this: until the rise of opium, only silver had sufficed – and of course Britain had largely to source that elsewhere. With opium, China shifted from being a net creditor to a net debtor, using all of its silver reserves to pay for its drug.

Opium was a commodity,[26] and its main traders were the private merchants who had risen from the late eighteenth century onwards, and who exploited the fact that, with the EIC's ships out of the picture, it was their own vessels that could now carry the various different kinds of the drug from the British-owned fields in which it was produced to the hungry market of China. All the private traders needed to do to enter this was to obtain licences to trade from the EIC, meaning that the latter kept its conscience clear, and the former were able to make money.[27] This whole business was performed on the basis of expediency – a demonstration of the ways in which modern capitalism, if allowed, was able to operate successfully, wholly divorced from moral restraint. Apologists did speak up for the medicinal qualities of the drug – just as later, in the 1950s, there were adverts praising the health benefits of smoking tobacco. However, for the Chinese – who had issued edicts under the Yongzheng emperor in 1729 outlawing the use of opium – this quickly became a social problem. As the *Chinese Repository* (a locally produced English-language news-sheet in Canton) stated in 1836: 'There is no slavery on earth to be compared with the bondage into which opium casts its victims.'[28] The number of addicts rose steeply, and may even have included the Daoguang emperor (1782–r1820–1850), who came to the throne in 1820 and was to reign for thirty years, over the period of the First Anglo-Chinese War.

One account in the *Chinese Repository* of September 1840 spoke of how a Chinese addict known to the author was betrayed by 'his pale and emaciated face, the relaxed tone of his mind, his occasional stupidity and unconquerable drowsiness'.[29] But as the British author Thomas De Quincey and others were to testify, once addiction set in (and addiction was almost always the outcome) it was destructive and deadly. Proclamations against the trade had been issued in Canton in 1828. But they had little impact on the tricks which merchants on both sides, Chinese and British, had developed to find ways around this. Sold in large cakes (which were then processed in-country into the paste that ended up being compressed in special pipes and smoked), the drug was physically brought to Lintin Island (close to the coast of what is today Shenzhen). There it was sold to Chinese traders and transferred onto their own junks. The contraband nature of the business meant that no duties or revenue were paid to either the local province or the central Chinese state. Another factor for the central government was that within China itself, the networks of collusion were massive: thus in effect there was a shadow economy and a shadow administration servicing it. There would have been little of this trade had there not been so many willing hands – both within and outside government – that were more than ready to make money. Opium, in the end, was a massive generator of wealth and of alternative forms of power and social influence. That was why it mattered to Beijing. And that was why it had to take action.

Despite the immense significance of the trade, it would be incorrect to say that the First Anglo-Chinese War from 1839 to 1842 was, as its name in Chinese today implies, solely (or even mainly) about opium.[30] The treaties that were signed after the conflict do not mention the drug, and it remained illegal until the Second Anglo-Chinese War in 1860. But as the American historian John King Fairbank has said, 'opium provided the occasion rather than the root cause'.[31] What was the root cause? It is true that there were powerful domestic reasons why Palmerston and his Whig party colleagues wanted to have an international distraction, and that this dispute offered a convenient opportunity. They were under attack from their Conservative opponents for appeasing radicals at home and for not protecting Britain's interests abroad, after a decade of protest over the need for wider political reform following the very limited increase in the voting franchise in 1832.[32] The 1839 war offered a good, unifying opportunity for Palmerston and his allies to demonstrate – in a relatively safe way – that they were strong and assertive on the global stage. But beyond this, the opium issue arose from the misapprehensions and misunderstandings of each of the parties involved about the nature of the powers of the other. Here the issues ran very deep. For the Qing central authorities, the assumption was that the British state had to be in control of this trade and was the directing hand behind it – because that was the model of the state it had in its own experience. The notion that the trade was largely in the hands of non-state actors – and above all actors that the British government seemed unwilling or incapable of reining in – didn't make sense.

The issue of power is key here. The Chinese had failed to understand just how much the British were creating a form of modernity, in which the part that could be seen from the imperial court – the economic component – was merely a piece of something far larger. At the heart of this was an appreciation that scientific knowledge produced not just ideas, but also processes and ways of influencing the world that provided new means of projecting power and promoting interests. The Qing, with their largely passive, defensive and reactive mindset, were almost doomed because they were facing, to use Palmerston's pithy phrase, a foe with an 'active' disposition. The whole dynamic of British economic and cultural development in the early modern and modern era had been about supporting this active disposition, reaching into the wider world to control, exploit and grow richer and more powerful through not just actions and processes, but also ideas. An active versus a passive partner is never an equal contest. Thus the first, crucial Anglo-Chinese war proved to be a highly asymmetrical and one-sided contest.

While these underpinning structural issues were well under way by the 1830s, Britain was not a uniform actor over this period in terms of delivering on its objectives. On the single issue of opium – much like the earlier debate about the moral abhorrence of slavery, before it was abolished in British law in 1807 – there were plenty of voices that regarded the trade with disgust, and recognised just exactly how hypocritical it was. Early on, in 1833, Scottish MP Charles Marjoribanks had declared in a letter to Charles Grant, president of the Board of Control in London, that 'to any friend of humanity it is a painful subject of contemplation, that we should continue to pour this black and envenomed poison into the source of human happiness and well-being'.[33] For author Horatio Montague Lay, writing in 1840, British merchants had pursued their own gain for half a century, sparing no expense 'to enrich themselves still further, by this merciless destruction of thousands of the people of China'. A vivid illustration of the kinds of moral compromises and self-justifications that had to occur to keep this whole trade in play was the journey in 1833 by W. McKay, assisted by the missionary Charles Gutzlaff, a formidable linguist employed by the company to interpret for it, who travelled up the Chinese coast on an exploratory mission to look for more inlets to deliver the drug into. Gutzlaff wrestled with his conscience, but justified it by the fact that while one side of the vessel was selling opium, from the other he was able to distribute religious tracts.[34]

As Elliot's posture during the build-up to the first conflict in 1839 shifted and adapted, so too did he impute hints of debate and resulting signs of change of policy to the Qing itself. In a despatch to Palmerston on 2 February 1837, he wrote that his informants indicated that the central government was considering legalisation of the whole trade. This was simply to ensure that it was able to gain revenue and could thus seek to control the business. A translation of the 'memorial' of a central court censor from October 1836 forwarded to London to back his report up stated that 'the sale of opium is the chief medium from which money is drained off and carried beyond the seas', and that the central government could address this by legitimising the trade, rather than forcing it underground.[35] These debates were indeed real enough. There were attempts by some officials to promote the merits of legalisation; but the internal contemporary politics of China was opaque to Elliot and his colleagues, and they merely caught a glimpse of what was happening on the surface.

Scholars have since documented the clash in the Daoguang court between the Spring Purification Party – a more conservative arm of officialdom which, according to one account, personified the true literati and were idealistic (and often unrealistic) in terms of their goals and political programme – and their more pragmatic, but less influential opponents. The Spring Purification group were 'perhaps better suited to an oppositional role. In office, they were exceedingly unsure of themselves and much inclined therefore to political adventures and militancy, perhaps as a diversion from the more serious and more intractable problems of the day',[36] putting them on that score in a similar position to Palmerston's beleaguered Whig party. To add to the problem, just as the British were ill-informed about the Chinese, so the Chinese had little good-quality intelligence and understanding of the British. A decade later, a member of the literati, Yao Ying, declared dismissively that despite all that had happened in the first war, 'the techniques of the Barbarians have never been greatly superior to those of China. Moreover in terms of strategic geography they fight in violation of the precepts of military science.' This makes him sound a bit like a soccer team manager blaming defeat on the cheating of the opposing side. Whatever such adherence to the correct 'precepts of military science' precisely meant here, the brute reality was that Britain had won the conflict and been able to impress its aims on the Qing. This critic made a more valid point when he said that where the Chinese made the greatest mistakes in the 1830s was that they had failed to 'study the international relations or domestic affairs of these barbarians from beyond the seas'. Thus, 'when their great ships suddenly hove into view [our scholars] were as terrified as if they had just seen a ghost or spirit, and as frightened as if they had been struck by a thunderbolt'.[37] The 1830s debates that Elliot excitedly referred to did not, in the end (and despite his high hopes), result in the legalisation of the drug. Instead, a campaign was mounted to go to the other extreme and eradicate the trade, destroy the supply routes and push those foreign traders engaged in it (which was almost everyone) out of the country.

The merchant princes and the mandarins

Private merchants were present in Canton and doing business with China from early in the eighteenth century. Confusingly, there were three individuals who represented this group, all of whom were called George Smith and all of whom were from Scotland. They figured as a constant thorn in the side of the EIC, often creating problems and acting in ways which the company found lawless and against its interests. The animosity was more than reciprocated. One George Smith, newly arrived in Canton in 1779, wrote to the EIC that 'I never admitted the authority of the Honourable Company [another name for the EIC] or their court of Directors, in any one shape whatever over me as a British subject.' He continued sharply, 'I trust for protection to a power capable to enforce it, whose duty it is, and will not permit its subjects to be oppressed.'[38] He was clearly making the point that, in his view, this was not something the company could do. Despite this significant mutual antipathy, the private merchants and the EIC had a common interest in bringing about change in the Canton system. They just differed about how that change might come about, and who would benefit most from it once it happened.

Of the enterprises of the 'merchant princes' (as they came to be known later in the nineteenth century, on account of their influence), the Jardine Matheson company, founded on 1 July 1832, was to prove among the most important.[39] This firm was one of a number of private traders that had come into existence over the period from

1820 onwards to exploit the new opportunities in the expanding Asian trade. Butterfields, Dents and American and European companies were of the same ilk. But Jardine Matheson came to assume an enormous significance in the development of Sino-British relations – right from the time of its foundation to today. In essence, it introduced private entrepreneurs as an organised force who, as they became more successful, represented not just the economic, but also the increasingly political and ideological importance of non-state actors.

The two founders were striking and driven figures, around whom was built a sort of mythology. William Jardine was from a humble background, the son of farmers from a hamlet in the Scottish county of Dumfriesshire. After training initially as a physician, he worked on ships plying their trade for the EIC in the Far East. James Matheson, his compatriot, was from somewhat more privileged circumstances, the son of a captain in the British army, and had graduated from the University of Edinburgh before he, too, found his way out to Bombay. Before 1830, they had formed a company together, seeking to grow opportunities for trade offered by the vessels going between India and China. They were clearly individuals with a formidable work ethic. Jardine was known for having only one chair in his office at their Canton factory, reportedly because this meant visitors who had to stand were quicker to transact their business and leave him to get on with his work.[40] Matheson was more outgoing and more willing to express his opinions in public, and was eventually to serve as an MP back home.

Their business was their life. But that business – being at the time it was and in the place it was – involved a large amount of politics and diplomacy, fields in which both participated, though Matheson was more active than Jardine. The two became principal representatives of the merchant princes, and came to take a far more hawkish, aggressive attitude towards dealing with China, largely dictated by their need for greater market access and better returns. One of the complaints in

Matheson's letters from the 1830s was about the poor profits so far from investments made in the Canton trade. In a letter to his nephew Daniel Matheson on 3 March 1832, he wrote 'our market for British manufacturing here is wretchedly low'.[41] Government figured in their thinking as a resource by which to remedy this situation. Matheson had been supportive of Napier on his arrival (though quickly cooled towards him personally), feeling that a firmer line needed to be taken to defend British commercial interests. The key thing was simply to get on with business. But in 1836, as Matheson complained, that was just not happening and the market was still very depressed.[42]

One could not fault either of the business partners for being zealously focused on their own interests. They were clearly formidably disciplined. The Chinese even recognised this, giving Jardine the nickname 'iron headed rat' – to express admiration (rather than disdain) at his indifference to being hit over the head with a stick of bamboo when insistently presenting a document at the Petition Gate in Canton.[43] Palmerston was to suffer another demonstration of iron-headedness before offering his own version in return, when Matheson, while back in London, called on him to vigorously promote his company's business interests. On being asked by the foreign secretary why the British merchants in Canton were always squabbling with the Chinese authorities, Matheson had retorted: 'We do not receive justice from their government.' Palmerston had then shot back: 'Ah, you are like the rest, do not know what justice is; you fancy justice is getting it all your own way.'[44]

In 1836, Matheson had publicly expressed his feeling unambiguously enough about the place he was dealing with in a pamphlet published in Britain. 'It has pleased providence', he began his polemic, 'to assign to the Chinese – a people characterised by a marvellous degree of imbecility, avarice, conceit, and obstinacy the possession of a vast portion of the most desirable ports of the earth.'[45] But it was not just the Chinese who attracted his fire. The EIC, in his view, was as much to blame for the crime of monopolising not just trade, but also knowledge of China; and it was because of the EIC that 'the ruinous exactions [China] inflicts on us' continued, forcing all British businesses to compromise, and ending up making them complicit in a system with which they did not agree.[46] The main objective, he made clear, was to 'cultivate the China trade in fair and honourable terms', rather than continue to suffer this iniquity.[47]

In many ways, the hardline attitude of private merchants like these represented a new force of modernity. They were not simply agents of a single nation. Matheson and Jardine had key partners in Calcutta, and traded with Australia and elsewhere in the Far East. Their main master was global capital and the accrual of rootless wealth. They were truly free agents, people whom the Chinese had great difficulty in understanding, because not only did they refuse to listen to the local authorities, but they also seemed largely indifferent to the instructions of their own authorities back home. Their energy had both its frightening and its admirable qualities. But what was clear was that a man like Matheson bowed to no authority and believed in the power of forceful lobbying to impose his own will, and thereby gain the good of the corporate, non-government entity he represented.

Opposing him and his occupation, from the Chinese side, was Lin Zexu (1785–1850). Appointed commissioner by the Daoguang emperor after an unprecedented sixteen imperial audiences in Beijing, when he had argued forcefully against the legalisation of opium and presented his own plans to wholly eliminate the trade, Lin arrived in Canton on 10 March 1839. A man who, to this day, holds a place of high esteem in the national story of modern China promoted by the Communist Party, he was clearly an impressive official, and one of the few (it would seem) to have had an impeccable reputation for moral rectitude. He had also troubled to get hold of some of the writings of the barbarians he was to deal with and have them translated, so that he might better understand their way of thinking. In an attempt to make direct contact, Lin wrote to the newly installed Queen Victoria in April 1839: 'We are of the opinion that this poisonous article [opium] is clandestinely manufactured by artful and depraved people of various tribes under the dominion of your honourable nation.' It is likely his letters did not reach their intended recipient, but they were published eventually in Britain, largely to illustrate the erroneous thinking of what was then called the Celestial Empire about the British.[48] From his arrival, the tempo of events accelerated. On 8 March 1839, even before he got to the city, he issued orders for all opium to be surrendered. To reinforce the seriousness of his intent, on 12 March a public execution of a Chinese opium trader was held before the British factory in Canton. Nine days later, the General Chamber of Commerce in the city met and offered 1,037 chests of the drug as a means of placating him. But it was with the commissioner's invitation to the merchant Lancelot Dent to present himself in Canton city that alarm bells really sounded. Elliot, who arrived in Canton a couple of days later, agreed to hand over 20,283 chests of opium, so long as the state of virtual martial law was lifted. These were the inauspicious roots of the first direct military conflict between China and a Western power.

Narrative of the war

The Chinese intentions towards the contraband opium they had amassed were unclear, at least to Matheson. Viewing matters through a purely commercial prism, he was convinced this was just a ruse to make money. 'You will be surprised to hear that the Chinese have no intention of destroying the surrendered drug,' he wrote to one correspondent, 'it being carefully sorted according to quality, weighed, packed and stored.'[49] For once his formidable intelligence-gathering skills had let him down: burning and destroying the drug, rather than trading with it, was precisely what Commissioner Lin intended to do. After a brief discussion about whether the whole hoard might be transported to Beijing to be presented to the emperor before its destruction (an idea that was rejected on practical grounds of logistics), huge pits were dug near Canton, foreign dignitaries invited, and over a few days, the opium trade of a season went up in flames. From that moment, the tempo of the conflict changed and the stakes grew higher. In essence, the Chinese had committed the ultimate cardinal sin in contemporary British eyes: they had illegally destroyed commercial property and deprived merchants of their just returns.

Over the next few months, arguments raged about the demand by the Chinese for bonds to be given by all traders coming to Canton, committing them not to engage in the opium business. While one renegade Briton, Thomas Coutts, signed, others took the advice of Elliot and refused. Elliot made it clear that this was an issue of national freedom and an exercise in sovereignty for the British, not just some piece of paper that could be agreed to for the sake of convenience and then ignored. As he wrote to Palmerston on 18 July: 'The difficulties in China are not confined to this matter of opium. The true and far more important question to be solved is whether there shall be honourable and extending trade with this empire.'[50] Honour was a key element in all of this interaction. The British and Chinese were, in different ways, highly status conscious, which made their disagreements even more intractable. Both wanted validation and hated to feel they were being humiliated or belittled. Just as Elliot was insistent on standing his ground, so Lin's behaviour from mid-1839 onwards was forceful and uncompromising, because of the notion that the British were being disrespectful and rude. He prosecuted his mission to push back against this with immense energy and effectiveness. After a brief detention in the city, on 24 August the British fled Canton for Macau; Commissioner Lin promptly ordered the governor there to expel them. On 31 August, the Chinese issued a further proclamation to fight them, escalating matters. An embargo placed on all English trade out of China brought in on 12 February 1840 meant that the British were forced to take more drastic measures, and with the arrival that same day of HMS *Volage* and HMS *Hyacinth* they had the germ of a solution.

The military campaign over 1840 and into 1842 constituted the heart of the First Anglo-Chinese War. It was a conflict that involved sporadic, brief, intense deployments of violence by the British, interspersed with long periods of inactivity. This led to large numbers of Chinese fatalities (one estimate put total Chinese casualties for the whole war at 20,000),[51] and very few British ones. As Lord Jocelyn, one of the key commanders on the British side, subsequently explained, engaging in some oxymoronic phrasemaking, the British felt 'obliged to use force to show them our purpose was amicable'.[52] The two sides' lack of familiarity with each other meant that they had a fundamentally different idea of the basic rules of war. The use of a white flag as a sign of temporary truce was one example: Elliot wrote in one despatch that he had 'to explain the nature of the flag of truce to the Chinese mandarins'.[53] Often, agreements were made by the Chinese which they then reneged upon, creating a lack of trust and bad blood. The cause of this was the often impossible demands issued by the central court, which – despite having no familiarity with the specific situation locally, thousands of miles away – expected quick results completely in China's favour, and frequently fired off commands instructing local officials to ignore what they had already promised. Despite all these differences, Lin and Elliot did have one thing in common: both were judged harshly by their overlords and paid for this with their positions.

The central moments of encounter and conflict during the years of war were a series of mini-campaigns which encroached fitfully, but remorselessly on the Chinese coastal territory. The first of these was the bombardment of Zhousan Island and the taking of Tinghai (today's Dinghai on the island) by ships under Sir Gordon Bremer in June 1840. Following the refusal of the Chinese in January 1841 to give compensation for the opium destroyed the previous year, the mouth of the Pearl River was sealed and the British seized the Bogue forts guarding ingress there. A truce was agreed, and on 18 January an agreement was signed, ceding Hong Kong Island to the British.

But with the Chinese refusing to concede more – and rejecting the demand for £60,000 compensation for the destroyed drug – forces under Sir Hugh Gough captured Canton in May 1841.

Dismissing Elliot for his failure to gain more from the Chinese, Palmerston appointed Sir Henry Pottinger, who arrived in Macau on 10 August. Moving north, Pottinger and his forces took Xiamen in late August, and retook Zhousan (earlier relinquished in one of the periods of truce with the Chinese). Ningbo was captured on 13 October, and despite a Chinese counterattack on 10 March 1842, remained in British hands. Chapu (today's Zhapu) was subsequently captured on 18 May 1842 (here the Chinese offered far fiercer resistance, perhaps because the forces they deployed were dominated by experienced Manchu soldiers, rather than novice Chinese troops). Gough and Admiral Sir William Parker captured Shanghai on 19 June and then proceeded up the Yangtze. With the British poised to launch an attack on the key city of Nanjing, the Chinese capitulated. There the Treaty of Nanjing was signed, ending the conflict, on 29 August 1842.

The war spawned many accounts. These broadcast its events and their significance back in Britain. One narrative by John Ouchterlony, an officer serving in the campaign, remarked on the part-fearful, part-intrigued reactions of the Chinese who witnessed the arrival of the British war vessels, these 'strange craft' that were about to mete out so much punishment on their compatriots.[54] British naval and military superiority was the key to the devastating imbalance in terms of ability to inflict fatalities and achieve core objectives in the war. The Chinese in this way were seeing some of the key innovations of a modernity that had so far passed them by. The British side was not a huge one: at full strength it had sixteen ships of war, with 540 guns mounted, four armed steamers, one troop ship and two English regiments, with ground forces numbering 4,000. More than half of these were not British at all, but soldiers brought from India. It was the technological advantages the ships had which mattered, and in particular, the innovative design of the *Nemesis*, a vessel which was 'perfectly flat-bottomed, and divided into seven water tight compartments', giving it flexibility to get into shallow waters and durability if it were struck.[55] Built in Liverpool, its beginnings were inauspicious, as it suffered an accident only two days into its first journey, at St Ives in Cornwall.[56] Its impact in China was critical, however, particularly during the attack on the Bogue forts. 'The excitement on board was general,' one eyewitness recorded at the time, 'now that she at length found her iron frame swinging side by side with the framed "wooden walls" of England's glory.'[57] For the Chinese dwelling in the villages along the banks of the river on which the *Nemesis* glided into view, the sight 'of the gigantic vessel moving, independent of wind and tide' elicited astonishment.[58] But for all the picturesque qualities of this scene, the vessel had one function – to supply force and engage in acts of violence. That it did this in novel and unexpected ways (in the eyes of the Chinese) only assisted in the delivery of its mission through the surprise it created and the confusion and panic that ensued. 'The Chinese,' another eyewitness subsequently wrote, 'not accepting quarter, though attempting to escape, were cut up by the fire of our advancing troops; others, in the faint hope of escaping what to them appeared certain death at the hands of their victors, precipitated themselves recklessly from the top of the battlements, and not a few vainly trying to swim and sinking in that effort.'[59]

For Doctor McPherson, the medic, 'the slaughter on the [Chuenpi] side was dreadful; independent of those bodies on shore, the sea was quite blackened with floating corpses and the beach for miles around was strewed with them. On shore the dead, in many places, lay heaped one upon another.' The sight that greeted witnesses in the Bogue forts

was horrifying in the extreme. There the round shot and shell had done fearful execution. The walls, in many places, were bespattered with brains; and it was difficult to discover whether the mangled remains before you ever possessed the human shape. Close to the site of the explosion of a mine, many of the enemy must have secreted themselves; but now a burnt, blackened, smouldering, stinking mass was all that remained to point out their mortal remains.[60]

The British side, while not suffering death on anything like the scale of their opponents, were afflicted by their own illnesses. Among other fevers, malaria – 'an endemic disease on the coast of China' – had incapacitated many.[61] War was a hard business for everyone, except those sitting far from the battlefields and airily declaring that Britain should do more to defend its honour and interests.

In all of this horror, too, there were signs on the British side of recognition of the heroism and humanity of those they had been sent to fight. One of the Chinese leaders in the field attracted John Ouchterlony's admiration for the way in which 'bravely but vainly' he had endeavoured 'with a handful of men who still adhered to him to resist the entrance of Sir H.F. Senhouse and his seaman'. This was the 'valiant old Admiral Kwan, whose body was found amongst the slain and recognised by the prisoners'.[62] According to one account, the Chinese 'under proper officers, and supplied with good arms, would make excellent soldiers; for they are accustomed to hardship and bad living'.[63] But in the field they were up against better-equipped, better-managed opponents. As one cruelly dismissive comment on the technical ability of their opponents put it, China was a country 'where steam is only known as proceeding from their own tea kettles'.[64] The same author added that for the British, the Chinese were 'an enemy so highly cultivated, and yet armed with bows and arrows'.[65] For another, the Chinese encounter with new British technology used in conflict proved too much: one Chinese farmer who had been placidly smoking his pipe as he watched the steam warship *Medusa*, was jolted from his reverie when the contraption ploughed into the bank next to him. 'The shock was of course considerable,' Robert Fortune wrote later, 'and the man who all at once seemed to awake from a trance, set off in the utmost terror, like an arrow, across the fields, without once looking behind him; and a Captain Hewitt who related the story, remarked, for anything he knew the man was running until this day!'[66]

What had it all been for?

The war had been won. But what precisely had it been about, and what did victory against China mean? Ouchterlony declared that the 'war was a just and avoidable one and the fault of the Chinese'. But writing after its conclusion in 1844, he admitted 'our commercial relations, under the new consular establishment, are not as yet proceeding in a very satisfactory manner'. The underwhelming results of the Treaty of Nanjing will be dealt with in the next chapter. But there was very early on a sense of anticlimax. Judging by Elliot's despatches – from a man sitting at the heart of the action until his abrupt dismissal – the issue for the British was one of fair treatment and honour. In his reply of 15 September 1840 to his Chinese interlocutor Keshen (the replacement for Commissioner Lin, who, despite his efforts, had been dismissed earlier by an angry emperor), he had written loftily of how Britain's aim was 'to demand satisfaction for the insulted dignity . . . In trade, there is mutual benefit. Each side makes exchanges, not gifts.'[67] Only through a shared understanding of the nature of reciprocity and rule-regulated free business could both sides hope to place 'our future trade and intercourse upon a secure footing'. In trying to achieve these objectives, however, Elliot had grown more and more aware of the huge difficulties either side faced in even trying to speak to the other, let alone actually do things: 'The manners and languages of our countries are so different that it is not at times certain that we may precisely understand each other in the way we wish.'[68] But his final despatch came back to the need to follow a policy that was – echoing his earlier words, so that they come to seem almost like an automatic mantra – 'consistent with the establishment of trade upon a secure footing.'[69] Hugh Hamilton Lindsay reinforced this point in a pamphlet arguing for the justness of the war, issued in London in 1840. It was not a question of trade having some moral point. 'The opium trade in China never can nor will be stopped', he stated. '[T]heir only resource is to legalise the trade and make it a source of revenue.' British objectives in China, however, were 'merely commercial intercourse, not territorial aggrandisement'.[70] If Britain had been at fault, it was 'in the vacillation of purpose and want of any fixed plan of conduct'.[71]

Others were far more sceptical and critical. During the long debates in the Houses of Parliament from 2 to 10 April 1840, the young rising star William Gladstone (1809–98) had declared: 'a war more unjust in its origin, a war more calculated in its progress to cover this country with permanent disgrace, I do not know, and I have not read of'. As he went on later, we 'the enlightened and civilized Christians, are pursuing objects at variance . . . with justice', the support of an immoral and contraband trade.[72] Palmerston's response defending the government was dismissive. On the practical issue of the claimed lack of precision in the instructions given to Elliot, he merely declared that his critics 'imagined that when you write to China, your letter should be as long as the voyage'. On the contrary, he held it to be 'the duty of a Minister to give his written instructions, distinctly, decisively, and without circumlocution, to write so as not to be misunderstood, at sufficient length but with not one word redundant'. As for the moral argument, the British foreign secretary was clear: China's morals were for China to police. Opium for the British was a matter of trade. How the Chinese handled it was up to them, but Britain's right to trade was sacrosanct, and in the eyes of British merchants there were willing customers in China and a ready market to which no impediment should be placed. Palmerston stated that the Chinese – like people everywhere – 'were disposed to buy what other people were disposed to sell to them' and that it was not the British government's job to police their morals.[73] Finally, the origins of the conflict, as Elliot indeed had surmised, involved a question of honour: 'the honour of the British flag and the dignity of the

British Crown. He thought that was the general opinion of the House, and of those parties in the country who were most interested in the question.' By a mere nine votes, his party won the debate.

In China, views on the discussion in parliament were negative. 'It is sadly unfortunate,' opined the *Chinese Repository*, 'that on great national questions of foreign policy deeply inviting both the interest and the honour of the country three successive days should have been spent in a mere trial of strength of the political parties.'[74] As for the war itself, many asked what the point of the whole venture had been: 'Never was there a war undertaken about which there was so much ignorance as to its causes, its objects, the manner of it being conducted, as there now is with regard to this war', the *Repository* stated. 'Even Her Britannic Majesty's Minister directing the war seems to be in doubt how to act and how to direct.'[75] The most obvious practical outcome was a treaty. Negotiating after the British were in sight of Nanjing, the Chinese adopted what Fairbank described as a set methodology which would be deployed later. First messengers were sent to convey basic information; then talkers 'who could attempt to fathom the British intentions by drawing them out in conversation'. Finally came the responsible officials. Once they had sorted out the detail, the commissioners and high leaders appeared.[76] Such a process occurred before the signing of this treaty in Nanjing, aboard HMS *Cornwallis*. Ouchterlony described the high theatre and drama of the occasion, with 'the commissioners ... in plain attire, but attended by a numerous and gorgeous retinue, composed of the elite of the vice-regal court in Nanjing and of the military force of the province'. The articles began with a declaration of lasting peace and friendship between the two nations – though at the price of 21 million dollars in compensation, to be paid over the next three years. Canton, Xiamen, Fuzhou, Ningbo and Shanghai were to be opened to British trade. The ceding of Hong Kong Island in perpetuity to Britain – initially agreed in the aborted Chuenpi treaty of a year or so before – was confirmed. The treaty also demanded that complete equality in terms of dialogue and access be accorded by each government to the other.[77] This agreement was the first of the infamous series branded 'unequal' by the Chinese, a label that has continued to the present day. The treaties established the basis of the treaty port system, which would provide the logistical backbone for British commercial and (increasingly) political interests in China over the coming century. They also set in place the main British ideas about diplomatic norms and legal foundations for international and economic interests within China. The key British objectives were access to a free market, and protection by law in the exploitation of that market. These demands prevailed over all others. This was a victory of the assertion of British material interests, with precious little heed given to values or any sense of justice. Ironically, opium did not merit a single mention.

Beyond the bad feeling created in China, the one completely tangible thing that resulted from the war – and the thing that would endure longest – was possession of Hong Kong. Palmerston's disdain for the island and his desire to have 'an insular possession', as Elliot had called it, more akin to the far larger, more northerly island of Zhousan, is well known. The concept of such a toehold in China, serving a function akin to that which Macau had had for the Portuguese for centuries, was mooted at the time of Macartney. But the specific place of Hong Kong was only first mentioned in English sources when it figured as the pick-up point for Sir George Staunton and Robert Morrison in July 1816, when they joined Lord Amherst's mission.[78] Descriptions of the island at the time of its acquisition were ambiguous. John Elliot Bingham recorded in 1843 that 'the bay of Hong Kong is a remarkable fine anchorage ... The site for the new British town is on the south side of [the bay] and north side of the island. A good road was quickly made along the sea face, and a gaol, court house and other buildings, have been erected.' Before long, Bingham surmised, this area would 'become a favourite residence with the British merchants.'[79] Botanist Robert Fortune had written in the same year of it being an 'island considerably longer than it is broad, perfectly mountainous, and sloping in a rugged manner to the water's edge'. The water in the harbour's ravines had, he went on, given the place its poetical name – Island of Fragrant Streams.[80] Within a decade, as the new colonial possession (its exact status was always a moot point – something that will be discussed later) was constructed and developed, views of it would become more complex. Social reformer Nathan Allen in 1853 remarked that it was only fit for opium trading.[81] Politician and author Laurence Oliphant seven years later described it as a 'beautiful woman with a bad temper'.[82] Its establishment as a British port simultaneously brought about a whole new structure of governance, with the creation of a governorship of Hong Kong as the key figure (the first governor – from 1843 to 1844 – was Sir Henry Pottinger). In the early years, this was a dual role, so that Pottinger also acted as plenipotentiary and superintendent of trade for the rest of the country: each of the first four governors had somehow to balance their diverse responsibilities in China and towards Hong Kong. But by 1857, the two roles had diverged, so that from that point on they became separate appointments, featuring two different people sitting atop alternative administrative structures. The governor of Hong Kong was answerable to the Colonial Office administration in Britain, rather than to either the Foreign Office or the British chief representative in China itself (which, not being a dependency or colony, was ostensibly still treated as a foreign affairs issue). This, needless to say, caused plenty of domestic tension right up to the time of the last governor, in 1997, with the two bureaucracies often squabbling and requiring mediation by higher political masters.

Knowing China after the war

The war and the period after it saw the production of an enormous volume of material about China – some of it by missionaries, who had acquired excellent language skills while living in the country, and some by those who had gained their knowledge while working as merchants trading with the Chinese. This material was to provide the basis for a more systemic and richer sinology in Britain. In the 1830s, lengthy and comprehensive treatments started to appear. The afore-mentioned Charles Gutzlaff had issued a long book in 1838 which contained detailed accounts of Chinese geography, politics and national character. Drawing on his years spent living in the country and mastering some of its local dialects, Gutzlaff somewhat patronis-ingly stated that the Chinese 'are an antiquated nation, the very tran-script of the ancient world, living in the present age, quick in intellect but slow to think of themselves'.[83] As for the emperor, he 'lives a very retired life, is little known even by his grandees, and has been remark-able neither for his great vices nor shining virtues'.[84] John Francis Davis, who served as the second governor of Hong Kong from 1844 to 1848, produced a two-volume work in 1836 which discussed, among many other issues, the works of Confucius, the ancient *Book of Changes* (*I-Ching*), the nature of Chinese religious belief, fengshui and the notion that Chinese language was based 'not on sounds but ideas'.[85] Davis also introduced some thoughts about the richness and length of Chinese history: 'The Chinese in the tenth century were not only further advanced than their contemporaries of Europe . . . but they had reached a higher point of civilization than the ancient Greeks and Romans.'[86]

That deepening awareness of the diversity and extent of Chinese culture and the need for the British to have some appreciation continued over the coming decade after the conflict. An exhibition by the American Nathan Dunn, 'Ten Thousand Chinese Things', held with some success at St George's Place, Hyde Park Corner, London in 1842, put before a large British audience physical examples of this new culture, with which they now needed to engage as never before. Samples of lacquered work, chinaware, Chinese boats, dragon fans, musical instruments and dwarf trees were placed before the public, with a well-illustrated catalogue to disseminate these images more widely.[87] In 1847, Thomas Taylor Meadows wrote of how 'the Chinese have been a literary people and great writers for upwards of 2,000 years', continuing, 'there is probably more written on practical business in China than in Great Britain'.[88] The issue in the country now was power imbalances, and the fact that 'mandarins are made responsible for a vast number of things over which they cannot normally exercise any control'.[89]

In among this material were other, often piercing, insights into the nature of the Chinese political system. In 1847, Robert Montgomery Martin, an Anglo-Irish civil servant working in Hong Kong, produced yet another monumental account of China's provinces, its relations with Britain and the most recent wars. For him, the fundamental principle on which the Chinese authorities operated was, despite all appearances to the contrary, to 'never oppose public opinion if too powerful, but to preserve for itself the privilege of making prohibitions; not to pursue the many transgressions, for that would endanger its very existence, but to choose a few individuals and make them scapegoats for the whole.'[90] This description of the highly strategic way in which the central government exercised power over citizens in China could serve well for explaining how things stand today: a remarkable system, where sometimes huge licence is combined with the harshest and often most arbitrary use of power to rein in particular figures, all guided at heart by a profound wariness and fear of what the public actually thinks and where and how their grievances and anger may manifest themselves. Chinese government in the 1830s was the same as it is today: the world's largest and oldest game of cat and mouse.

One of the issues that arose from this greater familiarity with each other was the use of terms in Chinese and how they might be conveyed in English translation. Of these, the most contentious was the character 'yi' (夷), which was more often than not rendered as 'barbarian'. The scholar P.P. Thoms argued that Chinese people were 'not likely to use coarse language', and that when it came to the term 'yi', the Chinese 'do not attach to it any offensive meaning', for 'the word barbarian should have been rendered foreigner'.[91] The problem was 'our ignorance of the Chinese language . . . which has led us to take offence where no offence was intended'.[92] Sir George Staunton had also waded in on this issue, saying in 1836 that 'barbarian' was not a correct translation.[93]

The root problem was that 'yi' was ambiguous. There were three contemporary ways by which to designate foreigners – to call them 'xi yang' (西洋 – people from the Western oceans); the more pejorative 'gui' (鬼 – devils); or 'yi' itself, though this term was not used before 1750. Rather than 'yi' being intrinsically *bad* in the original language, one reason the term attracted such negative attention in translation was the influential assertion of Charles Gutzlaff that its meaning was bad. Because of his status as a scholar of the Chinese language, his take on the issue proved decisive. Accepted now as insulting by English speakers, from 1858 the term 'yi' was banned and replaced with more palatable, less loaded characters like 'xi' (西 – the West) or 'wai' (外 – outsiders).[94]

Elsewhere, in more mainstream British culture, things were different. Certainly, neither considerations of the depth and longevity of China's culture, nor reflections on the complexities of its political system were on the mind of novelist Charles Dickens (1812–70) the day he caught sight of the only Chinese junk vessel to be sailed from China to Britain in the nineteenth century, which was something of a tourist novelty. Writing in *The Examiner* in June 1848 of his visit to the *Keying* (the name of the ship), he said: 'the shortest way to the celestial empire is by the Blackwall Railway'. There one could buy a ticket to board the junk. Dickens was not impressed once he had purchased his right to board: 'If there be any one thing in the world that it is not at all like, that thing is a ship of any kind. So narrow, so long, so low in the middle, so high on each end.' The Chinese love of disproportion and disorder that once impressed and influenced the Romantics held little appeal to Victorian Britain's greatest and most popular novelist. He drew a broader conclusion from what he had seen: 'Through all the immense extent of the strange Kingdom of China, in the midst of its patient and ingenious but never advancing art, and its diligent agricultural cultivation, not one new twist of curve has been given a ball of irony, not one blade of experience has been grown.' Towards the end of his life, his dim view of things Chinese would resurface in his uncompleted final novel, *The Mystery of Edwin Drood*, which begins with a salacious account of the visit to an opium den run by a Chinese person in London. But Dickens did have one interesting general comment to make as he was touring the *Keying* that day in 1848: 'It is a remarkable circumstance in China (which is found to obtain nowhere else) that although its institutions are the perfection of human wisdom, and the wonder and envy of all the world by reason of their stability, they are constantly being imperilled in the last degree by very slight occurrences.'[95]

This proved accidentally prophetic. Within two years, the disgruntlement of a failed candidate for the imperial exams would eventually lead to the titanic uprising of the Taiping, which posed an existential threat to the ruling regime. Many British had noted in their new sinology and reports the anomaly which underlay this sense of precariousness – the way a few hundred thousand Manchus were running a country with a population now approaching 350 million, overwhelmingly consisting of Han Chinese. Obtusely, the British did not try to take the further step of drawing any parallels with the way their own slender bureaucracy was running governance in India and elsewhere, with a few thousand people holding sway over similarly huge populations. Such an exercise, in any case, would not have detracted from acknowledging how inherently unstable and unsustainable the situation was in China. As Robert Fortune complained, after his travels tracking down tea plants in the mid-1840s, 'I think no country can be well governed where the government is powerless . . . China is very weak in this respect.' In his view, 'the only thing that keeps the country together is the quiet and inoffensive character of the people.'[96] With deepening trading interest,

Britain had to become, often very reluctantly, involved in these domestic politics. Within a decade, it would be faced with a choice of either continuing to maintain its position of studied neutrality or making deeper commitments to the ruling group (or some alternative to it). The 1850s and 1860s were to be turbulent decades. But they marked the start of the era of Britain's most profound involvement in Chinese affairs.

5

A World to Build

The Era of the Second Anglo-Chinese War and Its Aftermath, 1843–64

The 1839–42 war had ended in complete victory for Britain. The era in which that country's superiority in terms of technological, economic, geopolitical and cultural power was most complete and uncontested had begun in earnest. While this was a process that had been going on long before the violent military clashes across China and around its coasts starting in the 1830s, the First Anglo-Chinese War had made one thing clear: Britain was able to enforce its will when it chose to do so, and had a very high chance of prevailing. The high point of British power imbalance with China stretched for the next seven decades. After that, the long decline set in.

Despite this situation, China was not a passive, compliant plaything for British demands and desires. Far from it. From the moment the Treaty of Nanjing was signed, the Qing court was devising ways of resisting, adapting, revising and changing what it believed, from the start, to have been unfair and unequal arrangements. This mutated in time into a more self-searching realisation that China itself, its governance, its attitudes to itself and the world, and its vision of the modernity it was now learning about and having physical experience of every day, needed to undergo fundamental reform. But – as in the initial stages of grief – before any acceptance could set in, the dominant Chinese mode in the early years was one of denial. This was manifested in such physically small but symbolically loaded matters as foreign access to Canton city. The essence of the Canton system over most of the previous century had been to restrict and physically restrain foreign access to China, controlling the movement in particular of merchants, so that – apart from in a few designated places – they were almost invisible. The Treaty of Nanjing had ostensibly resolved this, with the promise of opening up the city. But there were still sporadic squabbles over the rights of the British to free movement – to such an extent that the successor to Pottinger as superintendent in China, Sir John Davis (1795–1890), authorised limited military action in 1847 to enforce entry. An agreement was put in place to allow this in two years.

The more important matter in the longer run was that – despite all the salivating by businesspeople when the supplementary treaty of commerce had been agreed with the Chinese in 1843 – trade levels had been disappointing. A report completed in 1852 by a Mr Mitchell for Sir George Bonham (1803–63), governor of Hong Kong and superintendent of trade in China from 1848 to 1854, was unambiguous: 'After ten years of open trade with this great country, and after the abolition of monopolies on both sides ... China with her swarming millions [does] not consume one half so much of our manufactures as Holland.'[1] In fact, since the signing of the treaty, things had regressed: 'Sir H. Pottinger found a larger trade in existence when he signed the supplementary treaty in 1843 than his treaty [has achieved] itself.'[2] Exports of British manufactures were £750,000 less at the end of 1859 than in 1844. The reason was not the lack of instruments to try to penetrate the Chinese market, in terms of business infrastructure, access and other facilities: these had existed since the end of the war. Nor was it lack of will on the part of the British traders. The key issue was the nature of the Chinese market itself, according to Mitchell: 'The habits of the Chinese . . . are thrifty.' There were few who wished to buy imported British clothing, because of its price and its unsuitability for domestic conditions. In any case, he went on (engaging in a bit of the essentialisation so common in documents about China at the time), for the Chinese 'his [sic] characteristic is a quiet energy that never tires . . . he looks upon labour as his natural inheritance'. China was full of people from 'the producing class', who exchanged what they needed with each other, and who lived in a situation with 'the almost total absence of political excitement and the utter indifference of the people to what dynasty is in power'.[3] It was an insular, inward-looking market – one that offered far more limited scope for growth and development than initial assessment of its size would suggest. For the British, Mitchell warned, 'we have nothing whatever to complain of if we will only view the thing properly, and forget forever the monster blunder of our first expectations', scale down expectations and be more realistic.[4] Those final admonishing words could have been inscribed across all the contemporary and future expressions of excitement and enthusiasm for what growth potential the China market offered.

This mismatch between initial hopes and reality constantly recurred throughout the relations between Britain and the West and China. Mitchell's report was, a few years later, in 1859, to attract the attention of Karl Marx (1818–83). In one of his few comments directly on China in his work (despite his massive posthumous influence on that country), the philosopher stated that Mitchell's report, and other facts, showed that the early 'high-flown anticipations had no solid ground to stand upon'.[5] For Marx, 'the main obstacle to any sudden expansion of import trade into China . . . [is] the economical structure of Chinese society', which depended on agriculture and a minute domestic industry (much as Mitchell had written). To attempt, as the British had done, to clear away these impediments by brute force was doomed to failure, because their root causes were structural. For those to change, the whole nature of Chinese society would need to be transformed. That would not happen by treaty; and nor would it occur quickly, if at all.

Taiping chaos

Mitchell was based in Canton when he wrote the report, with direct exposure to facts on the ground in China. But his airy analysis that the locals were not interested in the political situation within which they lived and blithely continued their day-to-day work, indifferent to the great movements of history going on around them, was largely wrong. In 1851, a year before he issued his report, rebels of the Taiping Heavenly Kingdom had commenced their vast insurrection. This was to lead to the death of 20–30 million people, and would bring chaos to large parts of the country, with some of the bloodiest and most bitter conflicts seen in the nineteenth century.[6] Compared to the contemporaneous American Civil War, this Chinese equivalent was significantly more devastating, while its impact on history was just as profound. For the Qing Manchu rulers, the essentially Han-led rebellion was a direct attack on their legitimacy. The great irony was that, as the historian Stephen Platt wrote in a 2012 history of the event, because the two sides (rebels and imperial government) were so intractably balanced, 'the final outcome was to a large degree determined by the diplomatic and military interventions of the British and other foreigners in the early 1860s'.[7] In this way, the British were to become the saviours of the very Qing regime they had been attacking so fiercely.

Early British assessments of the Taiping as a force were favourable, suggesting that they had 'high moral values'. This was a belief inspired more by the ostensible commitment to a form of Christianity by their charismatic, but unstable, founder Hong Xiuquan (1814–64) than by any cool appraisal of what the rebels stood for. But after this some-what rosy initial view, the attitude hardened into a realisation that the chaos they were provoking offered no great benefits to Britain's interests, and that the participants were little better than lawless bandits who would soon be dealt with by the central authorities. From that point on, neutrality became the default for Britain. British Foreign

Secretary Lord Clarendon had admonished local British representative George Bonham in 1852 that he should maintain a position of 'strict neutrality between the two contending parties' and 'abstain from taking any part whatever in the dissensions now prevailing'. The new plenipotentiary to China, Bonham's replacement Sir John Bowring (1792–1872), was given similar orders before he took up his new post in 1854 about seeking 'the most friendly intercourse with the Chinese authorities'.[8] On 24 January 1855, Clarendon reinforced this with the demand that Bowring 'remain a quiet observer of events passing around you . . . holding yourself aloft from all participation in the intestine troubles of the country'.[9]

John Bowring was a remarkable figure. He was a polyglot, able to speak French, Italian, Portuguese, German, Spanish and Dutch fluently, and with a good knowledge of Danish and Swedish. He could also read Russian, Serbian, Polish and Czech, and had learned Arabic. As an older man, to this formidable array of languages he also came to a good facility in Chinese.[10] As a boy, Bowring had recorded, he had had a dream in which he was sent by the king of England to be ambassador to China. 'To China', he wrote in his autobiography, 'I went as the representative of the Queen, and was accredited, not to Peking alone, but to Japan, Siam, Cochin China, and Corea – I believe a greater number of human beings – indeed not less than a third of the race of man – than any individual has been accredited with before.'[11] A close associate of the utilitarian philosopher Jeremy Bentham, and one of the editors of his works, Bowring's appointment to China, which sat at odds with his prior career, was akin to a reward for work he had done domestically. And while a man of high intellectual and cultural attainments, Bowring's role in the build-up and early stages of the Second Anglo-Chinese War was hardly a positive one. For someone of such wide and expansive intellectual interests, his philosophy towards the Chinese was defensive: 'All the superior authorities', he wrote in his autobiography, 'have received imperial instruction which may be summed up in two sentences: keep the barbarians at a distance . . . [and] take care not to involve the Emperor in annoying disputes.'[12]

The immediate issue resulting from the Taiping Rebellion was how to deal with the domestic political and social fractures that it was creating. One of the most pressing of these was the impact in the great new mercantile centre of Shanghai. This port city was not created by the British: it had existed as an important shipping and trading centre for centuries before. But first the British and then other Europeans and North Americans afterwards were to leave an indelible mark on the place, making it one of the great commercial centres of the world by the end of the century, a place of wonderful dynamic hybridity and energy. As early as 1848, the missionary Walter Medhurst (1796–1857) had said of the city that it was 'one of the greatest emporiums of commerce on the east coast of China. It communicates immediately with the rich districts of Suzhou and Hangzhou, receiving the rich brocades from the Arcadia of China, and conveying hither the inventions and commodities of the Western world.'[13]

The rebel action from 1853, when the Small Sword Society attacked Shanghai – one of a plethora of secret groups that had appeared once the Taiping emerged – created turbulence that impacted directly on Britain's interests in the city. Apart from the International Concession (a large area in the centre of Shanghai where Britain and other European powers enjoyed special legal and commercial rights, running it almost akin to a separate jurisdiction), the rest of the great new metropolis was under rebel bandit control. This caused such chaos and confusion that revenues for imported goods ceased to be collected. There were plenty of merchants who inevitably thought this an excellent outcome. But the punctilious British (and in particular their local officials) were uneasy and felt that for duties not to be collected, even though the cause was local dysfunction, was against the treaty signed a decade previously. Rutherford Alcock (1809–97), the British consul general at the time in Shanghai, proposed that an Inspectorate of Customs be established to collect revenue and to ensure that it was remitted to the central Chinese government. The rebellion in the city grew to such an extent that, on 11 April 1854, the British military were involved in a small skirmish, the Battle of Muddy Flat, rebuffing the invading parties. From that point, Taiping activity shifted its focus elsewhere.

The Shanghai Customs House was opened on 12 July 1854. Thomas Wade, a colleague of Alcock's in the consular service, was appointed the first inspector, though after a brief period he was replaced by Horatio Nelson Lay (1832–98). Initially, there was local resistance. The idea of having a foreign-managed entity saying it was collecting taxes which were clearly for the local government was a novel one. Initially, there was confusion about who had ultimate control over the newly established entity. But as a result of a case in 1858 when a ship was ordered to pay dues and protested, the Foreign Office in London made it clear that the Customs Service, and its head, were directly under the Chinese government and answerable to it.[14] The Chinese Imperial Maritime Customs Service, as it was formally named, went on under this unique arrangement to be, in the words of historian Hans van de Ven, 'one of the most, if not the most, powerful bureaucracies operating between the Taiping rebellion and the Communist Revolution [of 1949]'.[15] It became 'the all-powerful, all-knowing centre for a disciplined organisation with a self-confident, senior staff, bound together by a strong esprit de corps'.[16] In the next half century it was to be the key example of how Britain had inserted itself into the operation and functioning of the Chinese state in areas which are usually regarded as belonging solely to the sovereign power of the country in question. Not the least of its functions was to collect and publish immense amounts of data about China's economic situation.[17] A further manifestation of what became almost a British shadow administration on Chinese sovereign territory was the creation of the Shanghai Municipal Council, whose first meeting was held on 17 July 1854, and which, at least in the foreign concessions in the city, came to assume many of the policing and administrative duties.

The Arrow War, 1856–60

The Second Anglo-Chinese War had its origins in the unexciting issue of the hauling down of a British flag from a boat. The *Arrow*, manned by twelve Chinese sailors and registered until recently as a British vessel in Hong Kong, had, on 8 October 1856, when the event took place, no up-to-date registration. This meant that it was a viable target for Chinese officials, whose suspicions about its trading activity gave them the pretext for action. All of the sailors on board were detained. British demands for their release and for compensation of some sort were swift. From this squabble about the symbolic import- ance of another nation's flag – and what was seen as disrespect shown to it – flowed a whole series of far larger and more far-reaching events over the following four years. These dragged in French, Russian, American and other parties. They constituted perhaps one of the most unjust wars of the nineteenth century. Sir John Pratt, one of the pre-eminent British officials dealing with China in the next century, called it simply an 'unjustifiable war' and one about the justice of which even its chief participants seemed in two minds.[18]

One of the chief players on the British side was Harry Parkes (1828–85), the locally based man who had to deal with managing the *Arrow* issue initially and who then displayed a fiery temper and an uncompromising character that was to win him plaudits from the more hawkish on the British side. Parkes' broad approach, according to his biographer, was 'never giving up, never allowing himself to be slighted, but always resolutely maintaining the dignity and honour of his country before the eyes of the Chinese'.[19] He himself said that China was 'in the position of a diseased man whose whole system had [sic] to be cleared by violent remedies: they tear him and leave him prostrate, but then there is a reaction which, if not checked, works as a recovery'.[20] This Englishman evidently regarded himself as the person required to administer this tough love. As one assessment put it, among his contemporaries he had 'a reputation of a man determined to keep the East in an inferior position.'[21] A fluent speaker of Chinese (thanks to having been sent to the country when he was orphaned as an adolescent), he had been present at the signing of the Treaty of Nanjing. His future included imprisonment and brutal treatment at the hands of the Chinese (including the threat of execution) in the Arrow War, and then stints as the chief plenipotentiary in both China and Japan. He was the quintessence of a mid-Victorian diplomatic activist, a person who spent almost his entire life abroad, serving a cause and a country that he had only properly experienced up to the age of fourteen. But the ideal of Britain was a powerful one for him, even if his direct experience of its reality was hazy and brief; and his commitment to his country remained with him through decades of often hard, unrelenting work far beyond its shores.

The Second Anglo-Chinese War had the same stop-start narrative as the first. Initially skirmishes occurred in late 1856, when Commander-in-Chief Michael Seymour's forces took the Barrier forts and occupied the Macau passage. These continued until the end of the year. Things escalated in early 1857, when the bread supplied to the family of John Bowring in Hong Kong was poisoned with arsenic, an action that led to sickness in its victims rather than death, but which deepened the sense of crisis and antipathy towards the Chinese.[22] At this point, the situation in China became folded into domestic concerns in Britain. By 1857, Palmerston was prime minister. He had signalled some years before that China remained on his mind, despite the distraction of a myriad other international and domestic issues. 'The time is fast coming', he had threatened earlier in the 1850s, 'when we shall be obliged to strike another blow in China.'[23] In view of comments like this, the *Arrow* incident was simply the trigger that Britain had been waiting for. Had it not been this, something else would have caused the conflict that followed.

The parliamentary debates on the need for action in China were held in February 1857. Richard Cobden led the opposition, saying that 'the British government followed one policy towards the strong and another towards the weak'.[24] But it was the powerful peroration of William Gladstone which best expressed the moral case against the impending war. 'War taken at the best is a frightful scourge to the human race,' he boomed,

> but because it is so the wisdom of the ages has surrounded it with strict laws and usages, and has required formalities to be observed which shall act as a curb upon the wild passions of man, to prevent the scourge from being let loose unless under circumstances of full deliberation and from absolute necessity.

And yet Palmerston's government had 'dispensed with all these precautions. [It has] turned a consul into a diplomatist and the meta-morphised [sic] consul is forsooth to direct the whole might of England against the heads of a defenceless people.'[25] In a rhetorically masterly move, Gladstone shifted from statement of more abstract principle to the concrete reality of what this war would involve:

> You go to China and make war upon those who stand before you as women or children. They try to resist you; they call together their troops; they load their guns; they kill one and wound perhaps two in action, but while they are touching units you perhaps slay thousands.

There was no 'equality of ground' between the two, just imbalance, injustice and the exercise of raw power for the sake of it. In the context of the appalling suffering that was already being meted out to ordinary Chinese by the ongoing Taiping Rebellion, and the toll this was taking on the government, the words about the stronger inflicting misery on the weak gain added power and relevance. The tenor of Gladstone's argument was clear: Britain was kicking a country when it was down – and to make matters worse, clearly knew it was.

While the House of Lords approved the war, the House of Commons voted down the decision. That necessitated the only general election in British history to have been mainly about matters related to China. Palmerston's tactics succeeded. After a jingoistic campaign through mid-1857, when he played to his strengths, he was returned with a majority of eighty-five and the ability to act as he pleased.

James Bruce (1811–63), the eighth earl of Elgin, was appointed in mid-1857 to take a posse of troops to China to deal with the effrontery of the Chinese. Like his predecessor Charles Elliot, his writings reveal great ambiguity about the endeavour he was now engaged in. 'It is impossible to read the [official books about China] without feeling that we have often acted towards the Chinese in a manner which is very difficult to justify', he admitted. But he followed this with a compensatory sentiment, at least for Britain's behaviour: 'And yet [the Chinese] treachery comes out so strongly at times as to make anything appear justifiable.'[26] His view did not change when in the thick of the campaign. 'Uninvited and by methods not always the gentlest,' wrote the British commander to Foreign Secretary , the earl of Malmesbury, on 18 January 1859, 'we have broken down the barriers behind which these ancient nations sought to conceal from the world . . . the rags of rottenness and their waning civilisation'. Taking an approach very unlike that of Gladstone a couple of years earlier, in the parliamentary debate of 1857, Elgin alluded to the need for some moral justification for what Britain was doing. Surely the British had not come to China and undertaken this whole campaign simply to fill 'our pockets from among the ruins we have found or made?'[27] Since it was a rhetorical question, Elgin did not furnish it with a candid answer. He was evidently adept at what the American novelist F. Scott Fitzgerald called the genius of being able to think two wholly contradictory things at the same time and find them compatible.

Elgin's passage to China was interrupted by the need for the troops with him to go to help quell the Indian Mutiny. That event, replete with its own unspeakable violence and suffering, was one he was a partial eyewitness to, as he tagged along, waiting until his force could be restored to him in Mumbai. It was ultimately to consist of 1,500 men from Great Britain, with 350 Indian troops and 750 Europeans.[28] As historian Robert Bickers has written, 'The face of the British military was often an Indian face.'[29] Unlike in 1839, this time – symbolising a little of the new-found (and brief) European unity – British forces were working as part of an international group, alongside French soldiers under Baron Jean-Baptiste-Louis Gros. With this small force, the foreigners inflicted dizzying levels of violence and damage on their Chinese target. By the year end, a bombardment of Canton saw two hundred Chinese killed for only eight British dead and led to an infantry landing and the taking of the city.[30] 'The most striking element after this,' wrote Laurence Oliphant, who was serving in the invading forces,

> was that impressive silence, that absence of all movement on the part of the population of a million and a half, that lay as though entombed within the city walls, whose only desire, if they could think at all, appeared to be that the bare fact of their existence should be forgotten by the foreigners.[31]

Governor Ye Mingchen (1807–59), branded by Palmerston 'one of the most savage barbarians that ever disgraced a nation', who 'has been guilty of every crime which can disgrace a nation',[32] was, unfortunately for him, not accorded the luxury of being forgotten. Far from it. He was found, after an initial attempt to go into hiding in the house of the lieutenant general of the city's forces: 'his glance . . . [was] troubled and his fingers trembled with suppressed agitation'.[33] After detention on a boat, he was promptly sent to Calcutta as a prisoner of war, dying there two years later. As with the First Anglo-Chinese War, the imperial government played for time, bluffing and telling the combined forces then in Shanghai (which now had Russians and

Americans added to the French and British) to return to Canton and negotiate with the authorities there.

In April, the forces proceeded to the Haihe River, and by 30 May 1858 envoys were in Tianjin. With the signing of treaties, it seemed that an outcome had been arrived at that had resolved matters: the treaty with the British (the Treaty of Tianjin), ratified on 26 June, for the first time allowed British representation to be based at the capital, Beijing. Lord Elgin rewarded himself for his hard work by spending a few weeks voyaging up the Yangtze, before heading back to Britain. He was unaware that in reality the business was not over: matters would come to a head again because of the deep reservations held by the leadership in Beijing about the terms that those mandarins mandated to negotiate with the invading forces had agreed. By mid-1859, Lord Elgin was back in China to sort things out. This time he aggressively proceeded with French forces to Tianjin. Holding this city was, according to one observer, like 'holding the throat of the Chinese'.[34] It was during this part of the proceedings that Parkes and a number of other foreigners were taken prisoner and maltreated (these included the correspondent for *The Times*, who was covering the war as a very early example of an 'embedded reporter' and who tragically died).

Elgin's frustration was one of the contributory factors that led to the sacking of the Summer Palace on 5 October 1860. This infamous event saw predominantly British and French troops run amok once they reached the capital, pillaging and setting fire to the pleasure grounds and living quarters of the emperor on the outskirts. Ironically, these buildings had been inspired by designers from the Europe of their destroyers. Fragments preserved today by the government stand as stark monuments to foreign aggression. One eyewitness serving in the British forces, G.T. Wolseley, justified his compatriots' behaviour before and during the sacking by stating that 'our objective was not to weaken the Imperial government, but to show China how immeasurably stronger and greater in war we were'.[35] Wolseley did not acknowledge the fact that achievement of the latter objective involved near certainty that the former would occur; but he did admit that when troops entered the palace, 'they seemed to have been seized with a temporary insanity'.[36] Some of them, he stated, 'dressed themselves in the richly embroidered gowns of women' found on the site, giving a farcical aspect to a day that was to leave such deep historic wounds.

Once the looters had exhausted themselves, smoke from the smouldering ruins drifted across the evening sky towards the centre of Beijing city, miles away. 'In passing between our camp and the [Summer Palace] upon both of these days,' Wolseley noted, 'the light was so subdued by the overhanging clouds of smoke that it seemed as if the sun was undergoing a lengthened eclipse. The world around looked dark with shadow.'[37] During the orgy of pillaging, a Pekingese dog was found. It was subsequently taken to Britain, the first of its breed to make the journey, and was given to Queen Victoria, who (somewhat obtusely) named it Looty.[38] Despite the light-hearted nature of the name, there was nothing remotely humorous about the aftermath of that day. Indeed, even in the twenty-first century it stands as a symbol of Chinese humiliation at the hands of foreigners and a source of anger and shame.

Some eyewitnesses did admit to qualms about what was happening, with one, Henry Brougham Loch, speaking of 'natural repugnance . . . at the destruction of the beautiful building'; though he went on to say 'that no money indemnity could compensate for the insults inflicted on the British'.[39] An indemnity, after all, would have ultimately fallen on the heads of the people, rather than the elite. Attacking the palaces, which were known to be the main residence of the emperor for much of the year, was seen as striking directly at the rulers and teaching them a lesson – rather like sanctions against political elites in the twenty-first century are meant to hurt those that deserve it. But for the question of what precisely the war had been about, and what it had achieved, things are even more unclear than in the case of the First Anglo-Chinese War two decades before.

The treaties that were agreed during the second war – the Treaty of Tianjin in 1858 and the Beijing Convention two years later – broadly set in place the principle of complete reciprocity between the governments of Britain and China, and the right of each to speak directly to the other. The 1858 treaty, under Article 16, also set out in greater detail than before the basis of extraterritoriality, by which British subjects committing crimes in China had to be dealt with according to the laws of Great Britain, not the host nation. New ports were opened up to foreign trade – Jinjiang, Formosa (Taiwan), Tengchow (today's Penglai, near Yantai), Swatow (Shantou) and the island of Hainan. Use of the term 'yi', usually rendered in English as 'barbarian' (see discussion in the previous chapter), was forbidden. As a full expression of British power, these agreements set out how Britons wished to relate to China, where they wanted to do trade, and even how they were to be spoken about. The Convention of Beijing also stipulated a payment of 8 million taels (a local form of currency, each equivalent to 1.3 ounces of silver) in compensation, in effect underwriting the costs of the violence that the British had committed on their victims and funding the invasion. Tianjin port was opened for trade, and Kowloon (a major part of Hong Kong to the north of the island, which had, up until then, been in Chinese hands) was ceded in perpetuity to Britain. Above all, the whole administrative machinery by which China related to the outside world was reformed, so that the change affected not just external issues, but also the internal configuration of the Chinese state. Whether this was the British helping their recently defeated partner to modernise or was purely intended to make their own lives easier (or was a mixture of the two), it was still yet another remarkable demonstration of prescriptive power by one entity over another. A new body, the Zongli Yamen (as the prototype for China's Ministry of Foreign Affairs was first called), was to conduct relations with all foreign countries.

Established in 1861, it replaced the mixture of different, overlapping bodies – such as the Ministry of Rites – that had performed these functions hitherto. To take the lead in engaging with these new entities for the British was Lord Elgin's brother, Frederick Bruce (1814–67), appointed as minister in 1860.

Deeper involvement: The Lay–Osborn fleet and the defeat of the Taiping

The Second Anglo-Chinese War had cemented Britain's role both with and in China. Government traders – rather than private or even EIC businessmen – had emerged from the time of Macartney as key players, and they had brought a whole new dynamic into play because they had the resources and authority of the British state behind them, rather than more restricted corporate interests. Before this era, if the British had anything like a policy towards China, it was mostly about commercial interests and the delivery of profit and trade. But by 1860, the naval officer Sherard Osborn would write – intemperately but truthfully – that the idea that one could have just trade relations with China, and not political ones which inevitably involved the state, was 'humbug'.[40] As Member of Parliament Charles Beresford was to comment half a century later, 'In China, commercial and political questions cannot be separated.'[41] This was not just about the situation in China itself: it also came about because of the nature of modern trade and its relationship to, and reliance on, political power. Increasingly, larger and more complex issues were involved, which ran alongside the development of a modern state in Britain with its technical and administrative appurtenances. These entailed consideration of a balance of interests between different forces within the country, and how consensus between them was created. These had to be set within a holistic national framework. Therefore, one can say that, by the middle of the nineteenth century, a British policy was emerging towards China that had to set out and then manage the risks and opportunities, and also articulate the overall objectives that Britain, corporately, was trying to achieve, not just in commerce, but across the board.

That there were risks was clear enough. There were some things Britain clearly needed in its relations with China, and others it wished to avoid; thus the whole process was a balancing act. Despite its exercise of raw power and the use of force against the tottering state of the Qing, Britain certainly did not want the empire to fall. That was why it eventually shifted from neutrality in the Taiping Rebellion to siding with the imperial government. A China that was weak, wounded and dysfunctional, but that did not collapse and create regional chaos, was therefore desirable. Had implosion ever threatened to happen, Britain would have had to consider far more intrusive intervention. It would have faced the dreaded possibility of a second India – a country recently (in 1857) taken under direct British colonial control when the mirage of EIC management proved unsustainable. The costs to Britain of this were to prove steep.

If the British government was sceptical and reluctant about the benefits of having such control over this part of its empire – in the shaping of which it had had a far larger hand – with China its scepticism ran far deeper. Public opinion seemed to agree. As *The Times* newspaper stated in 1875, 'We are not in the mood to undertake . . . another India.'[42] In London, according to one historian, the government Board of Trade (in charge of much economic policy making), 'convinced the rest of Whitehall that the Chinese trade would never be worth the expense of war or sovereignty'.[43] That resulted in an outcome which veered between events that were coercive and intrusive (like the aftermath of the Second Anglo-Chinese War) and a constant desire to assert boundaries and zones where Britain would not find itself saddled with responsibility for a vast territory which it knew it understood poorly, and which threatened to burden it with massive administrative and political responsibilities. The ideal arrangement for British policy towards China post-1860 was, therefore, to have power without responsibility. This was subsequently labelled 'informal empire': Britain had legal privileges, a free-trade regime, instruments of intervention in domestic issues (like management of the Imperial Maritime Customs) and could engage in occasional use of force; but beyond this, it let China do as China wished.[44]

The new semi-official rulers of this so-called informal empire were the consuls. By 1869, the British consular network in China was the largest in the world.[45] These officials were the referees in this freshly created game of foreign direction and intrusion in the affairs of China. From that era up to the present, they have been among the most important actors in the China–Britain story. Some of the richness of their collective experiences, and the ways in which they supplied new forms of knowledge and expertise about the country in which they lived and worked, will be discussed in the following chapter, for their heyday was the latter third of the nineteenth century and the start of the twentieth. But already, some powerful examples of their impact could be seen in the 1850s and 1860s. Horatio Nelson Lay is a good example. Lay was the son of a botanist and missionary in China, George Tradescant Lay (c. 1800–45), whose early death meant that his adolescent son had to identify a career for himself. Direct approaches to Palmerston led to mixed outcomes, but he was able to move to China in the late 1840s, learning the language to the level of total fluency. In 1854, he was appointed acting consul in Shanghai and head of the new Imperial Maritime Customs. He served as the translator for Lord Elgin during the war.

In 1860, Lay had the idea of furnishing the Chinese with a modern flotilla built by the British. He had promoted this idea at the court in Beijing, with some success, and returned to Britain in order to commission the building of the vessels. There was a certain appropriateness in his interest in naval affairs, as he had been given his first and middle names in honour of the great British sea hero from earlier in the century. But unlike his namesake, Lay was no commander; he was but an intermediary, and one who had a habit of hearing what he wanted to hear, rather than what he was actually being told. In a pamphlet defending his ultimately abortive mission after its failure in 1863 (the Chinese were content with the ships, but not with the management and leadership of them under British-appointed command, and on that the whole project collapsed), he stated that he had long believed that the Chinese needed 'a European naval force, under Imperial authority'.[46]

Lay shared with his contemporary Harry Parkes a robust attitude towards the people he was dealing with. 'We must never forget', he wrote to Robert Hart (1835–1911), his successor as head of customs, 'that we have to control as well as guide the Chinese government.'[47] After all, he went on, speaking in the tone of European racial superiority so common at the time, these people were, 'when compared with ourselves, but children';[48] they were mere 'imbeciles in power'.[49] The British had therefore to ensure that 'the Chinese government is strong enough to fulfil its obligations';[50] but in trying to do this, they also had to avoid any tendency to 'drift into further entanglements and complications'.[51] How this circle was to be squared, Lay did not go on to say; but in essence, these were the two contrary poles through which the British had to manoeuvre, in order to fulfil their own interests – material enrichment and reward at the lowest cost.

The immediate issue, however, was the continuing crisis posed to Qing rule by the Taiping insurrection. By 1860, it had been tearing apart the fabric of the Chinese state for a decade. Throughout much of this time, it had impinged on British interests, but not so critically that further actions were needed. The British had attempted to protect these interests as far as they could – for example, by repelling Taiping forces from Shanghai in 1853 – while maintaining a show of neutrality and avoiding escalation. In the end, despite debate in Britain about getting sucked into internal Chinese affairs (and with huge amnesia over the recent war in China from 1856 to 1860, which demonstrated clearly the depth of involvement that already existed through the amount of debate it had generated in Britain and the resources that the British had devoted to the conflict), the fact that the Taiping authorities were opposed to opium (which had only just been finally made legal for trading in 1858) and the damage now being done to British trading interests more broadly precipitated a shift in attitude. By 1862, Britain had abandoned its position of neutrality.

Intervention was delivered by perhaps one of the most extraordinary and unsettling characters to take part in the relationship between Britain and China – General Charles Gordon (1833–85). Gordon was a charismatic, driven character, someone who captured the imagination of writers and the public both at the time and afterwards. The writer Lytton Strachey described a man of 'almost magical prestige', who was in the habit of 'walking at the head of his troops, with nothing but a light cane in his hand', passing through danger 'with the scatheless equanimity of a demi-god'.[52] Despite the misgivings of Frederick Bruce, the lead figure in charge of British interests in China at the time, about the mercurial character of this soldier, Gordon was appointed to lead a band of what were, in effect, mercenaries, who were granted the somewhat grand title of the 'Ever Victorious Army'. At the time, Gordon had people working assiduously to promote the myths demonstrating his singularity and bravery that had grown up around him since his time at military school in Britain, where his eccentric version of Christianity and his headstrong nature attracted devotion and irritation in equal measure. A career which typified the ways in which the world at that time often seemed like an open space for the British to criss-cross at will, in order to enjoy their adventures, had seen him take part in the sacking of the Summer Palace in 1860. ('It made one's heart bleed to burn [the palace]', he wrote in a letter back home, before continuing with somewhat less repentance: 'in fact, these palaces were so large, and we were so pressed for time that we could not plunder them carefully'.)[53] Of this looter, his contemporary biographer Andrew Wilson, writing in 1868, made the claim that the Taiping were about to meet 'a more formidable opponent than any they had encountered, and one who knew how to break their ranks, not less by his skill in the arts of war than by his personal prestige.'[54] Seen in this way, Gordon seemed to want to personify the British state he was ostensibly serving.

For all the large claims at the time that the intervention of the small force under Gordon had had such a significant impact on the final outcome of the rebellion, the reality was far less dramatic. The epic battles led by the great Qing commander Zeng Guofan (1811–72), which involved dizzying levels of violence and bloodshed, were the main actions that finally defeated the insurgency. Compared to Zeng's campaigns, Gordon's attack on Suzhou, the event for which he was most famed, was relatively minor. The most vivid single incident during his command as head of his modest army was the outcome of a clash with the newly emerged local leader Li Hongzheng (1823–1901), a figure who in the coming decades would be one of the key interlocutors of the British. Despite promises to the contrary given to the British, Li had executed rebel soldiers that Gordon had undertaken to protect. 'Do you see that? Do you see that?', Gordon had said to another British soldier who had come to find him soon after their execution. 'The light through the small Chinese windows was so faint that Macartney [the soldier] had at first some difficulty in recognising what it was, when Gordon then exclaimed, "It is the head of the Lar Wang, foully murdered."' And with that, he held up the dead rebel leader's head, which had somehow fallen into his hands.[55]

Gordon, were he alive today, would no doubt serve as a rich subject for a small army of psychologists, with his strange mixture of extreme narcissism, dislike of authority (while at the same time assiduously serving that authority) and God-complexes. After a stint in the riverside town of Gravesend back in Britain, rebuilding the fortress there and involving himself in local charitable work, 'Chinese Gordon', as he came to be called, briefly revisited China in 1880, before meeting his end famously in Khartoum at the hands of rebellious local forces – an event that embarrassed the government, which was accused of not doing enough to protect him. At the same time, his insistence on staying in such a dangerous place long after he had been ordered to leave aroused suspicions that he had called down his final demise on his own head through an advanced version of a martyr complex. However one assesses Gordon's impact on the end of the great internal conflict in China he had played a role in, his symbolic importance was great. The story of his struggles in China were one of the most accessible ways in which a British public, now able to enjoy news sent by cable from China far quicker, could understand more about the huge country its armies had so recently humiliated and where its compatriots were exercising, as never before, wide and systemic influence.

The Taiping's defeat and the disbandment of the Ever Victorious Army in 1864 marked a major inflection point. It was accompanied at the central court by a similar (though at the time far less remarked on) change in the elite. The Xianfeng emperor's (1831–r1850–1861) decade in power ended in 1861. His successor, the Tongzhi emperor (1856–r1861–1875), was an infant of five when he came to the throne. As he was far too young to exercise any power, a group of regents was authorised to administer the empire in his stead, until he came of age. But it was increasingly his mother, the formidable Empress Dowager Cixi who, after an early but brief struggle, was to be the true power until the end of her life. The China that she ruled was a place that was both increasingly resentful of the continuation of Manchu dominance and reliant on Britain and other Western powers for technology, finance and ideas to achieve the massive task of modernisation. It was over this era that Britain inserted itself in the financial and economic affairs of the country – and thereby in its politics and diplomacy – to an extraordinarily high degree. This was a period that marked the peak of its influence: the complex outcomes would shape both the new century and the China that emerged.

Robert Fortune's disguises and British understanding of China

Charles Gordon is the better-known figure in the British story in China in the mid nineteenth century. But it was almost certainly

Robert Fortune (1812–80) who had the greatest long-term impact. His main achievement was to undertake one of the most dramatic acts of intellectual property theft of all time. For through his efforts, tea plants – which had been grown predominantly in China – were finally transported to India and, after much trial and error, successfully cultivated in the different soils and climatic conditions there. Today, most of the tea drunk in Britain comes from India. Fortune was one of the key influences on the reasons behind this. As he himself wrote, he was able to procure 'upwards of twenty thousand tea-plants . . . from the finest tea districts of China' and convey them safely to the Himalayas. But he was also able to discover a range of different flowers and plants which, as he rightly predicted, 'will one day produce a striking and beautiful effect in our English landscape'.[56]

Fortune was a botanist, brought up in Scotland. In 1842 he was appointed a botanical collector of the Royal Horticultural Society of London and was sent to China to gather samples of plants, shrubs and flowers. China's unique ecology was appreciated early on as one of the most vivid points of difference with Britain. It was also a field of science where there had been much engagement and activity ever since the first collectors came at the end of the seventeenth century. Many of China's plants were unknown in Europe and offered something fresh and new. A writer in 1795 had spoken appreciatively of the abundance in China 'of the juniper, jujube, cypress, bamboo (a kind of reed, which grows to the height and size of large trees), acacia, tea-plants, cotton tree [and] Tong-Tsao, a kind of cane of bamboo, much resembling the European elder tree'.[57] In 1804, William Kerr, a Scottish gardener, was sent from Kew as the first professional plant collector to explore this important new world of plants. John Reeves (1774–1856) lived for forty years in Canton and Macau and supervised the collection for the Royal Horticultural Society, introducing wisteria into Britain.[58] Clarke Abel, a medical doctor but also a keen naturalist, was part of the 1816 Amherst embassy, tasked with discovering more about the flora and fauna of the place they were sent to.

The beautiful buddleia, clematis, azaleas and daphnes, and with several species of rhododendron, lilium and abies, all sourced there, had been brought back by naturalists in the nineteenth century to furnish British collections and then gardens. They offered an example, like tea, of the way in which things from China reached into and shaped the most intimate and domestic space in Britain. 'Nothing', as Fortune wrote, 'can give the Chinese a higher idea of our civilisation and attainments than our love for flowers, or tend more to create a kindly feeling between us and them.'

In order to gather yet more specimens, Fortune copied the trick of the missionary Walter Medhurst, and assumed the garb of a local Chinese mandarin to get around the country, avoiding the restrictions in place against freedom of movement placed on foreigners. 'I was, of course,' Fortune explained, 'travelling in Chinese costume; my head was shaved, I had a splendid wig and tail, of which some Chinaman in former days had been extremely vain, and upon the whole, I believe I made a pretty fair Chinaman.'[59] With the assistance of long-suffering local servants, he was able to pass himself off as a native from more remote provinces, whose dialect was therefore impenetrable to the citizens of the areas through which he was travelling. This gave him unfettered mobility. His main worry was dogs, which, he became convinced, 'manifest very great hatred to foreigners, barking at them whenever they see them, and hanging on their skirts until they are fairly out of sight', thereby nearly exposing his true identity.[60]

In this unique set-up, the botanist was able to undertake his initial research into tea plants, the secrets of their cultivation and how best to appropriate samples that could somehow be transported to India. This he eventually achieved through the use of new wooden seed and plant container cases, though it was an endeavour that incurred a large amount of frustration and danger. Fortune did not regard his work in terms of the commercial gain that would eventually derive from it when British growers in India finally had control of the supply of tea: he was far more excited by the contribution he was making to science. The immense new sources of wealth for importers, traders and other businesses flowing from this was purely accidental, however serendipitous for them. Fortune's epic travels were representative of something more generally important than simply the collection of plant material and the stealing of tea-growing technology. As the historian James Hevia has argued, projects like these were signs of the move from a more abstract and ideal understanding by the British of China, towards what could be called a 'new pedagogy' – a 'more scientific form', with things like 'precise empirical knowledge such as measurements, statistics, thermometer readings, botanical and zoological specimens, or exact plans'.[61] In the newly established Beijing legation, thanks to their facility with Chinese and their intimacy with matters in China, figures like Thomas Wade were producing 'novel understandings of China's previous diplomatic and commercial exchanges with regional powers'. They were assembling libraries of Chinese classical works and starting to deepen their understanding of how the Chinese, through their long history, had seen themselves, and how they thought in the present.[62]

In mid-century, the process of creating knowledge involving not just what to know about China, but what attitude to take to this newly accessible place was in its infancy. In the beginning, it was mostly a matter of presenting novel items to highlight the country's difference and strangeness. In Britain, there had been a Chinese pavilion at the Great Exhibition of 1851 in London. This was provided not by the Chinese government (which had been asked, and which was the only specifically invited nation to decline official participation), but was put together by merchants from Canton and private collectors. 'The result was an odd assortment of objects and the general consensus was that the China display was the most disappointing of all the nations', as one recent study puts it.[63] Things plonked down in this way – out of context and with no interpretive framework – could only go so far in creating an intelligent public understanding and engagement. One major impediment was that, despite the first Chinese student enrolling at a British university in 1850 (Huang Kuan, who studied medicine at Edinburgh), there was still no meaningful community of people of Chinese heritage in Britain to help with the work.

Neutrality may have been the starting point, but it could then either veer towards idealisation (as had occurred during the Chinoiserie craze of a century before) or go in the opposite direction and display manifestations of antipathy. Finding a middle path always proved hard. The writer Leigh Hunt (1784–1859) had clearly expressed this ambiguity at the heart of the British attitude towards the Chinese, as the two countries came to know each other better. In an essay from 1840 singing the virtues of tea ('at once a refreshment and an elegance'),[64] Hunt wrote that perhaps the British sipping their drink might have certain ideas about the Chinese – and at this point he veered into the worst kind of stereotypes, referring to 'little-eyed, little-footed, little-bearded, little-minded, quaint, overweening, pig-tailed, bald-headed, cone-capped and pagoda-hatted [people], having childish houses and temples with bells at every corner'. However, he went on, 'one gradually acquires a notion that there is a great deal more good sense, and even good poetry, among them than one had fancied from the accounts of embassies and the autobiographical paintings on the China-ware'. They were, after all, 'an ancient and great nation', whose great product, tea, had changed British insular customs.[65]

Increasingly, though, it was to be the prejudiced, rather than the open-minded, side of popular British opinion that held sway. A 'Chanson for China' which appeared in the satirical magazine *Punch* on 10 April 1858, gave full rein to the most offensive extreme of this, speaking of how 'With their little pig-eyes and their large pig-tails,/ And their diet of rats, dogs, slugs and snails,/ All seems to be game in the frying pan/ Of that nasty feeder John Chinaman'.[66] Pictorial representations of the Chinese, and of aspects of Chinese culture, were often no better. This reached its peak in statements by national leaders like Prime Minister Palmerston, who, during the parliamentary debates about the war in 1857, called the Chinese attacking the British 'a set of barbarians – a set of kidnapping, murdering, poisoning barbarians'. Statements from a figure in authority such as this gave licence to others to express similarly aggressive, discriminatory attitudes.[67]

Those who wished to see the Chinese as backward people who, in the words of the philosopher John Stuart Mill, had 'no history' and had been stationary 'for thousands of years', whose only hope was to be improved by foreigners,[68] had to avert their eyes from the evidence to the contrary that was increasingly prevalent in their environments. Ironically, much of this was derived from the cruel pillaging of the Summer Palace and elsewhere in China during the 1856–60 war. Artefacts found their way into Britain and into displays, and little by little into the great collections of the British Museum and other places. Like it or not, too, by its own actions Britain was now in direct contact with China more than ever before, and it had to create a framework where it avoided its worst fears – responsibility for a country it had weakened through its attacks, but which it did not wish to have collapse and implode. That would remain the principal aim of Britain until the end of the century.

6

Of Consuls, Customs and Commerce, 1864-1900

Britain in 1861 found itself with the right to have permanent representation in the capital of China, Beijing (then known by the British as Peking). This had been one of the perennial demands made to the Chinese government ever since the time of Macartney. Finally, it was realised. On 26 March 1861, the British took possession of a new legation compound, a building from the eighteenth century close to the centre of the city and the Forbidden Palace that had once been owned by the aristocratic Liang family. David Rennie, based in the building as a doctor when it opened, described it as 'two sets of quadrangular courts, running parallel between each other, north and south, with a covered passage between them'. There were buildings around these in the Chinese style, with a 'palatial portion' on the eastern side, and state apartments. 'The roofs . . . are covered with green glazed tiles and supported by heavy columns of wood . . . The interior, though out of repair, is still very handsome: the ceilings of the state apartments being beautifully decorated with gold dragons within circles on a blue ground.'[1] Harry Parkes, however, with his customary directness, was less positive. Writing to his wife in November 1860, he said, 'Peking is in a wretched state of dilapidation and ruins and scarcely one of their palatial buildings is not falling into decay. We have obtained the best and yet it is quite uninhabit-able.'[2] For A.B. Freeman-Mitford, working in the legation in June 1865, one had to 'fancy a residence in the heart of a great and popu-lous city where foxes, scorpions, polecats, weasels, magpies and other creatures that one expects to find in the wild country abound'.[3] This puts the perennial complaints about the cramped conditions of the current embassy in Beijing in the twenty-first century into perspec-tive. For the next ninety years, the old Liang Palace was the location for many of the key moments in the diplomatic field between the two nations. It was where the Boxer attacks took place in 1900, and where the plenipotentiaries from Britain did their work, directed their staff, met their Chinese guests, and tried to create and then implement British policy towards the country hosting them.

Dr Rennie, during his year-long stay, was able to pick up some of the dynamics, and the emerging tensions, between the groups from Britain now seeking to take advantage of the new treaties in place and promote their divergent interests. The diplomatists, after all, had their fresh headquarters, and were able to set up a swath of representation across the country. But the businesspeople were a more amorphous group, with Rennie commenting on the 'unreasonable attitude' of some of them. Rennie's reflections on observing this were that 'there are strong grounds for believing that in almost every dispute which arises between ourselves and the Chinese, we are in the first instance wrong'. The problem was that 'the Chinese equally invariably adopt the wrong method of putting matters right'.[4] This unpleasant situa-tion had its upside, because it meant that as ostensibly intermediaries, the consular staff had plenty to do. But of this group, too, Rennie had some criticisms: the Chinese speakers among them, he observed, 'lose themselves completely as soon as they have learned the Chinese language and try to carry everything by bullying and what they call "knowing how to manage the Chinese".'[5] It was already becoming clear that knowing about China did not automatically mean having much wisdom about the place – that quality would prove far rarer.

A network of competent intermediaries and administrators was necessary for a very simple reason. The final decades of the nineteenth century marked the peak in scale and scope of British imperial interests both globally and simultaneously in China. As one history of the period wrote, 'From 1860 to 1885, British companies had a virtual monopoly of the China trade.'[6] In 1874, Britain accounted for 40 per cent of the country's foreign trade. By the next decade, the British comprised over 50 per cent of foreign citizens in China and owned 60 per cent of all foreign firms.[7] By 1897, they had 65 per cent of all trade and shipping in the country. In 1894, of registered ships leaving the treaty ports then in existence, 85 per cent carried British goods; and of those entering, 65 per cent were British. Indeed, until as late as 1936, Britain was the main investor.[8]

The years from 1864 to 1900 were unmarked by any single event of similar significance to the Macartney or Amherst embassies or to either of the two Anglo-Chinese wars. Instead, this was an era of consolidation, one when – because of the inherent weakness of the Qing state – the levers of control open to Britain were freer than they would ever be again and easier to use. There was sporadic tension, such as the drama surrounding the Margary Affair of 1875, when a British official and four of his Chinese companions were murdered by local people as they travelled in the area adjoining Burma to explore business opportunities. But on the whole, this was a period when the main issues were the construction of institutions and the achievement of yet more commercial or industrial goals.

Only in the final decade of the century did the intervention of other Asian and European powers usher in the period that is now known as 'the scramble for China'. Until then, Britain promoted what it eventually called an 'open door' policy, where in theory all the benefits that had been obtained – largely through British military or political efforts – were also enjoyed by other allies. This was called the 'most favoured nation' principle and had been in place since the first treaty of 1843: basically, whatever benefits accrued to one power under a treaty signed with China became by default the norm for everyone else – assuming they improved on those available elsewhere. By the 1880s, Britain felt that the 'open door' it had expended so much effort on was bringing disproportionate free benefits to others. This prompted the creation of informal spheres of influence, which in turn resulted in the unseemly carving up of the country by different players witnessed in the final decade and a half of the nineteenth century. The Chinese did not watch this passively. The mistreatment of their country nurtured a strong sense of nationalism – a phenomenon that increased as further abuses by foreign powers occurred. In the last part of the century, new ideas and thinking about what it meant to be a nation and what constituted legitimate and illegitimate acts by one power towards another spread in China. Ironically, these had originally emerged in the West itself; but the principles they proposed about self-determination, international law and sovereign rights were ones which Chinese thinkers such as Kang Youwei and others applied to the situation locally.

Robert Hart and the Imperial Customs

Robert Hart is central not just to the story of Britain's late-nineteenth-century relations with China, but to the whole narrative of foreign engagement and involvement by the Qing, and its struggles to achieve a modernity that did not clash with its intrinsic sense of tradition and fear of instability and collapse. Hart, a native of the north of Ireland, must rank as the most influential British person ever to have lived and worked in China. He merits this epithet because, from 1864 – when he assumed leadership of the Chinese Imperial Maritime Customs Service (and thereby became a direct employee of the Chinese state) – until the first decade of the twentieth century, he was in charge of a large part of the Chinese domestic fiscal system. No foreigner before or since has had this sort of role within the Chinese government.

The Chinese Imperial Maritime Customs Service has been described as a 'state within a state'.[9] It had duties that extended far wider than collecting tariffs – although on its own that gave it immense influence and power. It established the Shanghai River Police in 1868; by 1891 it had grown from the three customs houses it had in 1861 to twenty-six, by which it managed China's ports; by 1892 it had built 104 lighthouses; and perhaps most significantly of all, it collected crucial, accurate and detailed data on the country's fiscal affairs.[10] In this way, it achieved the sort of knowledge revolution that was referred to in the previous chapter. It created a new set of ways of knowing about China that were not possible before it came into existence. The simple fact was that, prior to the accurate and largely incorrupt and fair collection of customs by the service, no one either in Beijing or elsewhere in the country really knew whether what needed to be paid was actually being paid. Hart and his colleagues were assiduous in their work and managed to gain the trust and respect of all sides – a unique achievement both at the time and later.

The Customs Service had initially a simple function: it took the customs duties from each port, managed by its chief representatives there, and then divided this amount according to pre-agreed proportions between the local and central government. It then made the necessary remittances. The service was unimpeachable in its commitment to its bureaucratic aims, meaning that the corruption that had once been rife among officials undertaking these duties vanished. The Chinese saw the value of this, because they enjoyed a steady and substantial revenue stream that required no effort on their part (except to fund the modest running costs of the service itself). The initial purity of the mission was, eventually, to be compromised. This set in as a result of the massive indemnities which were exacted from the Qing after the Sino-Japanese War of 1894–95 and the Boxer Rebellion in 1900. Both of these were paid from the customs duties to the foreign powers, meaning that what the Chinese state received from tariffs and charged on trade (mostly with foreigners), it paid back to some of them. Finally, too, as the hold of Chinese nationalism deepened, the fact that an important branch of what should have been domestic government was overwhelmingly managed and run by foreigners became a major source of resentment and complaint, leading to its abolition in the middle of the twentieth century.

Hart was a contradictory figure. He had a strong personal Christian faith, and on the surface the austere demeanour and habits of a Victorian-era public official. But he also managed to father three children by his Chinese mistress Ayaou in the 1850s, and his diaries record moments of piercing self-criticism when he was afflicted by further bouts of sensual longing. 'I am a hard working, earnest man,' he wrote on 14 August 1864, 'delighting (after my necessary outside work is done) on remaining quietly in the house with my books, and simple indoor pleasures . . . But I am mad upon the pleasures of the couch. O Woman, lovely woman!' He completes this confession to his diary with the disarmingly direct and candid, 'I like to have a girl in the room with me, to fondle when I please . . . for I have a great stock of love in my nature.'[11]

Despite the unique situation he was in, seemingly caught between two bosses, Hart had a clear understanding of where his chief loyalties lay. 'I am on the Chinese side,' he stated at one point, 'and I will help them to the best of my ability.'[12] He was also very critical of the way in which Britain had behaved in China. Of the eventual aid given in crushing the Taiping (see previous chapter), he wrote in July 1865 that 'we think we have the right to the thanks of the Chinese for the assistance we have given them . . . but it must be remembered that in so far as we have aided them . . . we have done so because we thought it in our interests to do so.'[13] But nor was he blind to the significant challenges that the Qing itself faced, or to the impediments that the often reactionary mindset of its leaders placed in the way of addressing these. 'Other countries have been going ahead & China has been going back', he wrote in October the same year, though he followed this with an expression of optimism: 'If we can only get a fresh start out of the old dame, what may she not be among the nations.'[14]

Hart proved consummate in building up and then maintaining the trust of the Chinese, but also in ensuring that the British regarded him well enough to offer him the position of minister in China in 1885 (an offer, after some soul-searching, he turned down). His balancing act was probably the most remarkable and unparalleled feat of dextrous diplomacy in the whole sweep of British–Chinese relations. One of the key means by which he maintained the confidence of the British was by ensuring that, in the very practical matter of how the customs were run, he maintained the dominance of appointees originating from his home country. In 1889, of the 993 European administrative employees, 503 were British.[15] In this way, he offered a model for how it might be possible to bridge the two very different political and intellectual cultures he worked with, by apportioning sides of his personality and allegiance to each. As the differences between the two sides grew, the inherent tensions stretched to breaking point. This occurred in his own lifetime, meaning Hart was the first and last of his kind.

To promote the interests of the British government – and by proxy, those it was meant to be serving (which at the time meant mostly businesses, and latterly missionaries and other British who happened to come to China) – there was a specific Chinese consular service. In 1844, eight people – consuls and superintendent assistants – were selected and sent out to work in this newly established service.[16] Over the next five decades, it would grow to be the largest consular network that Britain had in the world. By 1854, entrants were being trained in the Chinese language at King's College London, the only institution then teaching Mandarin.[17] King's was to continue to be the main language-teaching centre for China-bound diplomats, accounting for half of all those sent out between 1888 and 1907.[18] Despite this, there were perpetual complaints at the time that, even after all the training, 'we hear that most consuls spoke Chinese poorly'.[19]

However well prepared they were in terms of language and historical knowledge, almost all those sent to work for the British state in the Qing found that they had harsh and isolating experiences awaiting them. For each consular official who succeeded (Thomas Wade and H.A. Giles come to mind, both of whom spent their time in the service in China acquiring language skills and knowledge which was then used in scholarly output, such as translations or books), there were many more who were less driven and fortunate, and for whom the main aim was merely to survive. Rutherford Alcock recorded in an article in 1855 that since the opening of the treaty ports a little over a decade before, eleven consular officials had died, nine at home on sick leave, and 'several of those remaining at their posts were in a precarious state of health'.[20] Things did not improve much in later years: it is a sobering fact that of the ninety entrants between 1897 and 1920, five committed suicide and a good number suffered either a nervous breakdown or some other serious physical ailment.[21] For all the romantic notions associated with the career by non-diplomats, it was a hard life. The case of one Mr Morgan, a consul who opened the Tianjin consulate in 1860, might be read as typical. He spent seventeen years there, interrupted by two spells of home leave totalling five years. In 1877, while back in Britain on sick leave, he was widowed. In spite of this, he was given a new assignment as the consul in Canton. Despite himself being retired, a former British minister to China, Rutherford Alcock, sought to persuade the Foreign Office not to proceed with this new appointment on the grounds, Alcock wrote, that 'Morgan had become insane ... [and] was threatening to return to China at once with a Belgian mistress'.[22] The new appointee was promptly retired and never took up his position. Sometimes it was the place where people were sent that seemed to be cursed. Changsha, opened in 1905, was particularly ill-fated: the first consul got consumption and died there; the second needed to leave, having suffered some form of prostration; and the third temporarily went out of his mind. None of this was helped by a nasty attack on foreigners in the city in April 1910.[23]

The role of consuls was about more than just providing a practical support network for British interests across the country as these expanded. Consular staff also introduced a different kind of mindset – one increasingly framed by scepticism about the great opportunities that the Chinese market offered, as they gained deeper lived experience in the country. For business groups, optimism was a necessary part of their trade: they had to believe that, with effort, China would be able to repay their huge investments in time and resources. But just as the Mitchell Report of 1852 had articulated an early sobering note of caution, so from the Treaty of Tianjin onwards British officials and merchants 'were with few exceptions on opposite sides of the fence regarding Anglo-Chinese relations'.[24] In this clash, the 'old China hands', as the long-term traders and businesspeople in the country liked to be called, were ranged against the developing China cadre in the Foreign Office. The former had even set up their own organisation, called the China Association, in London in 1889 to represent their interests and project more positive views back in Britain. The merchant Matheson voiced the usual complaint levelled against officials by business as far back as 1847, when he said that 'the British authorities instead of protecting their own subjects almost invariably take the side of the Chinese'.[25] Fair or not, this became a perennial complaint thereafter. Officials were seen as being too risk averse, too conciliatory towards Chinese demands, and too pessimistic about what financial outcomes might result if the country were to be pushed in the right direction. Lord Elgin in 1858 had expressed this scepticism well, saying to Shanghai traders that even after they had broken down the impediments to trade, they would probably find 'an ancient civilisation in many respects effete and imperfect', which 'while not without claims on our sympathy and respect' was not so much unwilling to fulfil the heady promises expected to flow from trade with it, as incapable of doing so.[26]

What the merchants wanted came to be called a 'forward policy' – a course of action by Britain that was pre-emptive, proactive, less hung up on risks and potential problems, and ready to aggressively shape China in the desired image, rather than passively accept the country for what it was. For officials, their fears about doing this were founded on what they knew of the vulnerability of the whole Chinese empire and their dread (to revert to a theme explored in the previous chapter) of ending up with a collapsed central government and a resultant set of new responsibilities that Britain had neither the political nor the economic capital to cope with.

On 13 July 1869, a debate took place in the British parliament about the need for a more aggressive policy towards China; but the motion was defeated. As was made clear by Rutherford Alcock, the soon-to-be-retiring minister in China at the time, pushing the country too hard could result in its break-up. London-based officials like Louis Mallet (1823–90) at the Board of Trade favoured a gradualist approach and crafted central policy on this basis. From their vantage point, they did not see any strong sign of economic returns from the market. When the Alcock Convention of 1869 was sent for ratification, it was seen as typifying the soft attitude of officials towards the Chinese, and was voted down because of opposition from British merchants. The convention was relatively uncontentious, proposing a small increase in the very low duties previously set on silk and opium; in return, the British would be granted tax concessions, rights to non-steam navigation on inland waterways, and temporary residence privileges within the country. It would also have allowed the Chinese to have representation in Hong Kong. The massacre of ten French nuns in Tianjin in 1870 provided sufficient reason for the convention to be ditched.

Alcock and Thomas Wade, who worked together in China in the mid nineteenth century, embodied the character of consuls. Born in 1809 (making him an exact contemporary of William Gladstone), Alcock was assessed by his biographer Alexander Michie, who knew him personally, to be a person 'stamped with the hall-mark of duty, of unfaltering devotion to the service of the nation and to the interests of humanity'.[27] Sent out as one of the first consuls after the Treaty of Nanjing in 1844, he was initially made head of the British consular post in Fuzhou in the southeast, before being promoted to the consulate in Shanghai two years later. It was there that he first engaged with the Taiping, before moving to Canton in 1855. From 1858 to 1864, he was posted to Japan, but returned to China as minister from 1865 to 1869. After this rich experience, Alcock had no illusions about the basis of British power in the country in which he spent so much of his life in government service. 'In one way or another, however we may disguise it,' he wrote, 'our position in China has been created by force, naked, physical force'.[28] His job was to navigate between the imperial authorities, locally based compatriots and his home government. In Michie's words relations between the parties consisted of a 'never-ceasing struggle, under veiled appearances of amity', during which 'the treaty extorted by force is generally sought to be eluded by cunning'.[29] Nor for that matter did he have any illusions about the non-Chinese he was often serving: 'The worthless character of a numerous gathering of foreigners under no effective control is a national reproach as well as a public calamity'. These figures 'dispute the field of commerce with [more honest] men, and convert privileges of access and trade into means of fraud or violence'. Unscrupulous traders were 'unchecked by any fear of their own government, protected by the privileges granted them by the treaties', inflicting suffering on both the Chinese and the more honest peers in their own trades.[30]

What was Britain to do in this situation? Referring to the 'magnitude of dangers with which our relations, both political and commercial' in China were menaced, the question was whether there 'are any means which Great Britain singly, as most largely interested, or the three treaty powers [US, France and Britain] in combination, can employ to avert the mischief and put an end to the danger'.[31] The priorities, according to Alcock, were to promote 'the prosperity and good government of the country'. This was not an altruistic aim, for by doing this, Britain might 'rescue our commerce from its perilous condition'.[32] Very similar iterations were to be deployed over 160 years later, when Britain's policy had the aim of helping China with its internal reform, in order to ensure that it was a better and more reliable geopolitical and economic partner. The main objective was for it to fit into a system that was already in place, and to which it would do well to conform. Britain could certainly dictate this much more assertively in 1855. The anomaly was that the residue of this policy, built on an attitude dating from an age when Britain was much more powerful and had many more options, could last so far beyond the time when its achievement was even remotely feasible.

Working beside Alcock was Thomas Wade, archetype of the scholar diplomat. Wade's China career had begun in 1842, when he had served as a soldier during the endgame of the Anglo-Chinese War. Interpreting jobs in the army, and then for the Supreme court in Hong Kong, led him to be appointed assistant to Sir John Davis, while chief plenipotentiary to China, and then, in 1853, consul in Shanghai. Later in the decade, he was assistant to Davis's successor Bowring, and then to Lord Elgin in the military campaign. This led to service in Beijing and appointment to the top position of representing Britain from 1871 to 1875. After this, Wade returned to his home country and, in 1888, was elected the first professor of Chinese at the University of Cambridge. His four decades in China had given him immense facility in both Mandarin and Cantonese, and a broad and deep understanding of the culture, politics and society of the place. But for some, he was regarded as being too scholarly to be a statesman, even though he was 'beloved for his Irish geniality, open-mindedness and sincerity'.[33] Even as a scholar, he had the poor luck to take up his academic post when he was already elderly and had more or less retired from active scholarly endeavours. His time in Cambridge was largely bereft of any output and served more as a symbolic appointment and a declaration of intent by the university to do more about the teaching and understanding of China, rather than to achieve anything specific.

Opening up China: Finance and railways

Merchants were inevitably among the most important and influential players. While motivated by commercial gain and trade for themselves, their shareholders and partnerships, achieving that involved not just a supportive government network, but also the introduction of modern finance, infrastructure and trading standards into China. The foundation of the Hong Kong and Shanghai Banking Corporation (HSBC) in 1864 was a major landmark on this road. Initially, it had paid-up capital of 2.5 million US dollars, and was designed to act as the local bank for Hong Kong, the treaty ports and Japan. It was also granted the right to issue bank notes.[34] Over time, HSBC would become the British government bank, acting as a key instrument for policy. It illustrated well how the British were just as capable as anyone else of allowing a corporate face to sit on what was very often a government-run body, at least in the early era of its existence (today it exists as a wholly private enterprise).

HSBC quickly expanded internationally, opening branches in San Francisco in 1875, Singapore in 1877, New York in 1880, Lyons in 1881 and Nagasaki in 1891.[35] It operated as a kind of finance-sector equivalent of the consular service, but with even stricter rules on the personal lives of its employees: it expected its staff to put in ten years at the bank before they could marry.[36] Such strictures were less on the mind of one of its most illustrious workers in the early 1900s than the meagre initial recompense it gave in terms of wages. Speaking in 1954, the great P.G. Wodehouse (1881–1975) complained of how dismayed he was on his first morning with the company at its London offices to realise that with his starting wage 'all I would be able to afford in the way of lunch was a roll and butter and cup of coffee: I had come straight from a school where lunch was a solid meal'.[37] Wodehouse was to enjoy a brief and (by his own admission) undistinguished career as a banker, first in London and then in Hong Kong; but he immortalised the company under the name of the New Asiatic

Bank in his 1910 novel *Psmith in the City*. While initially an exchange bank, HSBC had become, by the turn of the century, a commercial and merchant one. Undertaking these functions, it exercised great political influence, even while its leaders declared their apolitical stance on most matters. Its main benefit for the British government was the high rate of return it delivered, largely focusing on modern finance, as that sector became increasingly specialised and technical.

There were other companies that developed over this era and that dealt with the more prosaic issues of making and carrying things. Swire, founded in Liverpool in 1816 by John Swire (1787–1847) as a shipping enterprise, started its China interests in 1861, first through agents and then opening an office of its own in Shanghai in 1866 and in Hong Kong four years later. Swire was to compete in earnest with Jardine Matheson, which had by then diversified away from import and export trade into manufacturing, logistics and finance. Swire opened the Taikoo Sugar Refinery, an enterprise which, through the services of a young German chemist called Dr Ferdinand Korn, was meant to educate the Chinese, in the words of the company in 1884, 'into preferring clean to dirty sugar'. It also acquired ownership in 1873 of the Union Steamship Company.[38] Swire was, according to Robert Bickers in a modern history, motivated by objectives which 'were in themselves never anything but rational, but which were undertaken for reasons that had more to do with pride' and 'the penchant for glory and not for £ and d'.[39] In this way, it stood for a set of principles and values which it believed were global and transferable, and which could be used to shape and have impact on the wider world, showing that for some British, business was about far more than business itself.

The location of much of this commercial activity was in the treaty ports. Here a specific way of life developed for the British (and eventually other foreigners). They were places of intrinsic hybridity, with their concessions and settlements full of different types of people transacting different kinds of business, all united by their desire to live in parallel with – but not among – the Chinese. Up to the Chefoo Convention of 1876, only the British government was able to rent from the Chinese state and then sublet to its own nationals. The 1876 convention had arisen because of the aforementioned Margary Affair, when a British official was murdered in China. Beyond extracting a formal apology from the Qing for this, the convention also ensured that there were permanent Chinese government representatives in Britain and stronger legal rights for the British in China. It also allowed individuals to rent direct from Chinese landowners, rather than through the government; the establishment of a new port at Chongqing; and revised taxes on opium. After a fashion, it also eradicated some of the effects of a dreaded and deeply unpopular local tax called the *liqin*: literally meaning 'one in a thousand', this was the bane of importers, since it allowed customs charges to be levied not just at the port of entry for goods, but also inland as they were transported onwards. Local officials often either deliberately or unwittingly ignored the central edict that foreign goods needed to pay only one set of duties – at the point of entry – and endeavoured to extract yet more charges. Despite the changes in 1876, this issue was to rumble on, never being fully satisfactorily resolved. Treaty ports were deeply contradictory places. As historian Frances Wood has argued, they were meant to exemplify and advertise the principles of free trade on which they had been founded; but more often than not, they served as holdouts for the assertion of special rights, extraterritorial privileges and the prioritisation of British and foreign interests over Chinese ones.[40] They were at the 'vanguard of foreign penetration' designed to open up the whole country, and seldom fully considered China's interests in this mission.

In the expanding city of Shanghai, perhaps the greatest of these treaty ports was being constructed. Hong Kong was, of course, increasingly significant, but as a wholly controlled British colony it operated under a completely different set-up – not least because it fell under the management of the Colonial Office in London, and its administrators came through a different career route. But Shanghai remained a bona fide Chinese city, one mostly under Chinese rule. Long before it matured, Robert Fortune had noticed its potential in the early 1840s, when, he wrote, it had 'large native trade, the convenience of inland transit by means of rivers and canals; the fact that the teas and silks can be brought here more readily than to Canton'. He went on that he saw 'this place as an immense mart for our cotton manufactures' and that 'in a few years it will not only rival Canton, but become a place of far greater importance'.[41]

Shanghai did indeed move to the centre stage as a basis for commerce and trade, just as he foresaw. The city largely achieved this through being physically remodelled around the work and the needs of the foreign community coming to live there. But despite its future greatness, in the early years visitors were underwhelmed by some aspects of the urban landscape. 'The city is ugly and unattractive,' complained A.B. Freeman-Mitford when visiting in 1865, 'the river dingy and the country a dead level plain.'[42] But over the coming four decades, the area beside the Huangpu and Suzhou rivers – 'little more than a muddy towpath in the 1840s' – was turned into an attractive esplanade through land reclamation. This became the Bund, a series of buildings which included the iconic headquarters of the Hong Kong and Shanghai Bank, and the city customs, and which still stands today as among the world's great historic waterfront monuments.[43] They were described by William Ferdinand Tyler in the 1900s, while he was working as acting harbour master in the city's port, as a 'river front of which we [i.e. the British] were so proud ... I know of no other river port possessed of such a charming footage and I watched it with a sense of satisfactory authority.'[44] This illustrated how the shaping of the urban landscape in their host country gave the British not just a sense of commercial returns, but a far deeper feeling of belonging and connection with the country.

HSBC and other British companies were inevitably interested in the opportunities to develop and fund technologies that could be exported from the outside world into China. Of these, railways were among the most promising. The genesis of the great project of laying locomotive lines across the vast and complex geography of the country, however, was rocky. The first railway ever to be constructed in the country was near the walls of Beijing. This was a 600 metre narrow-gauge track funded by a British merchant in 1865. It was promptly dismantled almost as soon as it had been laid, by order of the central government, which said it served no purpose and was dangerous to local people living near the tracks, who risked being run over by the relatively fast new locomotives. A similar fate awaited the next attempt, this time in Shanghai in 1876 and funded by Jardine. It, too, lacked the approval of the Qing court; to make things even worse, a local Chinese was run over and killed by a train operating on the track almost as soon as it opened, fulfilling the pessimistic predictions made earlier. It was dismantled a year later. British engineer Claude William Kinder had better luck when he laid a 10 kilometre track in Hebei province in the north of the country in 1881. Made to transport coal, it was extended over the coming decade.

Despite these early ventures, in 1894 China had a mere 312 kilometres of railway. By 1903, this had at least grown to 4,300 kilometres, and had doubled again by 1914. This was a sector where anticipation and expectation ran ahead of actual delivery: from 1895 to 1898, there were agreed concessions for twenty railway projects, but two decades later only half had been built.[45] Despite holding to their habitual scepticism about whether the Chinese market would deliver even a little of the huge promise imputed to it by excitable business-people, the British government recognised early on that there was a bigger picture, and that railways and railway technology were a key area for potential foreign influence. 'Railway concessions in foreign hands [other than Britain's] could threaten British trade in its many centres', comments one study.[46] The fact that Germany and France were starting to edge into the picture by the 1890s was a major cause for concern. By this stage, the scramble for concessions and other interests in China by foreign powers had started in earnest, with Britain's core interest concentrated in the Yangtze valley, where most of its commercial entities were. The plan for a Beijing–Guangdong railway, which was mooted at this time, was something that Britain insisted on being a part of, despite Germany's opposition and its active promotion of its own involvement.[47]

In May 1898, Jardine also negotiated a preliminary agreement for a Shanghai–Nanjing rail line – something that received the support of the British government, which regarded this as serving broader national interests than simply the commercial gains that would accrue to a single company. This line had an Anglo-Chinese board and a British engineer-in-chief. But Britain suffered a major setback in the 1900s, when, after much lobbying, the Beijing–Hangzhou line was awarded to a Belgian management team with French money. Things improved after the signing of the Entente Cordiale in 1904 between France and Britain, which saw more co-operation between the two nations on the financing and building of railways. Thereafter, international co-operation became the norm, rather than the exception. In 1909–10, the first China consortium embracing British, French, German and American banks was set up to identify and then explore rail opportunities. This sector was not one that enjoyed unalloyed support and appreciation. There were strong critics of the way railways had been developed, with future viceroy of India, Lord George Curzon (1859–1925) in 1896 stating sharply that 'the introduction of these . . . has been a corrupting operation, not undertaken of free will or inclination, but forced from the outside'.[48] Modernising China's transport system was not a negative aim in itself: the questions were about the way it was being done and who, in the end, made the greatest commercial gain.

The role of missionaries

To add to the consuls and the merchants batting for Britain in China, missionaries increasingly began to appear as actors. Their early influence was attested by the career of the great sinologist and Protestant missionary Robert Morrison from the 1810s (see chapter three). But China remained a harsh terrain for those seeking to spread the Gospel and save Chinese souls, with meagre returns for so much effort for most of the nineteenth century. The French had taken the lead in much of the proselytising activity, largely through an agreement in the Treaty of Beijing that opened up the whole of the country and allowed freedom of movement by missionaries from 1860. They had used this to position themselves as champions of the Catholic cause. For Britain, promotion of Protestant variants of the faith took priority. British missionary activity spread slowly, but steadily. By the late 1880s, there were 1,296 Protestants working in the country, about 55 per cent of whom were British. This figure doubled over the next decade, reaching 2,818 by 1900 – again, half of them British.[49]

Missionaries and their work were often regarded with at best ambiguity, and at worst distaste by many of the other key British players working on and with China. Rutherford Alcock believed that the right of Christian groups to own land and build in China served to antagonise locals and was a major cause of tension between the Qing and foreign powers.[50] The China Inland Mission was, according to one account, 'particularly aggressive in its assaults on the pagan customs of the Chinese'.[51] It was, despite this, the largest group active in the country. The Church Missionary Society, affiliated to the Church of England, took a softer line and ranked second in terms of size. The other player was the London Missionary Society, a more evangelical and congregationalist entity.

The zealousness of some of the missionaries, and the precarious-ness of the position they put themselves in, meant that tragic outcomes at some point were almost inevitable. The Chinese view of religion, or, for many commentators, their lack of a specific faith, was long a source of fascinated and often highly prejudiced commentary by British observers. George Lay in 1841 described Chinese beliefs as 'nothing more than congeries of canonised fables'.[52] In 1843, Alexander Murray, an officer who had served in the British forces in China during the First Anglo-Chinese War, categorically declared that the Chinese 'were devoid of any religious feeling'.[53] Naval officer Sherard Osborn, who served in the Second Anglo-Chinese War two decades later, echoed this, commenting on how the Chinese were indifferent to religion and 'completely absorbed in temporal interests', by which he probably meant trading and making money.[54] More sophisticated commentary did attempt to describe the different belief systems that the Chinese held and to engage with the complexity and variety of what could broadly be called their world view. But for those who adhered to a high Victorian commitment to a monotheistic spirituality, China seemed a ripe target for spiritual intervention and guidance.

Despite this, religious groups did sometimes serve some more positive purpose, by injecting a degree of moral concern into aspects of British relations with China. They had been instrumental in the setting up of the Society for the Suppression of the Opium Trade in 1874 and were also involved in the arguments about the export from China of indentured labour, the infamous 'coolie' trade, which had increased once restrictions on the Chinese side were removed in the 1860s. A report issued in Shanghai in 1876 that focused on the transport of Chinese labour to Cuba exposed the misery and exploitation that arose from this particularly unpleasant business, something that came close to being a modern form of slavery. 'During the past year,' the report's authors stated, 'a large number [of Chinese] have been killed by blows, have died from the effects of wounds, and have hanged themselves, cut their throats, poisoned themselves with opium, and thrown themselves into wells and sugar cauldrons.'[55]

For all their good intentions, the missionaries when in-country often – through inadequate preparation – placed themselves in great jeopardy, fired by a zeal which made them heedless of the suspicion and uneasiness that their work engendered among local Chinese.

The outbreaks of violence against some of their number in 1895 showed where things could go badly wrong. Rioters attacked missionaries in Sichuan, due to their conviction that tinned meats brought to the area by the foreigners were the boiled remains of children. Thankfully no lives were lost. But the Stewart family, working for the Church Missionary Society in Fujian, were not so lucky. A local secret society targeted them, murdering the mother and one of her daughters. In a neighbouring house, five other ladies were slashed to death. The British minister in China at the time, Sir Nicholas O'Conor (1843–1908), demanded the punishment of the local official responsible for the area. While the Chinese government did respond, the broader issue of the tensions provoked by missionary groups and the activities they engaged in was one of the main contributory factors in the Boxer Rebellion a few years later (see next chapter).

However terrible this and other similar events were, the British official position towards missionary activity remained sceptical. Many people believed that Christian groups, however laudable their aims, were jeopardising British commercial interests, which they regarded as far more important. The ways in which consuls ended up needing to act as referees (alluded to earlier) is particularly germane here. British officials had to find a balance between the competing demands of hardnosed businesspeople, who believed they were always caving in to the Chinese on economic and political matters, and missionaries, who, for very different reasons, believed they had to promote a set of values among the Chinese that was not about material gain, but belonged to the realm of the spirit. The officials were caught between the proverbial rock and a hard place, and more often than not ended up irritating everyone, including the Chinese.

For all of these problems, there were missionaries who made an exceptional contribution to Anglo-Chinese understanding. James Legge (1815–97) was an example of this. Born near Aberdeen in Scotland, he was almost crushed to death at a political rally at the age of sixteen. After studying Chinese with fellow missionary Samuel

Kidd in 1838, he was ordained in 1839, and assigned by the London Missionary Society to the Anglo-Chinese College at Malacca in 1840. Within a short time he was made director of the institute. He arrived in Hong Kong in 1843, re-establishing the college as a missionary station there after its move from its original base. During a return visit to Britain for health reasons, he met Queen Victoria on 9 February 1848 at Buckingham Palace, accompanied by three Chinese converts to Christianity. The sovereign apparently asked many questions about China and the Chinese (displaying a more intelligent engagement than her naming her Pekingese dog Looty may have suggested – see the previous chapter).

Legge's life work was his rendition of the great corpus of classical Chinese philosophy and other literature into English. Many of these works are still available in the editions he produced. His first, a translation of the Confucian *Four Books*, was funded by Jardine. His achievement was based on formidable linguistic knowledge; but it was also deeply collaborative, for while the translations were directed by him, he received huge assistance from Chinese fellow scholars. From 1861, he published the first formal volumes of the Chinese classics, issuing in the end the first full editions of the ancient works of Mencius, the *Dao De Jing* of Laozi, and the *Book of Changes*. Legge offers a study in how someone from one culture with its set of core beliefs and convictions was able to slowly move to a position of deeper sympathy with and understanding of another very different one. He was originally unable to regard Confucius as a great man; but according to his modern biographer, 'the rest of [his] long career represents a struggle to amend the severity of his initial understanding'.[56] As a missionary, he clearly failed, as he had very few converts. And of even the three whom he had introduced to Queen Victoria, far from following a holy vocation, two went into business and the other ended up as a criminal.[57] Even when he returned to Britain in 1876 to be installed as the first professor of Chinese at Oxford, his pedagogical attainments were questionable. He had, it seems, not a single student in his time there.[58] Despite this, he – more than any other figure – created for English speakers the possibility of some level of access and engagement with Chinese classical literature and thinking. This started the process of making the Chinese historical views of the world contained in the copious literature of the country accessible to a far wider foreign audience.

Chinese in Britain: The first embassies

One of the anomalies of the Anglo-Chinese story up to the 1870s was the almost complete lack of official direct exposure of Chinese to their British counterparts in their home country. Despite gaining the right under the Treaty of Beijing (1860) to send someone, for several years the Qing court refrained from sending a mission to Britain to remedy this situation. This meant that the British continued to travel to, live in, work in and learn about China, occupying its physical space, while hardly any traffic occurred the other way. Robert Hart was the initial inspiration behind the earliest idea of a delegation to London in 1866, when he took three Chinese mandarins with him, led by an elderly Manchu official, Pin Chun. While in London, the group was 'much impressed by English cleanliness, although they commented also on the dinginess of the city'.[59] This restored some balance to the endless accounts by the British over the previous decades of precisely that feature of Chinese cities. The delegation also had to go through the trauma of seeing material looted from the Summer Palace and now on display in the British Museum. Like Legge's Christian converts, they had the chance to meet Queen Victoria.

A more permanent embassy was established a decade later, after the arrival in early 1877 of Guo Songtao (1818–91), accompanied by Liu Xihong as his deputy. Guo had originally planned to bring both of his wives with him to London, but in the end was persuaded by Halliday Macartney (1833–1906), the secretary provided by the

British for him, to bring only one.[60] *Punch* magazine was to lambast his wife as the 'Tottering Lily of Fascination'. Their accommodation was in Portland Place, where the Chinese embassy remains to this day. Guo's first impressions of his temporary home were positive: 'The liveliness of the commercial centres and the beauty of the mansions and houses could scarcely be excelled', he wrote of a journey from Woking to London on 21 January 1877. On his meeting with Queen Victoria on 6 February 1877, he wrote that 'the sovereign, dressed in a black robe with a veil made of white cotton cloth on which there were flowery designs, stood there in the middle, facing the door'. Her face, he noted, 'was plump but dignified'. As for the message she had for her guests, that was the same sort of almost meaningless formal polite-ness that – as the British had so often complained – typified state-ments that came from the mouths of Chinese emperors: 'Your Excellencies have come from far away to establish good relations with us. From now on, let us live in peace and harmony together for ever.'[61] Guo had the less pleasant duty of explaining what the Chinese govern-ment had done in response to the Margary incident, which had occurred the year before in China (see above).

Guo departed in 1878 and was replaced by the Marquis Zeng Jize (1839–90), whose stay at the Portland Place legation was to last for over a decade. According to one contemporary account, he was 'of an affable yet firm temperament, well-informed on European affairs, conservative, yet liberal [and] trusted by his own government and received with every courtesy by the government to which he was sent'.[62] Perhaps extrapolating from the circumstances of his home country, where the true power no longer resided with the Guangxu emperor (1871–r1875–1908), but increasingly with the formidable empress dowager behind him, Zeng quickly worked out the dynamics of power in the place in which he served: 'England', he wrote, 'is nomin-ally governed by a Queen and parliament, but the Queen has no other power than the mere empty one of signing state papers and parlia-ment spends its time on empty talk.' The real power 'was in the hands of the Prime Minister'.[63] Of this illustrious group, Zeng was impressed by the incumbent for part of the time he was ambassador in Britain, Benjamin Disraeli (1804–81), whom he found to be 'a man of few words though of a kindly disposition and noble bearing'.[64] Such sentiments would have struck Disraeli's great contemporary nemesis Gladstone as being very wide of the mark.

The Chinese delegation was able to promote some of the Qing's interests directly to people in Britain, particularly leaders, without the need for intermediaries. From the end of the nineteenth century, there were also more signs of people from China moving to and working in Britain. Twelve Chinese students from the Fuzhou Academy attended the Royal Naval College in Greenwich in 1877, one of whom (Yan Fu) went on to translate the works of Adam Smith and J.S. Mill into Chinese. Another native of China with the family name Lu attended lectures at King's College London on political economy a couple of years later.[65] But most portentous of all was the opening of the earliest recorded restaurant selling Chinese food in Britain – a coffee shop in London, set up in 1886 by Zhang Quan and Zhang Shou, previously cooks on ships of the Blue Funnel Line. There they sold chop-suey, a dish originating from Chinese in the US and consisting of meat, egg and vegetables stir-fried in a savoury sauce.[66] This was a brave venture, for the earliest British encounters with Chinese food had sometimes been inauspicious, and there was little sign that this novel new food would appeal to British palates. Aeneas Anderson, accompanying the Macartney embassy, was among the earliest to complain (something we learned in chapter three he did a lot of), moaning of how the Chinese 'not only eat all animal food without distinction, but do not discard even such as die of diseases'.[67] Samuel Holmes, a companion on the same tour, had found not the state of the meat, but the style of cooking vegetables unsettling, 'hashed up in such a medley confusion, that we scarcely knew at times what we were eating'.[68] And yet a little over a century later, it was to be Chinese food more than anything else that promoted awareness and understanding among the British public of China as a place, and of how it was different from Britain in fundamental respects, and had interesting and attractive things to offer.

A less salubrious image was gained through representations of opium smoking. The legalisation of trading in this drug by the Chinese government in 1858 created domestic sources of supply (rather than Indian imports). This meant that by the late 1870s, there was a consistent decline in the trade until it was finally outlawed in the early twentieth century. That opium addicts, and then opium addiction, had started to figure in the domestic space of Britain was significant, because it brought the problem closer to home and offered stark refutation of the claims by some earlier on about the medicinal benefits of the drug.[69] The writer Thomas De Quincey's *Confessions of an English Opium Eater* from 1821 had been an early account of the toll that addiction took. Much later, in the short story 'The Man with the Twisted Lip' (1891), Arthur Conan Doyle's great creation Sherlock Holmes dealt with a case where the protagonist, ostensibly respectable, needed to beg in secret, in order to fund his habit. Perhaps most famously of all, Charles Dickens' final, unfinished novel *The Mystery of Edwin Drood* (1870) contained vivid descriptions of the inside of an opium den. His observations were based on a visit he and Joseph Charles Parkinson had made to a den in the centre of London, at Bluegate Fields, site of a Victorian slum in the northern part of the dock area. The Lazarus mentioned by Parkinson in a short article he wrote about the same visit was 'one of the poor wretched Chinamen, who shiver and cower and whine on our street corners, and are mean, and dirty, and squalid and contemptible, even beyond beggars generally'.[70] There seemed to be more here than simply a response to someone who was an addict, though the full force of sinophobia had to wait until the next century to show itself.

China was not only more visible in Britain, but the country itself was also becoming more accessible to travellers. The great Isabella Bird, penname of Isabella Lucy Bishop (1831–1904), a Victorian travel writer who had trekked extensively across much of Asia, wrote about her journey through the Yangtze valley in the late 1890s. Bird's was an even-minded, thoughtful voice, even though she had clear commitments to Christian activism. Despite at one point on her travels being attacked by local Chinese fearful of the foreign visitors and their intentions, Bird had time to reflect as she made her way around the country – sometimes on foot, sometimes by junk and occasionally by palanquin – on the complexity of what she was witnessing. She tried to balance the China 'with its crowds, its poverty, its risks of absolute famine from drought or floods, its untellable and pitiless greed, and its political and religious hopelessness' against the 'certain lovableness of its people' and the better aspects of the great country she was experiencing.[71]

Bird was in a China that had been, for almost four decades, open to and increasingly influenced by Britain. British traders, consular officials and merchants, missionaries and travellers like herself were the most numerous of all the Western Europeans. Some of them were able to continue the exploratory work of the new natural terrain of the country begun by pathbreakers decades before. These included figures like the botanist Augustine Henry who, following in Robert Fortune's footsteps, sent back to Britain 158,000 specimens of plants in 1881. The five hundred new species and twenty-five novel genera contained in these consignments brought about a complete reordering of knowledge about aspects of the natural world.[72] This was indeed an era when technologically, economically and politically Britain was still pre-eminent, and when many of its citizens had a thirst for knowledge about all aspects of the wider world. And yet the morality of some of the things that Britain had done in that period of intense influence clearly troubled someone like Bird, despite the fresh knowledge and new perspectives that were coming from her direct encounter with this new place. 'It is', she wrote, 'surely the height of unchristian selfishness to sit down contentedly among our own good things and practically to regard China merely as an area for trade.'[73]

As for the behaviour of the British government, too, 'by bullying the Central Government, it is made to "lose face" with its subjects and its authority is so much weakened'. That was, in her view, self-defeating, because ultimately 'the value of [British] treaties absolutely depends on the power of the [local] Government to give effect to them'.[74] These were valid points, made powerfully in a book that was dedicated to the then prime minister, Lord Salisbury. He was a proponent of the 'open door' approach to China – but alas, a mixture of Chinese domestic issues, which resulted in an eruption of very early nationalist aggression towards foreigners, and the political situation between Britain and those competing with it for greater trade benefits and political control, resulted in an explosion of violence in 1900 that launched the most exploitative and unhappy decades of China's modern history.

7

The Start of British Retreat, 1900-25

The journalist John Otway Percy Bland (1863–1945), a long-term resident of China who initially worked in the Chinese Imperial Maritime Customs Service, was enjoying the kind of life an expat could live in the first decade of the new century. Things were good. Meandering in a houseboat with a few friends along the waterways of the country, free to go wherever they pleased, the group had their minds set on that quintessentially Victorian British pastime of game shooting. 'In all the East,' declared Bland,

> few places I know afford so great a variety of small game as the lower Yangtsze ... For all round sport, combined with pleasant condition, the country which runs from Wuhu on the great river to the upper reaches of the Chientang in Chekiang [Zhejiang] offers an unequalled field to the sportsman who takes an intelligent interest in his bag.[1]

Bland's tone throughout his book is one of great familiarity with the landscape he was in. A place once written about as so different, full of features and flowers and buildings that were striking because they were so unlike anything British visitors had seen before, became in his work something that was almost domesticated, with nothing that might unsettle or startle. This was indeed a sign that for many British, China had become a second home, a place where they could feel in control and free of anxiety. The great 'other' of a century before had become almost humdrum and boring.

Did Bland have reason to adopt such a relaxed, almost nonchalant attitude as he holidayed around the country? Only a few years before, China had been torn by a brief uprising – the Boxers, as they were somewhat confusingly called, a local group first mentioned as early as 1727.[2] This sect was to emerge during the chaotic decade at the end of the nineteenth century, when a number of different causes all came together – increased foreign aggression and involvement in Chinese affairs; deepening crisis at the central court brought about by the Guangxu emperor's brief attempt to promote internal reforms in 1898; and the rise of Chinese nationalism. The Boxer Rebellion itself – particularly the attack on the British and other foreign legations in Beijing over the summer of 1900 – was part of a process that ran into the following years, through the collapse of the Qing in 1911–12 and through the long era of fragmentation and conflict before the communists came to power in 1949. This era was a key one, because for Britain it was marked by evidence both of its waning powers in China and of the ways in which dealing with the country was to increasingly involve co-operation with not just the Chinese, but also other international allies.

From the 1880s, the brute fact was that China became more crowded as far as foreigners were concerned. There were two significant new players, both of whom were to prove, for very different reasons, deeply problematic to British interests. The first was Japan. A country coaxed out of over two centuries of isolation by the visit of the fleet of ships under Commodore Matthew Perry of the US in 1853, it then underwent its own intensive modernisation during the Meiji Restoration of the 1860s. Japan proved itself a quick and eager student, adopting many of the industrial processes of Europe and

America, and building an effective, modernised military that was able to defeat China in 1895, exacting substantial reparations and extracting extensive concessions in the northwest of the country, codified in the Treaty of Shimonoseki of that year. The main impact of the war was to cede the special tributary influence that China had over the Korean Peninsula to Japan, which proceeded to govern Korea as a colony until the end of the Second World War. The island of Taiwan was also ceded. The Europeans and Japanese were not only therefore encroaching on China's domestic space, but shaping the regional environment in which it was located.

Britain had few grounds for complaint: it was, after all, a pioneer in this sort of colonisation. The gradual annexation of Burma from the 1820s up to the Anglo-Burmese wars of 1885–86 – which resulted in a large, unified and mostly British-run entity, with a boundary shared with China and agreed by convention in 1894 – serves as a good example. The French, too, were busily constructing their own Asian empire in Indo-China, with control of what is today's Vietnam, Thailand and Cambodia. All of these had historically been key areas of imperial Chinese interest, and their removal to another sphere of control continued to demonstrate the erosion of Qing power over its own affairs and those of countries over which it had once held great sway. In this context, Japan's annexation of Korea was not a novelty, but more like the new norm.

The scramble for China saw the unseemly carving up not just of peripheral space around its borders, but of the domestic terrain of the country, causing it eventually to be split into de facto spheres of influence. Russia was a fairly predictable name appearing among the chief agents of this process, because of its vast northern border with the Qing and its clear interests in having commercial and political relations with a neighbouring power, as well as deeper control over and within it. But Germany was less expected. This was a nation which, under Chancellor Otto von Bismarck (1815–98), had initially reined in its colonial interests in China (if not elsewhere); but it then appeared as a major intervener once the Sino-Japanese War had shown just how vulnerable the country was. The British views of this German involvement were negative and critical to begin with. Lord Charles Beresford (1846–1919), an admiral in the British navy, toured China in 1898 and produced a short report. His fears were about 'Britain's good name' not being helped 'by forcing concessions from China when she is prostrated by involuntary powers stronger than herself'.[3] The maintenance of a stable, unified Chinese empire 'is essential to the honour as well as the interests of the Anglo-Saxon race', he declared. Beresford was right in his prognosis of the undesirability of this outcome; but he made little recognition of the major role that Britain had played in its genesis.[4]

'Have we a policy in China?', a writer going under the pseudonym of Diplomaticus rhetorically asked more directly in 1900, observing the changes and contortions of Britain's evolving position. This was hardly the first time the question had been asked, and nor would it be the last. The author recognised, in ways Beresford did not, that 'our present troubles in the Far East . . . are the direct result of an infirm and erratic opportunism, which is being made to [stand in] for policy'.[5] But now that China was being carved up, and the government there increasingly dysfunctional, there had to be major question marks over the wisdom and sustainability of Britain's approach: 'What is our policy today? All our former schemes have broken down. We have no clear idea of how to act in the future.'[6] The issue now was that there was no policy: just a series of different demands by different people often pulling in contrary directions.

As colonial administrator Archibald Colquhoun (1848–1914) argued in 1898, 'We have entered into an era of competition, fierce competition.'[7] The monopoly Britain once enjoyed, and thanks to which it had gained most of its advantages in China, was coming to an end. The policy response to this became one of compromise and flexible opportunism. When Germany forced the central government to lease Kiaochow (Jiaozhou) on the northeast coast in 1898 and then weeks later Russia obtained Port Arthur, that prompted the British to extract their own prize – the ninety-nine-year lease for the New Territories in Hong Kong, a large area to the north of the already conceded Kowloon and Hong Kong Island, and the port of Weihaiwei in Shandong.

The former had its utility, as it expanded hugely the area of the increasingly important colony (although it was this lease that was to come back to bite the British decades later, as the term ran out). But Weihaiwei was much more of a vanity project, with symbolic prestige, but no real, practical utility. This was a place that, according to one assessment, was at 'a pre-industrial level of development'.[8] Even the question of who should administer it once it was in British hands caused argument: the admiralty initially had control; but it then transferred that to the army and finally, in January 1901, to the Colonial Office. For the next twenty years, it was under one official, James Stewart Lockhart.[9] From the word go, Weihaiwei was a side issue that barely merited any British interest. Even the Germans felt it was a strange endeavour: the kaiser acidly commented that it marked 'a departure from the practical common sense with which Englishmen were usually credited'.[10] Its lease had originally been on the understanding that once Russia returned Port Arthur to the Chinese, Britain would do the same. But even when the 1905 defeat of Russia by the Japanese caused the former to transfer many of its China interests, including the port, to its conquerors, the British blithely reneged on their word and continued with their own concession. In the future, Weihaiwei would be of some sporadic use: by April 1916 it had provided 40,000 locals to serve in the First World War in Europe in various capacities (all working behind the lines in support functions, and none involved in direct fighting).[11] The colony was returned to the Chinese in 1930, its final administrator being Reginald Johnston (1874–1938), the man who, after the fall of the Qing, had been tutor to Puyi (1906–67), the last emperor.

Russia's encroachment on China was, for some in Great Britain, a serious issue that required a muscular and firm response. Colquhoun, writing in 1898, made it clear that this sort of domination by China's great northern neighbour had wider knock-on effects, and 'would seriously affect our future position in India, and even create a grave danger'.[12] This was the era when the Great Game was emerging. Britain had to play an elaborate kind of diplomatic chess, moving personnel and military around the world to preserve its extensive interests. That all needed 'diplomacy [that] must be supported by force'.[13] In Britain, fear of Russia extended far beyond what that country was doing in south and northeast Asia. There were plenty of domestic politicians, among them the ardent imperialist Joseph Chamberlain (1836–1914), secretary of state for the colonies from 1895 to 1903, who filed a litany of complaints about Moscow's competing aims in Eastern Europe, Central Asia and even as far afield as Africa, and who urged tougher responses. Despite this, the prime minister at the time, the marquis of Salisbury (1830–1903), took a more pragmatic view, agreeing in 1899 to an Anglo-Russian agreement that committed the two powers to attempting to co-exist amicably in the Far East.

The rise of Chinese nationalism and the Boxers

It bears restating that China was not a static, passive sufferer while this fight continued over who possessed what within it. Far from it. Foreign incursions had shaped and changed the country's domestic politics profoundly. These influences manifested themselves intellectually as well as physically. Ideas about national autonomy and self-determination had entered China through interaction with foreigners. Much of this was through books being translated by those now learning European languages, or via the intermediation of Japan. This latter was the route by which Marx's writings first made their way into Chinese. All of this created complex outcomes. The so-called Hundred Days' Reform movement in 1898 was one such involving a modest set of proposals put forward by key intellectuals of the late Qing, like Kang Youwei (1858–1927) and Liang Qichao (1873–1929), demanding

modernisation of Chinese industry, military, governance and education. The proposals included scrapping the ancient exam system for
officials, which even at that stage was still heavily dependent on knowledge of ancient Confucian texts. The Guangxu emperor supported the
reformers, and for 103 days their ideas seemed to be having traction.
But in a brutally effective countermove, Empress Dowager Cixi and
the conservatives surrounding her struck back. Kang fled south, eventually ending up in Hong Kong, where he received British protection.

While there, he met Lord Beresford on his tour of China, telling
him that 'the great object of the reform party had been to introduce
western ideas' and that if China failed to do this, then 'she would
crumble to pieces'. In Kang's eyes, Britain was not a wholly malevolent
force. It did have a potentially positive role. What differentiated it from
the other great powers was that its links with China were the most
extensive and among the longest. That meant 'it was in [Britain's own]
interests to help China'.[14] Kang at least survived to carry on his agitation work outside the country. Some of his fellow reformers had worse
luck, with a few being executed and others spending lengthy spells in
prison. The main political victim was the emperor himself, reduced to
a wholly symbolic figure, who was detained as a house prisoner by Cixi
until the end of his life. He died somewhat suspiciously a decade later,
only a few days before Cixi's own demise, a tragic and poignant figure.

The attempt at reform may have failed, but discontent and anger
domestically at the incompetence of the government and its inability
to protect the country from the greedy demands of outsiders did not
dissipate. The nationalist sentiment that emanated from this disgruntlement partially fired the Boxer Rebellion of 1900. The movement
originated with a group of activists in the northern rural areas of the
Qing who, reportedly, practised boxing exercises as a means of self-
cultivation (hence their name). A combination of famines, local and
national government incompetence, and then rising awareness of
foreign exploitation, caused the protest to spread. While the majority
of the victims were local, it was the murder of foreigners that gave the

Boxers their international prominence. The first such casualty was a missionary, Sidney W.M. Brooks, who was killed on the last day of 1899 in Shandong, one of the Boxer strongholds. In the following year, the movement gained momentum, directly coming up against the interests of Britain and other foreign powers through violent assaults on their legations in the centre of Beijing in the summer of 1900. The chief British representative in the capital, Sir Claude MacDonald (1852–1915), was described by his biographer as 'a soldier, a man of action, and impatient of the subtleties of diplomacy', was the official who had to deal with the full brunt of this.[15]

In a despatch back to London on 5 June, MacDonald had complained about the lethargy of the central government in its response to the rising number of attacks on foreign legations. In his view, the onslaught was partly due to collusion with the imperial court, no matter how much it protested its non-involvement. His conviction prompted him to call for British and other troops, including Russian and Japanese, to go to Beijing via Tianjin and supply protective reinforcements. The murder by the protesters on 20 June of the German minister while he was himself on his way to the Chinese authorities to complain about the increasingly volatile situation caused things to escalate. A couple of days after this, MacDonald described a determined Chinese attack on the British and other legations: 'the greater part of the Hanlin [a building once housing an academy next to the British legation] was . . . set on fire by the enemy, the fire bell rang, and all hands were soon at work endeavouring to extinguish the flames'. Strong winds during the day meant that the flames were carried nearer to the legation buildings themselves, though in the end they were beaten back by firefighters. The Hanlin academy, however, with its books, examination rooms and library, was destroyed.[16] On 29 June, a further Chinese attack involving 'a tremendous fusillade that quite surpassed anything that had ever taken place before' meant that the whole of the small garrison available to the British was kept busy all night. Despite the fears of an even more concerted attack, eventually this bombardment stopped.[17]

Attacks of varying intensity continued throughout the summer until 14 August. Figures like Robert Hart had to take refuge in the compounds, because it was too unsafe to be outside. Elsewhere in China, those foreigners unfortunate enough to be in the wrong place at the wrong time were either seriously wounded or, in the worst cases, murdered. A contingent of British troops finally disembarked in Shanghai and made its way to the capital, forcing the central government to take action and start trying to rein in the protesters. It was not just in China that the crisis led to chaos and tumult: once it reached Britain (often weeks after the reported events were over), the news of what was happening had a long-term impact on public opinion there. Certain that the whole of the British contingent had been wiped out, a despondent Queen Victoria in the last few months of her life wrote to Lord Salisbury that she felt 'quite ill at the thought of the poor MacDonalds and the ladies and children' and what may have happened to them.[18] China was increasingly viewed with a mixture of horror and apprehension. Whereas previously the complaint had always been that the country was passive and unchanging, now it was that it was a place of dangerous revolt and simmering revolution.

Despite this, there was some criticism of how the British and other foreigners had behaved, and how they subsequently handled the crisis. The writer Bertram Lenox Simpson (1877–1930), going under the pseudonym of B.L. Putnam Weale, claimed to have been in the thick of the action in 1900 (though doubt was later cast on this). His writing, however, represented a common attitude that was held about officials and their remoteness and privileges:

When you glance at the eleven legations placidly living their own little lives, you can see them cynically listening to these old women's tales, while at heart they secretly wonder what political capital each of them can separately make out of the whole business, so that their government can know that Peking has clever diplomats.[19]

On the Boxer Rebellion attacks, the Foreign Office back in London had shown itself to be 'vacillating' and an organisation 'that never knows its own mind'.[20] The legation, far from being a well-trained entity where people were able to deal with emergencies, was filled by officials 'intensely jealous of everybody else, and determined not to give way on the question of supreme command'. It was unsurprising that when a real storm came, 'we are doomed because you cannot hold an area a mile square with a lot of men who are fighting among themselves and who have fallen too quickly into our miserable petty scheme of things'.[21] Despite this lacerating criticism, nothing prevented punishment being meted out to the defeated Chinese, once the situation had stabilised and the foreign troops had quelled the attacks. In a different way, this was as brutal as what had been happening over the summer. The Boxer Protocol, with its six demands (punishment of culprits, prohibition from importing arms, compensation, permanent legation guards, disarmament of the Taku fort, and military occupation of certain ports), saddled China with colossal indemnities amounting to £67.5 million (approximately £10 billion at 2023 values) that rank among the most severe ever levelled against a foreign power. Foreign banks like HSBC and others were only too willing to oblige in managing these.[22]

While in the legation when it was under attack, Robert Hart had experienced the real terror of the situation at first hand. Despite this, he had not lost his sense of perspective and gave lucid expression to misgivings about the long-term impact of these punitive reparations. Like them or not, 'Chinese feelings and Chinese aspirations . . . will never be stamped out, but will live and seethe and work beneath the surface', ultimately having some impact. Deliberately choosing to ignore it and to pretend the resentment was not there did not negate the fact that it was strong and important: 'National sentiment . . . must be recognised, not diminished when dealing with national facts.'[23] The Chinese, after all the humiliations they had endured over the last few decades, were a proud people. Burying them under such vast reparations would only strengthen their sense of having been wronged and the emotions that flowed from this. Hart's comments proved prophetic, for it was indeed these feelings of anger, injustice and exploitation that came increasingly to the fore as the country marched onwards in its great mission of achieving modernity, and which eventually led it so forcefully to reject any hint of foreign interference.

Back in Britain, the writer Goldsworthy Lowes Dickinson (1862–1932) was also critical of the role of the West and the very values it espoused when justifying the treatment meted out to the Chinese. Assuming the guise of a Chinese person writing to the British, the author complained about how the West was urging the country to adopt political and social institutions that worked for its interests, but not for those of China. That was because of the constant, obsessive quest for wealth creation and for seeking material returns, often through exploitation. The simple fact was, Dickinson argued, that Western society had a lack of morality. Its dominant rule was that 'it must devour or be devoured',[24] and for this reason (among others) it was forever failing to live up to its Christian ideals. Dickinson was a British writer who had never been to China; but at least he showed the distance that empathy could take someone when trying to imagine how the Chinese might feel after their recent experiences. Perhaps the most cutting comment of all, however, was made by no less a figure than the British minister in Beijing who had succeeded MacDonald, Sir Ernest Satow (1843–1929). In 1905, he commented: 'I may not love the Chinese, but it always seems to me that they have been most unjustly treated.'[25]

Borderlands

Britain often had to act in China to defend its broader regional interests, rather than simply to promote its bilateral aims. This entailed thinking about the real risk that Russia posed along the frontiers of the Qing empire, and in particular in the areas of Tibet and Xinjiang, and the knock-on effects this might have on India. According to Lord

Curzon in 1896, Russia was the 'real enemy', for it was 'Russia that threatens [China's] frontiers in Chinese Turkestan and on the Pamirs ... Russia who has designs on Manchuria, Russia whose shadow overhangs Korea' and 'Russia who is always hobbling in scientific disguise at Tibet'.[26] Over in the isolated legation that opened in the remote oasis town of Kashgar, close to the Sino-Pakistan border, George Macartney (1867–1945) served for over two decades. Son of Halliday Macartney (who among other things had worked in the Chinese legation in London) and a Chinese mother, he was a distant relative of Lord Macartney of the 1793 embassy. He was a man of quiet and sober personality, which stood him in good stead for the years in which he served in a place where hosting one or two visitors a year ranked as a busy time, and where the main task was to keep a close eye on an often erratic Russian counterpart serving in the city. Macartney was pragmatic in his approach, recognising the weak hold of the Chinese authorities locally and the need to pay lip service to the pre-eminence of the Russians. He saw his own function as one best served by the old tactic of simply focusing on trade. The consulate in Kashgar continued until 1948, when largely geopolitical issues (among them the brief existence of an independent state locally, and then the tussle between the Soviet Union and China, which ended up with control of the area being ceded to the latter) led to its closure.

The British involvement in Tibet was more invasive and eventually systemic. The main issue remained the same as it had been since the first visit by George Bogle over a century earlier (see chapter two) – i.e. what precise status to confer on the region. After a fashion, it was independent and had its own structures of leadership, along with a very distinctive culture and language. Yet it also clearly had a unique relationship with the Qing which verged on a client-state arrangement, even though nothing seemed to be formally codified. The notion of 'special influence', or 'suzerainty', became the term that captured this. But the British came to regard the looseness by which Tibet was linked with Beijing as reason to be uneasy about unhelpful

Russian interference there and the knock-on effect this would have on their Indian interests, if anything dramatic ever happened.

Colonel Francis Edward Younghusband (1863–1942) was the chief agent of British interests in the early twentieth century, a man mandated with trying to directly sort out the problem of why Tibet was so resistant to trading with Britain (or even speaking to it) and with coming up with ways to do something about this. An earlier attempt to address this issue in 1886 by Colman Macauley (1849–90), a British official based in India, had resulted in agreement to send a trade mission to the mountain kingdom. This was aborted, due to British military actions in neighbouring Sikkim; but it prepared the ground for a follow-up mission – albeit far more military – almost two decades later. A particular bone of contention throughout this period was the freedom that Tibet had to trade in neighbouring India, while rejecting reciprocity. Tibet also refused to accept a boundary that had been proposed by the British between it and India in 1890. Trying to ask for Chinese assistance in these matters had led nowhere, with the mandarins in Beijing saying they had no real influence on the monk officials who ostensibly ran Tibet at their behest. On 9 September 1903, Younghusband had written to the government of India from within Tibet that 'it may be taken as assumed that the Tibetans will refuse to negotiate in any way which we would consider satisfactory' and that therefore 'direct actions will be required'.[27] Whatever the direct action, the secretary of state for India told the viceroy on 6 November, it 'should not be allowed to lead us to occupation or to permanent intervention in Tibetan affairs in any form'.[28] Inevitably, that was precisely what Younghusband's mission ended up achieving.

In March 1904, a force led by Younghusband marched further into Tibet, where, on 10 April, it met two thousand Tibetans and quickly engaged in combat, rather than waste too much time talking. It was an unequal fight. 'The enemy was defeated and dispersed. Enemy's loss was 190 dead, many wounded. 70 prisoners', the reporting despatch went. 'Our casualties were three wounded.'[29] The surrender of Tibetan forts and the entry into Lhasa in July was effectively a British invasion, exceeding the demands of the viceroy and the British government. A convention was finally signed, in which Tibet agreed to pay compensation, opened itself up to trade and committed to a unique relationship with Britain (thus dealing with the jealousy that arose over the worries about Russian involvement). The indemnity would lead to a major rebellion in the area, and the fiscal burden would cause increased instability, precipitating the greater involvement of the Qing government in Tibet's affairs.

Younghusband was later to write more self-critically and reflectively that 'the Tibetans were . . . thoroughly nervous about the British'. Though the Tibetans were impressed by 'the moderation of our rule [in India], by the freedom we gave, and by the hospitals and schools', this positive note had to be balanced by the way 'these same Englishmen annexed other people's lands to their dominions'. The Tibetans ended up, naturally enough, with a split view of the British, according to which they were either 'benevolent and godly' or 'infernal and quite wicked'.[30] The Simla Convention of 1914, between the Republic of China (the successor state of the Qing), the British and the Tibetans, enshrined the unique notion of recognition of Chinese suzerainty. Contentious at the time for the Chinese – who wanted full sovereignty to be acknowledged, rather than this watered-down version – it remained in place right up to the wholesale change of position almost a century later (in 2008), when Britain abandoned this unique part of its policy and finally recognised full Chinese sovereignty over the region. Britain did not have formal representation in Lhasa until Hugh Richardson (1905–2000), who served there from 1936 to 1940, and then from 1945 to 1949. The post was subsequently closed before the communist invasions in the 1950s.

Collapse

When it came, the long-predicted dynastic implosion was more of a whimper than a bang. The 267 years of Manchu domination ended in the final months of 1911 and early 1912 with the Xinhai Revolution. Perhaps the ultimate indignity on this path to collapse was that the final war of the Qing era, fought in 1905 on Chinese soil, was between two partners – Russia and Japan – neither of whom was the sovereign owner of the territory they were fighting on. Never had China's impotence over control of its own affairs been so brutally demonstrated. Japan's victory in the conflict proved that an Asian nation could defeat a Western one under the conditions of modern warfare. This should have been a cause of some small celebration for the British, who – pragmatically realising the rapid shift in power and influence of others in China – had signed a treaty of friendship with Tokyo in 1902. The coming years were to show, however, that Japan, rather than any other power, was going to be the greatest threat to stability and peace in the area, despite all the diplomatic hopes invested in it early on in agreements such as that of 1902.

The British minister in China at the time of the Qing's final demise, John Jordan (1852–1925), went on to become one of the most influential ambassadors of the twentieth century in Asia. A native of the north of Ireland (like Robert Hart), he served in Beijing from 1906 to 1920. His career culminated in his being made a privy counsellor (an advisory position for the British sovereign) and playing a key role in devising British policy to deal with the evolving situation in China. His approach to the British position on the 1911 revolution was (much as had been the case during the Taiping Rebellion half a century before) to try to maintain neutrality and not take sides.[31] The priority was to safeguard British lives and property during the upheaval, and to protect what he called 'the unenviable state of the British concession in Hankou', located in Wuhan, where the revolution that toppled the Qing had first erupted.[32] As the situation deteriorated, he offered to mediate between the imperial forces and the revolutionaries, but soon faced up to reality. He retracted an earlier comment of his from 1911 that the country was unsuited to constitutional or republican government, and threw his support behind the newly emerging leaders. Charles Stewart Addis (1861–1945), head of HSBC at the time, was more committed and supple in his response, ordering the bank's athletic team in London to abandon their competition shirts of imperial yellow with a black Chinese dragon, in favour of something more neutral.[33]

With the formal end of the Qing on 26 January, Jordan was forced to acknowledge that, of the available options, a republic was the most feasible. In this, he was influenced by his strong relationship with the statesman Yuan Shikai (1859–1916). In his recollections, written in 1920 at the end of his time in China, he described Yuan movingly as 'the Chinese of all others for whom I had the greatest admiration' and 'the only high Chinese official whom I can claim to have known intimately'.[34] The Chinese leader, he recorded, 'was a true patriot', who died in 1916 'of a broken heart',[35] due to the rebuttal of his attempt to set up a monarchical system in the final year of his life and the opposition to the scheme from many of those around him, including the Japanese, who favoured maintaining the republican system. The failure of this plan ushered in an era in which domestic Chinese politics was divided between broadly different zones of interest, with the southern part of the country increasingly influenced by the nationalists and the northern coming under what was called the Beiyang administration. Other parts of the country fell under the sway of warlords. The outcome Britain had feared – of a country riven with deep internal fissures and threatening to splinter into a number of parts – was becoming a reality. This was a problem for Britain, because it no longer had the capacity to stop (or even mitigate) the worst effects of this lamentable process.

In the subsequent history of the development of Chinese nationalism over this era of painful national fracturing, Sun Yatsen (1866–1925) is regarded, both in China and Taiwan to this day, as a key figure, occupying a unique and symbolic role in the Chinese world. But among the British who knew him, he was viewed with deep scepticism. Once the Xinhai Revolution occurred, he lasted as president of the republic for only one month before resigning. Sun's early life was peripatetic and rootless, with periods of his student years and early adulthood spent in Hawaii, Japan and Hong Kong. Of the formative events in his life, one of the most significant occurred during a brief period of exile in London, when he was unable to return to China because he was on a wanted list due to his activities against the Qing. Approached on the street on 11 October 1896 by two people he believed to be friendly compatriots, he was steered towards the door of a house on Portland Place, the location of the Chinese legation. Bustled inside, he was kept in detention until the intervention of the British Foreign Office and some local contacts, who demanded he be released.[36] A forced return to his home country would most probably have resulted in his execution. The British assessments of him by those who had met him while in Hong Kong were underwhelming. One said that he was 'a curious character, hopelessly impractical in all he did, unintelligible in what he wrote and said, earnest and patriotic beyond a doubt'.[37] John Pratt (1876–1970), half-brother of the actor Boris Karloff and one of the key officials who shaped Chinese policy from the late 1920s onwards in Britain, wrote in a posthumous assessment of Sun in 1928 that he 'was a dreamer and a visionary', one who exercised tremendous power over the minds of his countrymen but was 'an utter failure as politician [because he could not] make any practical use of his power for the good of his people' – something that greatly irritated the 'practically minded British and prejudiced them against him'.[38] Sun's mercurial personality was one cause of this irritation; but the greater problem was his nationalism. Were his ideas to be fully adopted, the British feared they would almost certainly impact on Britain's interests and weaken its control over the country.

One of the ways in which Britain was able and willing to offer practical help to the new regime was through finance. This was administered through the Reorganisation Loan of 1913, originally planned at £60 million, with part of that sum secured against the largely foreign-controlled salt *gabelle* (the tax levied on the state monopoly on salt production). In the event, the amount was reduced to a £25 million tranche of money, of which HSBC supplied £7 million. Sir Charles Addis, director of HSBC in London after many years in Hong Kong (he went on to be governor of the Bank of England from 1918), saw clearly that finance was about far more than money: it involved support for 'a modernised and efficient China, achieved through controlled, apolitical leaning'.[39] The intention may have been apolitical, but the result – the shoring up of Yuan Shikai's leadership as the provisional president of China from 1912 to 1916, against his numerous opponents – was definitely not neutral. Throughout this period of revolutionary upheaval, there was one domestic entity in the country that managed to remain relatively stable: the still largely British-run Chinese Imperial Maritime Customs Service. With no functioning central government to remit revenue to, it sent what funds it continued to collect to foreign banks.[40] Through the Reorganisation Loan and the Customs, both of which had major British involvement, China remained under the tight control of non-Chinese, even as it edged closer to falling into complete chaos.

The rise of Japan in China and the Great War of 1914

The amity shown between Britain and Japan after the arrangement of their friendship treaty of 1902 was an uneasy one, prone to constant change and challenge. Prior to the First World War, Britain (despite the treaty) grew increasingly unhappy about Japanese encroachment on China. Initially it took a dim view of the Japanese support for a separatist movement in Manchuria and Inner Mongolia up to 1911. The Japanese proved as opportunistic as the British, fighting against the Germans in the First World War and then taking the chance, as soon as they could after the war, to evict them from Shandong province and acquire all the German possessions there. The most infamous expression of Japanese assertiveness came in 1915, when they issued twenty-one demands to the central Chinese government. These included control of Shandong province, rights to railways in Manchuria, the liberty to preach Buddhism across China, and the insertion of Japanese advisors into all levels of government. This was a forceful attack on Chinese sovereignty, and one of the main reasons why Yuan Shikai's own domestic political ambitions were undermined: the perception was that he was unable to face down such Japanese interference.

The twenty-one demands, the rise of Japan's militarism and the way in which its colonisation played out in practice in Korea (after secession of the peninsula to it in 1895), with high levels of brutality, all had a negative impact on Britain's views of its sole Asian ally. But it was the outcome of the First World War in terms of the Versailles Treaty and the replacement of German concessions and interests in China with Japanese that created the greatest problems and that fed a Chinese nationalism which, while it had been present in embryonic form, had failed up until then to become a countrywide, mass movement.

From 1917, China was an ally of the British and sent troops to Europe. These fought as part of the Chinese Labour Corps, performing crucial work in supplying the French and British troops on the Western Front. Around 140,000 were involved, some of them – like the soldier Liu Dien Chen – being awarded honours for their service and courage. At the end of the war, all but about 5,000 returned home. One author, Daryl Klein, even wrote an appreciative (albeit unfortunately titled) account of their service that was published in 1919, soon after the conflict: *With the Chinks*.[41] Chinese nationalists considered that the Chinese contribution merited kinder treatment at the hands of the allies.

G.E. Morrison (1862–1920), originally a native of Australia but based in Beijing since 1900, when he had become the correspondent for *The Times*, was one of those who sided with China on this issue. A vehement and influential supporter of the Japanese in their war against Russia in 1905, he had then served briefly as an advisor to

Yuan Shikai after the 1911 revolution – a role that contributed to changing his views about the Japanese, as he witnessed their bullying at first hand. In a letter to the editor of *The Times* in July 1919, he wrote of the Versailles outcome that 'it was an astonishing peace treaty which punishes China who gave considerable help to the allies, and would have given more'.[42] But the calculations of the allied powers at the peace conference failed to live up to the promise of self-determination that had been expressed in the idealism of then US President Woodrow Wilson. A Chinese delegation sat in the grand halls of the French palace in 1919, watching passively as their hopes disintegrated before their very eyes in negotiations and debates in which they were unable to take an active part. The British, financially and politically depleted after the colossal effort of the war, were unable to assist much either: they proved helpless to face down the pressure of the Japanese, with whom they fell into line. That they did so with grave misgivings is best illustrated by the fact that Lord Curzon, foreign secretary at the time, observed that the Japanese were guilty of 'old style imperialism'.[43] Coming as it did from a power that arguably invented many of the key attributes of modern colonisation, this criticism had real bite.

The years after the 1919 debacle ushered in an era of international conferences where country representatives sat in rooms with increasingly large numbers of other representatives, discussing Chinese affairs – usually with China on the sidelines, watching silently. Britain was a key member of this group. However, in a remarkably short period of time, it came to cede more and more voice and influence to the US, which had been coaxed from its period of relative isolation by the war and its involvement in it. The Washington Conference of 1921 typified this: a meeting where nine powers came together to decide issues of huge importance to China, even as they protested that they would stick by the independence and territorial integrity of the country. According to contemporaneous reports issued in London for the China Association, the Washington Conference had promoted 'a reconstructive policy in China . . . in ensuring the independence and integrity of China and the principle of equal opportunities for the commerce and industry of all nations'.[44] It meant, the report for the following year continued, 'peace with honour' for the country, and offered a way of helping it in the re-establishment of settled government. As for the increasingly reviled extraterritoriality condition granted to foreigners, the China Association felt that it was 'quite misleading to speak of [it] as oppressive'.

Britain's attempt to balance its pragmatic interests with what could be described as efforts to articulate a moral or values-based mission of seeking ways to help China and work with it was not new. Hints had appeared much earlier, particularly in the nineteenth-century debate about the rights and wrongs of the opium trade, which had pitted self-interest and the search for naked gain against claims of altruism and the need not just to exploit opportunities with China, but to care for the country. But as the twentieth century proceeded, explicit awareness of the tension between these aims came increasingly to the fore. On the one hand, there was the ever-stronger pull of the Chinese market, 'an industriously and commercially minded people of some 400 million . . . beginning to feel their feet in the industrial world'.[45] This market was 'undoubtedly a profitable one, but it is an expensive one to work properly'. That was why there needed to be concerted attention and support for business from government. But on the other hand, there was the position best exemplified by David Lloyd George (1863–1945), the British prime minister at the time of the Imperial Conference, held in London in June 1921. For him, empire more generally did have a moral justification, because it created unity in a world divided by race: 'The British empire has done signal service in bridging these divisions in the past . . . Our foreign policy can never range itself in any sense upon the differences of race and civilisation between East and West.'[46] These views are rightly subjected to coruscating criticism today – not least because it was precisely on the grounds of race that the empire operated, giving privileged position to overwhelmingly white, British interests over those

1. Queen Elizabeth I wrote at least three letters to the reigning Wan Li emperor of Ming China, the last of which is now in the Lancashire Records Office. Sent in a mixture of languages, from Latin, to Greek, to English, because of the uncertainty about which might be comprehensible to the recipient, all expressed a desire to trade, and none ever arrived.

2. Chinese-inspired designs in the eighteenth and early nineteenth centuries were so popular they inspired a specific term – Chinoiserie. The Willow Pattern design on porcelain plates made from technology taken from China and adapted in Britain was based on a story which had no obvious links with China.

3. Chinoiserie found its way into the most intimate spaces of the British, usually in the form of colourful wallpaper. This example is from the 1720s and, though made in Britain, was based on Chinese originals being exported to Europe at this time.

4. Henry Dundas, first Viscount Melville (1742–1811), the trusted confidant and aide to Prime Minister William Pitt the Younger, maintained a close interest in the affairs of the East India Company, and in particular attempts to establish formal relations with China. His support was crucial for the Macartney mission of 1792–94.

5. Lord George Macartney (1737–1806) led the first formal British mission to reach China in 1793. He had two audiences with the reigning emperor then, the octogenarian Qianlong. Qianlong's gravity and vigour despite his age impressed the visiting lord, who was suffering from gout – a factor that contributed to his unwillingness to kowtow.

6. The Qing authorities in Beijing forbade any trade in China with the outside world except that undertaken in the southern port city of Canton (today's Guangzhou). Here, in warehouses and workshops called 'factories', the British and other Europeans tried to do trade. It proved an often frustrating endeavour.

7. The perennial issue for Britain's relations with China in the early centuries was the lack of any common language. Missionary Robert Morrison (1782–1834) managed to compile the first Chinese–English dictionary and a grammar of the language in the 1810s.

8. Charles Elliot (1801–75) went from serving in the British navy to diplomacy. Before his appointment in China he worked on abolishing slavery in Guinea, Africa. Chief superintendent of trade to China from 1838 to 1841, a period covering the tumultuous years of the First Anglo-Chinese War, he was to subsequently serve as consul general in the then independent Republic of Texas.

9. Sir Henry Pottinger (1789–1856) replaced Elliot, negotiating the end of the Anglo-Chinese War in 1842 and serving until 1844 as the first governor of Hong Kong. Initially popular among the local British merchants, he was to fall out of favour with them at the end of his tenure.

10. The sacking of the Summer Palace during the Second Anglo-Chinese War marked the nadir of European aggression in China. British and French forces stripped the emperor's summer residence of its decorations. A small dog found in the ruins was sent back to Britain, where it was gifted to Queen Victoria. She named it Looty.

11. Charles George Gordon (1833–85) came to be called 'Chinese Gordon' due to his leading a group of mercenaries who helped the Qing government defeat the massive Taiping Rebellion in 1864. Gordon however enjoyed a fractious relationship with Chinese leaders, waving the head of an executed rebel leader whom he had promised would be spared in enraged protest.

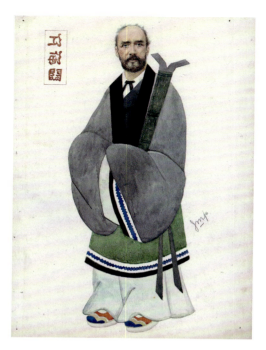

12. Sir Robert Hart (1835–1911) effectively ran a large part of the late Qing fiscal system through his leadership of the Chinese Imperial Maritime Customs Service for over forty years. A man of deep Christian faith, he felt he was a Chinese official rather than a British one, and in his early life managed to father several children with his local mistress.

13. The satirical *Punch* and other popular magazines promoted images of China which were mocking and dismissive. These typified attitudes in the late Victorian era towards a country seen as weak and backward. This marked a shift from earlier attitudes towards the country and its culture which were more admiring.

14. In the late nineteenth century, the 'scramble for China' saw Britain's attempt to preserve its interests through an 'open door' policy overtaken by the carving up of parts of China by Germans, Japanese and other European powers. Weihaiwei on the northeastern coast was isolated and economically unpromising, but Britain took possession from 1898 to 1930.

15. People of Chinese heritage first appeared in Britain in the late seventeenth century. But it was only with the advent of Chinese working on ships that small communities started to appear in Britain, around the end of the nineteenth century. Limehouse in East London served as the original Chinatown before it moved to today's Gerard Street area.

16. The collapse of British forces across Asia when confronted with Japanese power in the Second World War shocked observers. Hong Kong fell almost immediately after the attack on Pearl Harbor bringing the Americans into the war. The city remained under Japanese control until the end of the war, when, despite Chinese and American misgivings, it reverted to British control.

17. Joseph Needham (1900–95) started out as a biochemist, but developed an interest in China when he met a young researcher, Lu Gwei-Djen, in the 1930s. He started his immense history of science and civilisation in China after a period working at the British mission in Chongqing during the Second World War.

18. Former British prime minister Clement Attlee (1883–1967) led one of the first delegations to the People's Republic of China in 1954. He remained baffled when told during the visit that the law courts had to answer to the Communist Party, saying that he could not see this being viable in his home country.

19. The attack on the British office in Beijing by Red Guards during the Cultural Revolution in August 1967 left the building partially in ruins. Staff had to leave through a crowd of angry, chanting protesters, fleeing to nearby friendly embassies. The attack marked the nadir of Anglo-Chinese relations after 1949.

20. An ageing Mao Zedong (1893–1976) meets former British prime minister Edward Heath (1916–2005) in 1975, just a year before his death. Mao made a tremendous impression on his visitors, despite being incapacitated by Parkinson's disease. Heath was no exception, becoming a stalwart defender of the Chinese in the UK, and a critic of the management of Hong Kong's retrocession.

21. The meetings between Chinese paramount leader Deng Xiaoping (1904–97) and the first serving British prime minister to visit China, Margaret Thatcher (1925–2013), had to handle the contentious issue of Hong Kong. Thatcher found Deng cruel and was disarmed by his use of a spittoon – but she came to appreciate his formidable negotiating skills.

22. The first state visit by a British monarch to China: Queen Elizabeth II (1926–2022) in 1986. The trip proved a success and was seen as a reward by the Chinese for the agreement reached in 1984 over the future of Hong Kong. Despite this, controversial remarks by the sovereign's husband the duke of Edinburgh while in Xian distracted from the historic nature of the occasion.

23. The hand-back of Hong Kong in 1997 happened in torrential rain on 1 July. The last governor, Chris Patten (b. 1944), had referred in his final comments to the city now meeting its destiny. But the democratic reforms he had championed were gradually eroded in the years afterwards.

24. Leader of China since 2012, Xi Jinping (b. 1953) during his state visit to the UK of 2015. The pub in which he drank beer and ate fish and chips in the Oxfordshire countryside was near the constituency of his host, British Prime Minister David Cameron (b. 1966). It went on to be a popular spot for Chinese tourists.

of the territories and countries that were being administered. Yet they were sincerely offered at the time to explain that Britain was involved in countries like China for more than just reasons of trade. By the time of the Washington meeting in 1921, these notions had started to operate in a similar way to the twenty-first-century debate about defending human rights and liberal values, while still trading with communist China. The structural fault line between values and material gain in the British position appeared early and ran very deep, but it was to become more important as the twentieth century proceeded.

For Britain, the Washington Conference also provided a time when it was able to recognise that the Pacific was now much like a board game: one where its initial huge advantage had eroded and where its pieces in active play were increasingly being surrounded by others competing for space and influence. The conference was an attempt to maintain and protect British interests and assets, but also to start to balance relationships with the other (newer) players. The bilateral friendship agreement with Japan was allowed to lapse. A new consortium was brought into play, which included the US, France and others and which tried to address the growing worries about Japan's pushier attitude towards China and its other neighbours. While Japan ceded Shandong back to the Chinese in 1921, Britain maintained its interests in Weihaiwei until the end of the decade. Things were not helped by the increasingly chaotic situation within China itself. The relative lack of rule of law or proper administration in large swaths of the hinterland was – along with the chaos caused by competing power centres vying to control the situation – one of the reasons why extraterritoriality remained. 'Never,' opined the China Association annual report of 1923–24, 'during the history of foreign relations, except perhaps in the Boxer Years, have foreigners been the victims of such barbarous cruelty and outrages.'[47] The central government was a 'helpless spectator' to this, meaning that foreigners needed all the protection they could get from elsewhere.

The outcomes of the Paris Peace Conference, the May Fourth Movement of students and others across China in 1919 and the Washington Conference fed Chinese nationalism and brought about its renaissance. In July 1921, one of the manifestations of this feeling of anger was the meeting of thirteen people – constituting the fledgling Communist Party – in the French Concession area of Shanghai. Funded partly by the Russian Communist Party (the precursor of which had recently seized power in Russia in 1917), the movement was tiny and its activities wholly underground. It was several years before the British first started to pay serious attention to this grouping, which in the early years of the 1920s was pitifully small. The main focus, as the China Association said, remained on whether Great Britain could 'carry out her obligations to her own nationals and preserve that immense trade which she had built up by hard and patient work throughout several generations'. This was not just about the situation in China, but about Britain's 'prestige and her position in the Far East'. Britain's powers may have been dwindling in reality, but for Chinese nationalists it remained the country above all others that represented the chief causes of the parlous situation their own nation was now in, and which needed to be evicted in some way if national regeneration were to occur. Because of this, there were frequent boycotts of British goods throughout the mid-1920s, and a series of escalating attacks on British interests, some in Hong Kong and others around the network of treaty ports. The response to those was to shape London's attitude to China in the pre-Second World War years.

Changing Chinese and British minds

Britain was never a simple, singular actor in China, any more than China was a monolithic entity that was to be engaged with and acted upon that was to be acted on in one specific way. The British philosopher Bertrand Russell (1872–1970) represented this well, as he had a different attitude to that of the government of his country and many of its businesspeople. In the 1910s, he experienced a turbulent few years, following his early success as a writer and thinker on logic and meaning. His imprisonment for a few months in 1916 for his pacifist stance during the First World War led to his dismissal from his position at Trinity College, Cambridge. And it was not just in his professional life that he was experiencing stress: his marriage to his first wife had ended in separation, and he was living with the author Dora Black, a cause of some scandal at the time. The invitation to visit Beijing in 1921 therefore came at a good time to have a rest from Britain. And so the eminent philosopher accepted the chance to lecture at the relatively newly established Peking University.

Russell was a contentious figure. But – perhaps for the first time – here was a top-flight British intellectual, with no previous knowledge of China, experiencing at first hand the country and the ideas that were exciting its young people. 'After centuries of slumber,' he wrote in his autobiography decades later, 'China was becoming aware of the modern world . . . The English sneered at the Reformers, and said that China would always be China.' Russell found this attitude both short-sighted and arrogant, not least because it had very little basis in empirical reality: 'The Englishman in the East, as far as I was able to judge . . . is a man completely out of touch with his environment.'[48] These figures were unlikely either to offer their home country intelligent ideas about China or to convey in a coherent way Western ideas that could be of use to the Chinese. Soon after his visit, he produced a short book about what he felt he had learned while in Beijing. In it, he acknowledged the Japanese aggression and the Chinese nationalism that it was stoking. Russell saw Britain's position in the country as an anomalous and often hypocritical one, for the British had demonstrated what they regarded as their 'superior virtue' in the most curious way – by sacking the Summer Palace in Beijing in 1860 and then extracting huge indemnities to punish those who had already been punished enough. In key areas like customs autonomy, the treaties that were still in force with foreign powers meant that China had no effective control, despite being told that it needed to govern itself and look after its interests better.[49] Russell felt that foreigners needed to understand the profound and seismic changes going on in the country; but to do that, they required a different mindset, sensitive to noticing new things and interpreting them in a fresh way. 'If intercourse between Western nations and China is to be fruitful,' he wrote, 'we must cease to regard ourselves as missionaries of a superior civilisation, or, worse still, as men who have a right to exploit, oppress and swindle the Chinese because they are an "inferior" race.' This was an attitude he found untenable and reprehensible.[50]

Russell felt that he had learned from the Chinese, and that – far from being a teacher going to dispense wisdom – in many ways his brief tenure in Beijing had made him a student once more. A year after his visit, the writer W. Somerset Maugham (1874–1965) also gave an account of a tour around China – albeit one framed in more fictional, imaginative garb. *On a Chinese Screen* served as an account of at least some of the attitudes that Russell had lambasted in compatriots. In one, a missionary is described as being consumed by hatred and contempt for the Chinese, whose souls he is meant to be saving. In another, Maugham writes of the kind of expats that Russell had also mocked, 'the merchants who can live for thirty-five years in China without learning enough of the language to ask their way in the street'. They justified this, Maugham wrote, because the study of Chinese makes one 'grow a little odd'. And as proof of this, he offered the example of the Mandarin-speaking consuls who struck their fellow countrymen back home as eccentric and unstable.[51]

The career of Sir Edmund Backhouse (1873–1944) might be cited as proof that eccentricity and ability to learn Chinese occasionally did go together. However, the signs of strangeness in his character were apparent long before Mandarin had ever figured in his life. Backhouse came from a faded-gentry background. He offers a fascinating insight into another great perennial character type of Sino-British relations – the fraud. Had he put as much effort into valid scholarship as he clearly put into fabricating and forging documents and information during his life, he might have passed as a significant scholar. A proclivity to fantasising (which only intensified over the years) meant, however, that his career was a tantalising combination of verifiable, solid work intermixed with fabrications of the first order, which served to contaminate all his efforts and proved (to adapt an adage) that bad scholarship drives out good. The biography of the Empress Cixi which he co-authored with the journalist John Otway Percy Bland (see above) stands as a good example. It contains journal entries from a Qing official which – years later – were proved to have been forged. Backhouse also donated material to the Bodleian Library in Oxford, and very nearly gained the chair of Chinese studies there – before, to his disgust, it was offered to someone else. He was, his biographer the historian Hugh Trevor-Roper wrote, 'a marvellous linguist, and even those who disliked him in China admitted that he was a first-class sinologist ... But his writings had no power of thought' and he was 'socially and intellectually a snob' – one who ended his life protected in the British legation in Beijing, while earnestly hoping that the Japanese would be victorious in the war and his home country defeated.[52] It was a small tragedy that one of the few British who did have facility in the Chinese language at this time was to make such a flawed and often unhelpful contribution to the understanding of China for his home country.

Despite the misinformation promoted by figures like Backhouse, the knowledge of Britons about China and of the Chinese about Britain was undergoing a radical change over this period – as indeed were the sources from which that knowledge flowed. Overwhelmingly, in the period of bilateral engagement prior to this, it had been the British physically travelling to China, sometimes acquiring familiarity with the country through living, working and studying there. But in the twentieth century, thanks to the arrival of sailors on Chinese ships, of students (albeit in small numbers) and of Chinese officials and merchants, traffic started to flow in the other direction.

This phenomenon of people originating in China but being present in Britain was complex. On the one hand, there were clearly economic opportunities available to migrants – in laundries, for instance (the first of which to be opened by a person of Chinese origin was established in Liverpool in 1886); and in restaurants, as mentioned in the previous chapter. From quite early on, there were particular areas where Chinese communities lived: the oldest in Europe was in Liverpool, and another was in Limehouse in London. The *Pall Mall Gazette* labelled these 'Chinatowns' in 1900, coining a phrase still in currency today. These served, to some extent, to make the Chinese community more visible.[53] The number of people involved, however, was originally very small. The 1901 national census recorded 387 Chinese in Britain. Ten years later, the figure had risen to only 1,319, of whom 403 were in Liverpool and 247 in London.[54] For such a small community, it managed to attract a disproportionate amount of political and imaginative attention. Labour rights were one source of discontent, with the Seamen's Union complaining about the employment of Chinese aboard British ships in the early 1900s. Such anxieties were not new. As early as 1873, one Thomas Wright wrote in the *Journeyman Engineer* that 'the wholesale importation of coolie and China labour going on in some ports abroad is a thing to give pause to the thoughtful among the working classes'.[55] The breaking of a strike in Cardiff, Wales, in 1911 through the use of Chinese seamen who were not union members caused a riot, in which up to thirty Chinese-owned and -run laundries were destroyed.[56] Nor did the law offer any great comfort: an act of 1905 stripped British women who married non-natives of Britain of their citizenship – something that left some women effectively stateless in their own country if they married a man from China.[57]

The Limehouse Chinatown serves as a haunting monument to this very early phase of the Chinese presence in Britain. Today it is simply a collection of streets bearing Chinese names, with new houses erected on the old site (which was razed to the ground in the slum clearances after the Second World War). Canton Street, Pekin Street and Amoy Place are evocative names for what look like very typical post-war inner-London residential streets. Ironically, the one other feature of the landscape that alludes to this history is the distant sight of the grand HSBC building at Canary Wharf, a mile or so away. Limehouse, however, with its community of about 300 Chinese by the 1920s, was a place of pilgrimage for those attracted to the sense of difference and of mystery that this new community suggested to them. The most (in)famous was the Anglo-Irish writer Arthur Henry Ward (1883–1959), who, under the penname Sax Rohmer, produced the Fu Manchu series of novels from 1913. These lurid tales – often set in and around Limehouse – told of the inscrutable, fiendishly clever and cruel protagonist Dr Fu, and appealed to one side of the English imagination, which saw something negative and worrying about the Chinese. These stories set in place the lamentable foundations of what subsequently became labelled sinophobia.

That is not to say that they represented the majority view in Britain of people of Chinese heritage. There is plenty of evidence to show that attitudes were far more complex, and that there was also a market for the more positive character Charlie Chan, created by the American author Earl Derr Biggers and popular in the filmed versions in Britain from the 1930s onwards. Even so, Ward's character of Dr Fu appeared in written and filmed versions up to the 1970s, concluding with an extraordinary finale in which the archetypically British actor Christopher Lee assumed the leading role – a man with no known links, in terms of family or ancestry, to anyone in the Far East, and who hailed from solidly European stock.

8

Chaos and War, 1925-49

I t is a hot, sunny summer's day sometime in the early 1930s. Laura
Leroy, wife of a British diplomat based in the Chinese capital, has
plans for the entertainment of a lively group of visitors and friends
living in the city: they are to go to the nearby holiday home that the
mission maintains in the hills around Beijing. After much preparation, they travel to this place laden with food, furniture and practically everything else they need, embarking on a kind of adventure
along a mini-silk road; only this time not to trade or make money,
but to while away the time while the centre of the city is too dusty
and hot. Laura's time after her arrival at the weekend retreat is filled
with thinking about the dynamics, the shifts in sentiment and
emotions between individuals in her group of friends, none of whom
is from China itself. But little by little, she becomes more aware of the
unsettling state of the country they live in, and yet are seldom fully
aware of. As a sign of these troubles, bandits supporting one of the
contemporary rebel groups suddenly appear with guns from the
wooded hills around the summer villa, and almost kidnap the legation people. No one in the end gets harmed, but these gun-toting
interlopers are people who look as though they might turn nasty.
Uncomfortable memories resurface from over three decades before,

of the violence of the Boxer Rebellion, when protesters turned on foreigners. But the drama is resolved, and it remains sunny, pleasant and – despite the worrying interlude – mostly an edifying stay.

Laura Leroy may have been a purely fictional creation, but her creator, Mary Ann Dolling (1889–1974) – author of the 1932 novel *Peking Picnic* (writing under the penname Ann Bridge) – was writing from direct experience. Dolling was married to Owen St Clair O'Malley (1887–1974), who, like Laura's spouse, was a diplomat. At the time she wrote the novel, she too was living in Beijing while her husband served in the British legation there. There was indeed a residence, as she described in her novel, that belonged to the embassy outside the confines of the city, where diplomats and their friends could go for some rest and relaxation from the rigours of their daily rounds. More strikingly, through the words of her main character, Dolling's work conveys an oddly fantastical, often distant, idealising view of the Chinese. 'There is greater poverty here than anywhere else in the world,' Laura admits, before adding dismissively, 'but somehow no squalor.' Staring at a labourer who had just happened to pass by, she sees his 'superb limbs, freed for a moment from the rope . . . His hairless polished torso was modelled with the perfection of a god, his movements were full of grace and natural dignity.' The Chinese exemplified, Laura declares to her friend, 'the dignity of labour'.[1] They are, she says later, the 'most lovable race on earth'.[2] And yet, as the scene in the novel described above makes clear, once they allow their own conflicts and problems to become a little too real, so that they impact too much on the lives of the foreigners living among them, things become less convivial.

This separation between communities may be why the journalist Arthur Ransome (1884–1967) took a somewhat more jaded view of the British, when he was in China in the late 1920s. In the city of Shanghai, he met people who had witnessed some of the violence and upheaval that had occurred in April 1927. In that month, the newly emerging leader of the nationalists, Chiang Kai-shek (1887–1975), with the blessing of the Soviet Communist Party, turned on the small communist group with which, up until that point, he had been in a loose coalition and slaughtered several thousand of them in a deadly purge. Ransome found puzzling the mindset of these old China hands, some of whom had been based in the city for decades. They seemed 'to have lived in a comfortable but hermetically sealed and isolated glass case since 1901', he wrote, where they believed 'if they belong to England at all, [it is] to an England that no longer exists'.[3] Ransome was dismissive of Chinese communism, which he felt 'at this point of Chinese history is a wholly irrelevant slogan'.[4] But Chinese nationalism was a different kettle of fish, because it was led by people who were taught by the West, and who were their disciples. 'We ought to be rather flattered than surprised', wrote Ransome, 'that western educated Chinese have learnt something of this proud intolerance from ourselves.'[5]

Then there were the majority of the British actually living within China long-term, observing the country at first hand through their daily lives, rather than merely passing through. These were the people whom the historian Robert Bickers has described as 'not lovers or experts on China . . . nor . . . Sinologists. They were not led to China through any particular calling.'[6] What had led them there was the 'fact of empire', the opportunities for work and maybe even the creation of wealth that being in the country provided. By 1930, there were 13,000 British people living in the country.[7] These were neither glamorous nor necessarily exciting lives. The specific story that Bickers unfolds is that of Richard Maurice Tinkler, a British man who had found his way to Shanghai in the 1920s and who worked in the municipal police. The records that exist reveal someone who carried resentments about how he had been treated and why he had ended up on the other side of the earth; a figure who was sometimes violent and dismissive of those he disagreed with; and, perhaps most egregious of all, a man who held an antagonistic and deeply racist attitude to the people he was living among. This was despite the fact that some of them were his colleagues.

The anti-British movement and the final use of force

People like Tinkler lived in a China which was increasingly fragmented and unstable, and which their own country had limited scope to influence. In the mid-1920s, the northern and southern parts of the country often seemed as though they were unconnected, with the nationalist-dominated Guangdong administration under Sun's heirs, and the northern government still ostensibly meant to be running the whole country, but with diminishing authority. In this situation, Japan and the USSR offered particularly acute – albeit very different – competition to British interests. While the Japanese developed their own very brutal form of colonisation, the USSR – through the activities of the Comintern, the international arm of the Soviet Communist Party – was more amorphous, but perhaps even more potent in its quest for influence, bringing in new, subversive ideas and organisational forms. Both were more than willing to stir up anti-British feeling locally to promote their own ends. The British government was well aware of this, with the administration of Prime Minister Stanley Baldwin in 1924 openly expressing their fears of Russian Bolshevik influence over the nationalists.[8] The issue was that they had diminishing options for how to counteract and respond to this newly arisen form of Russian influence in China.

A good example of this rising tide of antagonism occurred in 1925–26, when there was a sixteen-month boycott of British goods in Hong Kong. This was precipitated by events on 30 May 1925, when a Chinese student protest in Shanghai and the death of a local activist at a British-owned mill during labour unrest led to the municipal police under one Inspector Everton firing into a crowd, killing at least nine people. Subsequently there were strikes involving 60,000 people in China and then 250,000 in Hong Kong and Canton. In the last few months, the China Association 1925 report stated, an 'anti-foreign campaign particularly directed against Great Britain, and accompanied by the full use of the weapons of strike and boycott' had entailed an 'attack on foreigners'. It concluded that 'the effect of this upon British trade has been extremely serious'.[9]

Just as they had in 1911–12 – before the pushback by Yuan Shikai and his monarchist supporters – in 1925 the nationalists emerged as the more powerful force after a period of division and internal turbulence, and the one likeliest to be able to govern the whole country. This caused Britain to shift from its position of protestations of neutrality and soft support for the status quo towards more decisively taking sides. An assessment of the nationalists from as late as 1925 by the Foreign Office in London had still written it off as 'the radical party of which the late Sun Yatsen was the leader. It is strongly nationalistic and its left wing is deeply infected with Bolshevism', and it was clearly 'under the influence of the Soviet government'.[10] But that hostile stance was already crumbling when, later that same year, a more pragmatic and conciliatory approach was adopted. Nationalist anger at recalcitrance over issues like tariff reform, the removal of extraterritoriality and, for some, the continuing colonial control of Hong Kong meant that Britain finally needed to take the sting out of these attacks and find a modus operandi with the new leaders. Policy makers had to admit that, whatever their faults, those leaders were the only ones who looked close to forming a functional administration that might hold the whole mess together and stop things deteriorating even more.

There was always the option of using force to deal with certain of the problems arising from the chaotic domestic situation, and some expressed a preference for this. A Foreign Office memorandum of 8 January 1930 stated this with disarming directness:

It is important to bear in mind from the outset that our prestige in China was originally built up on force. It was maintained up to the Great War on prestige, but the Chinese have now come to realise that unless there is force behind it mere prestige is another word for bluff.[11]

What specifically was meant by use of force, however, raised many questions – not least about the impact it would have on Britain's relations with the other powers it had to work with in China, many of whom did not share this view. The delicate situation in the country itself also meant that a violent intervention could end up creating a bigger mess than the one it was meant to solve. Finally, after the appalling losses of the First World War, public opinion in Britain was no longer inclined to favour the deployment of soldiers and arms and the use of resources.

In December 1926, under the auspices of British Foreign Secretary Austen Chamberlain (1863–1937), a new approach was articulated in an attempt to balance the various themes that were now emerging. Speaking to the China Association on 18 September 1925, Chamberlain said that 'our only wish is for a strong, united, independent, orderly and prosperous China'.[12] Such rhetorical altruism was to become the norm, rather than the exception, in the years ahead. It was rhetorical because the speaker, while expressing such worthy sentiments, did not say very much about how such a China might come about, or what Britain's precise role might be in working towards this goal. A memorandum from the British government of 1926 tried to codify these aspirations in a more detailed format. It made clear that Britain finally recognised the Chinese nationalist movement, and that after negotiation it would recognise Chinese tariff autonomy and the justice of Chinese demands for treaty revision.[13]

Old habits died hard, however. No sooner had this more conciliatory memorandum appeared than, in early 1927, the Hankou concession in what is today's Wuhan experienced a major attack on British interests. A Mr Goff, the British consul general serving in the city at the time, initially ordered a small group of British marines to bayonet-charge a protesting crowd that had formed at the entrance to the concession. But as the situation escalated, the marines retreated onto a nearby ship and the marauders were allowed to do their worst on British property. Such an unexpected and, on the surface, spontaneous event caused immediate divisions among the British. The minister in Beijing, Miles Lampson (1880–1964), claimed that Britain had 'reason in one hand and ample force in the other' to act more assertively.[14] This was a theme to which Lampson warmed on another occasion:

> There is only one way to do real business with [the Chinese] ... Conciliation is merely regarded as a sign of weakness; but let them realise that we are fully prepared and only too anxious to do the right and fair thing ... yet, if they refuse conciliation and if driven too far, we will without question stand up for our rights.[15]

Plenty of British businesspeople were also eager for the toughest possible response. In February, 20,000 troops, the largest number ever sent to China, were despatched from brigades in India, the Mediterranean and Britain itself, and named the Shanghai Defence Force.[16] The actions of the nationalists in an attack on Nanjing on 24 March, in which several dozen British were killed and wounded, made the situation look as though it was getting out of hand. Despite this, on 2 May the decision was taken by the Cabinet back in London not to follow the route of forceful retaliation. As Chamberlain subsequently said, 'It is becoming more and more clear that in practice such a policy must be discarded as a practicable and effective means of defending British treaty rights and established interests in that country.'[17] Britain was never again to unilaterally consider the use of force in China.

By the end of the decade, a further major policy change was achieved, when Lampson negotiated over two years the dismantling of the treaty port system and the extraterritorial privileges. The final agreement, reached in 1931, maintained rights in Shanghai and Tianjin for a further ten years. All such privileges were finally ended in 1943, the slight delay being caused by the spread of the Second World War. The 1920s had taught Britain a sobering lesson about the depth of resentment towards its regime of control and its history in China, and brought about the realisation that this necessitated a fundamental change in its whole posture. In future, as John Pratt wrote in a memorandum in May 1930, the aim was 'to assist China by every means in our power to secure peace, order and progress', but 'we should leave [it] to the Chinese to choose their own form of government and their own rulers'.[18] This was a dramatic transformation. It was a pragmatic acceptance both of the restrictions that Britain's own powers faced and of the seemingly intractable issues within China itself and the limited ways in which foreigners might intervene in these constructively. From 1931, more than any other single issue it was Japanese aggression that caused China and those working in and with China the most stress. The immensity of what was to unfold in the country over the next decade and a half was something far beyond what Britain alone could handle. Most of the time, it was reduced to the role of passive witness to one of the most enormous tragedies that humanity has ever faced – the Sino-Japanese War – as helpless and impotent as everyone else as the chaos unfolded.

Build-up to war

The series of attacks that Japan launched in China from 1931, resulting in full-out invasion and war in 1937, had a devastating impact on the economy, society and politics of the target country and a knock-on effect on every area of its relations with other powers. For as long as possible, Britain tried to maintain neutrality during this escalating crisis, even as its investments, people and property were directly affected by on-the-ground fighting. The Japanese seizure of Manchuria in 1931 was a brutal wake-up call, however: it demonstrated unambiguously the untenability of the hope that Japanese intentions in China – intentions that had been growing increasingly aggressive over the last two decades – could somehow be contained. Now Britain and others had to work out a far more realistic policy.

First indications were not good: unlike the US, which offered immediate recognition to the annexation of Manchuria, Britain prevari-
cated about accepting Japan's rights over the territory it had taken. In
typical obfuscating fashion, while it did not recognise these outright,
it refused to not recognise them! This served to achieve the remarkable result of irritating the Chinese as much as the Japanese.

Sir John Pratt was an example of a new kind of British actor in the
bilateral relations. He was never posted to China at the most senior
level, but largely served back in Britain, from where he exercised a
huge influence over policy towards the country from 1927 onwards.
Pratt was a Whitehall insider, the son of an Indian mother and a
British father. His world view was a coolly realistic one. The Japanese,
he wrote, despite their previous friendly relations with Britain, saw it
now as a major impediment to the realisation of their aims in China
as these unfolded through the 1930s. Britain therefore became for
them 'public enemy number one'.[19] The Japanese encroachments (and
the escalation of these) also meant that British policy towards China
became inextricably mixed up with that towards Japan and its other
regional ambitions. The two were one and the same thing in this
period.

As war became more likely from the mid- to late 1930s, Britain
had four options: it could continue to sit on the fence; it could give
the Chinese as much help as possible without full alliance; it could
co-operate with Japan and be its ally; or it could side decisively with
China. As one analysis put it, London was caught between 'a Chinese
nationalism on the defensive and a Japanese imperialism on the
offensive' – or in other words, the proverbial rock and a hard place.[20]
Economically, there were a few more options to try to be creative and
flexible. The government chief economist, Frederick Leith-Ross,
visited the country in 1935 and made positive recommendations
about the need for more commercial engagement. This was by no
means solely about preserving the integrity of China as a good in its
own right: it was also because there were strong self-interested

reasons for Britain to do this. In 1931, it still had £197 million of investment in the country. It had the concessions of Tianjin and Canton, and of course its legation in Beijing.[21] It also had the international concession in Shanghai, which, even though it was shared with other foreigners, was the destination for the bulk of British investment. These were things that gave it the incentive to remain deeply involved, despite the chaos and confusion unfolding.

The political and security costs of maintaining even this relatively low level of involvement continued to rise, however. Britain was in a position akin to a helpless bystander watching as a savage fight drew uncomfortably close to their own terrain. Sometimes it came more than uncomfortably close. On 26 August 1937, while travelling by car from Nanjing to Shanghai, the serving British ambassador, Sir Hughe Knatchbull-Hugessen (1886–1971), was strafed and badly injured by a Japanese fighter aircraft. The incident was accidental, and the Japanese apologised; but it offered a vivid illustration of how dangerous the country was becoming. That same month, the Japanese imposed a blockade on all shipping along the coast from Shanghai to Shantou – a direct impediment to British trading interests, despite the key target being the rebellious Chinese. On 27 September 1937, speaking at the League of Nations (predecessor of the United Nations, which existed between the wars), Under-Secretary of State for Foreign Affairs Lord Cranborne mentioned 'Her Majesty's profound horror at the bombing of open towns which is now taking place in China'.[22]

There were also lower-level (but very real and practical) issues, such as the constant intervention in the International Settlement in Shanghai, with Japanese local officials refusing to allow Chinese workers who were employed in the area to return there if they left temporarily for any reason. The Japanese demands also led to the eventual reform of the Customs Service in a Customs Agreement of 1938, whereby Britain lost its decisive role and simply became a creditor nation like everyone else. That marked the ultimate demise of British control over the organisation after over eight decades, though the service continued under different, locally appointed leadership until 1949. The Chinese generally were happy that the final piece of foreign interference and control over their domestic situation was gone, even though it had been achieved through Japanese involvement.

While these events contributed to deepening hostility towards Japan's role in China, the general policy of appeasement towards Japan's actions that Britain tried to pursue did not change until the last minute. Up until then there was an increasingly desperate attempt to maintain some semblance of neutrality. Occasionally Britain tried to devise a more active but low-key way of supporting China's cause: in 1937, for instance, it attempted to suggest sanctions. But that idea was opposed by the US and was therefore never pursued. The fact that London was increasingly obliged to confer with its ally across the Atlantic, and equally as frequently told that its ideas were not ones that could be supported, was a further sign of a new paradigm emerging.

The invasion by the Japanese of southern China in 1938 marked the real turning point and one that finally brought the British down from off the fence. It showed with piercing clarity that the Japanese, as Pratt had foreseen, regarded their interests in China as impossible to fully realise so long as third parties like Britain were still involved and complicating the picture. The rhetoric of the invader promising to protect foreign interests – even in spite of the war it was waging – was undermined by a simultaneous demand that this was only done on the basis of complete obedience to all it demanded. Later in the year, the Japanese orders became more specific and stringent. Settlements and concessions in China were regarded as places where foreigners had administrative powers, but had to be obedient to the new over-lords, which meant that they could not maintain any posture of neutrality. When in 1939 a Japanese customs official was assassinated in Tianjin and the British refused to hand over the Chinese suspects for fear of how justly they would be treated by the new authorities, the concession was punished by being blockaded. A struggle then ensued to prove who was more powerful – the British, until recently, or the new, assertive Japanese. Comments in parliament the previous year that Britain should stick to its course of sitting out the war in the Far East until it was over and then helping whoever won reconstruct the country seemed an increasingly bad idea, and by 1939 was untenable. Evidence of the daily dwindling of Britain's power was easy to find. The blockade on Tianjin in 1939, which crippled its trade interests there, was just one example of this. When the Japanese wanted, they could easily and quickly place their hands on the choke points of British interests and demonstrate who now had the upper hand.[23]

There were many British witnesses to the escalating crisis in China who gave varied testimony as to what was happening on the ground. One of them, the author Peter Fleming (1907–71), brother of the creator of the James Bond novels Ian Fleming, wrote an account of a tour he took around China just after the Japanese annexation of Manchuria in 1933. In *One's Company*, published the following year, he spoke of the Japanese being 'highly insular: temperamentally they are the worst – by which I mean most reluctant – colonists in the world'. He wrote of how the Japanese found it hard to recruit people to settle and work in the region, because of the harsh local conditions and low living standards. Geisha houses were an attempt to make the area a 'home from home', in order to supply at least some of the needs of the invading army, he wrote.[24] He was writing long before the full horror of enforced sexual slavery by what became known as 'comfort women' was properly understood, and before the Nanjing Massacre of 1937 had occurred. Events such as that would no doubt have changed his relatively benign views of the geisha business. A little later, between January and July 1938, the poet W.H. Auden (1907–73) and the writer Christopher Isherwood (1904–86) undertook a journey across China as it was convulsed by war, documenting this in a travelogue they published afterwards. In Suzhou, they were instructed by a missionary in the techniques of how to receive the Japanese when their armies finally arrived. 'Brick up all your compound gates but one', they were told. 'When the first soldiers arrive they must be given tea. You must argue with them patiently, you must be firm but very polite, and on no account must you show that you are frightened.' The problems happened when the Japanese drank alcohol. At that point 'the women will almost certainly be raped'.[25]

As these visitors tried to make sense of the rising signs of calamity in Asia, Britain's own situation in Europe transformed dramatically. With the failure of appeasement, in September 1939 war was declared on Germany after its invasion of Poland. Consumed by its own urgent needs, British attention shifted closer to home. Yet in spite of these immense distractions, there was still steady support for China's war effort against the Japanese across the political spectrum in Britain. Events like the Blitz 'evoked a new sense of shared suffering with China's heavily bombed cities', as one historian wrote.[26] Groups affiliated with the left – such as the Hands off China campaign (1925–27), the League against Imperialism, and the Friends of the Chinese People (in existence from 1927 to 1937) – were replaced by a China Campaign Committee, which ran from 1937 to 1949. These in different ways were indigenous expressions by British people of a rising awareness of their Asian ally's plight, and represented a deepening solidarity with its people. They were by no means mass organisations, but they did indicate some awareness of and sympathy with China's plight among a more mainstream audience in Britain. A further manifestation of that intensifying interest was the exhibition in London of some of the treasures that had been moved from the Imperial Palace in Beijing to various places of safety, away from the war in China. Under the auspices of the Royal Academy, 420,000 people were able to see selected items from this remarkable collection between 28 November 1935 and March 1936. The whole collection itself was finally to be transferred, in the most dramatic fashion, across the strait to Taiwan after the end of the war and before the victory of the communists. The artefacts are housed today in the great Palace Museum in Taipei.[27]

Trying to defend Hong Kong

Of all the interests Britain had in China, the preservation of its colony in Hong Kong was, by 1940, the most important. Over the previous half century, the city had increased the size of its population and had become a major logistics and trade hub. While very British in its mercantile and capitalist spirit, politically it was effectively run as a benign dictatorship, with a governor answerable only to the secretary of state back in Britain (and later, from the 1950s, after Legislative change, parliament). A small colonial office regulated the city's affairs via this structure in London, with the far larger and more influential Foreign Office having to take a back seat.[28] As war loomed, the Hong Kongese and the British local administrators were increasingly aware of the limitations of their support back in Britain, and suspicious that the government would sacrifice their interests in order to salvage its position in China itself, perhaps to the point of relinquishing the city if conflict necessitated this. They were forever aware that they were now a small part of a bigger picture and, in order to be heard, had to shout loudly to assert what they thought were their legitimate demands.

Despite being ceded to Britain, Hong Kong's links with the rest of China throughout the colonial era up to the 1930s had continued to be extremely close, with an intimate connection between the politics of the two places. In 1911, at the time of the Xinhai Revolution, the local population in the colony supported the nationalists and the revolution that had just occurred, even though it had no impact on their own governance. Many of the key protagonists in the uprising (including the first president of the new republic, Sun Yatsen himself) had used the place as a basis for their activities, with the city representing a refuge from the vengeful Qing authorities across the border. Local prostitutes at the time even announced that they were paying half their earnings to support the cause of revolution (and appealed for more clients, so that their contributions could increase).[29] The 1925 strike against British interests showed how powerful the sway of

China continued to be. This brought Hong Kong almost to a stand-still, as its workers stood in solidarity with those elsewhere in their vast neighbour. Despite this deep connection, both during the build-up to the Sino-Japanese War and in the war era itself, the city's admin-istrators had to face the great challenge of ensuring as far as possible that the Japanese accepted that Hong Kong was a separate territory, and that they had no cause to take a closer interest and intervene in its affairs. Support for the Chinese war effort therefore had to be discreet, so that it would not attract reprisals. An example of this occurred at the start of the war, when the covert transhipment of arms to support Chiang's nationalist armies was allowed.

This balancing act became impossible after the 7 December 1941 Japanese attack on Pearl Harbor brought the Americans into the war. Britain's declaration of war on the Japanese the following day meant that Japan now had more than sufficient reason to launch an invasion of Hong Kong – and it promptly did so. The subsequent fall of the city within a few days was part of a general series of defeats suffered by British forces across Asia at the hands of their new enemy. In a very short period of time, Burma (Myanmar), Singapore and Malaysia fell to well-equipped, well-disciplined, ruthlessly executed attacks by the imperial forces. Hong Kong's position was known to be vulner-able even during an earlier assessment by the chiefs of staff in London.[30]

It was left to Sir Mark Young (1886–1974), appointed governor in 1941, to try to hold out as long as possible when the attacks started. A short message from a British official back to London on 8 December captured the desperation of the situation with pithy simplicity: 'Japanese planes over Kowloon City, and Kai Tak airfield ... our planes flattened.'[31] British war leader Winston Churchill (1874–1965) regarded Hong Kong and the general theatre of war in Asia as a second front – one that would be sorted out once the more important conflict in Europe was over. Thus reinforcements were not sent in sufficient numbers to stand even a chance of putting up meaningful resistance. The small British force defending the city was able to delay the inevitable, but not stop it. By Christmas, Young was forced to request a ceasefire and had surrendered.

The British population certainly endured high levels of suffering during and after the actual conflict. One eyewitness account talks of how medical orderlies and those who were meant to be treating the wounded and dying were themselves 'taken out, stripped to the waist, lined up alongside a storm drain and, amid shouts of laughter, were bayonetted or hacked to death'.[32] However, the local Chinese were to suffer far more extensively. A doctor in Kowloon stated that there had been at least ten thousand victims of rape. Many others were bayonetted, with some having their hands tied together before being thrown into the harbour.[33] Lamentably, this kind of barbarity was the norm rather than the exception across the border in China. The British administrators became prisoners of war, running their own affairs under a 'camp committee', and the economy of the city became geared towards the delivery of the goals of the Greater East Asia Co-Prosperity Sphere set up by the Japanese. Those British who stayed had to work to achieve these. Understandably, most had opted to flee before the final denouement.

Despite the early brutality, during the rest of the war Hong Kong did not go on to see the same levels of cruelty and harshness that were experienced in other areas under Japanese occupation. The city was saved by its importance as a convenient commercial and logistics hub, and was largely left to its own devices under the Japanese governors sent from Tokyo to manage it. Despite the occupation, even as early as 1943 there were those back in London planning the continuation of colonial rule, once this dark phase was over. These plans were particularly supported by the business community, which foresaw that – once peace was restored – Hong Kong (rather than anywhere in mainland China) would be where some autonomy for foreign business interests could be maintained. Engaged in their life-or-death struggle against the Japanese – one that had even pushed them into an uneasy and unequal coalition with the communists – the nationalists were clearly distracted by trying to survive. However, whatever the ruminations going on in Britain, they were unlikely to wish any continuation of colonial rule after a conflict which was, at heart, about the survival and defence of an autonomous, unified Chinese state.

Such views had little impact on Churchill, who, in the latter stages of the conflict, was himself famously engaged in a fight with US President Franklin Roosevelt over how far, and where, Britain's imperial holdings could continue once the war was over. On Hong Kong, he had made clear his disregard for China as a great nation: he did not consider that it merited a seat at the main table when negotiations about the post-war settlement started, and assumed that Britain would indeed retake Hong Kong once hostilities ceased.

An early provisional agreement at the 1943 Cairo Conference hammered out between US President Roosevelt (1882–1945), Churchill and Chiang Kai-shek had come up with a process whereby Britain ceded the territory to China, which then made it a free port with a promise to protect British interests and commerce.[34] On 1 May 1944, Sir George Mann, in a Foreign Office note, mapped out options in more detail, writing that either the territory would revert to the same status it had had under the British prior to Japanese annexation, or it would come under Chinese control, but on the understanding that there would be better access for Britain's commercial interests in China itself.[35] Roosevelt, had he lived, may have insisted on the latter, softer option – one that was compatible with his largely critical view of Britain's colonial interests and the need for them to come to an end. But Harry Truman (1884–1972), his successor after his death in 1945, was more amenable to British desires. It was therefore the first of Mann's options (the one that Britain evidently preferred), rather than the second, that was pursued once war in the East had ceased. Once Japan surrendered, Britain simply announced in August 1945 that it was going to reoccupy the city and readminister it. American disillusionment with Chiang and the corruption of his nationalist forces helped strengthen Britain's hand when it made this audacious move. Chiang did offer some counterproposals, whereby British control over the territory would be reimposed but China would be allowed to regain sovereignty. But these were rebuffed.

In the end, after much negotiation, British Admiral Cecil Harcourt, briefly de facto governor of the territory after the defeat of the invaders, signed a surrender document from the Japanese on behalf of not just the British government, but also Chiang Kai-shek as China theatre commander.[36] Despite a last-minute push by Chinese forces towards the borders of the city, the arrival in late August of a British army contingent sent from Sydney, Australia forced Chiang to call his troops off. He assumed that the matter would be postponed to a later date and that there were more urgent issues to attend to. Hong Kong therefore came back under British colonial rule. Chiang was never able to revisit this matter, consumed as he was by the more urgent business of trying to save his own power base in the country, and the British remained in control of the city until its final retrocession, half a century later.

Aftermath of war

The Sino-Japanese War had physically destroyed 20 million lives and led to 50 million becoming displaced. It had divided the nation into nationalist, communist and Japanese-controlled portions, in ways that had almost destroyed any notion of a unified Chinese state. Much of the infrastructure of the country had been ruined. Those British who had worked for all or part of the war period in China had witnessed a country which, from 1941, had been a key ally struggling alongside them in a common cause against the Axis powers. The way in which support and help for Europe had been prioritised over assistance to the front in Asia was one of the great sore points after the conflict, creating resentment that would simmer in the years to come, even to the point where China's role as an ally was almost forgotten once the Communist Party took over in 1949.

As in so many other areas, the war had a transformative impact on Britain's relations with China. It meant initially acknowledging a far greater role for America, leading Britain to attempt to constantly balance and calibrate its interests with those of the US. Trying to achieve this created tensions which were evident even at the start, though they would become far more apparent in the future. In the early years, Britain simply sought to factor this new dimension into its policy making, appreciating that the space for its direct bilateral influence with China had become far more limited. The war and its immediate aftermath initially concealed the impact of this huge change, as – for both London and Washington – it had made possible a new and more collaborative relationship with China against a common enemy. But this collaborative ethos soon faded. Within a decade, Britain and China were once more on opposite sides of a geopolitical divide, one where America's diktat held increasing sway. Once China became communist, the US expected its allies, of which Britain was the most stalwart, to follow its lead and ostracise the new country. As the next chapter will show, this did not mean that there was no space for at least some independent action; but it was limited and had to be explained clearly to both the US and China. In essence, Britain lost much of its freedom of action and agency in Chinese affairs. That characterised the era from 1945, and continues ever more markedly to this day.

The war had also been the moment when the final vestiges of British privilege in China were swept away. This had been a long process, ongoing since the 1920s. The restoration of tariff autonomy to the Chinese, the loss of control over the salt *gabelle* and the customs were landmarks along this path for Britain, as it gradually let go and relinquished its former perks. It was indeed ironic that in the end the Japanese, through their invasion, had inadvertently swept away the imperial interests of others. All these privileges, apart from colonial control of Hong Kong, were removed when extraterritoriality was finally abolished in 1943. That provided the grounds for a reset. Symbolically, it was important, too, that throughout the war, Britain and British officials had maintained a constant presence in China, shifting their diplomatic representation from Beijing to Nanjing and finally to Chongqing, as the Japanese-controlled areas grew, but never abandoning the country, even if they were only able to offer limited help. Of those that helped, perhaps the most significant was a biochemist from Cambridge University, Joseph Needham, who had developed an interest in China and particularly in the history of science and technology in the country's past. His two years from 1943 as science attaché at the British legation in Chongqing and the opportunities they afforded him to travel around other provinces proved formative ones, although his work only appeared from the 1950s onwards. That will be dealt with in the next chapter.

The war inevitably brought about profound change within China, too, particularly its internal politics. The Foreign Office grew aware of this as it observed the rising role of the communists from the mid-war period. Assessments of them initially implied that they were of limited importance. But the wartime ambassador Archibald Clark Kerr (1882–1951) made note of what he understood to be their 'mild radicalism' in the Chongqing years, and how this was gaining them more adherents and might be significant in the future.[37] Once the Pacific War was over, Britain's attitude was tepid towards expanding its involvement in China beyond merely protecting its surviving assets. The Treasury, aware of the crippling debt that the country had assumed in its fight against Nazism, felt that China was too much of a risk for greater commitments to be made to it in terms of extending credit or supporting business investment. There was an initial debate about trying to restore Britain's prestige and its role in the country, but the new Labour government under Clement Attlee (1883–1967) had larger and more immediate issues to confront, including the final arrangements for the independence of India (which happened in 1947) and the management of critical domestic affairs, like the establishment of a social welfare system and the creation of the National Health Service. Matters concerning China slipped down a level, and that position was reinforced by the outbreak of fighting between the nationalists and the communists in 1946, which plunged the country into civil war leading to even more resistance in London to greater engagement.

For this final spate of national unrest, Britain was able once more to sincerely support a neutral stance. It had no illusions about the levels of corruption and dysfunctionality in the Chiang nationalist regime. But nor did it relish the rise of the communists, despite the debate in government circles about just how close the Chinese party was to the Soviet one. The Communist Party leadership proved harder to comprehend and remained to some degree shrouded in mystery after its years headquartered in the remote Yan'an area of central Shaanxi province. Generally, though, after the war the British public, if they had a view on China, were largely positive. There had been groups in Britain selling goods and trying to donate and give help to the Chinese in their struggle against the Japanese from the 1930s. Now there was a wider sense that the country deserved fairer treatment after the horror of the Japanese attacks and atrocities, and following its period as an ally.

The rise of Chinese Britain

In the period prior to the twentieth century, as we have seen in previous chapters, while there had been sporadic visits by Chinese people, some of whom settled in Britain, the numbers had been small. Chinese people had limited exposure to first-hand information – in their own language and from people with a similar cultural background – about what life was like in Britain, and about the culture, identity and history of the place. One of the most important tasks was the translation of works of literature. Whereas the earliest translations of Chinese classics into English had appeared in the eighteenth century (see chapter three), it was to be well into the twentieth century before the reverse process occurred. The first translation of any play by William Shakespeare, for instance, was in 1922, when *Hamlet* was rendered into Chinese by Tian Han – penname of Tian Shouchang (1898–1968) – a student then based in Tokyo. Tian subsequently went on to write the lyrics of 'March of the Volunteers', which serves today as the national anthem of the People's Republic. Zhu Shenghao (1912–44) then completed translations of most of Shakespeare's plays in the 1930s. While his work was highly regarded, he never studied or lived in Britain, but learned English entirely in China (not unlike one of his counterparts in Britain, Arthur Waley (1889–1966) – only in reverse).

The China Association had complained in 1922–23 that 'it is unfortunate that so few young Chinamen come to English for their education'; members of the audience let out an approving 'hear, hear' when this sentiment was expressed.[38] Things did improve, however, over the coming decade, as remarkable individuals came to study and work in Britain. The relative novelty of what they were doing, and the freshness and quality of their work, meant that it had a major impact in shaping some deeper understanding of the people of a country which had been influencing China for the previous hundred years or so, and yet which had remained largely inaccessible over that time. Xu Zhimo (1897–1931) is a good representative, someone who came to further his banking career in 1921 after an initial period in the US, but then shifted to being a student. Based at King's College, Cambridge from 1921, his brief time at the university was eventful, as he divorced his wife, visited Europe, translated poets like Samuel Taylor Coleridge, made friends with people such as the painter Roger Fry and the writer Lowes Dickinson, and wrote poetry – all in the space of just a few years. His most celebrated poem, 'Saying Goodbye to Cambridge Again' (published in 1928) is widely known and well loved across the Chinese-speaking world. Nostalgic and evocative in tone, and only two stanzas long, it expresses something of the atmosphere and appearance of the West, but in a strongly Chinese idiom.[39]

Shu Qingchun (1899–1966), far better known by his penname Lao She, was in Britain at around the same time as Xu. He worked as a lecturer at the School of Oriental and African Studies (SOAS) in London, and his novel based on his experiences over those years, *Mr Ma and Son* (published in 1929) expressed well some of the frustrations of being Chinese abroad at this time. The story tells of a father and son and of their experiences trying to get by in the new city they find themselves in, and is sprinkled with descriptions of the prejudices that British people sometimes had towards these new, very unfamiliar visitors. Mrs Wedderburn – their landlady in central London, for instance – holds fast to the 'absolute, unshakable truth, beyond all shadow of doubt, that the Chinese were poisoners'.[40] Her daughter, Mr Ma suspects, when talking to another Chinese visitor who has developed a crush on the girl, is 'an average young English person, and the average young English person looks down on the Chinese'.[41] Lao She was to return to China after stints in America after the war, and died there – most likely at the hands of revolutionary Red Guards during the Cultural Revolution, though the circumstances of his death remain unclear to this day.

A very different writer was the great Qian Zhongshu (1910–98), who studied at Oxford, where he was financed by the Boxer indemnity funds (by then largely allocated for scholarships and educational support for Chinese). He and his wife, the novelist and translator Yang Jiang (1911–2016), introduced the works of a host of European writers to the Chinese. Qian was not to suffer the same extreme outcome as Lao She, though the years he and Yang spent in a reform camp during the Cultural Revolution were movingly remembered in a short memoir that Yang completed in the 1980s, translated into English as *A Cadre School Life: Six Chapters*.

There were also, in the 1930s, Chinese writers who wrote about Britain and China principally in English. Chiang Yee (1903–77) was one such. Like Lao She, he worked from 1933 as a lecturer at SOAS in London and then survived as a freelance writer, largely due to the success of his *Silent Traveller* books. These alternate English text with watercolour paintings in a distinctively Chinese style, and cover places like London and the Lake District. As the British historian Herbert Read wrote, Chiang shows that his art 'is not bound by geographical limits; it is universal and it can interpret your English landscape just as well as the Chinese landscape'.[42] After centuries of British illustration and literary description of the Chinese landscape, Chiang's was an interesting inversion – a British world in English, but with Chinese views and illustrations exemplifying Chinese aesthetics. He had a wide circle of acquaintances in London, but despite his vehement opposition to Nazism was unable to fight on the allied side during the war because of his alien status. He moved to the US in 1955, and then back to China in 1975, just two years before his death.

For those Chinese who came to settle and work in Britain, and who were not students, the 1920s to the immediate post-war years were harsh ones. At the end of the First World War, the British government rewarded those who had helped in the war effort or who had come to Europe to fight in the Chinese Labour Corps by encouraging voluntary repatriation. This hostile attitude only intensified after the outbreak of race riots in 1919, calling for the repatriation of all non-whites. Some three thousand Chinese seafarers and labourers were subsequently threatened with deportation to France or Belgium to take part in reclamation work. Chinatowns that existed in Liverpool, Manchester and around Limehouse in London decreased in size: while the population of the latter stood at 4,000 before the First World War, by 1921 the figure was 300. Through the 1920s and into the 1930s, matters deteriorated, so that the 1931 census revealed a further fall in the number of those who were classified as Chinese in Britain from the decade before. The number of those identifying as Chinese at Limehouse had shrunk to a hundred by 1934. The Liverpool equivalent was torn down in 1934, with no compensation offered to its inhabitants.[43] During the Second World War, Chinese seafarers were engaged in the war effort, with Liverpool's Chinese community swelling to a total of 3,000. But once the war was over, the Chinese population in Britain continued to fall until the 1950s. Chinese who had fought in the war were forcibly repatriated, with some leaving behind British-born wives and children. It was only in the 1950s that there was a modest renaissance of people of Chinese heritage in Britain. This came in the wake of a combination of factors: a relatively liberal immigration environment for those who could claim British citizenship, on the basis of having been resident in one of Britain's overseas colonies; and the poor economy in Hong Kong, which encouraged some there to seek a better life in Britain.

To a certain extent, however, the single figure in this period who did most to promote better understanding of China in Britain was the scholar Arthur Waley. Appointed assistant keeper of oriental antiquities at the British Museum in 1913, during his time there he taught himself both classical Chinese and Japanese. Despite never visiting Asia, or being able actually to speak the languages he could read, he became a formidable and accomplished translator, introducing a wide English-language readership to the Tang-era poets of a thousand years before, rendering them into often lyrical, highly accessible poetry which gained critical acclaim on its own merits. Waley was also to write about classical philosophy and historic issues, working from 1929 exclusively as a professional translator and writer.

9

The Cold War Era

Britain Making Friends with the Communists, 1949–71

The first impressions gained by the British of the new force emerging in China, the communists, were not good. In 1949, as it followed the civil war unfolding in China, Britain became increasingly aware that the communists were going to be the victors. Through a mixture of poor judgement and lack of up-to-date information about where the demarcation line currently was between the nationalists and the communists, the British vessel HMS *Amethyst* set off in mid-April, in the midst of this complex, rapidly developing situation, on a journey from Shanghai up the Yangtze River to Nanjing, to undertake guard duties at the British legation there. From the start, things went badly. Guns targeted the ship from the northern, communist-controlled side of the river. The firing increased in intensity as the vessel progressed towards the city of Jiangyin, resulting eventually in shelling which caused enough damage for it to stop deep in enemy territory. Over the next few weeks, the British aboard and the local communist commanders negotiated. These discussions were to be the precursor to the new style of politics that Britain was to experience, since they were the first formal contact between the two systems. The communists demanded an admission that the ship had gone astray deliberately in order to spy on them, were deeply suspicious of British intentions, and came up with numerous different demands before they would even consider letting the *Amethyst* go free. And each of those demands prompted pushback from the other side.

As the incident unfolded, it attracted enough attention back in Britain to register in the House of Commons. There the Conservative member of parliament and future prime minister Harold Macmillan (1894–1986) lambasted the government's response for the impotence it showed in helping the vessel extract itself. This was 'an absolute gem', he said on 5 May 1949, 'a little cameo of incompetence, a miniature masterpiece of mismanagement, a classical illustration, which I have no doubt will long be studied by the staff colleges of the world, of exactly how not to do it'.[1] After weeks of fruitless and often painful negotiations, the *Amethyst* eventually made a bold dash for freedom in October. But the encounter was unsettling and one that had promoted much more thought among the British about who precisely the Chinese communists were, and impelled them to take this novel, unfamiliar force much more seriously.

Publicly and privately in British analysis from 1945 to 1951, there was debate about what to make of these people who were on the verge of taking over the world's most populous country, and yet who had seemingly appeared from nowhere. While the reports of figures like American journalist Edgar Snow (1905–72) in *Red Star Over China*, his seminal 1937 work, contained descriptions and interviews with the movement's key leaders and had introduced at least some ideas about this new political movement into the English language, contact was very limited for as long as the nationalists remained the dominant political force and the war raged. Michael Lindsay (1909–94), working in China during the 1940s, wrote in 1955 of how he had been struck by the fact that embassy officials from Britain in Chongqing 'not only knew nothing about the Communist areas but also made clear that they did not wish to know'.[2]

As the Second World War drew to a close, many in the British system realised that they needed to start showing at least curiosity towards this group and to move beyond the indifference that had characterised their attitude up to then. Examining the sparse sources available, a consensus soon emerged that – far from being mere puppets of the USSR – China's communist movement was significantly different. As *The Times* stated on 25 January 1945, unlike the Russians, whose revolution was urban in nature, the Chinese were 'an agrarian democracy'.[3] They were cut from different cloth to their Soviet brethren, and their leader, Mao Zedong had produced writings that provided evidence of a strongly distinctive and much more indigenous political ideology – one that prioritised rural revolution over urban proletariat revolt, despite what Marxist orthodoxy prescribed.

The Foreign Office supported some level of engagement. For it, the post-war policy was to aim to keep a foot in the door of the country as it stabilised and returned to some kind of normality. It did not share the American allegiance to the nationalists under Chiang Kai-shek. Maintaining links with everyone made sense, hedging until a final dominant winner emerged. In this, the Foreign Office mandarins were guided by awareness of Britain's parlous post-war trade and economic position. The country still had extensive interests in China, with £300 million invested there in 1941 – investments that had survived, even as the country had been ripped apart by conflict. The objective was to try to be in a position to pursue commercial opportunities, no matter who formed the government.[4] According to British analysis, the communists were a nationalist force, rather than one that bought into class warfare and revolutionary aims.[5] A similar view was articulated by Archibald Clark Kerr, ambassador from 1938 to 1942, when he talked of the communists as holding to 'mild radicalism'.[6]

The collapse of the nationalists in the course of 1949, and their flight to the island of Taiwan to continue the Republic of China there, was one of the great landmarks of twentieth-century history. The outcome – the victory of the communists under Mao Zedong's

leadership by October 1949 – had global and long-term reverbera-
tions. For Britain, it presented complex and difficult diplomatic challenges. Uppermost was how to maintain at least some influence in
China, while not alienating the US, which, it became clear very early
on, was antagonistic to the regime and continued to support Chiang's
cause across the water. Attempting to forge links with the new rulers
in Beijing was a first major test for the British, as they tried to factor
US interests and importance into their own policy towards China
(see the previous chapter) and create some kind of balance. It was to
prove a precarious and exhausting business. As they sought to defend
their course of action in Washington, the most important card that
the British held was their continuing management of Hong Kong and
the consequent need for at least some sort of relationship with the
new regime in Beijing. London argued that it had no choice in the
matter. In the end, with huge reservations, the US reluctantly came to
accept this.

Winston Churchill, still leader of the opposition in 1949, stated
the pragmatic case with clarity when speaking in parliament in
November of that year: 'When a large and powerful mass of people
are organised together, and are masters of an immense area, it may be
necessary to have relations with them.' Indeed, he argued, when
things were most difficult and there was most space for argument,
'that is the time when diplomacy is most needed'.[7]

It was not just the Americans, though, who were profoundly sceptical about building amicable ties with China. The French, with their
extensive interests across the Asian region, were also opposed to
British moves to recognise the new government. But if for no other
reason than Hong Kong, Britain needed to maintain some means of
talking to the Chinese. Happily, the original fears that the communists would undertake an invasive move on the city once they had
seized control proved erroneous. There were enough pragmatists in
the new capital established in Beijing to appreciate the merits of
having the city continue for the time being as a territory administered

by the British, thus allowing some access to capital, technology and controlled trade with the outside world.

Supplementing this, the British were far more realistic and sceptical of the grander, more ambitious designs for a new China to be constructed from the ashes of the old that the idealists in Washington were addicted to. America had hoped to see a radical transformation of Chinese politics and – through the concerted effort of missionaries – its world view and values system. This explains the bitterness of the disappointment it felt when the atheistic communists prevailed, because their victory snuffed out these hopes. The great Ernest Bevin (1881–1951), foreign secretary under the ruling Labour government of the time, had made it clear that the creation of a Western-style democracy in China was wishful thinking.[8] One had to work with what one had; and in the end, diplomatic recognition was a means by which to deliver much-needed influence over a new player, one with whom there were very limited options.

There were also broader strategic reasons: if China were to become isolated, it might be tempted deeper into the Soviet camp seeking stronger bonds there. That scenario would see a major part of Asia fall under Soviet communist sway, going the same way as Eastern Europe, creating a bamboo as well as an iron curtain. After their wartime collaboration from 1941, Moscow and the West had increasingly diverged, so that containment and pushing back against Russian hegemonistic designs was now a priority. In this way, the Cold War quickly reached Asia. For these reasons, and despite American protestations, Britain became the first major European power to confer diplomatic recognition on China, on 6 January 1950. Humphrey Trevelyan (1905–85), who served as the second British chargé d'affaires in Beijing from 1953 to 1955, later wrote that 'we had recognised the Communists not because we approved of them, but because they were in control of the mainland and it was normal practice to recognise the government in control, however much we disapproved of it'.[9] Despite these statements of official commitment to pragmatism, public opinion differed. A poll in November 1949 showed a majority of both Labour and Conservative voters opposed to what their government had done.[10]

Representation but no status: The early years of Britain in the new China

Recognition did not bring Britain quite the level of influence it wanted, but it did mean that (with only the briefest hiatus) it is the one major Western country to have maintained continuous contact with different Chinese regimes from the early decades of the nineteenth century right up to the twenty-first century. America refrained from direct contact with the People's Republic from 1950. The barriers between the two great powers deepened with the Korean War (1950–53), when they fought against each other – albeit the Americans under United Nations auspices, and the Chinese as a (vast) proxy force for the North Koreans. The two countries did not return to any form of meaningful direct contact for over two decades.

British diplomatic recognition was a big deal. But because London also maintained contact with the Republic of China on Taiwan – a major issue for Beijing, which did not recognise the legitimacy of Chiang's forces and actively planned a final invasion to resolve the issue – the new Beijing regime did not initially reciprocate. It was also irritated by another manifestation of Britain's historic habit regarding China of settling on neutrality until decisive action was forced on it. At the newly established United Nations, Britain did not actively support the People's Republic in its demand for the representative seat to be given to it, rather than Taiwan (to which the right was granted). Policy on this was to shift over the years, and was only finally resolved with a successful vote (which Britain supported) in 1971 in Beijing's favour. But in those early years, faced with strong US opposition, the best Britain managed was abstention, despite some sympathy for the communists' demand.

The combination of war in Korea, where Britain was fighting as part of the UN forces, and a Cold War heating up in Europe proved unconducive to warm and friendly relations. Trevelyan found that life in Beijing was like being in 'a superior mental home, with every comfort, but having no contact with the outside world beyond the limits of the British Embassy'.[11] Douglas Hurd (b.1930), a future foreign secretary in the 1990s, remembered his time from 1952 to 1954 serving in the city as one when 'we had no great problems, but then we had no great achievements. We waited for something to happen. We waited and we waited'.[12] Britain had had £110 million of assets in China when the communists came to power.[13] In 1949, there had been 4,000 British still living and working in the country.[14] But the following decade became one of almost perpetual retreat and abandonment. By 1954, investment levels had almost vanished and only 300 British were left. As one historian put it, Britain had shifted from keeping a foot in the door to keeping just a toe there.[15]

One of the new features of the Sino-British relationship from 1949 was a politicisation of the link in Britain itself. The former China hands – those that had worked for the major companies with interests in China, from Jardine to HSBC to British American Tobacco or Swire – were broadly conservative in outlook (there were exceptions of course), even if not actual supporters of the Conservative political party. From 1949, the fact that an entity clearly on the left was in power in Beijing meant it was far more likely that those with either Labour Party or more left-leaning sympathies would maintain a friendly view of the new People's Republic. Trade was an area of immediate focus. As a result of the Korean War, in which over 4,500 British died, Great Britain imposed export restrictions on trade with China on 25 June 1951.[16] This compounded the challenges that British companies with interests and personnel still in the country faced. As Trevelyan said, these people were 'in China as virtual prisoners', due to demands that they continue paying the staff they employed (and whatever other commitments they had), and they were not allowed to leave until deals had been done with the Chinese government.[17]

The staff of Jardine in Shanghai were particularly badly hit. Over the previous century or more of business activity across the country, they had accrued interests in engineering, logistics, breweries, mills and property. But as one of their local managers admitted in September 1954, in a telephone call to his colleagues in Hong Kong to update them, 'we are trying to get on as quickly as possible but we are at [the local Chinese officials'] mercy'.[18] The Chinese government locally had made its own views clear. Implementing the transfer of almost all forms of enterprise and business into the hands of the state, it placed a placard at the entrance to one Jardine building in Shanghai simply declaring 'Celebrate Transfer, Welcome Takeover'. Company personnel experienced some of the uncompromising tone from Chinese officials that their diplomatic counterparts were having to deal with in Beijing. Thomas Beesley, the local representative, while trying to wrap up business and get as much reasonable compensation as possible once it became clear that the company would not be able to continue in the country, encountered this problem. On 4 August 1954, he philosophically admitted that the outlook of the two sides was different. 'It would be in vain for us to discuss concrete problems, if we, after agreeing to certain principles, refuse to stick to such principles after a few days', he wrote in one report.[19] The new Chinese government's insistence on establishing the broad parameters for discussion before moving on to particular issues was to become standard practice and dominated discussions from simple trade deals to the huge tussle over Hong Kong retrocession years later. Often, only after the most senior leaders had set out the framework were officials lower down able to undertake their work. The Chinese also asked for Jardine staff to be 'sincere and friendly'. Such sincerity and friendliness was miraculously maintained until the two sides struck a deal that led to the complete withdrawal of the company from China by 1957. It was to return by the end of the century, however, when Jardine made a remarkable comeback on the mainland.

China wanted trade, but it wanted to be careful about its trading partners. In 1952, at the Moscow conference for sympathetic partners, a delegation led by the Nobel Peace Prize-winning scientist Lord John Boyd-Orr (1880–1971) reached agreement on potential trade with the Chinese side – which then set up a trade office in East Berlin to service Europe. The businesspeople who came to follow up on these trade opportunities were not from the 'old China hands' network. Far from it: they were largely individuals who had more left-leaning sympathies and almost no prior experience of dealing with China. From their number, the British Council for the Promotion of International Trade (BCPIT) was established and signed £30 million worth of two-way deals.[20] To support this, the Chinese finally sent a chargé d'affaires to London, followed by a commercial counsellor.

The appearance of these new actors who engaged with China split the business constituency in Britain as never before. While there had been friction and divisions in the past, this was a far more profound schism. John Keswick, a member of the family that had largely steered Jardine's business since the nineteenth century, expressed the antipathy clearly. It was 'irksome that these ridiculously uninformed businessmen would go hobnobbing with the Chinese at a time when we are being squeezed to death by them', he stated in April 1953.[21] Nor was the British government keen. Foreign secretary at the time (but soon to be prime minister), Anthony Eden (1897–1977) dubbed the BCPIT a Communist Party organisation.[22] This claim was repeated in 1963 by the secretary of state for industry, trade and regional development – no less a figure than future prime minister Edward Heath (1916–2005), who stated in parliament that year that it was 'a communist controlled organisation, and the advice given to business firms by Her Majesty's Government is that they should consider very carefully whether to become associated, directly or indirectly, with it' – a harsh command, particularly coming from a leader who, later in life, became associated with an almost slavish closeness to the Chinese government and its leaders (see next chapter).[23] Though export controls were lifted in 1957 and government-supported trade missions were sent to China (Frederick Erroll, parliamentary secretary at the Board of Trade, undertook the first ever ministerial-level visit to the People's Republic that year), the division between the two trade groups endured.

Withdrawal involved people, businesses and institutions. Only one British manufacturer, a knitting factory, remained in operation until 1959.[24] The actor and writer Michael Croft (1922–86) had heard of this venture when visiting Beijing as part of a theatre delegation in 1958, and recorded admiringly of the Yorkshire-born plant manager that his endurance in keeping the place running under wholly British management was 'a feat of economic acrobatics that came perilously close to calculated suicide'.[25] The network of official government representation was wound down until only limited personnel in Beijing and Shanghai remained. The physical delegation in the capital moved in 1958, after a long hiatus, from the old palace it had occupied for almost a century in the central legation quarter to a more purpose-built location further out, along a road called Guanghua Lu. The new embassy, with a residence next to it, was a functional, underwhelming building which, after several extensions, continues to operate to this day. As for Shanghai, remarkably the grand consulate along the Bund functioned until 1966, when, after the radicals supporting the Cultural Revolution just being launched in the city took control, it was peremptorily closed. After years of neglect, it reopened in the mid-2000s as a five-star hotel in the Peninsula chain.

Croft also reported the almost complete departure of the British from the capital Beijing. Apart from those serving at the British legation, there were only four compatriots working outside. Of these, Arthur Boyd continued as a journalist and, according to Croft, despite his fervently anti-communist views, was able to report on China in such a remarkably balanced and even-handed way that he attracted the praise of the premier, Zhou Enlai (1898–1976).[26] It was a lugubrious sight, Croft observed, 'the managerial left-overs, salvage men, scrap merchants in real estate, hanging on to what remained – a solitary floor in the Hong Kong and Shanghai Bank, a single room in the Chartered, a Sassoon hotel, an office block'.[27] It was to this that the once-mighty British interests in the country had been reduced.

Nor was China's new regime doing much to endear itself to the British public. Liu Ningyi (1907–94) was the first official from the People's Republic to come to Britain, visiting in 1950. Despite being the most travelled of the new leaders, according to Alan Winnington (1910–83), a journalist who covered Chinese affairs, 'travel had not broadened his mind'.[28] Liu's visit was striking for its counterproductiveness. Refusing almost every invitation, he instead stuck to gatherings in which only left-wing sympathisers were present. This was hardly likely to change the minds of opinion formers or policy makers, let alone the wider public. But it was, alas, to prove a good indication of things to come in the following decades.[29] Hosting such visits did not even curry much favour back in Beijing. Reporting to the National People's Congress – China's annual parliament – in February 1958, Zhou Enlai did not mince his words, categorising the British as 'double faced'.[30]

This antipathy arose from more than just ideological and geopolitical differences. From 1949, Britain faced Chinese leaders and a ruling party that had adopted a particular view of the country's recent history. This recounted how the previous hundred years had been a period of unjust humiliation at the hands of foreigners (see the introduction). The British occupied prime position in this cast of villains: they were regarded as the people who had carved the country up, exploited it, and caused it to lose face and prestige. That gave rise to an often angry and hostile posturing on the part of the new government towards any dialogue or relations with Britain. These attitudes rendered difficult any attempt by London to maintain even informal links with the communist government. Its past was already becoming an impediment in the present. As Lindsay wrote in 1955, 'Chinese policy is determined by emotional rather than by rational considerations.' The British aroused particularly deep feelings. This type of approach to things by Beijing may have sacrificed 'real advantages in the present and future in order to pay off grudges from the past'; but it proved an enduring position.[31]

Delegation game

Given this more controlled and restricted situation, one of the few ways in which the British could find out what was happening in China was through the new phenomenon of delegations. Prior to the Second World War, China had been a relatively accessible place, the only impediments being physical, rather than political. The 1860 Treaty of Beijing granted freedom of movement around the country: the issue for foreigners was not whether they had a right of access, but whether the trains, roads or waterways were in a fit condition to allow convenient travel. The communists when they came to power almost immediately imposed severe restrictions. The level of distrust towards all outsiders – not just the British – meant that even the ostensibly favoured Soviet experts being brought in large numbers to help with reconstruction were placed in compounds like the Beijing Friendship Hotel, where they could be confined and monitored. If this was the deal on offer to a supposedly friendly country, it is not difficult to appreciate the huge limitations placed on nationals from somewhere like Great Britain.

The Chinese came quickly to prefer delegations as the best way of allowing some level of access. An attendee of one of these, the distinguished British journalist James Cameron (1911–85), observed in 1955 that Beijing had become 'the headquarters, possibly the world's number one centre' for this activity. He himself found forty-seven such delegations ongoing the week he arrived in the country: they consisted of those he labelled the uncommitted, the partially committed and the truly supportive, who believed in the country's new socialist mission.[32] Nor was this a technique reserved just for

Britain. The era of the People's Republic of China might just as well be called the 'delegation dynasty', under which specific groups of visitors are allowed into the country as part of tightly controlled, organised tours. This has remained a universal feature of Chinese diplomacy to the present day, across all countries, subjects and business sectors, even though the conditions of entry have largely been relaxed and independent travellers have long been accepted.

An early delegation was led by the then leader of the opposition, Clement Attlee. As prime minister in 1950, he had overseen recognition of the People's Republic and therefore merited particularly warm treatment. Attlee wrote a series of articles about his 1954 visit, which were carried in the *New York Times*. The Chinese hosts were perhaps just as struck by his low-key personality and reticence as were many of those who worked with him in Britain. His was a sympathetic view of a regime – one which he appreciated had been established in the most tumultuous of circumstances. Even so, he found some things that he learned during his tour troubling. At a meeting with Premier Zhou Enlai, the two men fell into a discussion about law, from which the British politician quickly concluded that the Chinese 'had no real conception of the law as something quite apart from the will of the Government'. Having asked what happened if there was conflict between the judiciary and government, Attlee was told that this would never happen, since they were in agreement on policy. Attlee later curtly remarked: 'I said that in Britain I should regard this as a most disturbing thing.'[33] Trevelyan, the main British representative in Beijing at the time, observed a comical discussion over dinner at the legation, when Zhou asked if the British Labour Party practised a Chinese-style system of criticism and self-criticism. With a glance at Attlee, another member of the mission, Aneurin Bevan, a former minister of health, replied: 'Well clearly, we are so busy criticising each other we have no time for self-criticism.'[34] Attlee was also granted a meeting with Mao Zedong, at which he experienced a very early version of something that would – as time went by and the powers of the chairman increased – become akin to ritual: the 'audience' with the great Chinese leader in which guests were often reduced to awe-struck admiration (British Prime Minister Edward Heath's 1974 meeting with the Great Helmsman, cited in the next chapter, is an excellent and very typical example). Attlee found Mao 'vigorous but quite friendly' and was greeted by a Mao statement that the US had replaced Japan as the country's main enemy. He also recorded displeasure at the emergence of the newly created, but relatively short-lived, Southeast Asia Treaty Organization (SEATO), something he interpreted as an early attempt to contain China in its own region. SEATO was dissolved in 1977 after doing very little for its twenty-two years in existence – except irritate Beijing.[35]

Comedy – both intentional and (more often) unintentional – was a common feature of these delegations. What insights they gave the Chinese into British thinking is highly questionable. But they exposed eminent figures – from the poet Edmund Blunden to the philosopher A.J. Ayer – to ideas and ways of thinking that were coming to prevail in the country. General Bernard Montgomery (1887–1976), who visited in 1961, offered an extreme example of how embarrassing these visits could be, with the tight control exercised and the very limited access to local people or any opportunity to properly witness local conditions. When asked by a reporter on his return from Beijing whether he had discussed the recent invasion of Tibet by the People's Liberation Army in 1959, which resulted in the annexation of the local state and the flight of the key religious leader, the Fourteenth Dalai Lama (b. 1935), to neighbouring India, the great war leader noncha-lantly replied: 'I could have asked, but I didn't want to. I'm very friendly with Mao [Zedong], and I didn't want to irritate him in any way.'[36]

Sometimes the visitors were simply too eccentric for even their fellow delegates to properly understand. The artist Stanley Spencer (1891–1959), whose oddness and strange habits infuriated those who travelled around the country with him in 1954, stated grandly at a welcome banquet that he was 'possibly the most marvellous visitor to

China they had ever had . . . something on a par with the coming of Buddha.'[37] Trevelyan simply observed sharply that the main impact Spencer had on his Chinese hosts was when he expatiated 'on the delights of Formosa, which he did not explain was not Taiwan, but [a Chinese restaurant] at Cookham-on-the-Thames.'[38] Taiwan's situation was then (and remains) highly sensitive, with the British regarding the island as having a legally undefined status until such time as the nationalists and communists resolved their mutual differences and a solution emerged. That position was replaced several decades later by the One China Policy (see next chapter).

In terms of action going the other way, while China had some diplomatic representation in Britain from 1954, its emissaries undertook very little work there. What promotion of the wider understanding of contemporary Chinese matters there was came through the auspices of organisations like the Society for Anglo-Chinese Understanding, which was established in 1965 and largely continued the work of the Britain–China Friendship Association before it: political differences over some of the aims of that earlier group led the biochemist Joseph Needham to work on establishing the new body. Needham was perhaps the most significant figure in intellectual exchange between Britain and China in the twentieth century. He had come to study the country almost by accident, when he met Lu Gwei-Djen (1904–91), herself a biochemist who had come to undertake research at Cambridge University under Needham's wife Dorothy in 1935. Needham's collaboration with her extended far beyond learning about the long and (for Europeans) largely forgotten history of science in China over the last three millennia. They were romantically linked for over six decades, with Needham marrying her on the death of Dorothy in 1987. Lu's help was crucial for the undertaking that would consume most of his life after his return from a brief but dramatic and eventful period as director of the Sino-British Science Cooperation Office in Chongqing from 1942 to 1946. This work, the multi-volume *Science and Civilisation in China* – the first volume, a general overview of Chinese history, was issued in 1954 – continued for the next half century, producing its most recent volume in 2004, a decade after Needham's death.

Needham thought long and hard about the questions his encounter with China and Chinese culture raised for him. From the 1950s onwards, his non-technical writings addressed two broad issues. The first was why China had been bypassed by so much of scientific modernity, despite its being known and acknowledged in Europe since the time of Francis Bacon in the sixteenth century that the moveable-type printing press, the magnetic compass and gunpowder – three of the key drivers of technological progress – had all originated in China centuries before they appeared in the West. Why was it, Needham asked, that 'Chinese society of the eighth century had favour[ed] science as compared with Western society and that of the eighteenth century inhibit[ed] it?'[39] He was unable to produce the final work he intended in his series offering a comprehensive answer to this question, and it has continued to stimulate argument to this day. The second theme he returned to was a more pedagogical one: why had Europeans become so narrow-minded and largely confined within their own history and culture? He attributed this to what he labelled 'spiritual pride'.[40] The broad thrust of this critique was what he described as the 'tacit assumption that because modern science and technology, which grew up indeed in post-Renaissance Europe, are universal, everything else European is universal also'.[41] This meant that it was not just its technological methods and processes, but also its values and outlooks that were assumed to be of global applicability, negating the values of everyone else and being promoted to replace them. In essence, Needham was accusing Europeans of being parochial and bigoted.

It was not just Needham's left-wing views that attracted plenty of critics, but also his actions. His involvement in an investigation into claims of the use of chemical weapons by the United Nations forces against the North Koreans during the Korean War was the most controversial. He led a delegation to China in 1954 which addressed this question, producing a report largely accepting the Chinese and North Korean claims that these weapons had been deployed – claims that were ultimately discredited, due to evidence that the Chinese had doctored and manipulated laboratories and other places the delegation had gone to, in order to prove the Americans guilty. One of the outcomes of this unhappy situation was the relative sidelining of Needham for much of the next few decades, particularly by what might be regarded as the British establishment. It is an unfortunate fact that a figure so important in creating better-quality dialogue and increased understanding of China, particularly within the British intellectual elite, was isolated for political reasons for much of his career, despite the fact that his broader knowledge was of such huge public benefit.

The Cultural Revolution

Britain in the post-1949 years needed all the expertise on China it could get, so that the sidelining of a figure like Needham had a greater impact than would normally have been the case. The harsh reality was that sinological knowledge had stagnated – and in some areas deteriorated – partly because the country was physically increasingly inaccessible, and partly because the sources of information about it (i.e. from its own government) were severely restricted and subject to considerable manipulation. The only option for those interested in learning more was to go on delegations; but places on these were rare and often reserved for political or professional groups favoured by the hosts. This situation was only partially remedied by the fact that some insight was provided from Hong Kong, which served as a listening post and provided limited access to information about what was going on in the People's Republic. But for all that it offered a modicum of access to research materials and some exposure to Chinese culture, the colony was still not the mainland: it had a very different political, social and economic structure, and there was a strong, almost impenetrable border with its neighbour.

Even those on British delegations through the 1950s and 1960s who did manage to set foot in the country gained little real information on the dramatic changes happening, but undertook their visits in a kind of protective vacuum. It was often only afterwards, and via indirect sources, that news of such epic and consequential events as the Hundred Flowers Movement of 1956–57 (when the Party invited open criticism of its performance in power) and the Anti-Rightist Campaign of the following year (when many of those who had spoken out were punished) started to trickle out. The Great Leap Forward and then the tragic famines of the late 1950s and early 1960s were known about at the time – in the very broadest outline – through the testimonies of those seeking refuge in Hong Kong and through painstaking reading between the lines of official government statements. But it took many years for a clearer idea of what had happened to emerge.

This was even more the case with the complex political machinations in the central government around Mao and his inner court. Diplomats serving in Beijing tried to gather some evidence of what was happening and often had to resort to meticulous Kremlinology, when they had to make educated guesses about who was in or out of favour according to their place in public ceremonies or whether anyone had completely disappeared from the line-up. According to David Wilson, who worked in Beijing at the mission in the 1960s and who went on to be the penultimate governor of Hong Kong from 1987, 'We picked up one or two things, but a real sense of what was happening under the surface, we found it very, very difficult to find.'[42] There were occasional moments when observers felt they could see things a little more clearly. A telegram sent by British Foreign Office official Hugh Davies on 9 October 1969 observed that the *Red Flag* journal just issued in Beijing, carrying its monthly offering of domestic propaganda and radical ideology, had a picture of Mao on the front. The heavy editing of the image made Davies 'wonder whether this is not a picture from the files of Madame Tussauds. His hair has been resprung and every wrinkle on his face carefully ironed out. He almost appears to be wearing lipstick.' Davies had a more serious point, however: 'Mao is not so much a man as a sort of ideal concept', which made sense of the effort to present him in this ideal-ised, unrealistic fashion.[43]

The febrile nature of Chinese domestic politics from 1966 onwards meant that even the most talented external analysts often came up short in terms of predicting things or making sense of them after they had happened. A good example is the Cultural Revolution, which began that year and which consumed the political elite in Beijing in internal fights, at the same time creating instability across the rest of society, akin to a civil war between leftists and those accused of being revisionists. This perplexing and often violent movement was initially greeted with some degree of optimism by Needham and figures close to him, because of its aims which, super-ficially at least, looked utopian and well intended. The eminent Cambridge economist Joan Robinson (1903–83) was a particularly enthusiastic proponent. She was part of a delegation to China in 1953 and visited again seven times over the next twenty-five years. Her visit in 1967 formed the basis of a book two years later, which gave a largely positive assessment of the aims and implementation of the mass movement then sweeping the nation.[44] Detractors, however, believed they had firm grounds for thinking that she and the others like her had been taken for a ride, and that they were witnessing not an idealistic campaign to create a better new world, but an old-style power struggle, where Mao was simply finding new ways of dealing with those he regarded as his opponents.

Britain was hardly politically well favoured in Beijing at the time the Cultural Revolution started, and the escalating chaos made its position even more precarious. One major bone of contention was the war in Vietnam, where China was an ally of the northern, communist-led part of that country: even though Britain did not send any troops, Harold Wilson (1916–95), prime minister from 1964, supported the US intervention in support of the south. Wilson ironically was someone who had visited the People's Republic a decade earlier and had met Zhou Enlai. Such previous personal contact mattered little when arguments like this occurred, and his papier-mâché image was unceremoniously burned by zealous Red Guards for the crime of being a lackey of the Americans. Added to this were the perennial issues that arose from Hong Kong. In 1966, communist sympathisers in the territory took the anti-imperialist call to arms from across the border seriously and engaged in what were labelled by the city's government as riots. Some of the activists were rounded up and imprisoned, including individuals purportedly working as official Chinese journalists. This enflamed an already highly volatile situation and triggered huge rallies in front of the new British legation in Beijing. The chargé d'affaires at the time, Donald Hopson (1915–74), noticed on 21 August 1967 that Chinese staff working for the delegation had joined the melee outside, demanding the freedom of those incarcerated in Hong Kong. Over the following hours and into the next day, the situation spiralled out of control. London received the stark news in a secret telegram on 24 August that two days previously the building had been entered by the protesters, and that apart from the secure area, it was now 'completely gutted though roof and walls are still holding'.[45] Hopson was able to write that same day to George Brown (1914–85), the foreign secretary at the time, explaining what had happened. He described a carefully planned operation 'with special equipment to effect entry' by people who knew exactly where they needed to go. He suspected it was guided by the Cultural Revolution Group, an elite national level of radical leaders, with support from the security services. British staff were paraded up and down and forced to their knees once the surging crowd had managed to get inside the legation. All were beaten, with the women 'not spared lewd attention from the prying fingers of the mob'. In what must have been a terrifying experience, Hopson and his colleagues listened to the 'noise of breaking windows and smashing of furniture' as they took refuge in the safe internal area of the building. But soon liquid and then smoke were poured into the confined space through holes made in the outside walls. 'We could see the glare of many faces, and it was now clear that the mob would soon go through the walls and there was a danger we should be burned alive if we stayed.'

Hopson had a military background, having served with distinction in the Second World War and been awarded a decoration. This gave him some experience of conflict on which he could draw to lead his colleagues through the emergency exit into what he described in his despatch back to London as 'the glare of the fires and searchlights'. He continued, 'the mob greeted us with howls of exultation and immediately set about us with everything they had ... We were [hauled] by our hair, half-strangled with our ties, kicked and beaten on the head with bamboo poles.'[46]

In the aftermath of this onslaught, the British were able to find refuge in the property of friendly embassies and legations, such as the French. There they could tell others of what it had been like to experience at close quarters the raw fury of radical activists in a country that now seemed to be once more careering towards civil war. The sacking of the legation in 1967 brought to an end the idea that this post was a quiet, out-of-the-way and almost irrelevant one. In London, retaliation was still being considered in response to the outrages that British crown servants had suffered in Beijing when, in one of the more bizarre episodes of the period, on 27 August 1967 furious Chinese diplomats emerged from the legation in Portland Place with iron bars and bottles to signify their full support for their own government and express their fury over British actions in Hong Kong. They proceeded to clash for five minutes with police outside, resulting in wounds being inflicted on both sides. Others continued to engage in a stand-off for the rest of the day from the relative safety of the perimeter of the legation. An event like this hardly served to calm the diplomatic situation, and some politicians argued that all Chinese government personnel should be expelled. After expressing its dismay at the event, the Foreign Office, as usual, focused on more practical immediate issues, working over the coming weeks on ways of getting the women and children out of Beijing and back to Britain. This eventually happened, though it proved a stressful, long-drawn-out exercise.

The sense of crisis from the sacking of the mission in Beijing and the fracas at the Chinese legation in London was compounded by the continuing detention in China of other British people who were wholly unconnected to government business. The highest-profile case was that of the Reuters press correspondent Anthony Grey (b. 1938), who in July 1967 was placed under detention in his office and living quarters in central Beijing for over two years. Grey's account of his time – mostly in solitary confinement – describes the challenges of trying to keep sane, despite constant anxiety and an almost complete lack of information about what was happening in the wider world. He recorded his frustration at the British government, whose reluctance (as he saw it) to effect his release showed that it was 'weak-kneed'.[47] He was unaware of the embassy's own travails and of the disturbing fact that what seemed to him at the time to be evidence of its ineffectualness was down to its having very few options, with barely the means even to protect itself. Grey was subsequently to learn that Percy Cradock (1923–2010), then an official newly arrived in Beijing, had tried to use publicity via the British press to shame the Chinese; after meeting Grey, he deployed the accurate phrase 'he lives in a void'. Cradock subsequently wrote that he believed the storm of publicity that followed his comments helped resolve matters.[48] Added to this was the humiliation by the radical Red Guards in May 1967 of Peter Hewitt, British consul in Shanghai, who was physically evicted from the historic building the British occupied along the Bund there, causing the consulate to close and be repossessed by the Chinese.

Events like the treatment of Grey and the sacking of the Beijing mission meant that 1967 marked the nadir of Anglo-Chinese relations in the post-war era. The dysfunctionality and chaos at the heart of Chinese domestic politics was simply one aspect of a situation that was unmanageable and was only eventually resolved by the outcome of the power struggles in Beijing. These were largely domestic issues, which impacted mostly on China itself and in which relations with the outside world were usually a peripheral issue. While Maoism as an ideology over this period did have some traction elsewhere in Western Europe, and even in America, in the late 1960s its influence in Britain was limited. China regarded the Communist Party of Great Britain as too pro-Soviet; it tended to work – if it bothered to work at all – with the even smaller and more marginal Communist Party of Great Britain (Marxist–Leninist).[49]

Despite indifference to his ideas, Mao as a figure had some level of public recognition in Britain, gaining a reference in a Beatles song ('Revolution', released in 1968), with his image enjoying the same iconic status as elsewhere in the world. But beyond the confines of very small left-wing political parties, Maoism was not a live issue. Most British who did observe the situation as it unfolded on the other side of the world were bewildered and perplexed by what they saw. This was not the place where Confucian hierarchy ruled supreme, but one where images of young people dressed in quasi-military uniforms were shown screaming at people who were much older (and apparently more senior) and who were often wearing strange dunce-style hats and ink-stained placards around their necks. In the modern world, where the gathering of empirical evidence was becoming easier and the means of analysing it were growing more accurate, China seemed to be bucking the trend: it was becoming not more knowable, but far less.

Green shoots after the Red Terror

Over the 1960s and early 1970s, a fundamental realignment in China's international affairs dramatically altered the context of Sino-British relations. Far and away the most significant development was the eventual rapprochement with the US. After their heyday in the early 1950s, Moscow's relations with Beijing had plummeted to the point where, in 1969, the Chinese and Russian armies clashed on China's northeast border, leading to casualties. Mao even reportedly feared a nuclear attack on his country by his former ally, and mandated some of the generals who were languishing at the time in a soft form of detention to brainstorm what the country could do to manage this threat from across its vast northern border. They came up with something which, up until that point, had been unthinkable – to create some sort of relationship with China's ostensibly greatest foe, the US, in order to provide a counterbalance to the Soviet Union. In furtive, secret moves in Poland, at the United Nations in New York or in Pakistan – in the few places where the communist Chinese and the Americans might contrive to meet – discussions were held to establish how this might happen. The domestic situation in China also showed signs of calming down a little. The Cultural Revolution chaos peaked in 1969, and in that same year a Party Congress (the first for thirteen years) inserted a largely military leadership into top decision-making bodies to restore at least some semblance of order. The radicals – subsequently dubbed the Gang of Four – were increasingly balanced by more pragmatic forces associated with Premier Zhou Enlai. Mao continued to maintain his puppet-master role; but with the mysterious disappearance and then death in a plane crash over Mongolia in 1971 of his chosen successor, Marshal Lin Biao, there were increased signs that people were witnessing the closing of an era.

US–Chinese détente was marked by secret visits to China (from Pakistan) by then National Security Advisor Henry Kissinger (1923–2023) in late 1971; the final success of the People's Republic of China replacing Taiwan at the United Nations that same year; and the visit to Beijing by US President Richard Nixon (1913–94) himself in September 1972. These have taken their place as seminal events not just in China's modern history with the outside world, but in geopolitics more generally. For Britain, though, the new diplomatic openness of China to the outside world, after years of rejection, offered an opportunity to finally regularise its position in the country.

There were slight signs that dramatic change was afoot some time before the final breakthrough. By 1970, the fractious, unfriendly tone that had prevailed between Britain and China in previous years had changed. There were some tiny hints of this: for example, in 1971 the Chinese sent a telegram to mark Queen Elizabeth's birthday – something they had never done before. That same year, Mao even talked to the British chargé d'affaires at a meeting – a rare and auspicious act of imperial solicitude. Then there were the more practical things. Direct telephone lines between London and Beijing were reinstalled in April 1971. And a BBC film crew for the current affairs programme *Panorama* went to China in late 1970 to make a documentary about changes in daily life there. Most significant of all was the position Britain took on Taiwan. From 1961 it began to vote for the right of the People's Republic to have the United Nations seat. A high level of agreement was needed, however, to effect this change, with two thirds of voting members required for a motion to be successful (though this was changed to a simple majority in the late 1960s). Probably Britain assumed that, as this was unlikely, it was safe to vote for something that wouldn't actually happen. But British Prime Minister Harold Wilson stated in 1970 that the broader issue, 'the conflict in southeast Asia . . . cannot be decided on a world scale without the representation . . . in the United Nations of the Chinese government for the Chinese people'.[50] That meant getting the People's Republic back into the fold.

With US rapprochement imminent, Britain had the space finally to upgrade its relations. This happened on 13 March 1972, when a communique was signed, allowing ambassadors to be exchanged. The issue of Taiwan and British representation there was dealt with in the announcement of a form of words – the British version of the One China Policy. Alec Douglas-Home, foreign secretary at the time, announced it thus:

the Government of the United Kingdom acknowledges the posi-
tion of the Chinese Government that Taiwan is a province of the
People's Republic of China. Both the Government of the People's
Republic of China and Taipei maintain that Taiwan is a part of
China.

He went on to state that the Taiwan question was China's internal
affair, to be settled by the Chinese people themselves.[51]

The scholastic levels of ambiguity and nuance in such a statement
were the result of thousands of hours of pondering and revision by
officials on both sides. The all-important word was 'acknowledge'.
This avoided the question of which partner was right or wrong, and
meant that Britain was acting a little like someone at a party who
ends up standing between two people arguing vehemently from
diametrically opposed positions: they simply accept the very different
points that both are making, without trying to come down on one
side or the other. One can acknowledge many things – including that
others hold highly delusional ideas sometimes – without actually
sharing them. The obfuscation served its purpose (and to some
extent continues to do so half a century later), which was to allow
space for co-operation on both sides of the Taiwan strait. Similar
postures were adopted by the US and others. With this issue out of
the way, Britain and China could now try to grow closer to one
another, and once more endeavour to overcome the many other
potential problems that their mutual history presented.

10

Getting Closer

Resolution of the Hong Kong Issue, 1972–97

'It is in any case a fairly modest residence. There was nothing luxurious anywhere, and even our teacups were not of top quality.'[1] So wrote the British ambassador – in post since 1972 – after he had been ushered, alongside Edward Heath, into the presence of Mao Zedong on 27 May 1974. Despite the underwhelming quality of the tableware, Mao's personal study was not an easy place to gain access to. It was, after all, the inner sanctum: a kind of holy of holies, where the Great Leader, then already suffering from Parkinson's disease, sat amidst his piles of books, deep in the leadership compound of Zhongnanhai, exercising almost god-like power over the 900 million people in the country around him.

Edward Heath was not being received as an active head of government. He had lost his position as prime minister in February 1974, when the Labour Party under Harold Wilson joined with the Liberals to scrape together a coalition government. That he was out of office and merely leader of the opposition should have meant lower protocol to greet his arrival in Beijing. But the Chinese authorities were always willing to recognise the sterling service of a good friend – a category into which the visiting British statesman fell, thanks to the fact that he had presided over the upgrading of relations between the two countries. Accordingly, on his visit to Beijing in the summer of that year, he received treatment fit for a king. Maybe there was broader strategic planning behind such largesse: there was reason to believe that Heath could well return to power imminently, as the inconclusive outcome of the February election meant that a second one was likely to be held later in the year. This made some on the British side suspicious of the amount of attention the Chinese were giving their guest. Ambassador John Addis (1914–83) had written to the Foreign Office that the 'conspicuously high levels of reception accorded to Mr Heath was [sic] deliberately conceived at the highest level as an intervention in British internal politics', providing him with symbolic and propaganda material to bolster his position back home. This was perhaps the first time any such worry about Beijing messing in Britain's domestic affairs had been expressed, and marked an extraordinary turnaround from a century before, when the boot was firmly on the other foot: then it had been the British not so much interfering in Chinese affairs, as out and out running them. Half a century on, those who would return to this theme of China's claimed interference should take heed, however: Heath failed to win an outright majority at the second general election when it was called in May. Even if he had been Beijing's preferred candidate, he was never to return to power.

Regardless of these suspicions, the guard of honour at the airport, the meetings with leaders Zhou Enlai and Deng Xiaoping, and the general level of attention and fuss must have been welcome respite from a Britain buffeted by strong economic headwinds, with interminable arguments about the role of the European Economic Community which it had just joined, and the continuing demands of unions. The encounter with Mao was clearly the most important part of the whole tour. To Ambassador Addis, the chairman seemed 'stronger and more robust than I expected. He gives a very firm handshake' – though he clearly had great difficulty in speaking. However, his words, when they did come, posed penetrating questions, and he remained in 'complete control of the discussion'. Mao said that 'there were no problems between Britain and China' and that Hong Kong 'is a question left over from the past' that would be resolved in due course. The great surprise came at the end of the meeting, however, as Heath and his entourage were about to depart. 'I have an invitation from God. He has asked me to visit him', said Mao. As Addis continued in his report: 'Mr Heath said he hoped Mao would not accept the invitation for some time. Mao said "I have not yet replied" and threw himself back in his chair, laughing uproariously.'[2] Unfortunately for China, Mao's acceptance of God's offer was not taken up for two years, and he lingered jealously in position, fitting in an even later second meeting with Heath in 1975, and causing general political and economic stagnation with his capricious leadership until his final demise.

Quite what Britain made of the reports – both of the visit and of the new and increased ardour of their former prime minister towards China – was hard to gauge. A *Panorama* crew accompanied Heath, recording parts of his tour; but the main achievement of its members was to irritate their local handlers through their desire to film what they were told not to (rather than enlighten their audience back home with the very limited footage that they were finally able to send). As Hugh Davies – by then back at the Foreign Office in London – commented, the Chinese 'could have hardly expected much more' than this disappointing public relations outcome. He went on, 'The public reaction here was, I suppose, rather bemused bewilderment about Chinese motives.' This bemusement may have been compounded by comments like the one Heath made at his meeting on 14 June with Deng Xiaoping (1904–97), when he stated that 'the British did not aim to impose their own ideas on other people' and then went on to say in a speech in Kunming that 'Chairman Mao was quite right to call upon the Chinese people to resist hegemony'. Such sentiments – both in delivery and content – would not have sounded out of place coming from a Cultural Revolution Red Guard cadre.

Despite this, Heath deserves some acknowledgement: of all the prime ministers of Great Britain since the Second World War, he is the only one to have shown any deep interest in or commitment to relations with China, and to have recognised their importance. For most of his predecessors (and all of his successors), China was not a place with which they seemed willing to engage emotionally, and nor did they show much direct interest in it. Heath, by contrast, had an internationalist outlook, which was clear through his work to bring Britain closer to Europe. He was also a man with wide cultural interests – from classical music (he was an accomplished pianist and could conduct), to sailing, literature and art. That he had an open mind about China was laudable, even if he was later criticised for being overtly supportive of the government in Beijing, particularly over the issue of Hong Kong. This reached almost comical levels. In 1982, passing through the city after his sixth visit to Beijing, while dining with local businesspeople he berated them for being short-sighted in not accepting China's proposals for how retrocession would happen fifteen years later. When a member of the group lightly joked that he seemed 'to have been well brain-washed in Beijing', Heath 'leapt to his feet, said he had never been so insulted in all his life, and that he wanted an apology'. Even when the apology was proffered, he still stormed out, saying 'I am not eating with people like you.'³

Hong Kong: The great unresolved issue – prelude

Without Hong Kong, it is likely that Britain's post-war relations with China would have been very different. Mutual history in the earlier era would still have mattered, but it would have been a memory, rather than an issue that was live and topical. The ninety-nine-year leases taken out in 1898 on much of the territory that constituted the city meant that there was always a ticking clock, and that one day the situation of this 'borrowed place, living on borrowed time' (as the

British-Chinese writer Han Suyin put it) would need to be resolved.[4] In the Maoist period, the Chinese did very little to address the problem, leaving the matter dormant. The British to some extent hoped that a compromise would be reached – one that might even allow an extension of the ninety-nine-year lease due to expire in 1997 on 97 per cent of the city's territory, or a role for British administration beyond that deadline. All that the Chinese had said was, in the words of Percy Cradock (reporting the sentiments articulated by Zhou Enlai at a meeting with a British official in Beijing in 1971), that 1997 was a 'watershed'. The question was what kind of watershed and what role Britain might play on the other side.[5]

By the 1970s, Hong Kong had become what the locals called 'Asia's global city'. Achieving this had taken a combination of targeted government support and immense entrepreneurialism and hard work by the city's population. The early years after the Second World War were tough, with a struggling economy and outward migration, much of it to the UK. But in the 1960s, the territory's government introduced a combination of marketisation and capital investment in infrastructure – a model, according to one historian, 'where central planning was accompanied by rapidly increasing public expenditure'.[6] The governorship of Sir Murray MacLehose (1917–2000) from 1971 also introduced more socially oriented reforms (e.g. housing projects and healthcare reforms) in an attempt to address the inequalities in the city, and sought to root out corruption, which had increased due to its economic success. These measures contributed to making Hong Kong by the 1980s an increasingly prosperous and commercially attractive logistics and finance hub.

Of all the changes that occurred from the 1970s and into the 1980s and that impacted on the city's unresolved status, the most significant were within China itself. The death of Mao Zedong in September 1976 created great uncertainty about what would happen next. Anthony Crossland (1918–77), then the British foreign secretary, had visited China only a few months before the chairman's death and picked up on this lack of clarity. He was told by Hua Guofeng (1921–2008), the man regarded as Mao's final chosen successor, that whatever might happen (and no one, not even Hua, would dare to refer to Mao's mortality directly) there would be no change in foreign policy. This, Hua said, 'was laid down by Chairman Mao and the Central Committee'. He went on to say that there would also be 'no change in trade policy', though there 'might be some changes in the method of conducting trade'.[7] But Crossland's impression upon hearing these reassurances was that the future direction of the country remained uncertain. Hua himself was assessed as 'a follower, not a leader', and so it was unclear if he had any role in deciding what the future path for the country would be. Crossland was only able to state his hope that 'the moderates would come out on top', because 'if they did not there would be a serious risk of disintegration'.[8]

The radicals were indeed replaced swiftly in a bloodless coup only a few weeks after the chairman's death, but there followed an interim period of a year or so when very little seemed to change. When the decision to embark on economic reform was finally made under the newly rehabilitated Deng Xiaoping, who returned to his position of dominance domestically in late 1978, the subdued delivery of the news and lack of immediate clarity about the ways in which it might occur served to obscure the full import of what had just been announced. But within eighteen months, through acts like the establishment of Shenzhen just across the border from Hong Kong as a Special Economic Zone able to attract foreign capital, technology and management, the era of dramatic transformation had begun. China's radical change became a fact, rather than something people hoped for.

Part of China's 1980s reform process involved embracing some aspects of Western capitalism, which meant that Hong Kong – where this system was already practised – started to matter more to it as a place of finance, a provider of investment and an international port. Hong Kong also quickly became the principal source of much of the know-how, as China built its manufacturing and export sectors – the areas where it was to see the most spectacular growth in the coming years. The city had always figured as a portal to some degree; but it was now starting to operate on a wholly different level, gaining benefit from its unique role as the point of entry to a transforming Chinese economy and to the opportunities for the outside world that were starting to appear there.

In 1979, a secret memo (subsequently declassified) was produced in the Foreign Office about where the city was heading in the light of these dramatic new events and what the implications were for Britain's administration of the territory. The paper, 'Hong Kong in the 1980's', announced a little optimistically that 'there seems a strong possibility that the Chinese will agree to some satisfactory arrangement over [the city]'. Whatever the Chinese intentions, the British interests that needed to be safeguarded were clear: 'In the post-Mao era Hong Kong has proved a very positive factor in the development of relations between Britain and China.' The place was 'an increasingly important market for British goods', but one where Britain had a 'moral obligation' towards the Hong Kongese. There was a fear that, were the British to withdraw, hundreds of thousands might flee abroad. For the Chinese, the city now had increasing significance for their own economic planning, giving even greater cause to safeguard its prosperity. But Britain 'should stick with Hong Kong', because (though this was not explicitly stated in the paper) it had become much more valuable and significant as its neighbour's economy started to lift off.[9] The notion that, aside from purely practical economic reasons guiding its interests and involvement, Britain also had moral obligations was a new one. This was something that would figure more strongly during the negotiations, when they began in earnest from 1982.

For all its insight and comprehensiveness, however, the 1979 paper made no mention of the one thing that clearly did matter to the Chinese. This was not trade or economics, but the emotional and symbolic importance of sovereignty. It was precisely of this that Deng Xiaoping spoke when he met the visiting Hong Kong governor,

Murray MacLehose, on 30 March 1979. The governor's main interest in undertaking this visit was concern over land leases in the territory. It was now impossible to guarantee these for more than eighteen years, but the city government needed some means of offering clarity to those who were now intending to buy or rent land beyond this deadline, about what would happen when 1997 came. In reply to MacLehose's deliberately very specific point (officials optimistically believed that concessions on this – apparently relatively minor – point could lead to broader Chinese acceptance of continued British control in some form post-1997), Deng simply replied broadly that China had a consistent position on the future of Hong Kong, which was that sovereignty lay with the Chinese; and while the city would have its own special status, it should and would be returned in 1997. Hong Kong could continue with its capitalist system after reversion, while China persisted with socialism, but sovereignty would belong to China. The details would need to be worked out, Deng admitted, but on the matter of principles these had now been stated. And that was where the matter was left. This did nothing whatever to allay the legal concerns over the uncertainty about leases after 1997 – the very thing that the governor's visit had been undertaken to resolve.[10]

It is strange that the fundamental importance of sovereignty and why it meant so much to the Chinese should seemingly have been so hard for British politicians (and some officials) to understand. It didn't help that the first major visit by a senior Chinese leader to London since 1949 was by Hua Guofeng, who had made such an underwhelming impression on Tony Crossland some years before. Hua's visit in early November 1979 was hosted by the newly elected Prime Minister Margaret Thatcher (1925–2013). To those observing him, Hua was 'the master of his well rehearsed brief', but 'showed no gifts for repartee or wit. His . . . remarks were banal. Most of the time he was detached, impassive and impersonal. At the end of our visit we knew him little better than when he arrived.'[11] True to form, when the subject of Hong Kong did come up during one of his two meetings with Thatcher, he was anodyne to a fault. 'The Chinese government would keep in touch with the British government,' he stated, 'and would take account of the investors even after the problem had been solved.' For all Hua's significant role in the immediate post-Mao era and his support for the immensely consequential changes taking place in China, to his London interlocutors he was just irredeemably grey.

Getting serious: Thatcher versus Deng

Hong Kong mattered to the emotions of Chinese and British alike. That was one thing that the sides had in common. But the kinds of emotions it gave rise to were very different. For the British, the survival of this final significant colonial-era dependency offered at least some tangible link to a past when, for some, Britain had mattered globally and had worldwide reach. Those that visited the city, like the writer Jan Morris (1926–2020), found its unique hybridity deeply impressive: it was a place that was both indisputably culturally Asian and yet uniquely British, meaning that it straddled and belonged to two very different worlds.[12] This had nothing to do with defending the imperial legacy. It was much more because Hong Kong, as a point of fact, was a joint creation of the two very different cultures and outlooks – Western capitalism and rule of law sitting within a community that overwhelmingly identified culturally as Chinese, even if it increasingly saw itself as Hong Kongese. The residue of British influence was heavy: from the use of English around much of the city, to the side of the road that cars drove on (inexplicably the left – the same as in Britain, but not the same as in China), to the style of the older buildings, like the governor's residence. The city had an evocative feel to it – a place of subterfuge, perhaps of romance and mystery – with a transitory atmosphere, the great skyscrapers often rising out of mists around the harbour in ways that, visually, gave the place a spectral appearance. That made it an attractive place for writers of spy fiction like David Cornwell (the real name of John le Carré), who partially set his 1977 novel *The*

Honourable Schoolboy there. One scholar described the uniqueness of the city, placed as it had been 'at the interstices of empires. Its existence in this global liminal space has been marked by precarity, creativity and recalcitrance.' It was a city 'constantly on the edge', physically abutting great powers, but also symbolically edgy, because it was 'on the edge of being annihilated, and on the edge of breaking free'.[13]

For the Chinese, though, it summoned up a host of other emotions. Nostalgia was not one of them. Hong Kong in their eyes was the product of the century of humiliation, forcibly taken from the Qing at a time when it was weak and victimised, an issue left over from history that would need to be resolved, not looked back on with fondness and sentimentality. Hong Kong retrocession was, for the anti-colonial communist rulers, a matter of pride and honour, not regret and apprehension. One has to bear this viewpoint in mind constantly as one looks at the discussions about the future of the colony started in 1982. The weight of this history, and the two starkly contrasting attitudes of the main interlocutors, meant they were never likely to give each other an easy time. While arguing about the same place, the two sides were starting from very different points and proceeding with very different convictions and feelings.

The key players in the negotiations exemplified this deep contrast. On the British side was Margaret Thatcher, a figure whom Cradock, while ambassador of China from 1978, had had the chance to meet during the Hua Guofeng visit of 1979. This gave him his 'first experience of those bruising but searching meetings which were a distinguishing feature of her administration'.[14] As Cradock admitted, the 'Chinese were not favourites' for her. She had visited the country in 1977 while in opposition, and did not share her predecessor Heath's passion for what she found there. 'She was', as one official noted later, 'a great exception to the general rule among political and business leaders, that having reached Beijing and had their tummies tickled, they are captivated by the place.' She found it 'a rather unpleasant place governed by rather unpleasant people'.[15]

Her interlocutor Deng Xiaoping was unlikely to change her mind on this point. A ruthlessly and fully committed member of the Communist Party since the age of sixteen, Deng was – despite a few years in France in his youth – resolutely uncontaminated by influence from the outside world (the only sign he had ever been in Paris was apparently his lifelong love of croissants, which he had acquired there). His background was typical of many of the elite after 1949: he had served as a military leader in the Sino-Japanese Wars and in the Civil War, afterwards becoming a key person in Mao's administrations. But then he followed a more unusual trajectory. Felled in the Cultural Revolution in 1966 for being a so-called 'Capitalist Roader' and revisionist, who was supportive of the USSR, he was sent down to do manual work in a factory in Jiangxi province. Humiliated he may have been, but at least he survived, and could be brought back to Beijing and temporarily rehabilitated in 1974, when the political winds changed. Against all the normal laws of Chinese politics, where second acts were very rare, a further period of internal exile in 1976 did not stop him emerging soon after the death of Mao as a key leader. This marked his final return to power from the political graveyard. While he never occupied any formal position higher than vice premier from 1979, everyone knew that he was the power behind the throne, and that his decisions were key to the way in which China was going and what it intended to do.

Deng was a survivor par excellence and a formidable opponent for Thatcher. He was tough-minded, adept at balancing different interests, and more than a match for his relatively inexperienced British opposite number. The wonder in the end is that Thatcher did as well as she did in her encounters with him. A note of the famous meeting between the two in Beijing (the first ever visit by a serving British prime minister to the country) held on 24 September 1982 started off with Thatcher, in characteristic style, setting out Britain's position with lapidary clarity. 'The British and Chinese Governments had a common objective; they shared the aim of maintaining the prosperity and stability of Hong Kong in the interests of the people who lived there.' So stated the record of the meeting, summarising her words. While at least acknowledging the importance of sovereignty for the Chinese, she said that this was 'a difficult issue for her'. She had to make concrete proposals to the British parliament, which was the ultimate decision maker on this; if it was satisfied, then sovereignty would be manageable. Deng's response was categorical and unambiguous: 'On sovereignty there was no leeway for China; sovereignty was not a matter which could be discussed.' In 1997, sovereignty would certainly revert to China. The work now was to find a formula for the future of the city which maintained its prosperity.

Deng explained why sovereignty was so key: because it related to questions of history which profoundly influenced the Chinese view of the meaning of Hong Kong's return. As it had been taken from China against the latter's will, if the territory did not revert completely to the People's Republic in 1997 'it would mean that the new China was like the China of the [Qing] dynasty and the present leaders were like Li Hongzhang.' Li was a high official from the late Qing who had signed away the ninety-nine-year lease in 1898 and who was regarded after 1949 as the archetypal capitulator and foreign lackey. 'If in 15 years', Deng warned, 'they had not recovered Hong Kong, the people would have every reason no longer to put faith in the leaders and the Chinese government ought to retire voluntarily from the political arena.' In any case, for Britain, too, resolution was the right thing to do; for if the Hong Kong issue were to be resolved during Thatcher's term in office, Deng concluded, 'it would mean that Britain's colonial era had been brought to an end'.[16]

The Chinese believed their approach was guided by justice and morality – things Thatcher was hardly likely to agree with, in view of her own deep convictions about the political immorality of communism. Countering these appeals to high ethical issues, Thatcher's response was to focus initially on pragmatic matters. She cited the need to maintain stability and predictability in the city and to ensure that international business confidence was preserved. This implied that some role for Britain after 1997 was preferable, because it was the known quantity and would provide continuity. Not that ethical issues were absent from her calculation. But simply maintaining the status quo was the best way for Britain to ensure that it could fulfil its moral obligations to the city's citizens. Despite these arguments, Deng and Thatcher's standoff came down to one fundamental matter of principle: which was more defensible, Chinese people governing themselves, or Britain trying to continue its colonial history and governing for them. Unsurprisingly, Deng's vision was to prevail.

Facing each other across such a wide divide, Deng and Thatcher were clearly unlikely to bond well – particularly in view of the gaping differences between them culturally, politically and in terms of personality. But as Cradock observed, 'the Prime Minister was, despite herself, impressed by this short, barrel like figure, with bruised face and dismissive gestures and almost limitless authority, chain-smoking and spitting, a product of a totally alien political environment'. She found him cruel, but acknowledged that he was someone who had survived in a system with almost no mercy, managing to prevail in the end against the will even of Mao.[17] The person who had described herself in Britain as a lady 'not for turning', and who had been given the nickname by others of 'the iron lady', had met her match.

This did not deny the validity of one of the issues Thatcher had raised: what role the people of Hong Kong themselves played in all of this. It was clear in public opinion surveys that, as scholar Ho-Fung Hung put it, despite Beijing declaring the importance of the Chinese finally ruling their own affairs in the city, 'the colony's residents were willing to support any proposal about Hong Kong's future except returning to China'.[18] The quandary for Britain throughout the negotiations – and indeed, all the way up to 1997 and, to some degree, beyond – was how to take into account the views and sentiments of the Hong Kongese, even as London seemed to be negotiating these away over their heads. Here the sins of the colonial fathers were visited on their successors. The great vulnerability of the British position was that it had never made much effort to extend democracy in the territory, governing with a system that allowed very little (if any) popular representation, and leaving things mostly at the fiat of the administrators and the governor. Attempts to give residents a greater role in decision making had been few and far between, and had never achieved much.

Sir Mark Young, who headed the colony before and after Japanese occupation, had marked his post-war reinstatement in 1946 with a desire to introduce constitutional reform. This was motivated by a wish that 'the inhabitants of the Territory can be given a fuller and more responsible share in the management of their own affairs',[19] and involved the relatively mild idea of transferring some of the functions of government to an elected municipal council. The Foreign Office and other stakeholders in London were supportive; but before anything could be done, business and elite groups back in Hong Kong lobbied fiercely for the measures to be stopped, because they were regarded as introducing sources of potentially unwelcome instability. The Chinese themselves were vehemently opposed to ideas of self-government, stating in 1960 that 'We [Beijing] shall not hesitate to take positive action to have Hong Kong, Kowloon and the New Territories liberated', were this to occur.[20] The failure to address the governance of Hong Kong – whether principally due to Chinese pressure or to pressure from lobbyists in the city itself – left it with a political system that was non-democratic, meaning that from 1982 to 1984 it often seemed as though the place and its people were a passive negotiable commodity with no extant mechanism for the city and its population to have any direct say in their fate.[21]

Over the first twelve months after the Deng–Thatcher meeting, officials from Britain and China began their negotiations in earnest. The Chinese issued twelve points in 1983, the most important of which was a stark statement that, come what may, Hong Kong would revert to Chinese rule on 1 July 1997. In October 1983, the British acknowledged that their previous hopes of maintaining some role in the governance of the city in the future needed to be ditched; from this moment on, they shed their insistence on any form of continued British administration after 1997. To some extent, the ensuing process replicated this pattern, with tactical abandonment of various other once fervently held objectives until a resolution was reached which, for the British at least, could be presented as preserving some of the unique attributes of the city whose interests they said they were trying to protect. Maintenance of the legal and economic system, along with some core political freedoms – such as freedom of the press and the right to demonstrate – were the most important of these.

Thatcher signed the agreement with her Chinese counterpart, Zhao Ziyang (1919–2005), on 19 December 1984, during her second visit to China. It set out the broad framework for retrocession, agreeing to use the notion of 'one country, two systems' and promising Hong Kong – as a 'special administrative region' within the People's Republic – a high degree of autonomy to run its own economy, have its own currency, and be able to set its own interest rates and govern itself for fifty years up to 2047. Foreign affairs and defence were to be the responsibility of Beijing. The agreement meant that in June 1997 Britain would cease all direct involvement in Hong Kong's affairs, and a chief executive would be appointed to replace the governor. Whether deliberate or not, this change in nomenclature gave the impression that the city was more like a business than a geographical territory. There were plenty of critics at the time who were dismissive of the proposed arrangements. One reportedly stated that 'we have handed 5 million people over to a sovereign power by negotiation. But that sovereign power is [a] Marxist Leninist, thuggish, oppressive regime. That is the bottom line.'[22] Others felt that the arrangement would prove difficult to implement, with China at liberty to do whatever it wanted after the handover. Fearing what might happen, many in Hong Kong voted with their feet and emigrated to safe havens elsewhere, reversing the function of the city in more recent history as a place where people came to seek refuge. A balanced assessment of the 1984 deal, while acknowledging that it inevitably contained lacunae, also needs to recognise the immense work and dexterity shown by Cradock and his colleagues. Their lives were not made easy by Chinese tactics, which were often aggressive and unhelpful; so the very fact that there was an agreement at all in the end is remarkable. The Chinese had proved themselves formidable opponents, but they had held most of the main cards. At least the British had avoided the far worse outcome of no viable arrangement post-1997, with all the uncertainty that would have brought.

Britain had its rewards once the agreement was signed. In 1986, Queen Elizabeth II (1926–r1952–2022) undertook the first ever state visit to China by a British monarch – something that Deng had suggested to Thatcher in late 1984, at the time the Hong Kong accord was signed. Although the queen had visited Hong Kong itself in 1972 (again, the first monarch to do so), the mainland offered very different and distinctive challenges and pitfalls. One such was the opportunity for her husband, the famously tactless duke of Edinburgh, to give free rein to his mercurial skills. While speaking to British students studying in Xian, he made some unfortunate comments about the appearance of Chinese people. Apart from the 'Xian Incident', as this event was dubbed by the long-suffering diplomats who had to deal with its fallout in the British media, the visit went well enough in view of the heavy symbolism and history that was involved. Queen Elizabeth's forebears, after all, had sat atop a system that had not been kind to China in its period of greatest weakness and vulnerability a century before.

There were also high-level visits back to the UK (Hu Yaobang, the Communist Party boss, proved a popular visitor in 1985). Things were helped by the fact that this decade was a relatively easy time in China's relations with the outside world more generally. This was an era of relative optimism, with economic reforms looking like they presaged more wide-ranging political ones. The country was no longer so introspective and inaccessible, participating as never before in international fora and, beyond this, mostly playing a constructive role. As ever, of course, the mix also contained negative elements, such as the frequent clampdowns on dissidents and activists (which would get worse after the 1989 uprising) and the attempts to register a China Democracy Party in 1998 in Hangzhou, where over a dozen democracy supporters were given lengthy prison spells. 'Spiritual pollution' campaigns were also a phenomenon aimed at reducing the influence of Western culture domestically in China, by restricting on the availability of foreign films, publications and other pernicious imports. But for Britain, as indeed for other countries, it was easy to justify engagement in the present on the grounds that it would bring about desired change in the future. A more open China led to new forms of interaction and new actors taking part in them. British football teams, pop stars (George Michael and Andrew Ridgeley of Wham! went in 1986) and artists all visited in increasing numbers. All declared that they were discovering a country unexplored and unknown beforehand. In doing so, they showed their lack of awareness of the fact that Britain was now in the fourth century of its relationship with this place, and that they were simply revisiting an old, familiar partner.

1989: Tiananmen Square and its impact

This constructive atmosphere came to a juddering halt in June 1989, when the leadership, under an aged and supposedly retired Deng, sent in troops to fire live bullets at demonstrating students in the central Tiananmen Square in Beijing. Unfortunately for the Chinese government, the world's press were in the city to observe the first Sino-Russian summit for over twenty years, and it was therefore easy for them to train their cameras on the scenes of shocking violence that occurred during this major diplomatic event. It was one of those journalists who took the iconic 'tank man' image from a room in the Beijing Hotel – a picture that was flashed across the world and today still stands as a symbol of the horror of the event. Once the massacre occurred, Britain's condemnation was unequivocal: Thatcher, still in power, said she was 'appalled by the indiscriminate shooting of unarmed people'.[23] British citizens were urged to leave. Embassy personnel were reduced to a minimum. Students were repatriated, and businesses froze their work, waiting to see what would happen.

For a few weeks, it seemed as though China might return to the isolation in which it had existed during the Maoist era. But America was among the first to try to find a way forward and reopen lines of communication. Once George H.W. Bush (1924–2018), the then president, had spoken to Deng, some forms of contact and engagement resumed. The Bush administration argued that such a major and important player could not easily be ostracised and that hopes of political reform through economic engagement, while they had suffered a serious blow, should not be abandoned. While some sanctions were introduced, China suffered remarkably little for an event that had been so conspicuously brutal.

Thatcher was initially less forgiving than the Americans, and did consider returning to the 1984 deal and reviewing it to see if the new situation now prevailing meant it could be cancelled. According to Douglas Hurd, one of her colleagues at the time, she had 'nearly come to the point of saying "we are not going to give up Hong Kong"', in view of the horrific events that had occurred in Beijing.[24] While a laudable aspiration, it proved impossible to fulfil, as it would have violated international law and almost certainly created a direct confrontation between China and the West.

In Hong Kong itself, many people who were sympathetic to the students and protesters in China themselves took to the streets to protest. A number of prominent activists from within the People's Republic who had taken part in the events of June 1989 fled to the relative safety of the territory, smuggling themselves across the border or getting there by other indirect routes. Unsurprisingly, while rattled and on the defensive immediately after 4 June, China was insistent that everything was on track for the handover and that nothing had changed. In 1990, only six months later, it proceeded with the formulation and issuance of a Basic Law, something intended to serve as a de facto constitution for the city after 1997. That was endorsed by the National People's Congress in Beijing on 4 April. In Article 68 of this document, modest proposals for local representation in a Legislative Council, and for universal suffrage for the role of chief executive were set out – though, as ever with Chinese documents of this nature, the detail of how this might work was left for later. In practice, direct elections were allowed for half of the sixty seats in the council. The remainder were to be filled by what were called 'functional constituencies', broadly appointed by specific business and trade areas, officials and members appointed by the governor. The council's transition to direct, universal-franchise elections for all seats in 1995 under the final governor proved a major sticking point for Beijing, and was reversed almost as soon as the city reverted to Chinese rule.

The 1989 crisis brought attention once more to the reality of how narrow Britain's options with China were. Whatever dramatic events occurred, and however clearly they showed the two countries to be at variance, because of its interests in Hong Kong Britain had no choice but to maintain pragmatic relations with Beijing. Even while it joined others in the West in expressing abhorrence at the crackdown – and as much as it would have liked to walk away – it had to maintain dialogue because of that common link. This proved that it was as trapped in its past with China as China believed it was with Britain. Concrete, practical matters once more forced their relationship to continue, despite the profound mutual antipathy.

On this occasion, it was the plans to construct a new airport that served as the immediate excuse for intensified contact, only a few years after the 1989 events. Kai Tak Airport, in use since 1925, was reaching capacity by this time. Located in the centre of a dense residential area, and infamous for the close-up views it afforded passengers into the rooms of neighbouring blocks of flats, as the descending planes weaved their way onto the runway, it was not fit for purpose as an entry point to a supposedly global commercial and logistics hub. A new site – partially on reclaimed land at Chek Lap Kok Island – had been identified some years before; but the issue was that the substantial construction costs for the project would bridge the periods of British and Chinese administration, and therefore some form of agreement was needed on the part of the two sides before the project could proceed. As soon as the idea was broached with the Chinese, it became a source of complaint: they claimed that the British were intending to engage in a massive money-making ruse that would bring financial benefit to its own companies, saddle the city with debt and leave the whole burden for the post-1997 administration to shoulder.

Whatever else the airport argument did, it forced John Major (b. 1943), Thatcher's successor as prime minister, to become the first leader of a major Western nation to visit China after the 1989 massacre, in September 1991. He participated reluctantly in the visit, but seemingly had no viable alternative: the amount of money to be borrowed to fund the airport (and how it would be borrowed) needed the support of the Chinese government, as the impact would extend beyond 1997. Ever the consummate opportunist, Beijing had exploited British anxiety to finalise the matter, insisting that only the British leader presenting himself in Beijing would suffice to complete the negotiations and sign off on the memorandum. Major's anger at appearing to be forced to do this (at least according to contemporary speculation in the press) and his unhappiness during the trip itself were dismissed by Cradock, who accompanied him. 'I saw no evidence of this', he wrote, referencing both those claims. 'On the contrary, the Prime Minister was highly satisfied with his travels.'[25]

Major's unexpected re-election as prime minister in 1992 (despite predictions that he would be booted out of office) led to the final chapter in the story of British direct involvement in the city. His campaign manager during the election, the Conservative MP for Bath, Chris Patten (b. 1944), had succeeded in helping his colleague regain power, but had managed to lose his own seat. Burdened with a sense of obligation to his ally and friend, whose luck had run out while directly engaged in looking after Major's own interests, the newly re-elected prime minister allowed Patten to cast his eye over various appointments within the gift of the premier. The governorship of Hong Kong, a five-year term (usually renewable for a further five years), was the final jewel in the diplomatic-service crown. Well remunerated and high in status, it offered an interesting set of new challenges for an ambitious, relatively young public figure who was unexpectedly at a loose end. The timing worked, as did the nature of the opportunity; for although the incumbent in 1992, the distinguished sinologist and diplomat David Wilson (b. 1935), theoretically qualified for reappointment after he came to the end of his first five years, Major felt that a change was required, and that rather than the safer, more predictable option, a higher-profile and more political candidate might be in order. Patten was duly appointed the last governor of Hong Kong, setting up the final great British direct bilateral fight with the Chinese.

Patten had no previous experience of dealing with China – or, for that matter, of international affairs. His background was overwhelmingly domestic up to 1992. But he used this apparent weakness to his advantage when he started work in Hong Kong, aiming to supply fresh perspectives and a new way of thinking about an issue that had been dominated until then by a small, highly insular group of people. These he called the Foreign Office Sinophiles, people typified by the likes of Cradock and his various younger colleagues now sprinkled across government and steering Hong Kong and China-related policy. They were, as Patten wrote in his diary, people who 'took it for granted that ultimately you have to go along with Beijing rather than risk arguments. Beijing rules – OK.' Their attempts to gain his support by blinding him with sinological science cut little ice. 'It may be that if you spend years of your life learning Mandarin, reading Chinese history and immersing yourself in the country's culture,' he wrote, 'you inevitably fetch up taking this sort of view.'[26] In Patten's eyes, the main crime of this clique within government was its constant proclivity to err towards taking China's side and representing the views of Beijing better than those of the country they were meant to be serving. This became a theme throughout his time in the city, making its appearance early and not ceasing until the day he left. As he stated in 1994, 'we have produced a generation of Sovietologists who thought that it was right to stand up to the Soviet Union alongside a generation of Sinologists who thought we should cave in to China.'[27] Needless to say, many of those he castigated in this way would respond through numerous attempts to thwart and frustrate his programme. Britain, as ever in matters relating to China, was a disunited actor and expended as much effort in battling within itself as it did in taking the fight to Beijing. For this, and perhaps only this, the Sinophiles and Patten share equal responsibility, unhelpfully caricaturing each other and providing numerous opportunities for China to indulge in classic divisive tactics.

Patten decided early on in his time in office in Hong Kong where his priorities lay in the final five years of British administration. He acknowledged the huge commercial interests that needed to be preserved, along with the equal importance of looking after the welfare of the local people. But he also outlined bolder plans, and it was here that the real problems with China started. These broadly addressed the issue of how little Britain had done in the previous century or so of administration to introduce any meaningful democracy. 'I obviously', Patten wrote in his diary in July 1993, 'have to embed as far as possible the laws on human rights and freedoms in Hong Kong and to defend the independence of the judiciary, the whole question of due process and the cleanness as well as openness of government.'[28] His suspicions that this would prove 'more difficult as we get closer to 1997' proved correct.

Beijing's suspicions were inevitably that Britain was simply raising these matters so late in the day to cause problems and disrupt a process that had long since been agreed. Patten's fights with those in the British government back home who were similarly sceptical about what Britain could achieve with only five years to go, with the pro-Beijing parties in the city and with Beijing itself reached levels of rhetorical intensity not seen since the days of the Cultural Revolution. The last governor was (according to one of the more puzzling insults hurled at him by Chinese-language media) 'a tango dancer for a thousand years'. The most difficult of the tasks he set himself while this invective was going on was to push through an increase in those positions that were directly elected to the Legislative Council and reforms to the legal system. Many of these moves aroused deep suspicions in China that Britain's sole aim was to create sources of potential trouble after the handover, and that it was intent on planting timebombs that would go off once it had relinquished control. Even at the best of times, there was rarely much trust in Sino-British relations. Above all others, this issue brought out the full strength of Beijing paranoia. Small wonder that the years before 1997 were to prove so contentious and rocky.

Beyond this, Cradock and Patten represented strands of British thinking and attitudes towards China that had long been present, and therefore the clash between them had a far wider and deeper symbolic significance. On the one hand, there stood Cradock – the ultimate realist, a government insider who had served as Margaret Thatcher's foreign policy advisor and who had lived for years in China itself, including through the terrifying 1967 attack on the Beijing mission. This was a figure who certainly had a profound understanding of Chinese politics and who had been involved in perhaps the most complex set of negotiations with Beijing that Britain had ever undertaken. No one could deny the depth and breadth of his knowledge and his right to speak with authority. Ranged against him was Patten – someone who had worked with distinction and courage as a democratically elected politician at the highest level; someone imbued with a fundamental belief in the universal applicability of particular values involving human rights, freedom and the rule of law. As someone who was articulate, passionate and able to relate easily to people (in ways that officials never had to), it was easy to understand how Patten posed tricky problems not just for the Chinese, but also for his own side. The key difference between these two men was philosophical. For Cradock, the main thing was to be realistic, accept that Beijing held most of the cards and recognise that the best Britain could do was to play defensively and aim for smaller, tactical victories. Patten was more idealistic: he believed that Beijing would, at some point, have to back down because the British vision of rights ultimately had universal applicability, and Britain – not China – was on the right side of history.

The clash between Patten and Cradock embodied the twin strands of idealism and realism that had permeated Anglo-Chinese relations since the early eighteenth century. They were present when Palmerston – with his early realism and almost amoral stance – had squared up to the agonised moralism of Gladstone. Neither side had ultimately vanquished the other. Almost every step of the way, British policy on China involved compromise and attempts to create a workable consensus between these two poles. If anything, the realists usually ended up exercising more influence than the idealists. Patten's final stand – his assertion of some kind of defence of values – was entirely valid, but it came far too late. The date of the retrocession drew nigh with relentless and unavoidable certainty.

The night of the handover, 30 June 1997, was dominated by a downpour. The final governor, standing at the brand-new conference centre facing the famous harbour during the ceremony to mark the end of Britain's rulership of Hong Kong, ended up getting drenched. As the local newspaper, the *South China Morning Post*, put it the next day,

Mr Patten hailed the success of Hong Kong as a 'Chinese city . . . with British characteristics'. Britain's contribution was to have provided the 'scaffolding that enabled the people of Hong Kong to ascend'. But as the music swelled, the moment finally became too much for the Governor, his tears falling amid the rain.[29]

It was a poignant moment, and one that marked the end of the final tangible, direct residue of Britain's colonial history with China. Now, at last, a new history could start. The question was just how much the memory of the old would figure in that, or whether it would finally start to be forgotten.

11

The Great Shift

Britain in the Era of Chinese Dominance, 1997–2023

The year 1997 supplied Britain with that rarest of things – a fresh start in its relations with China. The status of Hong Kong, the final great issue left over from the long, contentious and problematic history of engagement, was seemingly now resolved, removing the key cause of argument and bad feeling. Not that there was a completely clean slate. Obligations that Britain had to observe still existed – six-monthly reports on the situation in Hong Kong needed to be produced by the Foreign Office up to 2047 and set before parliament, as one of the stipulations of the Sino-British agreement of 1984 during the fifty-year life span of the 'one country, two systems' arrangement. A certain amount of dialogue also continued through the work of the Joint Liaison Group, a body made up of representatives from both sides, which was finally folded on the last day of 1999. All of this was humdrum bureaucratic process, compared to the epic battles of the last decade and a half. Finally, there was the more abstract feeling of moral responsibility maintained by some people in the UK for the people of the city, as they grew accustomed to new rule. But nothing changed the stark reality that the affairs of Hong Kong were irrevocably in hands other than those of the British. Britain could radically simplify its China story by focusing finally on the commercial and trade opportunities that were starting to appear as the country continued with its reforms.

This most recent stage of the Anglo-Chinese story, however, is one marked by a dramatic, revolutionary change. This is the period that saw economically, militarily, geopolitically, and even intellectually and culturally the advantages that Britain had maintained over China in previous centuries and decades shift the other way. The asymmetry that had been so vast in the early era, and that had prevailed in Britain's favour for so long, started to narrow in the late twentieth century. Rather than settling on a harmonious balance, from 1997 China began to pull ahead. This was indeed a great reversal, a true paradigm shift – and one that happened with staggering speed. It was something that many others experienced as the People's Republic sped ahead economically. But because of their uniquely intense and extensive relationship, the psychological impact this had on the British and their link to the Chinese was to prove deeper and harder to adjust to. Before the millennium, the challenge was for China to get much attention from a Britain distracted by many other responsibilities. After that date, it was the other way around. Not the least of the problems this transformed situation created was that, for many in British politics in particular, this radical change passed them by, and they still referred to China in a way that was long out of date and that belonged to another age. Public figures talked airily of Britain having to work with China on the one hand, but needing to tell it whenever they were displeased or felt it had crossed a line. There was little sense that those using this language understood how transformed the positions of China and Britain were, and how likely it was that China – far from taking heed of, or even being offended by, this approach – was much more likely to ignore it, or not even hear it in the first place.

New Labour reset

In May 1997, the landslide election victory of the Labour Party under Tony Blair (b. 1953), after seventeen years of Conservative government, marked a sea change in British domestic politics. On relations with China, however, the impact was connected not to political events, but to the culmination of all the work on the Hong Kong retrocession. It was accidental that this happened after the change of government. Even if there had been no replacement of the ruling party, the long-planned hand-back meant that something was taking place which was bound to be transformative. Having attended the rainy ceremony mentioned in the previous chapter, Blair then had little else to do but enjoy a newly simplified relationship. Indeed, the initial challenges Hong Kong faced were nothing to do with the UK, but involved managing the unfolding Asian financial crisis, which impacted dramatically on the city's prosperity (as it did on other places across the region), raising unemployment and sending growth plunging. There was no immediate political impact, and the new chief executive, Liverpool University-educated Tung Chee-hwa (b. 1937), was able to slot into his new role relatively quickly. One of the first tasks his administration undertook was the swift removal of the final democratic reforms brought in by his predecessor, Chris Patten.

Symbolising the new era, the first ever state visit to the UK by a Chinese ruler took place in October 1999, when President Jiang Zemin (1926–2022) arrived. Never before had the most powerful leader of China, either in imperial times or subsequently, set foot in Britain. The visit, while big on status and symbolism, was also beset by a new tone of moralising, with Jiang being framed as the representative of a system that stood as the antithesis of British values. Demonstrations dogged his visit. Following a scuffle with police outside Buckingham Palace as Jiang was being entertained there, one supporter of the Free Tibet campaign stated that 'our banners have been snatched and our flags have been snatched. This shows how the British government is not interested in human rights but just in trade.'[1] A motion tabled in the House of Commons the same week stated

[T]his House welcomes President Jiang Zemin on his official visit to the United Kingdom; trusts that the visit will lead to an improvement in relations between the two countries; and expresses the hope that Her Majesty's Government will advise the President of the genuine feelings of concern in the United Kingdom about the Chinese occupation of Tibet and the denial to the people of Tibet of their right to determine their own future.[2]

This was a somewhat complex message to convey, but its broad thrust was that someone was welcome, but at the same time needed to work harder to be worthy of the invitation.

Concerns about Tibet had intensified in Britain from the 1980s onwards, as more and more people became aware of claims of forced abortions in the region, repression of local people's religious practices and what the Dalai Lama was to label 'cultural genocide'. The respect and high profile he enjoyed on his visits to Britain from this time helped raise the profile of the region. The Jiang visit itself provided a good illustration of the tensions in the new approach to China, one focused on engagement and trying to move on from the heavy burden of history. On the one hand, full pageantry was accorded to the visiting dignitary. He even went to Madame Tussauds to be modelled for a wax replica figure, and attended the newly opened Globe Theatre to hear some Shakespeare performed. But on the other hand, there were clearly vocal groups in the UK who felt that his government was deeply problematic, and that Britain had a responsibility to do something about it.

The question was what? China's reforms had produced a strange, hybrid economy, where high rates of growth had made the country, in the words of the much-admired premier at the time, Zhu Rongji (b. 1928), the factory of the world, providing goods to the capitalist West while maintaining its socialist and largely state-led system. Shops – from supermarkets to electrical appliance stores – were full of products made there, at far lower cost. This served to keep consumers happy – consumers who were often the same people who were complaining about the country's human rights record! In this sense, as never before, China was materially part of life in Britain, filling homes and offices with artefacts and products that had started their journey in vast factories along the Pearl River Delta. China's influence was also starting to appear in novel and unexpected ways. For the first time, Chinese companies, albeit very modestly, started to invest in Britain – seventy of them between 1997 and 2004.[3] While the Chinese investment was still overshadowed by that of other major economies, the fact that this was happening at all was of enormous symbolic importance.

The same could be said of the appearance of Chinese students at British universities. This commenced in the 1980s with the merest trickle, but within three decades had reached spectacular levels (180,000 were enrolled on university courses in Britain in 2023). The mindset of British immigration officials in the late 1990s was predominantly to regard people from mainland China as potential economic migrants. Tragic events, such as the discovery of fifty-eight dead Chinese on a lorry in the port city of Dover in June 2000, underlined this – people whose journey to the West was arranged by so-called 'snakehead' gangs, taking vast amounts of money to smuggle them across borders with the promise of a better life, all too often creating untold misery as they did so. Within a decade, however, people from the same nation were the target of British government-supported tourism campaigns, as it became clear that they were the highest-spending and most promising new cohort of visitors. The retail outlet which opened in 1995 at Bicester, near Oxford, quickly came to target Chinese visitors and was famous for its use of Chinese signage and train announcements. It was soon established as a standard element of any visit to the UK by people from the People's Republic.

The new focus on engagement for economic gain (with the underlying hope that this was justified, because China would politically transform via this route) was given a huge injection of energy by the country's entry to the World Trade Organization (WTO) in late 2001. Beijing had been working on its application for fourteen years, from the time when the organisation went under the name of the General Agreement on Tariffs and Trade (GATT). There were various stumbling blocks along the way, the worst being the 1989 uprising and the political obstacle this presented (see previous chapter). But the two main trading blocs – the European Union (of which Britain was then a part) and the US – felt that having China inside the global trading system would offer the blocs a new level of potential influence and a way of encouraging China to adapt and fit into what was later called the global, rules-based system. However, the assessments of many economists both inside and outside the country of how China might comply with the WTO demands were downbeat. There was a sense that it was likely to struggle, with its agriculture, finance and state-owned enterprise sectors exposed to a new intensity of foreign multinational competition.[4] While these did indeed pose real challenges, what was remarkable was not the problems, but the explosion of growth that occurred in the years after 2001. In a single decade up to 2012, China's GDP quadrupled. By 2005, the GDP of Britain and China was the same. Just five years later, China's was two and a half times larger; it had overtaken Japan and stood second only to America.[5] Since the beginning of the nineteenth century, China had never been economically more dominant than the UK. In the twenty-first century, the tables were dramatically turned and the story became one in which almost day by day, China pulled further ahead.

The opportunities this presented for Britain were clear. Through the first decade of the new century, as the WTO impact continued to unfold, British companies – supported by various state campaigns and often with the involvement of partially government-funded entities, like the China–Britain Business Council – made Beijing and Shanghai their chief targets. Ministerial visits were also common, though following the 11 September 2001 terrorist attacks in the US, the prime ministers Blair and then Gordon Brown (b. 1951) were not as frequent in their visits to China as their German or French counterparts, due to their fixation on Washington and making that relationship central to them. Blair visited Beijing in 1998 and attempted the new balancing act of talking about trade one minute, while trying to appease the human rights lobby back in Britain by addressing values the next. He visited again in 2003. Gordon Brown, as committed an Atlanticist as Blair, managed only one visit in his three years in office, in 2008. In return, Jiang's successor Hu Jintao (b. 1942) visited Britain in 2005. His far lower-key personality – together with his minders' heightened sense of risk aversion – meant that his visit was trouble free, largely by being almost invisible.

As a component of engagement, Britain sought to rebrand its image in China. The bilateral history from which it was trying to emerge meant that the vast majority of urban Chinese, better educated and wealthier than ever before, had some appreciation of Britain as a historically important place, but very little sense of anything more modern that it had to offer. America was seen as the place where cutting-edge technology was being created. Britain had a much older, more traditional feel: it was a place that, for many, was still dominated by fogs, men in bowler hats and ladies wearing long, traditional ballgowns. British government-supported campaigns in the mid-2000s to address this – one was called 'Think UK', for instance – attempted to rebrand the UK as a place that was cool and modern.

In the opposite direction, the Beijing Olympics of 2008 meant that a much larger British audience than ever before could see images of and read stories from China. The opening ceremony in the Bird's Nest stadium, with its massed ranks of drummers and its high-tech imagery, gave some idea of the nationalist pride and scale of the country. Other stories highlighted its economic success and the dramatic social changes its people were witnessing. There was also plenty of evidence of the more negative side, with the (at that time) much freer Chinese internet offering daily stories of protests, Chinese people fighting and petitioning against injustice, and potential political struggles in the top leadership. For those who were willing to look, China became more accessible and knowable than ever before. During the Olympics itself, a campaign in Britain, 'China Now', supported by a combination of British government and private-sector funding, tried to convey some of the complexity, creativity and dynamism of the place – a country that had only started to exist in its current form a few years before.

What's the policy?

With rising economic opportunities and the appearance of a China that had greater diplomatic status than ever before, Britain's need for a coherent policy position was pressing. In part, this was required to provide some coherence with its allies – in particular the European Union, where trade negotiations happened, and the US, where security partnership was uppermost. Britain had long had to devise its China policy in a context where it was never purely bilateral, but had to take into account the views and desires of others. This only intensified as time went on. Through the 2000s, London worked broadly in a consensus atmosphere, in which most people agreed that trade and economic engagement with China was justified on the grounds of what would happen through it.

To communicate its policy position more clearly, in 2009, for the first time, the British government issued what it called 'A Framework for Engagement' with China. There it spelt out the three key areas that were seen as priorities. The first was getting the best for Britain from China's growth. The second was fostering China's role as a responsible global player. And the final priority was promoting sustainable development, modernisation and internal reform in China.[6] The framework sought to achieve some sort of balance: there was naked self-interest in the first priority; an attempt in the second to optimise Britain's influence over China, in order to get it to fit into the existing global order; and in the third, a much bolder attempt to make it more like the West. These aims were all interconnected: a

China run more along the lines of a legal system like Britain's, and with a political structure that was the same, would presumably have been a place that managed to achieve the first and second objectives far more easily; how the third could be achieved was far less clear. Each of the priorities was also aligned with the positions of both the US and the European Union, the latter of whose 2006 strategic statement had also placed issues in very similar silos.

As a final piece of historic tidying up, Britain in 2008 finally relinquished its unique policy of recognising Chinese suzerainty over Tibet, shifting to an acceptance of sovereignty. In October that year, the then foreign secretary, David Miliband, recorded in a written ministerial statement that 'the outdated concept of suzerainty' meant that

> some have used this to cast doubt on the aims we are pursuing and to claim that we are denying Chinese sovereignty over a large part of its own territory. We have made clear to the Chinese Government, and publicly, that we do not support Tibetan independence. Like every other EU member state, and the United States, we regard Tibet as part of the People's Republic of China.[7]

This change had been made partially in the hope that improved access to the region would now be granted. It was also aimed at creating a better dialogue with China, removing one of the most longstanding sources of tension and resentment. But critics afterwards pointed out that few if any improvements had occurred either in the level of autonomy promised to the region, or in the position between the Beijing government and the representatives of the Tibetan government in exile.

The contentiousness of the Tibetan issue remained, despite this significant policy change. In 2012, the recently elected British Conservative prime minister, David Cameron (b. 1966), used a longstanding means of meeting the Tibetans' chief spiritual leader, the exiled Dalai Lama, as a religious rather than a political figure, in order to avoid Chinese accusations of Britain covertly acknowledging the territory's independence. He did so in the undercroft of St Paul's Cathedral in London, during an event that was being held there that day. Chinese fury over this kind of meeting had risen in intensity over the previous decades. Despite their largely positive views on engagement with China, other European leaders, such as German Chancellor Angela Merkel, had been strongly condemned for doing similar things. But Britain's historic role in Tibet provided an added piquancy to any activity concerning this issue. The Chinese government went into overdrive, stopping all high-level visits. Even the fact that Britain was hosting the Olympics in London later that year did not abate their rage. For over twelve months, the British embassy in Beijing, usually inundated with VIPs from Britain, remained deserted, its staff largely left to do domestic reporting, rather than making the usual labour-intensive arrangements for copious numbers of dignitaries coming through. Interestingly, there was no significant fall in the statistics for trade and investment, nor in the numbers of tourists or students. Everything was business as usual, apart from elite contact.

For the things that mattered to China, in fact, the state of the bilateral political relationship rarely had much impact. There were three principal objectives it had, as it emerged into the more muscular, assertive and self-confident Xi Jinping (b. 1953) era from 2012. The first was to have Britain host Chinese investment that showcased its new technologies. Nuclear power and telecoms, particularly through the major company Huawei, figured largely here. Huawei, active in Britain since the mid-2000s, had signed deals to provide British Telecom with over £1 billion of telecoms equipment, despite worrying reports of security issues arising from use of its equipment. To address these concerns, the government set up a joint scrutiny office at the Government Communications Headquarters (GCHQ) intelligence organisation. It was to issue technical reports each year assessing the threats and problems, and these were to be set before parliament.

Huawei was joined in London by the rising force of the Chinese internet, Alibaba. Chinese investment also appeared in utility companies such as Thames Water, and in the acquisition of brands like the restaurant chain Pizza Express. Following the great economic crisis of 2008, the opportunities that Chinese money offered British companies became increasingly of interest.

By 2012, this had been joined by a second major area of Chinese focus in Britain: the City of London, as a potential trading centre for Chinese currency. The renminbi remained inconvertible. However, there were ways in which it could be traded under licence, and used to settle at least Chinese business accounts. Along with Singapore and Hong Kong, London became a major finance centre for Chinese banks (with over forty based there from 2012) and for flows of Chinese money. It was also, at least until the vote to leave the European Union in 2016, used as a gateway into Europe. And thirdly, China was interested in the UK as an intellectual partner – a place with highly ranked, research-intensive universities, where large numbers of its young people came to study.

From the 2009 framework paper, therefore, it was clear that Britain was expending a lot of effort on doing what it could to maximise trade and economic benefits from engagement with China. Far less clear was how it was able to progress the third priority of the paper – working to bring about reform and change in China itself. This became increasingly difficult as a result of the general collapse of confidence in Western governance after the 2008 economic crisis, and an accompanying attitude in China that was far more sceptical of what the West was proposing and whether that would help China, or merely lead to the same chaos that had engulfed Russia after 1991. The ways in which the Americans and others had responded to the demise of the Soviet Union was key: what many Chinese perceived was outsiders foisting on a third country reforms that were inappropriate or self-interested. This had resulted in widespread corruption, rising poverty and very bad societal outcomes in terms of alcoholism, poor health and falling average mortality rates. And that proved what poor suggestions they had been. The 2008 crisis – from which China emerged relatively unscathed and where it was often seen as a potential source of aid for others – only reinforced this idea in Beijing of Western incompetence. From his earliest days in office, Xi Jinping – with his grand talk of the 'China Dream' and national rejuvenation – supplied the country with a new and confident tone with which to talk to the world. This confidence was built on a platform constructed over the previous decade. It did not come from nowhere.

There were issues of trust that Britain, with its long history of opportunism and of placing trade benefits above values, faced a particular challenge in answering. In the nineteenth century, it was more than happy to support a failing Qing regime, even when reform was in the air, because of its need for a China that was never too strong to threaten it, nor so weak that it would collapse and create problems that way. The Second World War produced a major change in the way that Britain and others thought about a sustainable global order, inspiring them to create a system that embodied beliefs and values which ensured that destructive global conflicts never occurred again. Even so, the People's Republic regarded this system as one that had been established largely without its active participation (it arrived late on the scene, after all, not being part of the United Nations until the 1970s), and which represented a world order that was already passing into history and needed reform. Americans and others were keen to integrate China into this extant order, on the assumption that it was the best and the only one that could work. But under Xi, there was a rejection of what was called 'Western universalism'. A document sent to Chinese academics was leaked in 2013: this paper made it clear that the Chinese leadership had set its face against attempts to use civil society, political parties or the rule of law to contest the Communist Party's monopoly on organised political power.[8] The strategy of using economic and other softer modes of engagement, as well as inducements to be part of the prevailing global order, were regarded as Trojan horses, aimed at influencing China to deliver for Western aims, rather than its own.

A British diplomat based in China in the early 2000s, Nigel Cox, stated about this time that 'the first priority for Britain in China was not our commercial interests, it was the strategic contribution to the integration of China into the international community in all senses'.[9] In the 2010s, China called an abrupt halt to the delivery of this aim, with the appearance of a more assertive and nationalist Chinese leadership under Xi Jinping. British non-governmental organisations found their space to operate in the country shrinking. Legal and other forms of engagement were conducted either on Beijing's terms or not at all. While the freeze in elite relations after Cameron met the Dalai Lama eventually lifted with a visit to Beijing by the duke and duchess of Cambridge in 2014, the position of the Xi administration made the whole ethos of engagement outlined in the 2009 British framework paper redundant. The paper was subsequently removed from official websites, and now only exists on those of third parties that are interested in this special period of Sino-British relations – a fitting sign of its transfer from statement of active policy to material of purely historical interest.

The golden age: Attitude and not policy

One of the striking characteristics of British relations with China that has remained remarkably stable over the last century or so is the relative indifference of British people towards the country. Efforts to inspire British students to learn the Chinese language or engage with Chinese culture have led from time to time to sporadic (albeit limited) outbursts of enthusiasm. The number of those studying Chinese at university reflects this consistently low level of engagement, with figures remaining small and steady, and with only a few places offering full honours degrees in Mandarin (Oxford, Cambridge, Leeds, SOAS and Edinburgh being the most prominent). Chinese New Year festivals, with their greater sense of drama and novelty, have become popular; but on the whole, the few opinion polls there have been indicate that the same level of indifference that prevailed in the twentieth century also pertains in the twenty-first.

A 2013 survey showed that trade engagement with China was largely supported, though there were reservations about deeper involvement through investment in the UK, and those questioned were fairly neutral on the subject of Chinese foreign policy more generally.[10] These findings were echoed two years later, though with an admission that although China might be admired as a potential economic partner, it was not particularly liked:

> The British public seems to have a pragmatic approach to economic relations with China, but there is not much evidence of great affection for the country. Of the 12 biggest economies by GDP excluding the USA and those in Europe, China comes in at 8th in terms of net positive impressions (29% positive, 55% negative).[11]

For the British, the China story seems to be one about a remote and strange place. It does not fill the nation with the same kind of often visceral fear that it does, for instance, the US (where there is far deeper geopolitical unease at rising tensions with the People's Republic) or Australia (with its much larger and more visible trading relationship).

In this context, George Osborne (b. 1971), the British chancellor of the exchequer (in effect its finance minister) from 2010 to 2016, was an anomaly. A tour of China as a backpacker in the 1980s gave him an appreciation of the country, and a lasting personal interest in it. When he came to power, two decades later, he was clearly energised and excited by the potential that the place offered. Despite the initial tensions because of the Cameron meeting with the Dalai Lama mentioned above, when in power, Osborne was able subsequently to move beyond this to perhaps the most pro-Chinese position ever taken by a British elite-level politician. There was much criticism and derision at this approach in the press, with many castigating him for seeming to jettison all talk of values for more mercenary ends. But Osborne's arguments for pursuing that line were perfectly rational: everyone else seemed to be capitalising on the China opportunity, while Britain's rewards in terms of investment, finance engagement and bigger exports to the country's rising middle class were relatively poor. It was merely a statement of fact that, in the 2010s, in view of the respective size of their economies, Britain and China should have been doing far more business with each other than they were.

What Britain needed, according to Osborne's prognosis, was a changed attitude towards China, rather than the continuation of a policy that tried to balance the increasingly incompatible elements of seeking trade benefits and trying to square this with the challenges that the country presented in terms of its human rights and politics. Speaking at a bilateral summit before a visiting Chinese dignitary in September 2014, he stated 'we want our relationship to be based on more than just pounds and yuan – it must also be based on a deep understanding and respect between our civilisations'. He went on to say that the present moment marked a 'new chapter in the Britain–China relationship'.[12]

Osborne was willing to go further than any other major British leader since Edward Heath, visiting the People's Republic in 2015. At the invitation of the Chinese government, he also went to the highly controversial area of Xinjiang – a visit that received very positive coverage in the Chinese domestic media, while at the same time attracting harsh criticism back in Britain. Xinjiang, like Tibet, while in name an autonomous region of China, had been subject to increasingly draconian governance from the 1990s onwards. This had intensified as fears of separatism by the region's majority-Muslim Uyghur population grew in the 2000s. At the time of Osborne's visit, policies that eroded local culture and language were being condemned in

Britain. Since 2017, there has been increased concern about the region, following reports of over a million people there being incarcerated in so-called re-education centres.

The new Osborne-inspired approach reached its climax in October 2015, with the visit to Britain by Chinese President Xi Jinping – the first state visit for a decade. Xi proved a very different kettle of fish from his ultra-low-key, almost non-communicative predecessor Hu Jintao. Famously accompanying his host, David Cameron, to the Plough Inn at Cadsden, Buckinghamshire, and pictured sipping a pint of bitter and eating fish and chips there, he was also able to visit Manchester and promote his famed love of football. The Xi visit allowed the very vocal, extrovert Chinese ambassador in the UK at the time, Liu Xiaoming, to declare that a golden era was now dawning in the relationship. The joint communique issued at the end of the visit was certainly full of language that stressed reciprocity, mutuality and common purpose: 'The UK and China', it stated, 'regard each other's development as providing important opportunities for bilateral co-operation. Both sides will enhance bilateral trade and investment, and support mutual economic competitiveness and innovation for the benefit of both peoples in the decade ahead.' It went on to talk about enhancing political trust, 'based on equality and mutual respect and, in that spirit, recognise the importance each side attaches to its own political system, development path, core interests and major concerns.'[13] The language of 'golden age' certainly worked well enough in Chinese material. But in English, it immediately created problems, because of the sense that things were being overstated, and that fundamental underlying problems were being brushed under the carpet. Inevitably, in future years, as the relationship deteriorated, 'golden age' was replaced by less flattering terms, like 'bronze age', 'ice age' or 'stone age'.

Domestic British politics was another factor at this time, reconfiguring the relationship not just with China, but also with the rest of the world. The referendum to leave the European Union (EU) in June

2016 had a massive impact. Britain's domestic politics became divided, with major arguments about whether the country should leave the EU – and if so, how. Ultimately, the outcome of the vote heralded the end of Cameron and Osborne's period in power and created major challenges for Britain in its European policy. Britain was not alone in experiencing such upset: in the United States, the election of Donald Trump as president in 2016 delivered another shock.

This all meant that the politics in China – which in the past had been beset by unpredictability and uncertainty – was now far more stable than in the once-solid, long-established Western democracies. Whereas Xi Jinping's brand of populist nationalism seemed to have answered the question for the Chinese of who they believed they were and what their national mission was, the British people were visibly more divided and conflicted about their own identity. Whereas a century and a half earlier it had been a powerful Britain worrying about how sustainable the Qing empire was and when it might collapse and cause huge problems, now the situation was reversed. There were moments when Britain seemed to be caught in a trap from which there was no exit; it seemed to be slowly destroying itself.

China flung at Britain a series of sharp challenges, which exposed this stark power asymmetry. Of these, the most striking was the situation in Hong Kong. Arguments over how best to elect a chief executive, something that had been promised in the Basic Law of 1991, came to a head in 2012–13. There were major demonstrations in the central area of the city in 2014 against the Beijing-supported proposals, under which – instead of people being able to stand directly for election – an electoral committee would put forward nominations. This proposal was contested, but no alternative was allowed to go forward, so the current system of someone being appointed by the Legislative Council without a wider vote was maintained. The imposition of very wide-ranging national security laws in 2020 meant that any action that was regarded as undermining the governance of the city – whether it was undertaken in Hong Kong or abroad – was defined per se as unpatriotic and would attract draconian punishment. These laws led to the detention by the authorities of individuals who had previously been able to speak out and criticise the city's government and Beijing policy relatively freely. Martin Lee, a veteran activist and pro-democracy politician, was among the best known. *Apple Daily*, a very popular, non-mainstream newspaper, was closed down, and its founder Jimmy Lai jailed after being accused of organising illegal protests.

Britain's response to these events was vocal, and often delivered in concert with America, the Europeans and other powers. Its departure from the EU in 2021, however, meant that it needed to stand alone when speaking to China on values and rights issues, rather than as part of a much larger (and therefore better-protected) trading bloc. The decision in 2021 to grant Hong Kong citizens an accelerated pathway to citizenship in the UK allowed 160,000 of them to move to Britain between that date and 2023.[14] This inevitably angered Beijing, which saw it as interference in its affairs and a further reason to question Britain's good faith. In the end, the bottom line was this: China felt that, with retrocession having taken place a quarter of a century before, and despite the fifty-year period of transition, it had the right and the authority to exercise its sovereignty the way it chose. Britain's points, therefore, were sometimes treated with brutal dismissiveness.

Britain's China story: The 2020s

The outbreak of the COVID-19 pandemic in the central Chinese city of Wuhan in late 2019 had an immense impact on Sino-British relations – as indeed it did on relations with much of the rest of the world. The ways in which the virus spread, and the practical impact it had on the British people's social and economic life from March 2020 (when the first lockdowns were imposed to stop the spread of the disease) brought to the surface attitudes towards China that had never before been exposed. A poll in 2022 by YouGov delivered stark evidence of just how much the indifference registered during earlier surveys had shifted to dislike: only 13 per cent of those questioned admitted that they had a positive view of the country; a staggering 54 per cent disliked it; while 32 per cent remained neutral. In terms of people's perceptions of various countries, in early 2024 China ranked 111th on the list, slotting in between Benin and East Timor.[15] For all the effort made around the 'golden era' narrative, this was a truly terrible return. China had become distrusted; its involvement in critical infrastructure investments increasingly unlikely; and the overall narrative of engagement scaled back, so that risk management, rather than opportunity maximisation, became the key consideration. By the end of 2022, the newly appointed British prime minister, Rishi Sunak (b. 1980), was able to declare that the golden era was officially over.

There was a sharp and symbolic downward spiral in relations: when a group of British MPs was sanctioned in retaliation for measures imposed on Chinese officials dealing with Xinjiang and the human rights abuses in that region. That in turn led to the Chinese ambassador to the UK being banned from entering parliament. This was an unprecedented measure.

Speculation online about the origins of the virus, with claims that it had been deliberately created in a laboratory, fuelled a spate of attacks on people of Chinese heritage. The restrictions on travel meant that, whereas in 2020–22 Chinese had made up the largest group of foreign tourists shopping in Oxford Street, London, now barely any were able to visit the UK (nor British go to China). There was a reversion to a previous period, as interpersonal contact shrank.

In terms of engagement with China, little attempt has been made in the years since 2000 to reach beyond the well-established business, academic and official networks. HSBC, Jardine and Standard Chartered, along with the Foreign, Commonwealth and Development Office and the Russell Group universities, have to some degree dealt with China ever since the nineteenth century, and will continue to do so. Confucius Institutes in Britain have attempted to encourage a wider public to learn about Chinese culture and language; but since the 2010s they have been stymied by claims about their political bias in favour of the Chinese government, which provides some of their funding. Despite the rich, extensive and complex history between the two countries, knowledge of China remains stagnant and since the announcement of a golden era in 2015, there has been no significant uptake in terms of the numbers studying Mandarin. What activism there is for an upgrade in relations has come largely from the Chinese side, with an ever-increasing number of students arriving in Britain to study since 2015.

The perennial search continues for a coherent policy framework by which to capture the complexity of working with China, acknowledging its importance, but also shielding against its less palatable and more problematic aspects. An Integrated Review undertaken by the Cabinet Office, sitting directly under the British prime minister, produced at least one attempt to achieve this in 2022. In it, China was framed as a competitor, collaborator and adversary – the same framework used by the United States and the European Union. Thus in theory at least, the review indicated that there was space to explore commercial relations with the country and to have dialogue on areas of clear mutual concern, where there is a need for concerted action (such as combating global warming); but there was also a clear admission that in security areas, Britain and China were not aligned.

The document made it clear that Britain did not agree with China's behaviour in the South China Sea, where, since the 2000s, it has supported its territorial claims against its neighbours (e.g. the Philippines or Vietnam) through clashes between sea vessels, some of which have threatened to escalate into something far more serious; it does not agree with China's stance on Taiwan, or its policies in Xinjiang, Hong Kong and Tibet. The document also voiced concerns about the rule of law in the country and the predictability of the business environment there. And it mentioned frequently the lack of transparency and the need for greater reciprocity in global issues. This last point, in particular, became problematic when Russia brutally invaded its neighbour Ukraine in March 2022, and China largely sat on the fence, doing nothing to intercede with its ally to stop the violence and disruption that the war caused.

The Integrated Review, which was revised in 2023, was a rational attempt to solve a problem whose resolution had been sought many times before, almost always with limited success. In the latter half of the nineteenth century, Britain had the main tools by which it could have influenced affairs in China. But it decided then that, so long as its material and economic interests were looked after, it had no desire to take responsibility for potentially governing a colony that included a fifth of humanity and that stretched for thousands of miles from the coast in towards inner Asia. Pragmatism carried the day then. In the twenty-first century, the irony is that an almost messianic language of saving the Chinese from their cruel government has started to appear – language that is all the more striking because Britain has never been in a *less* favourable domestic position to do anything about the noble cause it is espousing. Instead, there has been constant tension between the hawks and the doves, to some extent mirroring the US, though never quite reaching the same intensity of anger and emotional engagement.

And yet there clearly is a China story in Britain, despite the swirling storm of argument and anger about what China means to British people in the contemporary world. In 2023, the British still consumed vast quantities of a drink that had originally been discovered in China, and which had reshaped their tastebuds and fundamental parts of their social culture from the seventeenth century onwards. Some of them (still) drank this tea from porcelain cups, the technology of which was originally developed in China, even though it was adapted and transformed by new processes invented during the Industrial Revolution. They frequently wore scarves and ties and other clothing made of silk, first imported indirectly from China hundreds of years ago; and they sat in gardens, the flowers in which were often originally from China, and the design of which had been profoundly influenced by debates about Far Eastern aesthetics through the eighteenth century. Many enjoyed food reportedly sourced from (or at the very least inspired by) the various cuisines of China, and available in innumerable restaurants across Britain. Despite all the bad blood of the previous years, British people when they shopped were more than likely to purchase goods that were manufactured in China, a country that so often figured in news stories as a challenger and a problem for global order. And they sent their children to universities in Britain where, more often than not, the largest single source of revenue was Chinese students paying high tuition fees.

Britain's China story is woven through the fabric of daily life – very rarely acknowledged explicitly, but undeniable when pointed out. The issue is not so much that Britain does not have a policy towards China – a country which it has affected so profoundly and which in turn has had such a profound impact on it. Rather, it does not have a clear narrative – a tale that makes sense of this often traumatic, fascinating and transformative story. That is what I have found to have been most lacking over the past three decades in discussions about China in Britain's life. And that is why I decided to write this book. It is the story of four hundred years of encounter, change, suffering and collaboration. It is a story that is rich, deep and undeniable. And it is a story that is one of the great cornerstones of modernity and of the creation of the modern world.

Chronology

13th century	Records of unnamed English interpreter in Mongol armies
1583	Seaman John Newbury carries a letter to Chinese emperor from Elizabeth I, but it does not reach its destination
1600	Founding of East India Company (EIC)
1613–23	English factory in Hirado, Japan, under Richard Cocks, which does limited business with China. Dissolved 1623
1636–37	John Weddell's visit to China
1642–44	Defeat of Ming dynasty and replacement with Qing
1658	Tea imported from China to Britain first advertised in *The Gazette* in London
1687	Shen Fuzong becomes first recorded person from China to visit Britain
1699–1700	Allen Catchpole becomes first British consul to the Chinese empire, representing East India Company interests, after attempts to set up an initial trade base there
1715	EIC opens first factory in Canton

1720	John Bell from Scotland becomes first recorded British person to meet a Chinese emperor, Kangxi
1741–43	Commodore George Anson takes first British ship of war to China
1757	Establishment of Canton system, under which the Qing Chinese authorities in Beijing only allowed foreigners to trade in the southern city and obliged them to stop all their business elsewhere. The members of business guilds (called *cohongs*), established slightly before this date, became the only Chinese who were able to engage in this trade – a situation that continued until the First Anglo-Chinese War
1774	First visit by a British person, George Bogle, to Tibet
1787	First attempt at a formal embassy to China, by Charles Allan Cathcart. He dies en route and the mission is aborted
1792–94	Lord George Macartney leads first successful formal mission from Britain that arrives in China and meets the Qianlong emperor. Despite this, the delegation fails to get improved market access and trading terms
1816	Lord William Pitt Amherst leads second formal embassy to reach China. Fails to meet the Jiaqing emperor and returns to Britain
1833–34	British government ends EIC monopoly, allowing private merchants to do trade in China. William Napier sent as first official superintendent of trade to China
1839–42	First Anglo-Chinese War, ending with the Treaty of Nanjing and the ceding of Hong Kong Island in perpetuity to the British, with Henry Pottinger as first governor
1850	Huang Kuan enrols at Edinburgh University, the first Chinese student at a UK university

1854	Establishment of Imperial Customs Shanghai, during the Taiping Rebellion, 1850–64
1856–60	Second Anglo-Chinese War. Sacking of Summer Palace in 1860, and Convention of Beijing opening more treaty ports for British and other foreigners
1864	Hong Kong and Shanghai Banking Corporation (HSBC) founded
1866	First Chinese embassy to London led by Pin Chun, who meets Queen Victoria
1875	Margary Affair in which a British consul is murdered in southwestern China, causing a diplomatic clash with China
1895	Japan's defeat of China in war results in ceding of Korea and Taiwan to Japan and marks rise of Japanese influence in the country
1898	Ninety-nine-year lease of New Territories to the British in Hong Kong
1900	Boxer uprising
1904	Invasion by Francis Younghusband of Tibet
1905	Japanese–Russian war
1906	Ban on opium in China
1911–12	Xinhai Revolution ends the 267-year Qing dynasty, replacing it with a republic
1914	Republic of China recognised by Britain
1917	China enters First World War on the side of Britain and its allies
1919	Versailles Peace Conference, transferring German colonial territory to Japan, causes May Fourth protest movement in China
1931	Japan's annexation of Manchuria marks start of over a decade of hostility between it and China
1941	Fall of Hong Kong to the Japanese. The British take back control in 1945 when the war ends

1946–49	Chinese Civil War between nationalists and communists
1949	Establishment of the People's Republic of China under communists. Britain recognises the new regime on 6 January 1950
1950–53	Korean War; Britain enforces sanctions on China
1957	Last full active British manufacturing organisation in China closes down, although HSBC and Standard Chartered continue their business in the country
1967	Sacking of British legation in Beijing by Red Guards
1972	Formal ambassadorial-level diplomatic relations established with sending of first ambassador, John Addis
1974	Edward Heath, leader of the British opposition, visits China and meets Mao Zedong
1976	Death of Mao Zedong. Within three years, China starts the reform and opening up process, allowing far greater engagement with the outside world
1979	Hong Kong Governor Murray MacLehose visits Beijing to discuss the future of the city with new paramount leader, Deng Xiaoping
1979	Chairman Hua Guofeng becomes highest-level visitor from China to Britain
1982	First ever visit to China by a serving British prime minister, Margaret Thatcher
1984	Sino-British agreement on Hong Kong after 1997 signed
1986	Visit by Queen Elizabeth II, first ever British monarch to go to China
1989	Tiananmen Square uprising
1990	Basic Law for Hong Kong serving as city's post-1997 de facto constitution agreed by Chinese parliament, the National People's Congress

1997	Retrocession of Hong Kong from British to Chinese rule
1999	Jiang Zemin becomes first ever Chinese president to visit Britain
2005	President and Communist Party leader Hu Jintao visits Britain
2009	Change in Tibet policy by British government from suzerainty to sovereignty
2015	Visit of President Xi Jinping to Britain
2023	British government labels China a 'threat' and over 180,000 people from Hong Kong move to the UK as a result of a 'pathway to citizenship' offered to them

Notes

Introduction: The Great Reversal: Britain's China Story

1. The National People's Congress of the People's Republic of China, 'Constitution of the People's Republic of China', revised 2004, www.npc.gov.cn/zgrdw/englishnpc/Constitution/2007-11/15/content_1372962.htm
2. See British Cabinet Office, 'The Integrated Review', 16 March 2021.
3. See Loren Brandt, Debin Ma and Thomas G. Rawski, 'From divergence to convergence: Reevaluating the history behind China's economic boom', *Journal of Economic Literature*, 52:1 (2014), 45–123.
4. Smith, 1776, vol. 1, 173.
5. Smith, 1776, vol. 1, 63–64.

Chapter 1 Partners at the Edge, 1550–1720

1. Scott, 1606.
2. Farrington, 1991, vol. 1, 67.
3. Farrington, 1991, vol. 2, 23.
4. Farrington, 1991, vol. 2, xi.
5. Iwao, 1958, 28.
6. Iwao, 1958, 35.
7. Iwao, 1958, 45.
8. Morton, 2023.
9. Mandeville, 2012, 23.
10. Hakluyt, 1972, 39.
11. Hakluyt, 1972, 90.
12. Burton, 1927, 314.
13. Bourne, 1574, 68.
14. Bourne, 1574, 70.
15. Bourne, 1574, 71.
16. Bourne, 1574, 72.

17. Dimmock, 2019, 4–6.
18. Quoted Liu, 2023, 285.
19. Pritchard, 1929, 45.
20. Eames, 1909, 7.
21. Quoted Liu, 2023, 290.
22. Eames, 1909, 8.
23. Huang, 1981.
24. Fontana, 2011, 204.
25. James I was to subsequently send his own letter in 1612 to the Chinese emperor, via John Sarris, acting as the first manager in Hirado. That also failed to achieve a result; Eames, 1909, 11.
26. Markley, 2006, 150–151.
27. Puga, 2013, 31.
28. Jackson, 2022, 36–37.
29. Jackson, 2022, 48.
30. Puga, 2013, 38.
31. Jackson, 2022, 99.
32. Eames, 1909, 14.
33. Mundy, 1919, 191.
34. Mundy, 1919, 302.
35. Mundy, 1919, 305.
36. Mundy, 1919, 191.
37. Mundy, 1919, 207.
38. Mundy, 1919, 210.
39. Mundy, 1919, 213.
40. Morse, 1926–1929, vol. 1, 26.
41. Puga, 2013, 49.
42. Morse, 1926–1929, vol. 1, 33.
43. Morse, 1926–1929, vol. 1, 45–46.
44. Fu, 1966, 48–49.
45. Wills, 1984, 69.
46. Morse, 1926–1929, vol. 1, 57.
47. Morse, 1926–1929, vol. 1, 64.
48. Poole, 2019, 339.
49. Dimmock, 2019, 22.
50. In Act 2, Scene 3, lines 75–76. There has been controversy over whether the phrase Cataian is used here to allude to trickery and sneaky behaviour, or simply grand and imperious bearing. See https://shakespeare-navigators.ewu.edu/TN_Navigator/2_3_76.html
51. Jonson, 2002, 11.
52. Jonson, 2002, 8.
53. Settle, 1676, 2.
54. Settle, 1676, 9.
55. Settle, 1676, 62.
56. Markley, 2006, 70.
57. Purchas, 1614, vol. 4, 336.
58. Purchas, 1614, vol. 4, 376.
59. Purchas, 1614, vol. 4, 377.

60. Dimmock, 2019, 93.
61. Hsia, 1998, 52.
62. Poole, 2021, 14.
63. Lack of an accepted transliteration system up to the nineteenth century meant that different methods were used to render Chinese names and words into English.
64. Poole, 2021, 6.
65. Hsia, 1998, 89.
66. Webb, 1669, 17.
67. Webb, 1669, 21.
68. Webb, 1669, 44.
69. Webb, 1669, 87. This single term was to prove a loaded, contentious one in the argument among Jesuits about whether or not it served as the equivalent of the Christian notion of a single, all-powerful God.
70. Hooke, 1686, 63.
71. Morse, 1926–1929, vol. 1, 300.
72. Pritchard, 1929, 70; Beevers, 2008, 31.
73. www.pepysdiary.com/diary/1660/09/25/
74. Billie Cohen, 'The true story behind England's tea obsession', BBC, www.bbc.com/travel/article/20170823-the-true-story-behind-englands-tea-obsession
75. See Porter, 2010, 83–84 for an illustration of this.
76. *Measure for Measure*, Act 2, Scene 1, line 91.
77. Appleton, 1951, 91.
78. Dimmock, 2019, 134.
79. Ovington, 1699, 1.
80. Ovington, 1699, 10.
81. Ovington, 1699, 26.
82. Ovington, 1699, 14.
83. Defoe, 1719, 171.
84. Defoe, 1719, 172.
85. Defoe, 1840, 211.
86. Defoe, 1840, 243.
87. Defoe, 1840, 244.
88. Appleton, 1951, 59.
89. Temple, 1814, vol. 3, 326.
90. Temple, 1814, vol. 3, 334.
91. Temple, 1814, vol. 3, 342.
92. Temple, 1908, 54.
93. Temple, 1908, 54.
94. Hsia, 1998, 53.
95. Addison, 1890, Essay 415.

Chapter 2 Coming Within Sight, 1720–87

1. Settle, 1676, 19.
2. Apart from once, in the seventh century, it had always been a male.
3. Pines, 2012, 44.
4. Curzon, 1896, 270.
5. Curzon, 1896, 271–273.

6. Satow, 2006, vol. 1, 32.
7. Bell, 1763, vol. 1, 332.
8. Bell, 1763, vol. 1, 333.
9. Bell, 1763, vol. 2, 7.
10. Bell, 1763, vol. 2, 30.
11. Bell, 1763, vol. 2, 46.
12. Bell, 1763, vol. 2, 97.
13. Bell, 1763, vol. 2, 103–104.
14. Morse, 1926–1929, vol. 1, 154.
15. Morse, 1926–1929, vol. 1, 155.
16. Phipps, 1835, 99.
17. Pritchard, 1929, 122.
18. Harrison-Hall and Lovell, 2023, 222.
19. Morse, 1926–1929, vol. 1, 174–175.
20. Morse, 1926–1929, vol. 1, 135.
21. Eames, 1909, 71, states that the standard tax was 10 per cent on goods, first imposed in 1728.
22. Maeve Kennedy, 'Sailor's rape confession uncovered in 17th-century journal', *Guardian*, 18 September 2018, www.theguardian.com/artanddesign/2018/sep/18/secret-unearthed-sailor-17th-century-journal-edward-barlow-national-maritime-museum
23. Lubbock, 1934, 541.
24. Lubbock, 1934, 528.
25. Morse, 1926–1929, vol. 1, 285.
26. Anson, 1748, 463.
27. Anson, 1748, 464.
28. Anson, 1748, 474.
29. Anson, 1748, 477.
30. Anson, 1748, 479–480.
31. Morse, 1926–1929, vol. 1, 285.
32. Morse, 1926–1929, vol. 2, 67.
33. Fairbank, 1953, 13.
34. Morse, 1926–1929, vol. 1, 276.
35. Cranmer-Byng, 1967, 247.
36. Morse, 1926–1929, vol. 1, 303.
37. Fu, 1966, 216.
38. Fu, 1966, 221.
39. Eames, 1909, 86–87; Fu, 1966, 223.
40. Cranmer-Byng, 1967, 248.
41. Dalrymple, 1793, 302.
42. Pritchard, 1938, Part III, 497.
43. *Canton Register*, vol. 1, no. 11, 15 March 1828, 3.
44. King, 1988, vol. 1, 188.
45. Hickey, 1921, 196.
46. Hickey, 1921, 198.
47. Hickey, 1921, 201.
48. Hickey, 1921, 218.
49. Davis, 1846, vol. 2, 32.

50. Pritchard, 1929, 133.
51. Pritchard, 1929, 147.
52. Davis, 1846, vol. 2, 30.
53. Hickey, 1921, 203.
54. Hickey, 1921, 205.
55. Hickey, 1921, 218.
56. Hickey, 1921, 223–224.
57. Hickey, 1921, 229.
58. Peyrefitte, 1993, 15.
59. Markham, 1875, lvi.
60. Markham, 1875, 5.
61. Markham, 1875, 12.
62. Markham, 1875, 24–25.
63. Markham, 1875, 84.
64. Markham, 1875, 132.
65. Teltscher, 2006, 6.
66. Markham, 1875, 101.
67. Markham, 1875, 122–123.
68. Markham, 1875, 134.
69. Turner, 1800, 245.
70. Turner, 1800, 250.
71. Turner, 1800, 368–369.
72. Markham, 1875, 265.
73. Markham, 1875, 274.
74. Morse, 1926–1929, vol. 2, 22.
75. Morse, 1926–1929, vol. 2, 95.
76. Auber, 1834, 38.
77. Fu, 1966, 175.
78. Fu, 1966, 200.
79. Fu, 1966, 212.
80. Fairbank, 1953, 7, 25.
81. Morse, 1926–1929, vol. 2, 65.
82. Beevers, 2008, 55.
83. Beevers, 2008, 13. 'Chinoiserie' was first used in 1883.
84. Chambers, 1772, 12.
85. Chambers, 1772, 11.
86. Beevers, 2008, 18.
87. Beevers, 2008, 17.
88. Chase, 1943, 21.
89. Chase, 1943, 21.
90. Beevers, 2008, 19.
91. Fan, 1945, 9.
92. Fan, 1945, 10.
93. Fan, 1945, 14.
94. Yang, 2011, 148–149.
95. *The Chinese Traveller*, 1775, 69.
96. Benton and Gomez, 2008, 346.
97. Price, 2019, 14–15.

Chapter 3 A Time of Diplomats: Macartney and Amherst, 1787–1830

1. Cranmer-Byng, 1962, 314.
2. Alexander, 1793–1794.
3. Alexander, 1793–1794.
4. Alexander, 9 Nov. 1793.
5. Pritchard, 1929, 177.
6. Morse, 1926–1929, vol. 2, 159.
7. Pritchard, 1936, 244.
8. Morse, 1926–1929, vol. 2, 160.
9. Pritchard, 1936, 237.
10. Morse, 1926–1929, vol. 2, 164.
11. Morse, 1926–1929, vol. 2, 166.
12. Pritchard, 1936, 309.
13. Cranmer-Byng, 1962, 19.
14. Hevia, 1995, 26.
15. Peyrefitte, 1993, xvii.
16. The massive challenges that Li faced in this whole endeavour and its aftermath is well covered in Harrison, 2021.
17. Staunton, 1798, vol. 1, 366.
18. Pritchard, 1938, Part I, 213.
19. Pritchard, 1938, Part I, 221.
20. Morse, 1926–1929, vol. 2, 214.
21. Cranmer-Byng, 1962, 123–124.
22. Holmes, 1798, iv.
23. Holmes, 1798, 66.
24. Holmes, 1798, 95.
25. Holmes, 1798, 97.
26. Holmes, 1798, 252.
27. Staunton, 1798, vol. 2, 17.
28. Staunton, 1798, vol. 2, 112.
29. Staunton, 1798, vol. 2, 366.
30. Staunton, 1798, vol. 2, 309.
31. Anderson, 1795, 91.
32. Anderson, 1795, 110.
33. Anderson, 1795, 132.
34. Anderson, 1795, 152.
35. Barrow, 1806, 274.
36. Barrow, 1806, 512.
37. Barrow, 1806, 343.
38. Cranmer-Byng, 1962, 238.
39. Cranmer-Byng, 1962, 239.
40. Cranmer-Byng, 1962, 237.
41. Cranmer-Byng, 1962, 234.
42. Cranmer-Byng, 1962, 264.
43. Cranmer-Byng, 1962, 190.
44. Cranmer-Byng, 1962, 210.
45. Cranmer-Byng, 1962, 210–212.
46. Auber, 1834, 200.

47. Pindar, 1812, 133.
48. Staunton, 1798, vol. 2, 38.
49. Staunton, 1798, vol. 2, 215.
50. Barrow, 1806, 594.
51. Pritchard, 1929, 190.
52. Pritchard, 1936, 144.
53. Hsu, 2000, 149.
54. Auber, 1834, 218.
55. Mundy, 1919, 210.
56. Fu, 1966, 325. One of the pretexts of the Macartney mission had been to congratulate Qianlong on his eightieth birthday, though in the end they arrived two years too late for this.
57. Harrison, 2021, 213.
58. Tuck, 2000, 32.
59. Ellis, 1817, 179.
60. Ellis, 1817, 425.
61. Ellis, 1817, 410.
62. Rowe, 2009, 182–184.
63. Ellis, 1817, 428.
64. Ellis, 1817, 464.
65. Markham, 1875, cix.
66. *A Delicate Enquiry*, 1818, 4–5 and 14.
67. *Diary of a Journey Overland*, 1822, 5.
68. *Diary of a Journey Overland*, 14.
69. *Canton Register*, vol. 1, no. 3, 30 November 1827, 1.
70. There were hardly any Chinese visitors to Britain at this stage. The most striking anomaly was the case of John Anthony. A Cantonese who had arrived in Britain on an EIC ship in 1799 and set up a barracks for Asian seamen in London, he became the first Chinese to naturalise as a British subject, for which a special Act of Parliament was passed in 1805.
71. Kitson, 2013, 33. The novel was *Haoqiu Zhuan* in modern Mandarin. Wilkinson's translation was probably from a Chinese version, and Percy added annotations and notes, and translated the final portion, but from Portuguese.
72. Lovejoy, 1960, 135.
73. Chang, 2010, 36.
74. Kitson, 2013, 190.
75. Kitson, 2013, 161.
76. J.F. Blacker, quoted Chang, 2010, 88.
77. Kitson, 2013, 53–55.
78. Kitson, 2013, 60.
79. Morrison, 1839, vol. 1, 68.
80. Morrison, 1839, vol. 1, 158.
81. Gutzlaff, 1838, 139.
82. Morrison, 1839, vol. 1, 197.
83. Morrison, 1839, vol. 2, 255.
84. Morrison, 1839, vol. 1, 518.
85. Morrison, 1839, vol. 1, 430.
86. Liu, 2023, 95.

Chapter 4 The Era of Conflict: The First Anglo-Chinese War, 1830–43

1. Select Committee, 1830, 5.
2. Select Committee, 1830, 6.
3. Select Committee, 1830, 159, line 1358.
4. Select Committee, 1830, 30.
5. Select Committee, 1830, 205, line 1863.
6. Select Committee, 1830, 307, line 3040.
7. Select Committee, 1830, 426, lines 3501a and 3509.
8. Wright, 1950, 42.
9. Houses of Parliament, 1840, 4.
10. Houses of Parliament, 1840, 12.
11. Houses of Parliament, 1840, 14.
12. Wong, 1998, 22–23.
13. Houses of Parliament, 1840, 23.
14. Houses of Parliament, 1840, 43.
15. Houses of Parliament, 1840, 105.
16. Houses of Parliament, 1840, 121.
17. Houses of Parliament, 1840, 193.
18. Houses of Parliament, 1840, 258.
19. Houses of Parliament, 1840, 318.
20. Houses of Parliament, 1840, 194.
21. Blake, 1960, 18.
22. Murray, 1843, 208.
23. Mackenzie, 1842, 52.
24. Bullock, 1840, 105.
25. Hibbert, 1970, 83.
26. Thilly, 2022, 3.
27. Fairbank, 1953, 60.
28. Allen, 1853, 32.
29. *Chinese Repository*, vol. 9, September 1840, 289.
30. It was called 'Opium War' at the time, however, in English, with the first such use so far found dating from 1 January 1840, when the *London Standard* (quoting the *Morning Herald*) deployed the term; Chen, 2017, 133.
31. Fairbank, 1953, 74.
32. Melancon, 2003, 98.
33. Marjoribanks, 1833, 16.
34. Fairbank, 1953, 70.
35. Houses of Parliament, 1840, 168.
36. Polachek, 1992, 102.
37. Polachek, 1992, 179.
38. Hanser, 2019, 73.
39. Grace, 2014, 123.
40. Grace, 2014, 106.
41. Jardine Archives, JM/C5/1.
42. Jardine Archives, JM/C5/2.
43. Blake, 1999, 37.
44. Chen, 2017, 119.

45. Matheson, 1836, 1.
46. Matheson, 1836, 8.
47. Matheson, 1836, 29.
48. Chang, 1964, 135.
49. Jardine Archives, JM/5/4.
50. Houses of Parliament, 1840, 431.
51. Bingham, 1843, vol. 2, 366.
52. Jocelyn, 1841, 86.
53. China Records Miscellaneous, vol. 4, IOR/R/10/71, Dispatch no. 2, 17 July 1840.
54. Ouchterlony, 1844, 56.
55. Hall and Bernard, 1847, 2–3.
56. Hall and Bernard, 1847, iv.
57. Hall and Bernard, 1847, 68.
58. Ouchterlony, 1844, 125.
59. Hall and Bernard, 1847, 87.
60. McPherson, 1843, 73–74.
61. McPherson, 1843, 168–169.
62. Ouchterlony, 1844, 118.
63. Murray, 1843, 220.
64. Cunynghame, 1853, 153.
65. Cunynghame, 1853, 202.
66. Fortune, 1847, 6.
67. China Records Miscellaneous, vol. 4, IOR/R/10/71, Dispatch no. 4, 29 September 1840.
68. China Records Miscellaneous, vol. 4, IOR/R/10/71, Dispatch no. 7, 18 November 1840.
69. China Records Miscellaneous, vol. 4, IOR/R/10/71, Dispatch no. 3, 8 January 1841.
70. Hamilton Lindsay, 1840, 31, 36.
71. Hamilton Lindsay, 1840, 33.
72. Hansard HC Deb 7 April 1840, vol. 53 cc669–748669.
73. Hansard HC Deb 7 April 1840, vol. 53 cc669–748669.
74. *Chinese Repository*, vol. 9, September 1840, 415.
75. *Chinese Repository*, vol. 9, September 1840, 2.
76. Fairbank, 1953, 100.
77. Ouchterlony, 1844, 450–452.
78. Coates, 1966, 119.
79. Bingham, 1843, 220–224.
80. Fortune, 1847, 15–16.
81. Allen, 1853, 57.
82. Oliphant, 1860, 65.
83. Gutzlaff, 1838, 292.
84. Gutzlaff, 1838, 367.
85. Davis, 1846, vol. 2, 139.
86. Davis, 1846, vol. 1, 207.
87. Dunn, 1842.
88. Meadows, 1847, 38.
89. Meadows, 1847, 155.

90. Martin, 1847, 102.
91. Thoms, 1853, 3.
92. Thoms, 1853, 14.
93. Staunton, 1836, 35.
94. Chen, 2017, 87, 93, 97; see also Liu, 2004.
95. Dickens, 1848, 3.
96. Fortune, 1847, 7.

Chapter 5 A World to Build: The Era of the Second Anglo-Chinese War and Its Aftermath, 1843–64

1. Foreign Office, 1859 (1852), 243.
2. Foreign Office, 1859 (1852), 244.
3. Foreign Office, 1859 (1852), 248.
4. Foreign Office, 1859 (1852), 251.
5. Brown and Deng, 2022, 107.
6. Platt, 2012, 358.
7. Platt, 2012, xxv.
8. Gregory, 1969, 4.
9. Costin, 1937, 194.
10. Bowring, 1877, 4.
11. Bowring, 1877, 216.
12. Bowring, 1877, 219.
13. Wright, 1950, 73.
14. Wright, 1950, 114–115.
15. Van de Ven, 2014, 4.
16. Van de Ven, 2014, 11.
17. Ladds, 2013, 2–3.
18. Pratt, 1943, 81.
19. Lane-Poole, 1901, 146.
20. Lane-Poole, 1901, 272.
21. Kiernan, 1939, 121.
22. Hurd, 1967, 35.
23. Costin, 1937, 149.
24. Hurd, 1967, 47.
25. Gladstone, 1857, 30.
26. Hurd, 1967, 96.
27. Costin, 1937, 279.
28. Costin, 1937, 231.
29. Bickers and Howlett, 2017, 62.
30. Oliphant, 1860, 134–135.
31. Oliphant, 1860, 130.
32. Quoted Wong, 1998, 8.
33. Oliphant, 1860, 147.
34. Osborn, 1860, 50.
35. Wolseley, 1862, 207.
36. Wolseley, 1862, 227.
37. Wolseley, 1862, 279.

38. Price, 2019, 96.
39. Loch, 1900, 168.
40. Osborn, 1860, 74–75.
41. Beresford, 1899, 7.
42. Pelcovits, 1948, 124–125.
43. Pelcovits, 1948, vii.
44. Osterhammel, 1999, 148.
45. Osterhammel, 1999, 156.
46. Lay, 1864, 4.
47. Lay, 1864, 12.
48. Lay, 1864, 20.
49. Lay, 1864, 37.
50. Lay, 1864, 52.
51. Lay, 1864, 65.
52. Strachey, 1948, 230.
53. Boulger, 1896, 60.
54. Wilson, 1868, 126.
55. Boulger, 1896, 125.
56. Fortune, 1852, vi.
57. Winterbotham, 1795, 222.
58. Pratt, 1944, 28.
59. Fortune, 1847, 252–253.
60. Fortune, 1847, 258.
61. Hevia, 2003, 128.
62. Hevia, 2003, 130.
63. Matthewson, 2022, 86.
64. Hunt, 1840, 23.
65. Hunt, 1840, 23.
66. Matthewson, 2022, 100.
67. Matthewson, 2022, 97.
68. Matthewson, 2022, 101.

Chapter 6 Of Consuls, Customs and Commerce, 1864–1900

1. Quoted Hoare, 1999, 19.
2. Cranmer-Byng, 1963, 63.
3. Cranmer-Byng, 1963, 69.
4. Rennie, 1865, 133–134.
5. Rennie, 1865, 290.
6. Wilgus, 1987, 20.
7. Wilgus, 1987, 23.
8. Wilgus, 1987, 22–23; Shao, 1991, 3.
9. Van de Ven, 2014, 4.
10. Van de Ven, 2014, 87, 117.
11. Fairbank, Smith and Bruner, 1991, 179.
12. Van de Ven, 2014, 51.
13. Fairbank, Smith and Bruner, 1991, 299.
14. Fairbank, Smith and Bruner, 1991, 326.

15. Wilgus, 1987, 101.
16. Coates, 1988, 13.
17. Coates, 1988, 75.
18. Coates, 1988, 338.
19. Kiernan, 1939, 19.
20. Alcock, 1855, 225.
21. Coates, 1988, 438.
22. Coates, 1988, 282.
23. Hewlett, 1944, 50.
24. Pelcovits, 1948, 1.
25. Pelcovits, 1948, 14.
26. Pelcovits, 1948, 18.
27. Michie, 1900, vol. 1, vi.
28. Michie, 1900, vol. 2, 221–222.
29. Michie, 1900, vol. 1, 411.
30. Sargent, 1907, 103.
31. Alcock, 1855, 250.
32. Alcock, 1855, 250.
33. Michie, 1900, vol. 2, 132–133.
34. King, 1988, vol. 2, 4.
35. King, 1988, vol. 1, 91.
36. King, 1988, vol. 1, 153.
37. King, 1988, vol. 1, 177.
38. Bickers, 2020, 99.
39. Bickers, 2020, 108.
40. Wood, 1998, 6.
41. Fortune, 1847, 123.
42. Freeman-Mitford, 1900, 47.
43. Hibbard, 2007, 37.
44. Tyler, 1929, 131.
45. King, 1988, vol. 1, 291–292.
46. Edwards, 1987, 32.
47. Edwards, 1987, 33–34.
48. Curzon, 1896, 314.
49. Wehrle, 1966, 12.
50. Michie, 1900, vol. 2, 237.
51. Wehrle, 1966, 13.
52. Lay, 1841, 94.
53. Murray, 1843, 219.
54. Osborn, 1860, 126.
55. Cuba Commission, 1876, 1.
56. Girardot, 2002, 60.
57. Girardot, 2002, 47.
58. Girardot, 2002, 199.
59. Biggerstaff, 1937, 313.
60. Frodsham, 1974, xlviii.
61. Frodsham, 1974, 119–120.
62. Parker, 1891, Part 1, 298.

63. Parker, 1891, Part 1, 300.
64. Parker, 1891, Part 2, 351.
65. Price, 2019, 104.
66. Benton and Gomez, 2008, 110.
67. Anderson, 1795, 63.
68. Holmes, 1798, 136.
69. McPherson, 1843, 248.
70. Parkinson, 1866, 421.
71. Bird, 1899, 213.
72. Pratt, 1944, 30.
73. Bird, 1899, 514.
74. Bird, 1899, 527.

Chapter 7 The Start of British Retreat, 1900–25

1. Bland, 1909, 49.
2. Purcell, 1963, 160.
3. Beresford, 1899, 2.
4. Beresford, 1899, 1.
5. Diplomaticus, 1900, 329.
6. Diplomaticus, 1900, 336.
7. Colquhoun, 1898, 423.
8. Atwell, 1985, 23.
9. Atwell, 1985, 39.
10. Young, 1970, 72.
11. Atwell, 1985, 106.
12. Colquhoun, 1898, 411.
13. Colquhoun, 1898, 416.
14. Beresford, 1899, 196–197.
15. Wilgus, 1987, 80.
16. Stationery Office, 2000, 158–159.
17. Stationery Office, 2000, 179–180.
18. Young, 1970, 143.
19. Putnam Weale, 1921, 18.
20. Putnam Weale, 1921, 19.
21. Putnam Weale, 1921, 53.
22. Young, 1970, 214–215.
23. Hart, 1901, 49–50.
24. Dickinson, 1901, 15.
25. Chow, 2017, 73.
26. Curzon, 1896, 276.
27. Younghusband, 1999, 140.
28. Younghusband, 1999, 186.
29. Younghusband, 1999, 244.
30. Younghusband, 1910, 299.
31. Kit-chin, 1978, 30.
32. Kit-chin, 1978, 36.
33. King, 1988, vol. 2, 71.

34. Jordan, 1920, 953.
35. Jordan, 1920, 959.
36. Sun, 1897, 34–36.
37. Tyler, 1929, 225.
38. Louis, 1971, 112.
39. King, 1988, vol. 2, 517.
40. Chow, 2017, 96–97.
41. Klein, 1919.
42. Lo, 1976, vol. 2, 770.
43. Chow, 2017, 122.
44. China Association collection, SOAS, 1921/1922 report.
45. China Association collection, SOAS, 1915 report, 20.
46. Louis, 1971, 58.
47. China Association collection, SOAS, 1923/1924 report.
48. Russell, 1968, 128–129.
49. Russell, 2021, 36.
50. Russell, 2021, 2.
51. Maugham, 1967, 269.
52. Trevor-Roper, 1976, 340–341.
53. Price, 2019, 146.
54. May, 1978, 122.
55. May, 1978, 113.
56. Benton and Gomez, 2008, 92.
57. Price, 2019, 139.

Chapter 8 Chaos and War, 1925–49

1. Bridge, 2010, 78.
2. Bridge, 2010, 102.
3. Ransome, 1927, 29.
4. Ransome, 1927, 38.
5. Ransome, 1927, 63.
6. Bickers, 2003, 8.
7. Friedman, 1940, 6.
8. Fung, 1991, 40.
9. China Association collection, SOAS, 1924/1925 report.
10. Fung, 1991, 60–62.
11. *Documents on British Foreign Policy 1919–1939*, second series, vol. viii, 1960, 1.
12. China Association collection, SOAS, 1925/1926 report.
13. Fung, 1991, 101.
14. Fung, 1991, 117.
15. Louis, 1971, 156.
16. Fung, 1991, 124.
17. Fung, 1991, 149.
18. *Documents on British Foreign Policy 1919–1939*, second series, vol. viii, 373.
19. Pratt, 1943, 231.
20. Clifford, 1967, viii.
21. Clifford, 1967, 16.

22. Clifford, 1967, 31.
23. Friedman, 1940, 201.
24. Fleming, 1934, 82–83.
25. Auden and Isherwood, 1939, 91.
26. Buchanan, 2012, 84.
27. Brookes, 2022, 106.
28. Kit-chin, 1990, 8.
29. Kit-chin, 1990, 103.
30. Snow, 2003, 40.
31. Snow, 2003, 53.
32. Welsh, 1997, 417.
33. Welsh, 1997, 417.
34. Snow, 2003, 192.
35. Shai, 1984, 109.
36. Shai, 1984, 121.
37. Shai, 1984, 132.
38. China Association collection, SOAS, 1922–1923 report.
39. Lyons, 2021.
40. Lao She, 2013, 49.
41. Lao She, 2013, 176.
42. Chiang, 1937, Preface.
43. Benton and Gomez, 2008, 26–27.

Chapter 9 The Cold War Era: Britain Making Friends with the Communists, 1949–71

1. Murfett, 1991, 145.
2. Lindsay, 1955, 170.
3. Porter, 1967, 5.
4. Tang, 1992, 33.
5. Watson, 1996, 23.
6. Shai, 1984, 132.
7. Tang, 1992, 45.
8. Watson, 1996, 23.
9. Trevelyan, 1971, 16.
10. Porter, 1967, 26.
11. Trevelyan, 1971, 22.
12. Kandiah, 2012, 20.
13. Porter, 1967, 29.
14. Broadman, 1976, 82.
15. Tang, 1992, 118.
16. Porter, 1967, 112–121.
17. Trevelyan, 1971, 54.
18. Jardine Archives, JM/J12/2/2.
19. Jardine Archives, JM/J12/2/2.
20. Broadman, 1976, 83, 86.
21. Tang, 1992, 160.
22. Luard, 1962, 145.

23. Trevor-Roper, 2020, 26.
24. Luard, 1962, 151.
25. Croft, 1958, 201.
26. Croft, 1958, 72–73.
27. Croft, 1958, 198.
28. Winnington, 1986, 207.
29. Lindsay, 1955, 13.
30. Luard, 1962, 173.
31. Lindsay, 1955, 20.
32. Cameron, 1955, 58.
33. Attlee, *New York Times* article, 8 September 1954.
34. Trevelyan, 1971, 119.
35. Wright, 2010.
36. 'Red China: In the jungle with Monty & Mao', *Time* Magazine, 27 October 1961.
37. Wright, 2010, 454, 274.
38. Trevelyan, 1971, 120.
39. Needham, 1979, 83.
40. Needham, 1979, 11.
41. Needham, 1979, 13.
42. Kandiah, 2012, 22.
43. Foreign Office Archives, FCO 21/427, 1 January 1969.
44. Robinson, 1969.
45. Foreign Office Archives, FCO 21/34/292, 24 August 1967.
46. Foreign Office Archives, FCO 21/34/248, 31 August 1967.
47. Grey, 2009, 24.
48. Cradock, 1994, 84.
49. Broadman, 1976, 142.
50. Broadman, 1976, 147.
51. Hansard HC Deb 13 March 1972, vol. 833, cc31–35, https://hansard.millbank-systems.com/commons/1972/mar/13/china-exchange-of-ambassadors

Chapter 10 Getting Closer: Resolution of the Hong Kong Issue, 1972–97

1. FCO 21/1239 1974.
2. FCO archives.
3. Cottrell, 1993, 117.
4. Cottrell, 4.
5. Cradock, 1994, 162.
6. Welsh, 1997, 75.
7. Foreign Office Archives, FCO 21/1505, 8 May 1976.
8. Foreign Office Archives, FCO 21/1505, 19 May 1976.
9. Foreign Office Archives, FCO 21/1735/137, 14 March 1979.
10. Foreign Office Archives, FCO 21/1735/123, 30 March 1979.
11. Foreign Office Archives, FCO 21/1712, 4 November 1979.
12. Morris, 1988.
13. Hung, 2022, 15, 198.
14. Cradock, 1994, 118.
15. Cottrell, 1993, 83.

16. Record of meeting 10 Downing Street, 24 September 1982. Available at www.margaretthatcher.org/document/138470

17. Cradock, 1994, 179.

18. Hung, 2022, 123.

19. Welsh, 1997, 434.

20. Hung, 2022, 120.

21. Cottrell, 1993, 177.

22. Cottrell, 1993, 177.

23. Robert McFadden, 'The west condemns the crackdown', *New York Times*, 5 June 1989, www.nytimes.com/1989/06/05/world/the-west-condemns-the-crackdown.html

24. Kandiah, 2012, 33.

25. Cradock, 1994, 243–244.

26. Patten, 2022, 16.

27. Patten, 2022, 173.

28. Patten, 2022, 39.

29. Chris Yeung, 'Tung and his team sworn in as Patten bids tearful farewell', *South China Morning Post*, 1 July 1997.

Chapter 11 The Great Shift: Britain in the Era of Chinese Dominance, 1997–2023

1. Audrey Gillan, 'Pomp and protests mark Jiang visit', *Guardian*, 20 October 1999, www.theguardian.com/uk/1999/oct/20/audreygillan

2. https://edm.parliament.uk/early-day-motion/16806/visit-to-the-uk-by-the-president-of-china

3. GLA Economics, 'Enter the dragon', 2004, www.london.gov.uk/sites/default/files/enter_the_dragon.pdf, 4.

4. The work of Yasheng Huang, in particular *Selling China* (Cambridge University Press, 2004) and *Capitalism with Chinese Characteristics* (Cambridge University Press, 2008) cover these general challenges well.

5. Kandiah, 2012, 47.

6. Foreign and Commonwealth Office, 'The UK and China: A framework for engagement', 2009, available at www.lancaster.ac.uk/fass/projects/ndcc/download/uk-and-china.pdf

7. Hansard, 29 October 2008, https://hansard.parliament.uk/lords/2008-10-29/debates/08102936000006/Tibet

8. China File, 'Document No 9', www.chinafile.com/document-9-chinafile-translation

9. Kandiah, 2012, 42.

10. YouGov, 'How Britain sees China', 29 November 2013, https://yougov.co.uk/topics/politics/articles-reports/2013/11/29/How-Britain-sees-China

11. YouGov, 'British public bullish on Chinese prospects, keen on closer partnership', 19 October 2015, https://yougov.co.uk/topics/politics/articles-reports/2015/10/19/british-public-bullish-chinese-trade

12. George Osborne, 'Chancellor's speech to the first UK-China Bilateral Investment Conference', 12 September 2014, www.gov.uk/government/speeches/chancellors-speech-to-the-first-uk-china-bilateral-investment-conference

13. Gov.uk, 'UK-China Joint Statement', 22 October 2015, www.gov.uk/government/news/uk-china-joint-statement-2015

14. Gov.uk, press release, 1 March 2023, www.gov.uk/government/news/government-announces-a-third-year-of-support-to-help-hong-kongers-settle-into-life-in-the-uk#:~:text=Since%20its%20launch%20at%20the,on%20a%20pathway%20to%20citizenship

15. https://yougov.co.uk/topics/travel/explore/country/China

Bibliography

Online and physical archival material consulted

Alexander, William. *Journal of the Lord Macartney's Embassy to China 1792–1794*, British Library Additional MS 35174.

Canton Register. 1827–1843, online archive of complete series, Heidelberg University, available at https://ecpo.cats.uni-heidelberg.de/ecpo/publications. php?magid=247

China Records Miscellaneous. *Letter book of Capt. Charles Elliot and other British Plenipotentiaries at Canton*, British Library, vols 4 and 5, IOR/R/10/71 and IOR/R/10/72.

Chinese Repository. Volumes 1–20, 1832–1850, available at https://guides.library. yale.edu/c.php?g=296315&p=1976866

Foreign Office Archives (using reference number and year), kept at the National Archives.

Hansard. China (Treaty Of Tien-Tsin), Volume 197: debated on Tuesday 13 July 1869, available at https://hansard.parliament.uk/Commons/1869-07-13/debates/ eaef49f9-45fc-4996-a33b-1faa8f978445/China(TreatyOfTien-Tsin)

Jardine Archives, held at Cambridge University Library.

Select Committee. *Report from the Select Committee of the House of Commons Appointed to Enquire into the Present State of the Affairs of the East India Company – China Trade*, London, 1830.

Anonymous authored material

'A Chinaman in London', *Blackwood's Magazine*, 170:1032 (1901), 492–498.

A Chinese Tale: Written originally by that prior of China the facetious Sou Ma Quang, London, 1740.

The Chinese Traveller, Containing a Geographical, Commercial and Political History of China, London, 1775.

A Delicate Inquiry into the Embassies to China and a Legitimate Conclusion, London, 1818.

Diary of a Journey Overland through the Maritime Provinces of China from Manchou on the South Coast of Hainan to Canton in the Years 1819 and 1820, London, 1822.

A Digest of the Despatches on China with a Connecting Narrative and Comments, James Ridgeway, London, 1840.

'Red China: In the jungle with Monty & Mao', *Time* magazine, 27 October 1961, https://content.time.com/time/subscriber/article/0,33009,873470,00.html

Remarks on Occurrences in China since the Opium Seizure in March 1839, to the Latest Date, by a Resident in China, London, 1840.

Documents on British foreign policy 1919–39

First Series, vol. VI, ed. E.L. Woodward and R. Butler, HMSO, London, 1956.

First Series, vol. XIV, ed. R. Butler, J.P.T. Burn and M.E. Lambert, HMSO, London, 1966.

Second Series, vol. VIII, ed. Rohan Butler, J.P.T Burn and M.E. Lambert, HMSO, London, 1960.

Books and articles consulted in writing this history

Abbott, Jacob. *China and the English; Or, On the Character and Manners of the Chinese*, New York, 1835.

Acton, Harold. *Peonies and Ponies*, Chatto and Windus, London, 1941 (reprinted Oxford University Press, Oxford and Hong Kong, 1983).

Addison, Joseph. Essay 414 from *The Spectator*, 25 June 1712, in Henry Morley, *The Spectator: A new edition*, vol. 2, George Routledge and Sons, London, 1890.

Akhtar, Ali Humayun. *1368: China and the making of the modern world*, Stanford University Press, Stanford, CA, 2022.

Alcock, Rutherford. 'The Chinese Empire and its Destinies', *The Bombay Quarterly Review*, 4 (October 1855), 219–250.

Alcock, Rutherford. 'Despatch from Sir Rutherford Alcock respecting a supplementary convention to the treaty of Tien-tsin signed by him on October 23, 1869', Houses of Parliament, London, 1870.

Allen, Nathan. *The Opium Trade Including a Sketch of its History, Effects, etc., as Carried on India and China* (2nd edn), Lowell, London, 1853.

Anderson, Aeneas. *A Narrative of the British Embassy to China in the Years 1792, 1793 and 1794*, Dublin, 1795.

Andrade, Tonio. *The Last Embassy: The Dutch mission of 1795 and the forgotten history of Western encounters with China*, Princeton University Press, Princeton, NJ and Oxford, 2021.

Anson, George (retold to Richard Walter). *A Voyage Round the World in the Years MDCCXL, I, II, III, IV* (2nd edn), London, 1748.

Appleton, William. *A Cycle of Cathay: The Chinese vogue in England in the seventeenth and eighteenth centuries*, Columbia University Press, New York, 1951.

Ash, William. *Red Square: The autobiography of an unconventional revolutionary*, Howard Barker, London, 1978.

Astley, Thomas. *A New General Collection of Voyages and Travel*, vol. IV, London, 1747.

Attlee, Clement. *As It Happened*, William Heinemann, London, 1954.

Attlee, Clement. Four articles in the *New York Times* on his visit to China on 8, 9, 13 and 15 September 1954.

Atwell, Pamela. *British Mandarins and Chinese Reformers: The British administration of Weihaiwei (1898–1930) and the territory's return to Chinese rule*, Oxford University Press, Hong Kong, Oxford and New York, 1985.

Auber, Peter. *China: An outline of the government, laws and policy and of the British and foreign embassies to, and intercourse with, that empire*, London, 1834.

Auden, W.H. and Christopher Isherwood. *Journey to a War*, Faber and Faber, London, 1939 (reissued 1973).

Ayer, A.J. 'Impressions of communist China', *The Listener*, 2 December 1954, 941–944.

Baker, Wyndham. 'An artillery officer in China 1840–1842', *Blackwood's Magazine*, 296 (1964), 73–86, 150–167.

Barker, Russell and George Fisher. 'Henry Dundas, first Viscount Melville', in *Dictionary of National Biography 1885–1900*, vol. 15, Smither, Elder and Co., London, 1900.

Barrow, John. *Travels in China*, Cadell and Davies, London, 1806.

Bassett, D.K. 'The trade of the English East India Company in the Far East', *Journal of the Royal Asiatic Society*, 92:1–2 (1960), 32–47.

Batchelor, Robert. 'A taste for the interstitial (間): Translating space from Beijing to London in the 1720s', in David Warren Sabean and Malina Stefanovska (eds), *Space and Self in Early Modern European Cultures*, University of Toronto Press, Toronto, 2013, 281–304.

Beevers, David. *Chinese Whispers: Chinoiserie in Britain 1650–1930*, Royal Pavilion and Museums Trust, Brighton, 2008.

Beevers, David. *The Royal Pavilion: The official guide to the palace of King George IV*, Royal Pavilion and Museums Trust, Brighton, 2020.

Belcher, Edward. *Narrative of a Voyage Round the World Performed by Her Majesty's Shio Sulphur*, London, 1843.

Bell, John. *Travels from Saint Petersburg in Russia to Diverse Parts of Asia in Two Volumes*, Glasgow, 1763.

Benton, Gregor and Edmund Terence Gomez. *The Chinese in Britain, 1800–Present: Economy, transnationalism, identity*, Palgrave Macmillan, Basingstoke, 2008.

Beresford, Charles. *The Breaking of China*, Harper and Brothers, London and New York, 1899.

Bickers, Robert (ed.). *Ritual and Diplomacy: The Macartney mission to China 1792–1794*, Wellsweep, London, 1993.

Bickers, Robert. *Empire Made Me: An Englishman adrift in Shanghai*, Allen Lane, London, 2003.

Bickers, Robert. *The Scramble for China: Foreign devils in the Qing empire, 1832–1914*, Allen Lane, London, 2011.

Bickers, Robert. *Out of China: How the Chinese ended the era of Western domination*, Allen Lane, London, 2017.

Bickers, Robert. *China Bound: John Swire and Sons and its world 1816–1980*, Bloomsbury, London, 2020.

Bickers, Robert and Jonathan J. Howlett (eds). *Britain and China 1840–1970: Empire, finance and war*, Routledge, London and New York, 2017.

Biggerstaff, Knight. 'The first China mission of investigation sent to Europe', *Pacific Historical Review*, 6:4 (1937), 307–320.

Bingham, J. Elliot. *Narrative of the Expedition to China from the Commencement of War to the Termination in 1842* (two volumes), London, 1843.

Bird, Isabella. *The Yangtze Valley and Beyond*, John Murray, London, 1899 (reprinted Virago, London, 1985).

Black, Jeremy. *George III: America's last king*, Yale University Press, New Haven, CT and London, 2006.

Blake, Clagette. *Charles Elliot RN 1801–1875: A servant of Britain overseas*, Cleaver-Hume Press, London, 1960.

Blake, Robert. *Jardine Matheson: Traders of the Far East*, Weidenfeld and Nicolson, London, 1999.

Bland, J.O.P. *Houseboat Days in China*, Edward Arnold, London, 1909 (reprinted Heinemann, 1919).

Bland, J.O.P. and Edmund Backhouse. *China Under the Empress Dowager*, 1910 (reprinted Earnshaw Books, Hong Kong, 2010).

Blue, Gregory. 'Opium for China: The British connection', in Timothy Brook and Bob Tadashi Wakabayashi (eds), *Opium Regimes: Britain and Japan 1839–1952*, University of California Press, Berkeley, CA, 2000, 31–54.

Boulger, Demetrius Charles. *Gordon: The career of Gordon of Khartoum* (originally in two volumes), T. Fisher Unwin, London, 1896 (reprinted Leonaur, London, 2009).

Bourne, William. *A Regiment for the Sea*, London, 1574 (reprinted 1620).

Bowring, John. *Autobiographical Recollection of Sir John Bowring*, Henry King and Son, London, 1877.

Braam, Andre Everard Van. *An Authentic Account of the Embassy of the Dutch East-India Company to the Court of the Emperor of China in the Years 1794 and 1795*, trans. M.L.E. Moreau de Saint-Mery, 1798.

Bridge, Ann. *Peking Picnic*, Capuchin Classics, London, 2010.

Broadman, Robert. *Britain and the People's Republic of China 1949–1974*, Macmillan, London, 1976.

Brook, Timothy, Jerome Bourgon and Gregory Blue. *Death by a Thousand Cuts*, Harvard University Press, Cambridge, MA, 2008.

Brookes, Adam. *Fragile Cargo: China's wartime race to save the treasures of the Forbidden City*, Chatto and Windus, London, 2022.

Brown, David. *Palmerston: A biography*, Yale University Press, New Haven, CT and London, 2010.

Brown, Kerry and Gemma Chenger Deng. *China Through European Eyes: 800 years of cultural and intellectual encounter*, World Scientific, Singapore, 2022.

Bruijn, Emile de. *Borrowed Landscapes: China and Japan in the historic houses of Britain and Ireland*, Philip Wilson Publishers, London, 2023.

Brunero, Donna. *Britain's Imperial Cornerstone in China: The Chinese Maritime Customs Service, 1854–1949*, Routledge, Abingdon, 2006.

Buchanan, Tom. *East Wind: China and the British left 1925–1976*, Oxford University Press, Oxford, 2012.

Bullock, T.H. *The Chinese Vindicated*, W.H. Allen, London, 1840.

BIBLIOGRAPHY

Burton, Robert. *The Anatomy of Melancholy*, Chatto and Windus, London, 1927.

Cameron, James. *Mandarin Red: What life looks like in communist China*, Michael Joseph, London, 1955.

Carrol, John. *A Concise History of Hong Kong*, Hong Kong University Press, Hong Kong, 2007.

Chambers, William. *A Dissertation on Oriental Gardening*, London, 1772.

Chang, Elizabeth Hope. *Britain's Chinese Eye: Literature, empire and aesthetics in nineteenth century Britain*, Stanford University Press, Stanford, CA, 2010.

Chang, Hsiao-pao. *Commissioner Lin and the Opium War*, Harvard University Press, Cambridge, MA, 1964.

Chang, I. Tung. 'The earliest contacts between China and England', *Chinese Studies in History and Philosophy*, 1:3 (1968), 53–88.

Chase, Isabel Wakelin Urban. *Horace Walpole: Gardenist; An edition of Walpole's The History of Modern Taste in Gardening*, Princeton University Press, Princeton, NJ, 1943.

Chen, Song-chuan. *Merchants of War and Peace: British knowledge of China in the making of the Opium War*, Hong Kong University Press, Hong Kong, 2017.

Chiang, Yee. *The Silent Traveller*, Henderson and Spalding, London, 1937.

Chow, Phoebe. *Britain's Imperial Retreat from China, 1900–1931*, Routledge, London and New York, 2017.

Clifford, Nicholas Rowland. *Retreat from China: British policy in the Far East 1937–1941*, University of Washington Press, Seattle, WA, 1967.

Coates, Austin. *Prelude to Hong Kong*, Routledge and Kegan Paul, London, 1966.

Coates, P.D. *The China Consuls: British consular officials 1843–1943*, Oxford University Press, Oxford, 1988.

Cocks, Richard. *The Diary of Richard Cocks 1615–1622*, ed. N. Murakami, Tokyo, 1899.

Collar, H.J. 'British commercial relations with China', *International Affairs*, 29:4 (1953), 418–428.

Colquhoun, Archibald. 'The China question: How it may affect our imperial interests', *Royal United Services Institution Journal*, 42:242 (1898), 406–437.

Costin, W.C. *Great Britain and China: 1833–1860*, Oxford University Press, Oxford, 1937.

Cottrell, Robert. *The End of Hong Kong: The secret diplomacy of imperial retreat*, John Murray, London, 1993.

Cradock, Percy. *Experiences of China*, John Murray, London, 1994.

Cranmer-Byng, J.L. *An Embassy to China: Being the journal kept by Lord Macartney during his embassy to the Emperor Ch'ien-lung, 1793–1794*, Longmans, London, 1962.

Cranmer-Byng, J.L. 'The old British legation at Peking: 1860–1959', *Journal of the Hong Kong Branch of the Royal Asiatic Society*, 3 (1963), 60–87.

Cranmer-Byng, J.L. 'The first English sinologists, Sir George Staunton and the Reverend Robert Morrison', in F.S. Drake (ed.), *Symposium on Historical, Archaeological and Linguistic Studies*, Hong Kong University Press, Hong Kong, 1967, 247–260.

Croft, Michael. *Red Carpet to China*, Longman, London and New York, 1958.

Crossman, R.H.H. 'A Chinese notebook', *Encounter*, 12:3 (1959), 11–22.

Cuba Commission. *A Report of the Commission Sent by China to Ascertain the Condition of Chinese Coolies in Cuba*. Chen Wen Publishing Company, Taiwan, 1970 (originally published by Imperial Maritime Customs Press, Shanghai, 1876).

Cunynghame, Arthur. *An Aide-de-Camp's Recollections of Service in China, a Residence in Hong Kong and Visits to Other Islands in the Chinese Seas*, London, 1853 (originally published in London, 1844 in two volumes).

Curzon, George N. *The Problems of the Far East*, Constable and Co., London, 1896.

Dalrymple, Alexander. *Oriental Repertory* (two volumes), London, 1793.

Dampier, William. *A New Voyage Around the World*, London, 1699.

Davis, John Francis. *The Chinese: A general description of the empire of China and its inhabitants* (two volumes), Harper and Brothers, New York, 1846.

Dawson, Raymond. *The Chinese Chameleon: An analysis of European conceptions of Chinese civilisation*, Oxford University Press, London, 1967.

Dean, Britten. *China and Great Britain: The diplomacy of commercial relations 1860–1864*, Harvard University Press and East Asia Research Centre, Harvard, Cambridge, MA, 1974.

Dean, Britten. 'British informal empire: The case of China', *Journal of Commonwealth and Comparative Politics*, 14:1 (1976), 64–81.

Defoe, Daniel. *The Consolidator*, London, 1705 (reprinted in *The Novels and Miscellaneous Works of Daniel Defoe*, vol. 9, London, 1840).

Defoe, Daniel. *The Farther Adventures of Robinson Crusoe*, London, 1719.

Deiwiks, Shu-jyuan, Bernhard Führer and Therese Guelen (eds). *Europe Meets China, China Meets Europe: The beginnings of European–Chinese scientific exchange in the 17th century*, Institut Monumenta Serica, Sankt Augustin, 2014.

Devine, Thomas Martin and Angela McCarthy (eds). *The Scottish Experience in Asia, c.1700 to the Present: Settlers and sojourners*, Palgrave Macmillan, London, 2017.

Dickens, Charles. 'The Chinese junk', *The Examiner*, 24 June 1848, 3.

Dickens, Charles. *The Mystery of Edwin Drood*, Collins, London and Glasgow, 1956.

Dickinson, G. Lowes. *Letters from John Chinaman*, R. Brimley Johnson, London, 1901.

Dimmock, Mathew. *Elizabethan Globalism: England, China and the Rainbow Portrait*, Paul Mellon Centre for Studies in British Art, Yale University Press, New Haven, CT and London, 2019.

Diplomaticus, 'Have we a policy in China?', *Fortnightly Review*, 68:404 (1900), 327–336.

Douglas, Robert. *Europe and the Far East 1506–1912* (revised and corrected by Joseph H. Longford), Cambridge University Press, Cambridge, 1913.

Dunn, Nathan (written by W.B. Langdon). *Ten Thousand Chinese Things: A descriptive catalogue*, London, 1842.

Eames, James Bromley. *The English in China*, Curzon Press, London, 1909 (reprinted 1974).

Eden, Anthony. *The Memoirs of Sir Anthony Eden: Full circle*, Cassell, London, 1960.

Eden, Anthony. *The Eden Memoirs: Facing the dictators*, Cassell, London, 1962.

Eden, Richard. *Of the North-East Frostie Seas and Kingdomes Lying That Way*, London, 1555 (reprinted in Sigmund von Herberstein, *Notes upon Russia*, Cambridge University Press, Cambridge, 2010, 175–256).

Edwards, E.W. *British Diplomacy and Finance in China, 1895–1914*, Clarendon Press, Oxford, 1987.

Ellis, Henry. *Journal of the Proceedings of the Late Embassy to China*, John Murray, London, 1817.

Esherick, Joseph W. *The Origins of the Boxer Rebellion*, University of California Press, Berkeley, CA, 1988.

Esherick, Joseph W. 'Cherishing sources from afar', *Modern China*, 24:2 (1998), Symposium: Theory and Practice in Modern Chinese History Research. Paradigmatic Issues in Chinese Studies, Part V, 135–161.

Fairbank, John K. *Trade and Diplomacy on the China Coast: The opening of the treaty ports 1842–1854*, Harvard University Press, Cambridge, MA, 1953.

Fairbank, John K., Richard J. Smith and Katherine Bruner. *Robert Hart and China's Early Modernization: His journals 1863–1866*, Harvard East Asian Monographs, Harvard University Press, Cambridge, MA, 1991.

Fan, Tsen-chung. 'Dr Johnson and Chinese culture', Lecture at the China Society, London, 1945.

Farrington, Anthony (ed.). *The English Factory in Japan 1613–1623* (two volumes), British Library, London, 1991.

Fay, Peter Ward. *The Opium War: 1840–1842* (revised edition), University of North Carolina Press, Chapel Hill, NC, 1997.

Feng, Zhong-ping. *The British Government's China Policy 1945–1950*, Ryburn Publishing, Keele, 1994.

Feuerwerker, Albert. 'The foreign presence in China', in John K. Fairbank (ed.), *The Cambridge History of China*, vol. 12: *Republican China 1912–1949, Part 1*, Cambridge University Press, Cambridge, 1983.

Fleming, Peter. *One's Company: A journey to China made by the author in 1933*, Cape, London, 1934 (reprinted Penguin Books, Harmondsworth, 1956).

Fontana, Michela. *Matteo Ricci: A Jesuit in the Ming court*, trans. Paul Metcalfe, Rowman & Littlefield, Lanham, MD, 2011.

Foreign Office. 'Copy of a report by Mr Mitchell on the state of trade in China', in *Correspondence Relative to the Earl of Elgin's Special Mission to China and Japan, 1857–1859*, London, 1859, 242–251.

Fortune, Robert. *Three Years' Wanderings in the Northern Provinces of China*, John Murray, London, 1847.

Fortune, Robert. *A Journey to the Tea Countries of China*, John Murray, London, 1852.

Fox, Grace. *British Admirals and Chinese Pirates 1832–1869*, Routledge, London, 1949.

Freeman-Mitford, A.B. *The Attaché at Peking*, Macmillan, London, 1900.

Friedman, I.S. *Britain's Relations with China: 1931–1939*, Institute of Pacific Relations, New York, 1940.

Frodsham, J.D. (trans. and ed.). *The First Chinese Embassy to the West: The journals of Kuo Sung-T'ao, Liu His-hung and Chang Te-yii*, Clarendon Press, Oxford, 1974.

Fu, Lo-shu. *A Documentary Chronicle of Sino-Western Relations (1644–1820)*, University of Arizona Press, Tucson, AZ, 1966.

Fung, Edmund S.K. *The Diplomacy of Imperial Retreat: Britain's South China policy 1924–1931*, Oxford University Press, Hong Kong and Oxford, 1991.

Gerson, Jack. *Horatio Nelson Lay and Sino-British Relations 1854–1864*, Harvard East Asian Monographs, Cambridge, MA, 1972.

Girardot, Norman J. *The Victorian Translation of China: James Legge's oriental pilgrimage*, University of California Press, Berkeley, CA, 2002.

Gladstone, William Ewart. *War in China: Speech of the Rt. Hon. W.E. Gladstone, MP, March 3rd 1857*, London, 1857.

Goldsmith, Oliver. *The Citizen of the World: Or, letters from a Chinese philosopher residing in London, to his friends in the East*, Allen Bell, London, 1837.

Grace, Richard J. *Opium and Empire: The lives and careers of William Jardine and James Matheson*, McGill-Queens University Press, Montreal and Kingston, 2014.

Gray, John Henry. *China: A history of the laws, manners and customs of the people* (two volumes), Macmillan, London, 1878.

Greenberg, Michael. *British Trade and the Opening of China 1800–1842*, Cambridge University Press, Cambridge, 1951.

Gregory, J.S. *Great Britain and the Taipings*, Routledge and Kegan Paul, London, 1969.

Grey, Anthony. *Hostage in Peking*, Michael Joseph, London, 1970.

Grey, Anthony. *The Hostage Handbook: The secret diary of a two year ordeal in China*, Tagman Press, Huntingdon, 2009.

Gutzlaff, Charles. *China Opened*, Smith, Elder and Co., London, 1838.

Hakluyt, Richard. *Voyages and Discoveries*, Penguin, Harmondsworth, 1972.

Halfpenny, William. *Rural Architecture in the Chinese Taste, Being Designs Entirely New*, London, 1750.

Hall, W.H. and W.D. Bernard. *The Nemesis in China* (3rd edn), 1847.

Hamilton Lindsay, H. *Letter to the Right Honourable Viscount Palmerston on British Relations with China*, London, 1836.

Hamilton Lindsay, H. *Is the War with China a Just One?*, London, 1840.

Hancock, Christopher D. 'Robert Morrison: Missionary mediator, surprising saint', in G. Wright Doyle (ed.), *Builders of the Chinese Church: Pioneer Protestant missionaries and Chinese church leaders*, Lutterworth Press, Cambridge, 2015, 30–48.

Hanser, Jessica. *Mr Smith Goes to China: Three Scots in the making of Britain's global empire*, Yale University Press, New Haven, CT and London, 2019.

Hargrave, Jennifer L. 'Marco Polo and the emergence of British Sinology', *Studies in English Literature*, 3 (2016), 515–537.

Harrison, Henrietta. *The Perils of Interpreting: The extraordinary lives of two translators between Qing China and the British empire*, Princeton University Press, Princeton, NJ, 2021.

Harrison-Hall, Jessica and Julia Lovell. *Creators of Modern China: 100 lives from empire to republic 1796–1912*, Thames and Hudson, London, 2023.

Hart, Robert. *'These from the land of Sinim': Essays on the Chinese question*, Chapman and Hall, London, 1901.

Hertslet, Godfrey. *Hertslet's China Treaties: Treaties &c. between Great Britain and China*, vol. 1, London, 1896.

Hevia, James L. *Cherishing Men from Afar: Qing guest ritual and the Macartney British embassy of 1793*, Duke University Press, Durham, NC and London, 1995.

Hevia, James L. *English Lessons: The pedagogy of imperialism in nineteenth-century China*, Duke University Press, Durham, NC and London, 2003.

BIBLIOGRAPHY

Hewlett, Meyrick. *Forty Years in China*, Macmillan, London, 1944.

Hibbard, Peter. *The Bund, Shanghai*, Odyssey Books, Hong Kong, 2007.

Hibbert, Christopher. *The Dragon Wakes: China and the West 1793–1911*, Longman, London, 1970.

Hickey, William. *Memoirs of William Hickey*, vol. 1: *1749–1775*, ed. Albert Spencer, Hurst and Blackett, London, 1921.

Hilleman, Ulrike. *Asian Empire and British Knowledge: China and the networks of British imperial expansion*, Palgrave Macmillan, Basingstoke, 2009.

Hoare, J.E. *Embassies in the East: The story of the British and their embassies in China, Japan and Korea from 1859 to the present*, Curzon Press, Richmond, 1999.

Holliday, John. *Mission to China: How an Englishman brought the West to the Orient*, Amberley Books, Stroud, 2016.

Holmes, Samuel. *Journal of Mr Samuel Holmes, Sergeant Major of the XIIth Light Brigade during his Attendance as one of the Guards on Lord Macartney's Embassy to China and Tartary 1792–3*, London, 1798.

Hooke, Robert. 'Some observations and conjectures concerning the Chinese characters', *Philosophical Transactions of the Royal Society*, 16:180 (1686), 64–81.

Houses of Parliament. *Correspondence Relating to China*, London, 1840.

Hsia, Adrian. *The Vision of China in the English Literature of the Seventeenth and Eighteenth Centuries*, Chinese University, Hong Kong, 1998.

Hsu, Immanuel C.Y. *The Rise of Modern China* (6th edn), Oxford University Press, Oxford, 2000.

Huang, Ray. *1587, A Year of No Significance: The Ming dynasty in decline*, Yale University Press, New Haven, CT and London, 1981.

Hugo, Victor. 'The sack of the Summer Palace', 1860, available at www.napoleon.org/en/history-of-the-two-empires/articles/the-chinese-expedition-victor-hugo-on-the-sack-of-the-summer-palace/.

Hung, Ho-fung. *City on the Edge: Hong Kong under Chinese rule*, Cambridge University Press, Cambridge, 2022.

Hunt, Leigh. 'Breakfast: Tea drinking', in Leigh Hunt, *The Seer: Or common-places refreshed*, part 1, Edward Moxon, London, 1840.

Hurd, Douglas. *The Arrow War: An Anglo-Chinese confusion 1856–1860*, Collins, London, 1967.

Hutcheon, Robert. *China-Yellow*, Chinese University Press, Hong Kong, 1996.

Iwao, Seiichi. 'Li Tan, chief of the Chinese residents at Hirado, Japan, in the last days of the Ming dynasty', *Memoirs of the Research Department of the Toyo Bunko* (The Oriental Library), 17, 1958, 27–83.

Jackson, Nicholas D. *The First British Trade Expedition to China: Captain Weddell and the Courteen Fleet in Asia and late Ming Canton*, Hong Kong University Press, Hong Kong, 2022.

Jocelyn, Robert. *Six Months with the Chinese Expedition*, John Murray, London, 1841.

Johnston, Reginald F. *Twilight in the Forbidden City*, Oxford University Press, Oxford, 1985.

Jonson, Ben. *The Key Keeper: A masque*, Foundling Press, London, 2002.

Jordan, J.N. 'Some Chinese I have known', *The Nineteenth Century and After*, 88: XIX–XX (1920), 942–960.

Kandiah, M.D. (ed). *The Role and Function of the British Embassy in Beijing*, Foreign and Commonwealth Office, London, 2012.

Kang, David C. *East Asia Before the West: Five centuries of trade and tribute*, Columbia University Press, New York, 2010.

Kidd, Samuel. *China*, London, 1841.

Kiernan, E.V.G. *Britain's Diplomacy in China: 1880–1885*, Cambridge University Press, Cambridge, 1939 (reprinted Octagon Books, New York, 1970).

King, Frank H.H. *The Hongkong Bank in the Period of Imperialism and War, 1895–1918*, Cambridge University Press, Cambridge, 1988.

Kit-chin, Chan Lau. *Anglo-Chinese Diplomacy in the Careers of Sir John Jordan and Yuan Shih-k'ai*, Hong Kong University Press, Hong Kong, 1978.

Kit-chin, Chan Lau. *China, Britain and Hong Kong: 1895–1945*, Chinese University Press, Hong Kong, 1990.

Kitson, Peter J. *Forging Romantic China: Sino-British cultural exchange 1760–1840*, Cambridge University Press, Cambridge, 2013.

Klein, Daryl. *With the Chinks*, John Lane – the Bodley Head, New York, 1919.

Ladds, Catherine. *Empire Careers: Working for the Chinese Customs Service, 1854–1949*, Manchester University Press, Manchester, 2013.

Lamb, Alastair. *Britain and Chinese Central Asia: The road to Lhasa*, Routledge and Kegan Paul, London. 1960.

Lamb, Charles. *The Letters of Charles Lamb* (two volumes), ed. W. MacDonald, J.P. Dent and Sons, London, 1909.

Lamb, Charles. *Selected Prose*, Penguin Books, London, 2013.

Lane-Poole, Stanley. *Sir Harry Parkes in China*, Methuen and Co., London, 1901.

Lao She. *Mr Ma and Son*, trans. William Dolby, Penguin Classics, London, 2013.

Lawson, Philip. *The East India Company: A history*, Longman, London and New York, 1993.

Lay, George Tradescant. *The Chinese as They Are*, London, 1841.

Lay, Horatio N. *Our Interests in China: A letter to Earl Russell*, Robert Hardwicke, London, 1864.

Lee, Adele. *The English Renaissance and the Far East: Cross-cultural encounters*, Fairleigh Dickinson University Press, Vancouver, 2018.

Lindsay, Michael. *China and the Cold War: A study in international relations*, Melbourne University Press, Melbourne, 1955.

Liu, Lydia H. *The Clash of Empires: The invention of China in modern world making*, Harvard University Press, Cambridge, MA, 2004.

Liu, Xin. *Anglo-Chinese Encounters Before the Opium War: A tale of two empires over two centuries*, Routledge, New York and London, 2023.

Lo, Hui-min. *The Correspondence of G.E. Morrison*, vol. 1: *1895–1912*; vol. 2: *1912–1920*, Cambridge University Press, Cambridge, 1976.

Loch, Henry. *Personal Narrative of Occurrences During Lord Elgin's Second Embassy to China in 1860* (3rd edn), John Murray, London, 1900.

Louis, William Roger. *British Strategy in the Far East: 1919–1939*, Clarendon Press, Oxford, 1971.

Lovejoy, Arthur O. *Essays in the History of Ideas*, Johns Hopkins University Press, Baltimore, MD, 1948 (reprinted Capricorn Press, New York, 1960).

Lovell, Julia. *The Great Wall: China against the World 1000 BC–2000 AD*, Grove Press, London, 2006.

Lovell, Julia. *The Opium War: Drugs, dreams and the making of China*, Picador, London, 2011.

Lovell, Julia. *Maoism: A global history*, Bodley Head, London, 2019.

Lowe, Peter. *Britain in the Far East: A survey from 1819 to the present*, Longman, Harlow, 1981.

Luard, Evan. *Britain and China*, Chatto and Windus, London, 1962.

Lubbock, Basil (ed.). *Barlow's Journal of His Life at Sea in King's Ships, East and West Indiamen and Other Merchantmen from 1659 to 1703*, Hurst and Blackett, London, 1934.

Lyons, Stuart. *Xu Zhimo in Cambridge*, King's College, Cambridge, 2021.

Mackenzie, Keith Stewart. *Narrative of the Second Campaign in China*, London, 1842.

Mandeville, John. *The Book of Marvels and Travels*, trans. Anthony Bale, Oxford University Press, Oxford, 2012.

Mao, Haijian. *The Qing Empire and the Opium War: The collapse of the Heavenly Dynasty*, trans. Joseph Lawson, Craig Smith and Peter Lavelle, Cambridge University Press, Cambridge, 2016.

Marjoribanks, Charles. *Letter to the Right Hon. Charles Grant, President of the Board of Control, on the Present State of Intercourse with China*, Hatchards, London, 1833.

Markham, George (ed.). *Narrative of the Mission of George Bogle to Tibet and the Journey of Thomas Manning to Lhasa*, Trubner and Co., London, 1875.

Markley, Robert. *The Far East and the English Imagination, 1600–1730*, Cambridge University Press, Cambridge, 2006.

Martin, G. Currie. *China in English Literature*, East and West, London, 1916.

Martin, R. Montgomery. *China: Political, commercial and social, in an official report to Her Majesty's Government* (two volumes), London, 1847.

Matheson, James. *The Current Position and Prospect of the British Trade with China*, Smith, Elder and Co., London, 1836.

Matthewson, Amy. *Cartooning China: Punch, power and politics in the Victorian era*, Routledge, London and New York, 2022.

Maugham, W. Somerset. *Liza of Lambeth & On a Chinese Screen*, Heron Books, London, 1967.

Maverick, Lewis. *China: A model for Europe*, Paul Anderson Co., San Antonio, TX, 1943.

May, J.P. 'The Chinese in Britain: 1860–1914', in Colin Holmes (ed.), *Immigrants and Minorities in British Society*, Allen and Unwin, London, 1978.

McPherson, D. *The War in China: Narrative of the Chinese expedition*, London, 1843.

Meadows, Thomas Taylor. *Desultory Notes on the Government and People of China and on the Chinese Language*, W.H. Allen, London, 1847.

Medhurst, W.H. *China: Its state and prospects*, London, 1838.

Medhurst, W.H. *A Glance at the Interior of China*, J. Snow, London, 1850.

Melancon, Glenn. *Britain's China Policy and the Opium Crisis*, Ashgate, Aldershot, 2003.

Meredith, George. *The Egoist: A comedy in narrative*, Heron Books, London, 1969.

Michie, Alexander. *The Englishman in China During the Victorian Era* (two volumes), Blackwood, London, 1900.

Montagu, Horatio. *A Voice for China Which Must Be Heard*, London, 1840.

Moore, Charles. *Margaret Thatcher: The authorized biography*, vol. 2: *Everything She Wants*, Penguin, London, 2016.

Morris, James. *Farewell the Trumpets: An imperial retreat*, Faber and Faber, London, 1978.

Morris, Jan. *Heaven's Command: An imperial progress*, Faber and Faber, London, 1973 (reissued 2012).

Morris, Jan. *Hong Kong*, Knopf, London and New York, 1988.

Morrison, Eliza. *Memoirs of the Life and Labours of Robert Morrison DD Compiled by His Widow* (two volumes), London, 1839.

Morrison, Robert. *A Memoir of the Principal Occurrences During an Embassy from the British Government to the Court of China in the Year 1816*, London, 1819.

Morse, H.B. *The International Relations of the Chinese Empire* (three volumes), Longmans, Green and Company, London, 1911.

Morse, H.B. *Chronicles of the East India Company Trading to China 1635–1832* (five volumes), Clarendon Press, Oxford, 1926–29.

Morton, Nicholas. 'How an English exile ended up at the court of Genghis Khan's Grandson', *Smithsonian Magazine*, July 2023, www.smithsonianmag.com/history/how-an-english-exile-ended-up-at-the-court-of-genghis-khans-grandson-180982598/

Mosca, Matthew W. 'The Qing state and its awareness of Eurasian interconnections, 1789–1806', *Eighteenth-Century Studies*, 47:2 (2014), Special Issue, 103–116.

Mundy, Peter. *The Travels of Peter Mundy*, vol. 3, part 1: *Travels in England, Western India, Achin, Macao and the Canton River, 1634–1637*, second series, XLV, Hakluyt Society, London, 1919.

Murfett, Michael H. *Hostage on the Yangtze: Britain, China, and the Amethyst Crisis of 1949*, Naval Institute Press, Maryland, 1991.

Murphy, Arthur. *The Orphan of China*, London, 1797.

Murray, Alexander. *Doings in China*, London, 1843.

Needham, Joseph. *Science and Civilisation in China* (four volumes), Cambridge University Press, Cambridge, 1954–71.

Needham, Joseph. *Within the Four Seas: The dialogue of east and west* (2nd edn), Allen and Unwin, London, 1979.

Nieuhoff, John. *An Embassy from the East India Company of the United Provinces to the Grand Tartar Cham Emperor of China*, London, 1669.

Nutting, Anthony. *Gordon: Martyr and misfit*, Constable, London, 1967.

Oliphant, Laurence. *Narrative of the Earl of Elgin's Mission to China and Japan in the Years 1857, '58, '59* (two volumes), William Blackwood and Sons, Edinburgh and London, 1860.

Osborn, Sherard. *The Past and Future of British Relations in China*, London, 1860.

Osterhammel, Jurgen. 'Britain and China: 1842–1914', in A. Porter (ed.), *The Oxford History of the British Empire*, vol. 3, Oxford University Press, Oxford, 1999, 146–169.

Ouchterlony, John. *The Chinese War*, London, 1844.

Ovington, J. *An Essay upon the Nature and Qualities of Tea*, London, 1699.

Pan, Lynn. *The Encyclopaedia of the Chinese Overseas* (2nd edn), Editions Didier Millett, Singapore, 2006.

Parker, A.P. 'Diary of Marquis Tseng', *The China Recorder*, XXII:7 (July), 297–304, and XXII:8 (August) (1891), 345–353.

Parker, E.H. *Chinese Account of the Opium Wars*, Shanghai, Singapore and Hong Kong, 1888.

Parkinson, Joseph Charles. 'Lazarus: Lotus eating', *All the Year Round*, XV:368 (12 May 1866), 421–425.

Patten, Chris. *The Hong Kong Diaries*, Allen Lane, London, 2022.

Pelcovits, Nathan A. *Old China Hands and the Foreign Office*, King's Crown Press, New York, 1948.

Percy, Thomas. *Miscellaneous Pieces Relating to the Chinese* (two volumes), London, 1762.

Perdue, Peter. 'The First Opium War: The Anglo-Chinese War of 1839–1942', undated essay available at https://visualizingcultures.mit.edu/opium_wars_01/ow1_essay01.html.

Perkins, Franklin. *Leibniz and China: A commerce of light*, Cambridge University Press, Cambridge, 2004.

Peyrefitte, Alain. *The Collision of Two Civilisations: The British expedition to China in 1792–4*, trans. Jon Rothschild, Harvill, London, 1993.

Phipps, John. *A Practical Treatise on the Chinese and Eastern Trade*, Calcutta, 1835.

Pindar, Peter. *The Works of Peter Pindar*, vol. III, London, 1812.

Pines, Yuri. *The Everlasting Empire: The political culture of Ancient China and its imperial legacy*, Princeton University Press, Princeton, NJ, 2012.

Platt, Stephen. *Autumn in the Heavenly Kingdom: China, the west and the epic story of the Taiping civil war*, Atlantic Books, London, 2012.

Polachek, James A. *The Inner Opium War*, Council on East Asian Studies, Harvard University, Cambridge, MA, 1992.

Pomeranz, Kenneth. *The Great Divergence: China, Europe and the making of the modern world economy*, Princeton University Press, Princeton, NJ and London, 2000.

Poole, William. 'The Chinaman and the librarian: The meeting of Shen Fuzong and Thomas Hyde in 1687', Lecture for the Oxford Bibliographical Society, New College, Oxford, 2010.

Poole, William. 'Early English Sinology 1577–1688', in Elizabeth Sauer (ed.), *Emerging Nation: Early modern British literature in transition 1660–1714*, Cambridge University Press, Cambridge, 2019.

Poole, William. *Epistola de mensuris et ponderibus Serum seu Sinensium (Oxford, 1688) by Thomas Hyde: A forgotten chapter in the history of sinology*, Editions Rariores No. 1, Oxford, 2021.

Porter, Brian. *Britain and the Rise of Communist China: A study of British attitudes 1945–1954*, Oxford University Press, Oxford, 1967.

Porter, David. *The Chinese Taste in Eighteenth-Century England*, Cambridge University Press, Cambridge, 2010.

Pratt, John T. *War and Politics in China*, Jonathan Cape, London, 1943.

Pratt, John T. *China and Britain*, Collins, London, 1944.

Price, Barclay. *The Chinese in Britain: A history of visitors and settlers*, Amberley, Stroud, 2019.

Pritchard, Earl H. *Anglo-Chinese Relations During the Seventeenth and Eighteenth Centuries*, University of Illinois, IL, 1929 (reprinted Octagon Books, New York, 1970).

Pritchard, Earl H. *The Crucial Years of Anglo-Chinese Relations: 1750–1800*, University of Virginia, Charlottesville, VA, 1936 (reprinted Octagon Books, New York, 1970).

Pritchard, Earl H. 'The instructions of the East India Company to Lord Macartney on his embassy to China and his reports to the company 1792–1794', *Journal of the Royal Asiatic Society of Great Britain*, Part I, 70:2 (April 1938), 201–230; Part II, 70:3 (July 1938), 375–396; Part III, 70:4 (October 1938), 493–509.

Pritchard, Earl H. 'Private trade between England and China in the eighteenth century (1680–1833)', *Journal of the Economic and Social History of the Orient*, Part 1, 1:1 (1957), 108–137; Part 2, 1:2 (1957), 221–256.

Proudfoot, William Jardine. *Barrow's Travels in China: An investigation*, London, 1861.

Puga, Rogerio Miguel. *The British Presence in Macau 1635–1793*, Hong Kong University Press and Royal Asiatic Society, Hong Kong, 2013.

Purcell, Victor. *The Boxer Uprising: A background study*, Cambridge University Press, Cambridge, 1963.

Purchas, Samuel. *Purchas his pilgrimage. Or Relations of the World and the religions observed in all ages and places discovered, from the Creation unto this present. In foure partes*, London, 1614.

Putnam Weale, B.L. *Indiscreet Letters from Peking*, Kelly and Walsh, Shanghai, 1921.

Ransome, Arthur. *The Chinese Puzzle*, Allen and Unwin, London, 1927.

Redfern, Rebecca C. 'Going south of the river: A multidisciplinary analysis of ancestry, mobility and diet in a population from Roman Southwark, London', *Journal of Archaeological Science*, 74 (2006), 11–22.

Rennie, David Field. *Peking and the Pekingese During the First Year of the British Embassy in Peking*, John Murray, London, 1865.

Robinson, Joan, *The Cultural Revolution in China*, Pelican, Harmondsworth, 1969.

Rose, Sarah. *For All the Tea in China*, Hutchinson, London, 2009.

Rowe, William T. *China's Last Empire: The Great Qing*, Harvard University Press, Cambridge, MA, 2009.

Russell, Bertrand. *The Autobiography of Bertrand Russell, 1914–1944*, vol. 2, George Allen and Unwin, London, 1968.

Russell, Bertrand. *The Problem of China*, Routledge, New York, 2021 (new edition of George Allen and Sons, London, 1922).

Sargent, A.J. *Anglo-Chinese Commerce and Diplomacy (Mainly in the Nineteenth Century)*, Oxford University Press, Oxford, 1907.

Satow, Ernest. *The Diaries of Ernest Satow, British Envoy to Peking (1900–1906)* (two volumes), ed. Ian C. Ruxton, Lulu Press, Morrisville, NC, 2006.

Scott, Edward. *An Exact Discourse of the Subtilties, Fashions, Pollicies, Religion and Ceremonies of the East Indians, as well Chynese*, London, 1606.

Settle, Elkanah. *Conquest of China by the Tartars: A tragedy*, London, 1676.

Shai, Aron. *Britain and China: 1941–1947. Imperial Momentum*, Macmillan, London and Basingstoke, 1984.

Shao, Wenguang. *China, Britain and Businessmen: Political and commercial relations 1949–1957*, Macmillan, Basingstoke, 1991.

Skrine, C.P. and Pamela Nightingale. *Macartney at Kashgar: New light on British, Chinese and Russian activities in Sinkiang, 1890–1918*, Oxford University Press, Oxford, 1987.

Smith, Adam. *The Wealth of Nations*, London, 1776 (reprinted in two volumes, Everyman, London, 1920).

Snow, Philip. *The Fall of Hong Kong: Britain, China and the Japanese occupation*, Yale University Press, New Haven, CT and London, 2003.

Soothill, W.E. *China and England*, Oxford University Press, Oxford, 1928.

Spence, Jonathan D. *The Memory Palace of Matteo Ricci*, Faber and Faber, London, 1983.

Stationery Office. *The Siege of the Peking Embassy 1900*, The Stationery Office, London, 2000.

Staunton, George. *An Authentic Account of an Embassy from the King of Great Britain to the Emperor of China* (two volumes), Dublin, 1798.

Staunton, George Thomas. *Remarks on the British Relations with China and the Proposed Plan for Improving Them*, London, 1836.

Strachey, Lytton. *Eminent Victorians*, Penguin, Harmondsworth, 1948.

Sun Yat-sen. *Kidnapped in London*, Bristol and London, 1897.

Tang, James Tuck-hong. *Britain's Encounter with Revolutionary China: 1949–1954*, Macmillan, London, 1992.

Teltscher, Kate. *The High Road to China: George Bogle, the Panchen Lama, and the first British expedition to Tibet*, Farrar, Straus and Giroux, New York, 2006.

Temple, Sir William. 'Of heroic virtue', in *The Works of Sir William Temple*, vol. 3, Weybridge, 1814, 325–345.

Temple, Sir William. *Upon the Garden of Epicurus: With Other XVIIth century garden essays*, Chatto and Windus, London, 1908.

Thilly, Peter. *The Opium Business: A history of crime and capitalism in maritime China*, Stanford University Press, Stanford, CA, 2022.

Thoms, P.P. *The Emperor of China v. the Queen of England: A refutation of the arguments contained in the seven official documents transmitted by Her Majesty's Government at Hong Kong*, London, 1853.

Topolski, Felix. *Holy China*, Houghton Mifflin Company, Boston, MA, 1968.

Toynbee, Arnold. *A Journey to China or Things Which Are Seen*, London, 1931.

Trevelyan, Humphrey. *Worlds Apart: China 1953–5, Soviet Union 1962–5*, Macmillan, London, 1971.

Trevor-Roper, Hugh. *Hermit of Peking: The hidden life of Sir Edmund Backhouse*, Macmillan, London, 1976.

Trevor-Roper, Hugh. *The China Journals: Ideology and intrigue in the 1960s*, ed. Richard Davenport-Hines, Bloomsbury Academic, London, 2020.

Tsang, Steve. *The Cold War's Odd Couple: The unintended partnership between the Republic of China and the UK, 1950–1958*, I.B. Tauris, London and New York, 2006.

Tseng, Marquis. 'China: The sleep and the awakening', *Asiatic Quarterly Review*, 3 (January 1887), 1–11.

Tuck, Patrick (ed.). *Britain and China Trade 1635–1842*, vol. X: George Thomas Staunton, *Note of Proceedings and Occurrences, during the British Embassy to Pekin in 1816*, Routledge, London and New York, 2000.

Turner, Samuel. *An Account of the Embassy to the Court of the Teshoo Lama*, London, 1800.

Tyler, William Ferdinand. *Pulling Strings in China*, Constable, London, 1929.

Van de Ven, Hans. *Breaking with the Past: The Maritime Customs Service and the global origins of modernity in China*, Columbia University Press, New York, 2014.

Waley, Arthur D. *The Opium War Through Chinese Eyes*, George Allen and Unwin, London, 1958.

Wang, Gungwu. *Anglo-Chinese Encounters Since 1800*, Cambridge University Press, Cambridge, 2003.

Watson, E.H. *A Naturalist in Western China*, Methuen and Co., London, 1913 (reprinted Cadogan Books, London, 1986).

Watson, Robert Emerson. 'The Foreign Office and policy making in China – Anglo-American relations and the recognition of communist China', University of Leeds unpublished PhD thesis, 1996.

Watt, George. *China 'Spy'*, Johnson, London, 1972.

Webb, John. *An Historical Essay Endeavoring a Probability that the Language of the Empire of China is the Primitive Language*, London, 1669.

Wehrle, Edmund S. *Britain, China, and the Anti-Missionary Riots 1891–1900*, University of Minnesota Press, Minneapolis, MN, 1966.

Welsh, Frank. *A History of Hong Kong* (revised edn), Harper Collins, London, 1997.

Westad, Odd Arne. *Restless China: China and the world since 1750*, Bodley Head, London, 2012.

Wilgus, Mary. *Sir Claude Macdonald, the Open Door and British Informal Empire in China 1895–1900*, Garland, New York and London, 1987.

Wills, John E. Jr. *Embassies and Illusions: Dutch and Portuguese envoys to K'ang-hsi, 1666–1687*, Council on East Asian Studies, Harvard University, Cambridge, MA, 1984.

Wills, John E. Jr. *China and Maritime Europe 1500–1800: Trade, settlement, diplomacy, and missions*, Cambridge University Press, Cambridge, 2011.

Wilson, Andrew. *The 'Ever-Victorious Army': A history of the Chinese campaign under Lt-Col. C.G. Gordon*, William Blackwood and Sons, London, 1868.

Winchester, Simon. *Bomb, Book and Compass: Joseph Needham and the great secrets of China*, Viking, London and New York, 2008.

Winnington, Alan. *Breakfast with Mao*, Lawrence and Wishart, London, 1986.

Winterbotham, William. *An Historical, Geographical, and Philosophical View of the Chinese Empire*, London, 1795.

Wodehouse, P.G. *Psmith in the City*, A. & C. Black, London, 1910.

Wolseley, G.J. *A Narrative of the War with China in 1860*, Longman and Roberts, London, 1862.

Wong, John. *Deadly Dreams: Opium, imperialism, and the Arrow War (1856–1860) in China*, Cambridge University Press, Cambridge, 1998.

Wood, Frances. *No Dogs and Not Many Chinese: Treaty port life in China 1843–1943*, John Murray, London, 1998.

Wright, Patrick. *Passport to Peking: A very British mission to Mao's China*, Oxford University Press, Oxford, 2010.

Wright, Stanley. *Hart and the Chinese Customs*, Mullen and Son, Belfast, 1950.

Xu, Zhimo. *Selected Poems*, Oleander Press, Cambridge, 2012.

Yang, Chi-Ming. *Performing China: Virtue, commerce and orientalism in eighteenth-century England, 1660–1760*, Johns Hopkins University Press, Baltimore, MD, 2011.

Young, L.K. *British Policy in China 1895–1902*, Clarendon Press, Oxford, 1970.

Younghusband, Francis. *India and Tibet*, John Murray, London, 1910 (reprinted Book Faith, New Delhi, 1998).

Younghusband, Francis. *The British Invasion of Tibet 1904*, The Stationery Office, London, 1999.

Index